LESBIAN, GAY, AND BISEXUAL YOUTHS AND ADULTS

AND ADULTS

Knowledge for Human Services Practice

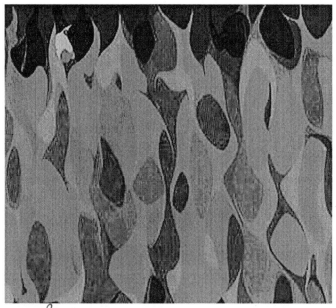

Ski Hunter / Coleen Shannon
Jo Knox / James I. Martin

What r the key diffs betw L+G+ heterosexuals do
across the life span?

What difficulties do L+G experience across
the lifespan?

What r key diffs do experienced
b-r L+6 # youth

SAGE Publications
International Educational and Professional Publisher
Thousand Oaks London New Delhi

For information:

 SAGE Publications, Inc.
2455 Teller Road
Thousand Oaks, California 91320
E-mail: order@sagepub.com

SAGE Publications Ltd.
6 Bonhill Street
London EC2A 4PU
United Kingdom

SAGE Publications India Pvt. Ltd.
M-32 Market
Greater Kailash I
New Delhi 110 048 India

Printed in the United States of America

Library of Congress Cataloging-in-Publication Data

Main entry under title:
  Lesbian, gay, and bisexual youths and adults: Knowledge for human
    services practice / by Ski Hunter ... [et al.].
      p. cm.
  Includes bibliographical references and index.
    ISBN 0-8039-5886-2 (cloth: acid-free paper). —ISBN 0-8039-5887-0
(pbk.: acid-free paper)
    1. Social work with gays. 2. Lesbians. 3. Gay men. 4. Bisexuals.
  5. Sexual orientation. 6. Gender identity. I. Hunter, Ski.
  HV1449.L483   1998
  362.8—dc21   98-8872

  98 99 00 01 02 03 10 9 8 7 6 5 4 3 2 1

Acquiring Editor:	C. Terry Hendrix
Editorial Assistant:	Dale Marie Grenfell
Production Editor:	Diana E. Axelsen
Production Assistant:	Lynn Miyata
Typesetter/Designer:	Marion Warren
Indexer:	Trish Wittenstein
Cover Designer:	Candice Harman

CONTENTS

PART II

◆

Identity Development and Disclosure

PART III

◆

Family

PART IV

Life Course

PART V

Human Services Practice With Lesbian, Gay, Bisexual, and Transgenderist Clients

PREFACE

AND

ACKNOWLEDGMENTS

◆ UNTIL THE PAST SEVERAL DECADES, research on the same-gender sexual orientation focused primarily on origins, "diagnosis," and pathology. Increasingly, research now focuses on the lives of lesbian and gay men and across many areas such as friendships, couples, parenting, and the life course. Lesbians and gay men are also addressed across many fields of study such as history, literature, and the arts, in addition to the traditional fields of medicine and psychology. In recent years, the literature has also increased on the lives and concerns of bisexual men and women and, to a lesser extent, of transgenderist men and women.

The purpose of the this book is primarily to look at the life experiences of lesbian, gay, and bisexual persons. First, controversial issues are examined regarding causation, choice versus no choice, language, perime-

ters of sexual orientation, numbers, and research issues (Chapter 1). The book also addresses heterosexism (Chapter 2) and how, as a result of this ideology, alternative lesbian, gay, and bisexual communities and culture developed (Chapter 3). The topics of coming out or identity development (Chapter 4) and identity disclosure (Chapter 5) are examined. Families are explored in couples (Chapter 6) and in couples with children (Chapter 7). Various issues related to life course development are addressed from adolescence through older adulthood (Chapters 8, 9, and 10). The final chapter presents affirmative guidelines for practice and the ecological/systems approach to practice assessment. Due to constraints on the size of the book, some topics are addressed only briefly (e.g., health, immigration) or not at all (e.g., friendships). In addition, some topics are restricted in exploration to lesbians and gay men because of the more limited research to date on bisexual men and women.

Most students in human services programs who later will be practitioners, supervisors, administrators, and/or professors will work with gay, lesbian, bisexual, and transgenderist persons as their clients, staff, or students. This book is intended for use by both undergraduate and graduate-level students. It can serve as a required main text in courses on oppressed populations and as a supplemental text for many courses that prepare students to practice in applied human services fields (e.g., social work, counseling, mental health, nursing, medicine, psychology, sociology, and education). The book can also be used by practicing professionals in human services such as social workers, clinical psychologists, policy planners, and human resource providers. It can be used for in-service training and workshops. It should also be of interest to members of the lesbian, gay, bisexual, and transgenderist populations and to others in the general population.

◆ Acknowledgments

We wish to acknowledge lesbian, gay, bisexual, and transgenderist persons throughout history. We are indebted to many people such as those whose courage leads the way to greater visibility, those who work hard for civil rights, those writers and researchers who engage in challenging the myths and stereotypes, and all persons who proudly tell and write about their lives.

We also want to thank Terry Hendrix and Dale Grenfell at Sage for their support of this project. We appreciate the opportunity to work with them and this fine press. Dale's quick and caring responses to questions were particularly welcomed.

We also thank many friends, colleagues, and partners for their encouragement and patience during the writing of the book. This includes David, Donna, Wilma, Jane, and Cathe. Appreciation is also extended to Lee, Carole, Shirley, Gary, Raymond, and Ron.

P A R T   I

ISSUES, OPPRESSION, AND COMMUNITY

INTRODUCTION

◆ THIS IS A BOOK ABOUT sexual identity. Several researchers divide sexual identity into various components (e.g., Morales, 1996; Shively & De Cecco, 1977). These components include (a) *biological sex,* or genetic and morphological maleness and femaleness, usually clear at birth; (b) *gender identity,* the psychological sense of being male or female; (c) *gender identity constancy,* the enduring perception of oneself as male or female; (d) *gender role behavior,* conformity to culturally defined norms of masculinity or femininity; (e) *sexual orientation,* feelings of attraction to males, females, or both; (f) *sexual orientation identity,* self-acknowledgment as heterosexual, lesbian, gay, or bisexual; and (g) *sexual behavior* (same gender, other gender, or both). Sometimes people feel uncomfortable with certain components of their

sexual identity, or there is ambiguity in the components. This includes, for example, transvestite and transsexual persons (e.g., Blanchard, 1989; Blanchard, Clemmensen, & Steiner, 1987).

Transvestite persons are almost always heterosexual men who are usually married and have children (Bailey, 1996). As children themselves, their gender identity was masculine (Talamini, 1982). They attain sexual gratification, however, from cross-dressing, which is usually a compulsive desire and done in private (Bailey, 1996).

Transsexual persons feel that their biological sex does not match their gender identity. Their desire to live as female (if born male) or as male (if born female) is a long-standing one (Denny & Green, 1996). They frequently cross-dress throughout childhood and adolescence and attempt to pass as a member of the gender not present at birth (Seil, 1996).

There are two groups of transsexual persons: primary (or classic) and secondary. The *primary* or classic situation involves women or men who feel that, for as long as they can remember (from about the age of 5 or 6), nature assigned them the wrong body. This gender confusion intensifies during adolescence. The situation is usually more stressful for feminine males, who are more frequently teased and rejected by families and peers. Unless there is understanding and support in the family, males tend to drop out of school and run away from home. On the streets, they are vulnerable to drugs, prostitution, and HIV. Usually living in poverty, they are unable to obtain treatment (Seil, 1996).

Because of their subjective discomfort with their biological sex, transsexual persons who can will often seek medical intervention in gender-reassignment clinics. The objective is reassignment of their biological sex to match their gender identity. This typically happens during the early twenties (Bailey, 1996; Denny & Green, 1996; Seil, 1996). Transsexual persons reassigned from male to female were usually distinctly feminine boys in childhood, whereas those reassigned from female to male were distinctly masculine girls (Bailey, 1996).

Not everyone who experiences a discrepancy between gender identity and biological sex will grow up to be a transsexual adult. Most boys identified with atypical childhood gender identity or "gender identity disorder of childhood" will probably be feminine gay men. Girls with this assessment are also not usually candidates for a transsexual outcome (Bailey, 1996). Seil (1996) pointed out that the prevalence of transsexual persons is relatively low. It is reported as 1 per 30,000 males and 1 per 100,000 females (American Psychiatric Association, 1987). The issue of whether atypical childhood gender identity

is a disorder is one of considerable debate (Bailey, 1996).

The *secondary* group of transsexual persons is almost entirely composed of men. Their histories also include discreet cross-dressing as well as images of themselves as possessing a woman's body. These experiences are often accompanied by sexual arousal (Bailey, 1996). The rest of their developmental history fundamentally contrasts with the history of primary transsexual persons. For example, they did not appear unusual in their childhood gender identities. They were able to suppress their discomfort with their assigned anatomic gender and what they felt was their appropriate gender until puberty or later (Seil, 1996). Their desire to change sexual anatomy also occurred much later, usually in their thirties (Blanchard et al., 1987). Prior to this transition, secondary transsexual persons are often so successful in performing an appropriate gender role that the announcement of their true gender identity is a shock to family and friends. Not many marriages survive such an announcement. There may also be rejection from one's children, and one's job may be lost. These losses often result in isolation and loneliness (Seil, 1996).

This book focuses mainly on the sexual identity issues of women and men whose sexual and affectional interest is focused on the same gender (lesbians and gay men) or on both the same and the other gender (bisexual women and men). A transsexual person may or may not fit these categories. Increasingly, human services professionals are required by their professional associations to deliver knowledgeable, unbiased services to gay, lesbian, and bisexual persons and to advocate against discrimination directed at these populations. Knowledge of these populations is the educational foundation from which unbiased human services practice with them begins (Croteau & Kusek, 1992; Larsen, Cate, & Reed, 1983; Serdahely &

Ziemba, 1984). Critical self-examination must be conducted for myths and negative attitudes and beliefs about these groups derived from living in a heterosexist society (see Chapters 2 and 11).

An increasing number of texts are now available for increasing one's knowledge of gay, lesbian, bisexual, and transsexual persons (e.g., Beemyn & Eliason, 1996; Blumenfeld & Raymond, 1993; Bohan, 1996; D'Augelli & Patterson, 1995; Firestein, 1996b; Garnets & Kimmel, 1993c; Greene, 1997a; Greene & Herek, 1994; Laird & Green, 1996; Savin-Williams & Cohen, 1996; Woodman, 1992). Journals also exist such as the *Journal of Gay & Lesbian Social Services,* the *Journal of Gay and Lesbian Psychotherapy,* the *Journal of Homosexuality,* and the *Journal of Gay, Lesbian, and Bisexual Identity.* The purpose of this book is to add to the available resources for use by human services professionals. Part of the knowledge requirement about bisexual, gay, and lesbian persons is awareness of important but contentious issues surrounding them. The remainder of this chapter addresses several of these issues: What causes same-gender sexual attractions? What language is acceptable? Who qualifies as lesbian, gay, or bisexual? What are the problems of doing research on these populations?

◆ Perspectives on Causes of Same-Gender Sexual Orientation

Although many other aspects of the lives of lesbian, gay, and bisexual persons are now addressed by researchers, the interest in causes is still prevalent. Today, a variety of theoretical concepts exist that attempt to explain the origins of a same-gender sexual orientation. Each concept is associated with proponents and opponents (Herek, 1991). The concepts can usually be categorized on one side or the other of a dichotomy: nature/

biological (essentialism) or nurture/social (social constructionism) (Herdt, 1993; E. Stein, 1990). Is sexual orientation a universal category found in every culture or an arbitrary social construction (Bailey, 1995)? Or, as posed by Baumrind (1995), "Do people develop a permanent sexual orientation or identity early in life and then discover what they are, as the essentialist believes, or is their sexual identity and even their preferred object of erotic attraction socially created, bestowed, and maintained, as the constructionist believes?" (p. 130).

Many studies fail to find associations between various proposed causative factors and same-gender sexual orientation. There is suggestive, but still insufficient, evidence for a biological basis (e.g., Bailey & Pillard, 1991; LeVay, 1991). Evidence for various environmental or social causes is also insufficient (e.g., Kitzinger, 1995). Most social and behavioral scientists assent to the view that same-gender sexual orientation results from a complex interaction of factors that is not well understood (Herek, 1991). It is also unlikely that a definitive set of components or a single path to same-gender sexual orientation will be discovered. There may be different forms of same-gender sexual orientation, resulting from different origins (T. Stein, 1993). Some forms, for example, may be primarily genetically determined whereas other forms may be less directly controlled by genes. Other forms may have a genetic basis but require social input for fruition (Blumenfeld & Raymond, 1993). Also, the route to same-gender sexual orientation may not be the same for men and women, possibly involving different biological and/or social factors (Burch, 1993). Dynes and Donaldson (1992) suggested that even a single form of sexual orientation may have multiple causes. At best, a cluster of routes may be discovered that lead to some forms of same-gender sexual expression. They are not likely, however, to account for the majority of the phenomena.

Because of so many unanswered questions about etiology and the probability that full clarity will not be discovered, Burch (1993) recommended shifting the focus from etiology to a descriptive portrayal of same-gender sexual orientation. There are also other reasons to shift the focus away from etiology. The search for causes implies pathology. There is also the fear that biological markers will be used to identify and thereby control these populations such as by preventing the birth of a "homosexual" child (De Cecco & Elia, 1993). Nevertheless, interest in the etiology issue is not likely to subside. A related issue is whether same-gender sexual orientation is a choice.

◆ Same-Gender or Bisexual Sexual Orientation: Choice or No Choice?

Out of all the issues in the essentialist/social constructionist debate, whether or not same-gender or bisexual sexual orientation is a choice is probably the sole interest of many individuals and groups. It is one of the most fiercely debated issues among scholars, scientists, and the lay public. It is also debated by some members of gay, lesbian, and bisexual communities. Essentialists assume that no sexual orientation, whether same-gender, bisexual, or heterosexual, is a conscious choice (Gonsiorek & Weinrich, 1991; Herdt, 1990). Instead, a "fixed, independent biological mechanism steers individual desire or behavior either toward men or toward women irrespective of circumstances and experience" (De Cecco & Elia, 1993, p. 11). In distinct contrast to this view is the claim that one's sexual orientation is chosen or constructed. This is one of the most basic tenets of social constructionism (Golden, 1987; Hart & Richardson, 1981; Longino, 1988; Vance, 1988; Weeks, 1991; Weinberg & Williams, 1974). Instead of *sexual orientation,*

the phrase *sexual preference* is often used by social constructionists to indicate that people take an active part in constructing their sexuality (Weinberg, Williams, & Pryor, 1994) or make a conscious, intentional choice of sexual partners (Baumrind, 1995).

During the last decade, Golden (1987, 1994, 1996) conducted in-depth interviews with more than 100 lesbian, bisexual, and heterosexual women. They were mostly White but of different ages and social classes. Golden found that women in all of these groups think that choice is a major influence on sexual orientation. Compared with gay and bisexual men, the notion of choice is far more likely to match the experiences of lesbians and bisexual women (e.g., Card, 1992; Esterberg, 1997; Faderman, 1984-1985; Golden, 1990; Gonsiorek & Weinrich, 1991; Kitzinger, 1995). Ponse (1978) used the phrase "elective lesbians" for those who see their sexual orientation as a conscious choice versus "true" or primary lesbians who do not see it as a choice. Elective heterosexual women, identified by Golden (1996), currently identify as heterosexual but believe that in certain circumstances they could prefer to link up with a woman. Golden (1996) pointed out that although no similar research addressed the issue of sexual fluidity with gay or heterosexual men, probably few of them are elective. Other researchers also suggest that biology may play a larger role in male sexual orientation than it does in female sexual orientation (e.g., Hu et al., 1995).

◆ Changing Views on Language

The language or terminology applied particularly to lesbians and gay men is another contentious issue. Not only is there a lack of universal agreement about terminology but it changes across time and varies across different geographical areas and cultures (Ameri-

can Psychological Association, 1991; Donovan, 1992; Herek, 1991; Hyde, 1985; Rothblum, 1994). A historical review of language
development reflects these changes and variations.

"Homosexual"

The terms *homosexual* and *homosexuality*
did not exist until the second half of the
1860s when they first appeared in Central
Europe. They were invented by a German-
Hungarian publicist and translator who opposed German sodomy laws, K. M. Benkert.
Writing under the noble name of his family,
Károly Mária Kertbeny, he first used the term
homosexual in private correspondence in
1868 and in two anonymous German pam-
phlets in 1869 (Herzer, 1985). He invented
this term to distinguish those who participated in same-gender sexual behavior from
those who engaged in male-female sexual
behavior. He associated "homosexuality"
with sickness and deviance but not with sin
or criminal behavior (Bullough, 1994; Donovan, 1992).

Kertbeny also invented the term *heterosexuality* in 1869 (Herzer, 1985). The con-
trasting pair of words, *heterosexual* and *homosexual,* were not popularized, however,
until the 1880s. Krafft-Ebing (1892) adopted
and popularized the term *homosexual.* Toward the end of the nineteenth century, both
terms moved from German to other European languages (Dynes, 1990c). They were
introduced into the English language in
1897 (Bardis, 1980). In the early years of
the twentieth century, the popularity of the
term *homosexual* escalated through its use
by Havelock Ellis (1942) and Magnus
Hirschfeld (1948).

The term *homosexual* was not without
rivals. Alternate terms such as *homophile*
were used in the United States. Historical
accounts sometimes refer to the years between 1950 and 1969 as the homophile period

(Dynes, 1990d). *Homophile* is still mentioned in contemporary discussions of useful
terminology (e.g., Garnets & Kimmel,
1993a). Coming from the Greeks, it means
"loving the same." In contrast to the term
homosexual, homophile is broader in its inclusion of affectional, nonsexual links between people (Dynes, 1990d).

Terms of the Community

Gay. In the wake of the 1969 Stonewall
Rebellion (see Chapter 3), the term *homophile* was rejected as not fitting the times.
Even more dismissed was the term *homosexual* due to its various past associations with
a string of negative stereotypes (American
Psychological Association, 1991; Cruikshank, 1992; Gonsiorek & Weinrich, 1991;
Herek, 1991; T. Stein, 1993). Although *homosexual* reigned supreme for more than a
century, the term *gay* began to overtake it
(Herdt & Boxer, 1992). The origins of *gay*
are unknown, but the term has been used in
the United States since the 1920s and in Great
Britain since the 1950s (Dynes, 1990b). By
the late 1960s, it was in widespread use
(Cruikshank, 1992). Cruikshank proclaimed
that "homosexuals became gay when they
rejected the notion that they were sick or
sinful, claimed equality with heterosexuals,
banded together to protest second-class citi-
zenship, created a subculture, and came out
in large numbers" (p. 3). "Above all, 'gay'
was a name chosen by the group itself, as a
sign of its refusal to be named by, judged by,
or controlled by the dominant majority" (p.
91). By the 1970s, use of this term was increasingly common; by the 1980s, it was the
standard term in the lesbian and gay culture
(Herdt & Boxer, 1992) although not in the
American culture at large.

Gay is not a term without critics. It can
convey frivolousness or triviality (Gonsiorek
& Weinrich, 1991). In addition, according

to Rust (1996a), some men who have sex with other men still prefer the term *homosexual.* They do not adopt a gay identity or share in the political implications of the term *gay.*

Lesbian. The term *lesbian* was used as early as the sixteenth century. It was probably derived from the home of the poet Sappho, the Aegean island of Lesbos (Nakayama & Corey, 1993). In the United States, the term was not in wide use until the nineteenth century. Before it achieved much popularity within the lesbian and gay community, it was customary to apply *gay* to both women and men (American Psychological Association, 1991). This was problematic for many women, however, because *gay* was most often identified only with men. It reflected men's experiences and culture and left out the separate and distinct experiences of women (Jeffreys, 1994; T. Stein, 1993). For these reasons, it became important to many women that the term *lesbian* be used to differentiate them from gay men. By the late 1980s, groups for both genders almost always included *lesbian* in the group name (Cruikshank, 1992).

Bisexual. The term *bisexual,* indicating attractions to both men and women, has existed in the psychological literature since the process of psychosexual development was first conceptualized by Freud and his contemporaries (Fox, 1995). Although this term was not selected by the bisexual community, it was not a pejorative term to Freud (1905/1953), who thought that bisexual potential existed in everyone. This was not, however, the general view of the psychoanalytic community, which thought that bisexual men and women were "homosexuals" trying to outwardly conform to social norms (Bullough, 1994). *Bisexual* appears to be a term accepted by contemporary bisexual

men and women. Current affirmative books, networks, and other resources use it or sometimes the shorter version *bi.*

The most important perspective on language for human services professionals is to use nonbiased terms. The Committee on Lesbian and Gay Concerns (GLGC) of the American Psychological Association identified representations of nonbiased language in 1991, many of which are now included in the *Publication Manual of the American Psychological Association* (1994). These terms are summarized in Box 1.1. They are recommended for use in the human services by researchers, writers, educators, students, and practitioners.

This text uses no terminology that signifies negative stereotypes about lesbian, gay, or bisexual persons. In discussions about history and research efforts, the terms *homosexual(s)* or "homosexuality" are sometimes used. Use of quotation marks with them, however, indicates that they are not acceptable terms unless, as noted earlier, individuals prefer to apply them to themselves.

Denny and Green (1996) referred to persons who identify with both male and female gender roles or the other gender as *transgenderist* persons. This term, which represents both transvestite and transsexual persons, will be used unless reference is being made to one particular group.

Several other terms that are frequently used in this book also require definition. The term *relationship* appears less often than an alternate term, *linkup.* The latter term refers to any kind of relationship from short term to long term and any couple whether gay, lesbian, bisexual, or heterosexual (FM-2030, 1989). The terms *coming out* and *disclosure* are used to distinguish two different processes. *Coming out* refers to the process of identity development whereas *disclosure* refers to the declaration of one's identity to others (Strommen, 1989).

Box 1.1. Nonbiased Language

1. The term *sexual orientation* is preferred over *sexual preference.* It refers to sexual and affectional relationships whether of lesbian, gay, bisexual, or heterosexual persons. Terms that are preferable to *lesbianism, homosexuality, heterosexuality,* and *bisexuality* include *lesbian sexual orientation, heterosexual sexual orientation, gay male sexual orientation,* and *bisexual sexual orientation.*

2. When referring to specific women and men or groups, the adjectives *lesbian* and *gay male* are preferred to the adjective *homosexual,* and the nouns *lesbians* and *gay men* to the noun *homosexuals.* If the meaning of the term *gay* is not clear (e.g., reference only to men), gender should be specified (e.g., gay men).

3. *Same-gender sexual behavior, male-male sexual behavior,* and *female-female sexual behavior* are recommended for instances when individuals engage in same-gender sexual behavior unrelated to their sexual orientation. An example is a heterosexual man who in adolescence experienced a single same-gender sexual experience.

4. When reference is made to people who relate sexually and affectionally to both women and men, the terms *bisexual women and men* and *bisexual persons,* or *bisexual* as an adjective, are preferred. ◆

Emerging Terms

Whether or not *gay, lesbian,* or *bisexual* will remain the standard terms is uncertain. Terms applied by community members rise and fall in popularity (Champagne, 1993) and the meanings applied to terms change over time within given social and political contexts (Rust, 1996a). The term *queer* illustrates these phenomena. Once applied to lesbians and gay men with derogatory meaning, it recently reemerged within segments of the lesbian and gay community. *Queer,* which applies to both males and females (Donovan, 1992; Elton, 1990; Heller, 1990), symbolizes a challenge to the traditional heterosexual ideas of gendered sexuality. Bisexual and transgenderist women and men may identify as queer because they challenge the traditional gender categories associated with heterosexual and same-gender sexual orientations. The categories of lesbian and gay can also be challenged when a lesbian and a gay man call themselves queer because they are attracted to each other (Rust, 1996a). Currently, however, the term *queer* remains controversial because of its past negative connotations as well as its present politically radical associations (Jeffreys, 1994).

Rust (1996a) pointed out that terms develop and change along with socially available sexual identities. For example, the number of these identities expanded with the growth of the bisexual and queer political movements (e.g., Queer Nation). Rust (1995) found in a recent study of bisexual women that their most common sexual identifications, other than *bisexual* and *queer,* included *lesbian-identified bisexual* and *bisexual lesbian* or *bi dyke* and *byke.* Women who used these identifications did not think that lesbian and bisexual identifications completely described their sexuality. In another study, some women identified as "bisexual lesbians" because, although they chose sexual involvement with women and identification as lesbians, they might also experience sexual desire for men (Golden, 1996). Other women chose to use these terms to signify a previous lesbian identification or a political commitment to women or to the lesbian community (Rust, 1995). There are also "transient lesbians" who identify as lesbians and are sexually involved with women for a time, then subsequently become involved with men (Golden, 1996). In certain lesbian communities, however, bisexual lesbians and transient lesbians are not readily accepted. They are viewed as "not real" or "false" lesbians versus "born" or "real" lesbians (Golden, 1987).

A recent identification among men is *gay bisexual*. Among both men and women, there are identifications such as *bisensual* (sensuality better expresses forms of human relating other than genital sex), *polysexual* or *polyamorous* (terms preferred by individuals who want to define their sexuality independently of gender and sexual dichotomies), and *polyfideltious* (fidelity to a group of three or more people) (Rust, 1996a). Most of the identifications and accompanying terms discussed here are not yet known to the mainstream heterosexual society.

◆ **Racial and Ethnic Groups:**
   Terminology and Membership

Racial and ethnic lesbian, gay, and bisexual persons are discussed in various sections of the book when there is existing research. The most research exists on Asian Americans, Latinos, Black Americans, and Native Americans. By way of introducing these groups, terminology and those included in the groups are identified in Box 1.2. The terminology or nouns used to refer to racial and ethnic groups follow the recommendations in the *Publication Manual of the American Psychological Association* (American Psychological Association, 1994).

Among racial and ethnic men who have sex with men and racial and ethnic women who have sex with women, terms of the gay and lesbian community may or may not be used. González and Espin (1996), for example, used the term *homosexual* rather than *gay* when discussing Latino men in same-gender sexual relationships. Although many of them do not identify as *gay*, they do identify with the term *homosexual*. González and Espin emphasized, however, that no term actually fits the diversity of motivations, behaviors, and identities of Latinos. Manalansan (1996) suggested using only the description *men who have sex with men*.

Among Indian Americans, at least six "gender styles" exist: women, men, not-men (biological women who perform some male roles), not-women (biological men who perform some female roles), lesbians, and gay men. Not-men and not-women are usually considered bisexual because they experience sexual attractions to both men and women (L. B. Brown, 1997). Rather than this or other standard terms, however, the term *two-spirit* is often used. It represents more of a spiritual/social identity that encompasses alternative sexuality, alternative gender, and an integration of Native spirituality (Tofoya, 1996, 1997). Williams (1996) explained that Indian American religions view persons with both a male and a female spirit as more blessed than persons with only one spirit. This includes, for example, men who are feminine and women who are masculine. Some Native individuals feel strongly that they are best represented and feel empowered by the term *two-spirit* and reject more standard terms as culturally biased. Other Native individuals, however, identify just as powerfully with the labels *lesbian, gay, bisexual, transgenderist,* or *queer* depending on their social-economic, regional, or generational locations or their political attitudes (Tofoya, 1996).

◆◆◆

Box 1.2. Terms and Membership in Racial and Ethnic Groups

For people of African ancestry, the terms *Black* and *African American* are acceptable. African Americans are diverse. Their cultural origins are in the tribes of Western Africa with some Indian and European mixtures (Greene, 1997b).

The terms *Asian* or *Asian American* are preferable to *Oriental*. More specific terms are also useful such as *Chinese* or *Korean. Asian/Pacific Islander* is a recent category that includes a range of people descended from families on the Asian continent and the Pacific Islands. The Asian continent includes people or their descendants from East Asia (Japan, China, Korea, Taiwan, and Mongolia), South Asia (Bangladesh, India, Nepal, Sri Lanka, and Pakistan), and Southeast Asia (Indonesia, Singapore, Philippines, Vietnam, Cambodia, Thailand, and Malaysia). Pacific Islanders include people or their descendants from Hawaii, Micronesia, Melanesia, and Polynesia. The discussion here is limited to Asian Americans, traditionally viewed as from East Asia, who themselves have disparate histories, cultures, and languages (Manalansan, 1996). Liu and Chan (1996), however, described *East Asians* (namely, Chinese, Japanese, and Koreans) as sharing Confucian and Buddhist influences, similar sociocultural dynamics and historical connections, and comparable conditions for lesbian, gay, and bisexual persons. The largest group of Asian Americans includes Japanese and Chinese people. Most of the research on gay, lesbian, and bisexual persons to date has focused on these two groups (Greene, 1994a).

The terms *Latino* or *Latino American* are preferred to more general terms such as *Hispanic*

and *Chicano*. These terms represent diverse racial and cultural backgrounds. They apply to Mexican Americans, Puerto Ricans, Cubans, and Central and South Americans (González & Espin, 1996). E. S. Morales (1996) pointed out that although Latinos may share the same language, all types of races are found among the different Latino nations, including Black, Asian, Native American, and Caucasian. Greene (1997b) cautioned that these groups may differ from one another as much as from the dominant Euro-American culture.

The terms *Indian American* and *Native American* are both acceptable for indigenous peoples of North America. Tofoya (1996) indicated that the term *Native* is preferred when including Native people from Canada and Central and South America. Most of the data available on lesbians and gay men, however, are primarily based on Native Americans. They are diverse in tribal groups, cultures, and languages. The number of differences is in the hundreds. For example, in the United States, there are more than 500 federally recognized and 200 nonrecognized tribes and more than 200 languages (U.S. Bureau of the Census, 1994).

In this book, the terms generally used, unless more specific ones are required, include *Black* or *African American, Latino, Asian American,* and *Native* or *Native American.* Sensitivity, however, to what a person from a racial or ethnic group wants to be called is always necessary (American Psychological Association, 1994). ◆

◆ Perimeters: Who Are Lesbian, Gay, and Bisexual Persons?

In Western society, the general public as well as scientists usually presume that two categories of sexual orientation exist: heterosexual and "homosexual" (Bohan, 1996). If these distinct categories exist, however, inclusion and exclusion criteria are far from clear (Bohan, 1996; Weinberg et al., 1994). This was shown in the work of Alfred A. Kinsey and his associates (called the Kinsey group) in the 1940s and 1950s (Kinsey, Pomeroy, & Martin, 1948; Kinsey, Pomeroy, Martin, & Gebhard, 1953).

The Kinsey Group

Early in his research, Kinsey recognized that substantial numbers of people participated in both same-gender and other-gender sexual activity (Kinsey et al., 1948). Sexual orientation appeared to be more often a mix of "homosexual" and heterosexual sexuality. As such, it was impossible to divide people into the two categories. This led to the development of the Kinsey group's seven-point rating scale, which classified a range of human sexuality from "homosexual" to heterosexual. An individual's location on this continuum was established by determining the proportion of sexual behavior that was oriented to one or the other gender. A score reflected the established proportion, ranging from 0 (exclusive heterosexual behavior), through a midpoint 3 (equal heterosexual and "homosexual" behavior), to 6 (exclusive "homosexual" behavior). Important contributions resulted from the use of the rating scale but there were also important limitations, noted in Box 1.3.

Later Developments in the Study of Sexual Orientation

The Kinsey scale implied that the more same-gender orientation that characterizes a person, the less other-gender orientation the person can have and vice versa. Later proposals suggested that these positions are relatively independent. An individual can show high levels of both same-gender and other-gender sexual behavior, low levels of both, or levels of each that vary in strength (Shively & De Cecco, 1977; Storms, 1980). Based on these possible variations, amendments to the Kinsey scale began in the 1970s and are ongoing (e.g., Bell & Weinberg,

1978; Berkey, Perelman-Hall, & Kurdek, 1990; Blanchard, 1989; Blanchard et al., 1987; Cass, 1979, 1983-1984; Chung & Katayama, 1996; Coleman, 1987; De Cecco & Shively, 1983-1984; Devor, 1993; Grimm, 1987; Holden & Holden, 1995; Klein, Sepekoff, & Wolf, 1985; Laumann et al., 1994; Money, 1988; Shively & De Cecco, 1977; Shively, Jones, & De Cecco, 1983-1984; Storms, 1980; Weinberg et al., 1994; Weinrich, 1988). Examples of amendments include (a) additional factors such as love and affection (e.g., Klein et al., 1985; Shively & De Cecco, 1977); (b) development of two continuous scales with separate ratings, one for measurement of same-gender orientation, the other for measurement of other-gender orientation (Kinsey used only one continuous scale) (e.g., Shively & De Cecco, 1977); and (c) measurement of intensity level of emotional and sexual attraction (e.g., Storms, 1980).

The work of Klein et al. (1985) represents one of the more influential advances of the Kinsey scale. Proposing that sexual orientation is multivariate and dynamic, Klein et al. developed the multifactoral Klein Sexual Orientation Grid (KSOG) to test this view. The grid contains seven components of sexual orientation: (a) sexual attraction, (b) sexual behavior, (c) sexual fantasies, (d) emotional preference, (e) social preference, (f) self-identification, (g) and living as a lesbian, gay man, heterosexual woman or man, or bisexual woman or man. Each component can be located on Kinsey's seven-point scale; the ratings can be highly congruent or incongruent. Some researchers added even more components (e.g., Coleman, 1987; Grimm, 1987). Developments of these kinds provide a more complex way to understand sexuality than was originally proposed by the Kinsey group, mainly by including an increasing number of variables (T. Stein, 1993). In addition, more attention was given to changes in one's location on the ratings over time.

Box 1.3. Contributions and Shortcomings of the Kinsey Studies

Contributions of the Kinsey Studies

Because of its scope alone, the Kinsey et al. (1948, 1953) work was a pioneering effort. A sizable amount of data were collected on 5,300 males and 5,940 females. The seven-point scale revolutionized theorizing about sexual behavior. It not only challenged traditional views of sexuality but in effect undermined them. For example, the category, "homosexual," which puts together all persons engaged in same-gender sexual behavior, was inaccurate (Bullough, 1994; Dynes & Donaldson, 1992). Kinsey's work also indicated that self-designated positions along the continuum were not always stable. They can shift over time.

The most startling result of the studies was the finding of a greater incidence of same-gender sexual behavior than was formerly believed to exist either casually or long term. At about the same time, these results were substantiated by cross-species and cross-cultural comparisons done by Ford (1948) and Ford and Beach (1951). These researchers discovered, for example, that in 76 human societies, same-gender sexual behavior of some degree was considered normal. Another important result from the Kinsey studies was the indication that same-gender sexual ex-

perience is best reported using several types of numerical information. For example, approximately 50% of men and 28% of women reported some degree of same-gender sexual experience. Only 4% to 5% of males and less than 3% of women, however, reported exclusive same-gender sexual activity since adolescence. Overall, women reported lower levels of same-gender sexual activity.

Shortcomings of the Kinsey Scale

Since the time of Kinsey's research, theoretical and methodological shortcomings have surfaced in the methodology, findings, and interpretations. Problems include (a) the narrow target of measurement (mostly sexual behavior or number of orgasms), which thereby leaves out many other possible aspects of sexual orientation; (b) reduction of sexual orientation to numerical categories leading to the presumption that all people who attain the same number are of the same sexual type; and (c) problems with the pool of respondents, which included volunteers or those purposefully recruited (Gagnon & Simon, 1973; Laumann, Gagnon, Michael, & Michaels, 1994; McIntosh, 1981; Michael, Gagnon, Laumann, & Molata, 1994). ◆

The KSOG (Klein et al., 1985), for example, attempted to distinguish patterns of the scale factors in three time periods: present, past, and ideal future.

Inclusion of Bisexual Sexual Orientation

One of the advantages of the multidimensional scales is the acknowledgment of bisexual sexual orientation as a valid category (Fox, 1996). Bisexual sexual orientation challenges the dichotomous conceptualization

of sexuality in which people are divided by gender identity (male or female), gender role (masculine or feminine), or sexual behavior (same gender or other gender). Whatever does not fit these dichotomies is often ignored. The bisexual experiences of most of the Kinsey respondents, for example, were not commented on because "homosexual" experiences were the main interest (Firestein, 1996a). Reasons for disinterest in bisexual sexual orientation are tied to several myths about its existence or permanence. See Box 1.4.

Box 1.4. Two Major Myths About Bisexual Sexual Orientation

Myth 1: Bisexual sexual orientation does not exist. Bisexual men and women are bombarded with messages that there is no such thing as a bisexual identity. Due to the same-gender/other-gender dichotomization of sexuality, men and women who claim they are "bisexual" are often viewed as actually either heterosexual or lesbian or gay: They are covering up their real sexual orientation, or they refuse to admit it, or they simply have not decided in which of the two categories they fit (Firestein, 1996a; Pope & Reynolds, 1991). Rust (1993a) found that some bisexual men and women also do not think that their identity is distinctive but, instead, additive such as heterosexual plus same gender.

Myth 2: Bisexual attractions constitute a temporary form of sexuality. A typical view of individuals who claim a bisexual identity is that this is merely a phase adopted when either coming out as lesbian or gay or returning to a heterosexual sexual orientation. When bisexual persons finish coming out or choose a single partner, their "real" sexual orientation is revealed. Then they are no longer perceived to be bisexual (Rust, 1996a). ◆

Rust (1996a) advocated against thinking that bisexual identity does not exist or that a person's bisexual sexual orientation should be questioned at times when single or with one or more persons of one gender. Most individuals who consider themselves bisexual feel attracted to both women and men, believe they could potentially become involved with either women or men, or had experienced former linkups with both women and men. They do not wish to adopt a lesbian, gay, or heterosexual identity that would deny part of their sexual feelings or experiences. The Kinsey studies established that more men and women display bisexual rather than exclusively same-gender attraction or sexual behavior. Even so, the myths about bisexual sexual orientation make it difficult for individuals to develop and maintain a bisexual identity.

Multiple Perimeters

Another complicated issue is the unsettled state of what components make up different sexual orientations (Halley, 1994; Michael et al., 1994). Do they include sexual desire and/or affectional desire for someone of the same gender; sexual acts with someone of the same gender; thinking of oneself as lesbian, gay, or bisexual; or participating in lesbian, gay, or bisexual communities? If they are made up of some combination of these components, which ones (L. S. Brown, 1995a; Halley, 1994)? Consider the components in Box 1.5. Which sexual orientation do they fit?

Based on the assumption that people who identify as heterosexual, lesbian, gay, or bisexual are in discrete, nonoverlapping, and permanent categories, it is typically thought that components such as sexual desire, sexual behavior, and self-identity are concordant. Consequently, a gay- or lesbian-identified person has only same-gender sexual desires and experiences, a heterosexual-identified person has only other-gender sexual desires and experiences, and a bisexual-identified person has both same-gender and other-gender sexual desires and experiences. In other words, one can accurately infer an individual's sexual desires and behaviors from

Box 1.5. Sexual Orientation Identification: Which Components Are Required?

The components considered here, in different arrangements, include sexual behavior, community participation (Golden, 1987), self-identity (as lesbian, gay, or bisexual) (Rothblum, 1994), sexual desire (Laumann et al., 1994), and affectional desire (Shively et al., 1983-1984).

1. *Sexual desire only.* Psychological literature emphasizes internal states related to sexual desire, especially the desire for or sexual interest in same-gender individuals, as more fundamental than behavior (Marmor, 1980). Should individuals be considered lesbian, gay, or bisexual, however, if they experience same-gender sexual desire but never participate in same-gender sexual behavior?

2. *Affectional desire only.* Same-gender bonding or deep friendships exist that are not sexual. The bonds between women in "Boston marriages," for example, are psychologically but not sexually intimate (e.g., Diggs, 1995; Rothblum & Brehony, 1993; Rupp, 1992; Smith-Rosenberg, 1975). The women may appear outwardly to others as if they are in a lesbian love linkup. The women themselves, however, do not identify as lesbian (Rothblum & Brehony, 1993).

3. *Affectional desire, self-identity, but no sexual behavior.* Sometimes self-identified lesbians and gay men desire same-gender affection but not sexual behavior. Either they do not ever include an overtly sexual component in their intimate partnerships, or sex is temporarily present but becomes unimportant later (Peplau & Cochran, 1990). Esterberg (1997), however, made a distinction between women who define themselves as lesbian and as celibate or choose not to be available for a sexual linkup and those who are currently not in a sexual linkup but are open to one.

4. *Sexual desire, sexual behavior, no self-identity.* If a person desires same-gender sexual contacts and participates in them but does not

identify as lesbian, gay, or bisexual, is this self-assessment wrong? This combination is present especially among some men. It also occurs among individuals in gender-segregated institutions such as prisons (e.g., Wooden & Parker, 1982).

5. *Self-identity incongruent with sexual behavior.* Should only men and women who are involved exclusively with members of their own gender be called lesbian or gay? What if some women and men identify as lesbian or gay, participate in same-gender sex, but also at times participate in other-gender sex? What about the person who claims a bisexual sexual orientation but chooses to participate in sex with only one gender?

6. *Sexual desire, sexual behavior, self-identity, no community.* Some people self-identify as lesbian, gay, or bisexual and desire and experience sex congruent with their self-identity but do not participate in lesbian, gay, or bisexual social or political occasions. This may result from various reasons such as lack of interest or time. It may also result from private affirmation of sexual orientation but no public disclosure, or what is often referred to as being "closeted" (Bell & Weinberg, 1978; Herek, 1991).

7. *Community participation incongruent with sexual behavior and self-identity.* People who do not desire or participate in same-gender sexual behavior or self-identify as lesbian or gay may participate in lesbian or gay communities for social or political purposes (Rothblum, 1994). A sample described by Silber (1990), for example, included feminist women who did not define themselves as lesbians or experience sex with other women but nevertheless participated in a lesbian feminist community.

8. *Community participation and/or self-identity incongruent with sexual behavior.* An example of this category is a woman who prefers sex with men but adopts a lesbian identity to express emotional and political solidarity with

the lesbian feminist community (Faderman, 1984-1985; Klein, 1990; Rich, 1980). In the 1970s, a politically radical branch of feminism advocated that its members adopt a lesbian identity as an alternative to patriarchal heterosexuality. Political lesbians may also decide because of political beliefs that sexual relationships with women are preferable to ones with men. This is a political as well as erotic choice (Golden, 1994). ◆

the label with which she or he identifies (Firestein, 1996a). As just explored, however, there is nothing this certain about what can be inferred from the various labels.

Findings from Golden's (1987, 1994, 1996) interviews with lesbian, bisexual, and heterosexual women who were engaged in sexual self-identification highlight many of the seeming inconsistencies appearing in Box 1.5. For example, whether a woman considers herself to be lesbian, bisexual, or heterosexual cannot be determined on the basis of sexual attractions and involvements. Nor do sexual attractions neatly predict sexual involvements. Some women experience same- and/or other-gender attractions but never act on them, while other women make a conscious decision to experience and pursue these attractions. Identifications are also not neatly predictable. There are women who report that they are lesbians even though they only experience sex with men; women who report that they are heterosexual or bisexual but they are currently experiencing sex only with women; women who report that they are either lesbian or heterosexual but experience sex with both genders; and women who report that they are bisexual even though they only experience sex with men. In addition, the gender of those to whom women are sexually attracted may change over time as well as the gender of those with whom they become sexually involved.

Different cultures also construct sexuality differently. Not all cultures, for example, define sexual orientation as does the Euro-American culture, in terms of the genders of the people one is sexually attracted to or involved with sexually (Rust, 1996a). Modern lesbian and gay identities are Western constructs. In East Asian cultures, there are no similar sexual identities (Chan, 1997). As indicated above, in Latino cultures, it is not uncommon for men to engage in same-gender sex without developing a gay identity (Carballo-Diéguez, 1989; Espin, 1984). This is also often the case for African American men (Greene, 1997b). In Latino cultures, this is especially common with men who take the masculine active or insertive sexual role (Carballo-Diéguez, 1989; Espin, 1984). Another reason these men do not identify as gay is their view of this identity as not a sexual orientation but as part of the White gay political movement (E. S. Morales, 1990). They more easily view themselves as participating in bisexual experiences (but not identity). Manalansan (1996) explained that bisexual practices are in part extensions of heterosexual machismo, or accommodated in the Latino concept of masculine heterosexuality, and in part hidden same-gender sexual orientation practices.

Similarly, in some Native communities, if a "masculine" male engages in active, insertive sex with another male, he is not viewed as "homosexual." Gender of the partner is irrelevant for the "masculine" man. The passive, receptive partner, however, is labeled as "homosexual" (Tofoya, 1996). Tofoya (1997) also pointed out that most Native communities do not apply the Western binary categories to classify the world such as male/female, gay/heterosexual, or good/bad. Depending on the situation, categories are used that range from appropriateness to inappropriateness. As indicated earlier, although many Native people strongly identify as lesbian, gay, or bisexual, other Native people find these categories too confining. Their concept of sexual expression is more fluid.

◆ Problems With Numbers

The ambiguity of definitions of gay, lesbian, and bisexual persons makes it exceedingly difficult to answer the question of how many people belong to these groups. Basically, there is no straightforward way to determine the numbers. In addition to the unsettled issue about what components make up different sexual identities, there is the issue of what degree of the various components is required. For example, is one declared gay or lesbian if one scored a 6 on the Kinsey scale, or will a 5 do? On multidimensional scales (e.g., Klein et al., 1985), how many components must be rated high, and how high? What about changes over time? Or does one always have to be a 5 or a 6? What about occasional or situational same-gender attractions? In addition to these ambiguities about what gets counted as various sexual identities, there is the question of how many respondents are willing to openly identify a sexual orientation other than heterosexual (Bohan, 1996).

Because of the barriers to establishing who is to be included or not in sexual orientation categories, some researchers call for the abandonment of such categorical labels as *heterosexual, bisexual,* and *"homosexual"* (e.g., De Cecco & Shively, 1983-1984; Paul, 1985). Such a move seems unlikely, however, as long as the interest in categorization and particularly the number of lesbians and gay men continues. Starting with the Kinsey reports in 1948 and 1953, attempts to determine the true proportion of this population

still persist (e.g., Billy, Tanfer, Grady, & Klepenger, 1993; Fay, Turner, Klassen, & Gagnon, 1989; Gagnon & Simon, 1973; Gebhard, 1972; Gebhard & Johnson, 1979; Janus & Janus, 1993; Laumann et al., 1994; Rogers & Turner, 1991; Sell et al., 1990; Sell, Wells, & Wypij, 1995; Wellings, Field, Johnson, & Wadsworth, 1994). Despite the many definitional and measurement problems, Gonsiorek, Sell, and Weinrich (1995) concluded that an approximation of the prevalence of predominantly same-gender sexual orientation in the United States is in the range of 4% to 17%. Based on the current research, the most reliable estimates of either exclusive same-gender sexual behavior or substantial same-gender attraction are probably somewhere in the middle of this range. These estimates, however, are only guesses. The actual figures are not likely ever to be determined. Stokes, McKirnan, Doll, and Burzette (1996) reported that the exact prevalence of bisexual behavior and attraction is also unknown.

◆ Research Issues

For the most part, this book is research based. There are considerable difficulties, however, in carrying out research projects in bisexual, gay, and lesbian communities. Certain social, political, and methodological issues affect both the conduct of research and its conclusions. Heterosexist research models, for example, which assume that heterosexual sexual orientation is the only acceptable form of affectional and sexual expression, lead to inadequate or distorted knowledge of lesbian, gay, and bisexual persons, their communities, and their cultures (see Chapter 2). Research may use identification of sexual orientation to devalue or stigmatize gay, lesbian, or bisexual persons or ignore sexual orientation altogether (Herek, Kimmel, Amaro, & Melton, 1991), thereby disavowing real differences that exist between these individuals and heterosexual individuals (Kitzinger, 1987).

Numerous methodological issues also challenge research on gay, lesbian, and bisexual populations such as sampling and generalizability, measurement and instrumentation, and research methodologies. As evident in prior discussions in this chapter, the most basic challenge of sampling has to do with the definition of the group of people (or population) the sample is meant to represent and to which generalizations about findings can be made. Because of the ambiguity about which components characterize same-gender sexual orientation, for example, operational definitions of this variable can vary widely. In addition, although lesbian, gay, and bisexual persons experience common bonds, they are heterogeneous and culturally diverse. They represent social groups that differ in such factors as gender, socioeconomic class, race, ethnicity, region, religion, age, cohort, parenthood, types of jobs and careers, marital history, current relationship status, educational attainment, being "out" or not, types of support groups, and other ways of life (Bohan, 1996; L. S. Brown, 1989b; Cruikshank, 1992; D'Augelli & Garnets, 1995; Donaldson, 1990; Greene, 1997b). Each social group is also characterized by its own particular culture that includes values, beliefs, and prescribed behaviors. Some social groups are also characterized by unique collective experiences such as political oppression, colonization, and emotional or physical disability (Greene, 1997c).

Because there is no conceivable sampling frame for lesbian, gay, and bisexual persons, a true random sample of this population cannot be drawn. Often, purposive or convenience samples are used, limiting the generalizabiity of study findings. Gay, lesbian, and bisexual persons are also unevenly distributed across the country. Their proportions are much higher in urban as opposed to rural settings (Laumann et al., 1994). Depending on where samples are selected, therefore, these populations can be either under- or overrepresented.

Measurement error reduces the probability that the concepts the research claims to measure are in fact occurring. Although measurement error cannot be completely eliminated, it can be reduced. For example, key variables such as sexual orientation are best conceptualized, operationally defined, and measured multidimensionally (e.g, Berkey et al., 1990; Klein et al., 1985). In addition, it may be essential to identify how far an individual has progressed in forming a gay, lesbian, or bisexual identity. The Sexual Identity Questionnaire (Cass, 1984) and the Gay Identity Questionnaire (Brady & Busse, 1994) are a few of the measures that are available to assess the progress of identity development.

To increase our understanding of gay, lesbian, and bisexual persons, it is also essential that both quantitative and qualitative methods be used. Quantitative methods are most appropriate for describing large samples, for correlational studies, and for testing predictive causal models. Qualitative methods are most appropriate for exploring or expanding upon the unknown, describing social processes, and understanding subjective, personal, and cultural experiences.

Research in gay, lesbian, and bisexual communities must also use a collaborative approach between researchers and study participants. Both researchers and the community can benefit from collaborative efforts, which will also contribute to reducing measurement errors and biases. An example of collaboration occurred in a recent study of interpersonal influences on HIV risk behavior among gay men in Dallas, Texas. Two authors of this book (J. I. Martin & Knox, 1997) involved members of a social service agency for gay men and lesbians in every step of planning the project such as development of the survey instrument, critique of the questionnaire, and dissemination of the questionnaire.

◆ **Summary**

The major issues centered on lesbian, gay, and bisexual persons are all unsettled. The debates about these issues are contentious, such as whether same-gender or bisexual attractions and behavior are a choice. Language, or the terms persons who experience same-gender or bisexual sexual attractions and behaviors use for self-identification, not only changes over time but varies in different segments of these populations. Which components are involved in the various sexual orientations is also an unsettled issue. The only clarity since the Kinsey studies is that sexual orientation is not bipolar and that many components are involved other than sexual behavior. There is also the complication of change in components and identities over time for any given person. This fluidity as well as ambiguity about the components of different sexual orientations makes the determination of how many persons are gay, lesbian, or bisexual a difficult if not impossible task. This also creates one of the numerous problems in research on these populations, that is, how to determine operational definitions for measurement. Although this is a research-based book, the various limitations of the research on gay, lesbian, and bisexual populations are recognized. No doubt the social, political, and methodological problems noted above affected much of the research. Thus the knowledge presented here can best be considered tentative and in an early stage of development.

2

THE
OPPRESSION
OF
HETEROSEXISM

◆ Only recently did the study of attitudes toward gay, lesbian, and bisexual persons become an inquiry separate from the identities themselves. One discovery in this new approach is that, in contrast to other "outsider" groups, contempt and hatred for lesbian, gay, and bisexual persons can still be openly expressed with minimal social disapproval (Johansson, 1990d). Personal and institutional hostility and intolerance are not just acceptable but expected (Byrne, 1993; Gonsiorek, 1993; Herek, 1995). In addition to the bias against their sexual orientation, HIV/AIDS is also used as a justification for antagonistic reactions toward lesbian, gay, and bisexual persons (Garnets & Kimmel, 1993a). Bisexual men, for example, are perceived as spreading HIV/AIDS to the heterosexual population (R. Pope & Reynolds, 1991; Rust, 1995).

This chapter addresses the continual rejection of gay, bisexual, and lesbian persons, or what is referred to as heterosexism. Topics include issues of terminology; different levels of heterosexism; factors associated with psychological heterosexism; psychological benefits for perpetrators; psychological consequences for gay, lesbian, bisexual, and transgenderist persons; and issues and interventions related to combating heterosexism.

◆ Terms and Definitions

Often the term *homophobia* is used to describe the rejecting attitudes toward lesbians and gay persons, and *biphobia* toward bisexual persons. Herek (1995) recommended using an alternate term, *heterosexism,* which is defined as "the ideological system that denies, denigrates, and stigmatizes any nonheterosexual form of behavior, identity, relationship, or community" (p. 321). Although no single word is sufficient to address issues such as prejudice, discrimination, violence, morality, and legality, a term such as *homophobia* is less suitable than the term *heterosexism.* First, the literal meaning of *homophobia,* "fear of sameness," is an ill-fitting term for the prejudice, discrimination, and violence against gay and lesbian persons (Herek, 1995). The term does not indicate the extent of oppression directed toward same-gender identities (Blumenfeld, 1992). Second, homophobia implies that prejudice against gay and lesbian persons is a form of psychopathology. This puts the focus on the individual rather than on the larger cultural context (Herek et al., 1991). In addition, translating the oppression of lesbian and gay men into a pathology of the oppressors could presumably mean that they be treated with compassion (Kitzinger & Perkins, 1993) or, as stated by Card (1996), elicit sympathy because they are victims of a "fear." Logan

(1996) found considerably more prejudicial responses than phobic responses in an investigation of anti-lesbian-and-gay attitudes. A phobia is a clinical condition at the extreme end of the fear continuum. It is characterized by avoidance of situations because of overwhelming psychological or physiological outcomes. Herek explained that prejudice and discrimination against lesbians and gay men do not represent a phobia or fear on the level of claustrophobia or agoraphobia. Nor are they irrational and dysfunctional behaviors.

◆ Different Levels of Heterosexism

Heterosexism appears in many forms. The two most comprehensive forms operate at the cultural and individual levels.

Cultural Heterosexism

The cultural level of heterosexism is manifested in the belief in and promotion of the inherent superiority of the heterosexual sexual orientation, that it is the only acceptable form of affectional and sexual expression. This belief is reinforced by social customs and institutions (Cruikshank, 1992; D'Augelli & Garnets, 1995; Neisen, 1990). Cultural heterosexism is like institutional racism and sexism in these ways and is sometimes referred to as institutionalized heterosexism (Blumenfeld & Raymond, 1993). It is so pervasive and taken for granted that it is rarely even noticed (Herek, 1995).

Cruikshank (1992) explained that, to maintain the supremacy of heterosexuality, the lives of persons other than heterosexuals are "erased." For example, translations of Greek poetry celebrating love between men were altered. The erotic meaning of Walt Whitman's poetry in the nineteenth century was overlooked. After her death, Emily

Dickinson's passionate love letters to women and her poems were altered by her family, a coverup that survived for a hundred years. If not erased, the existence of persons other than heterosexuals is simply not acknowledged. For example, even though research in the humanities and the social sciences claims to pursue knowledge about humankind, lesbian, gay, and bisexual persons were not mentioned in college textbooks until recent years, except in sections on deviance and mental illness. As another example, when do you read about news of lesbian, gay, bisexual, or transgenderist graduates in alumni magazines? Kitzinger (1996) noted that racial and ethnic lesbian and gay persons also experience omission in the dominant Euro-American gay and lesbian communities. Either their needs are not discussed or the needs of the dominant group are discussed as if they fit all gay and lesbian persons.

Discrimination

Cultural heterosexism is expressed in subtle forms such as in lack of acknowledgment or in brazen acts of discrimination (Neisen, 1990). Johansson (1990a) defined *discrimination* as "treatment that disadvantages others by virtue of their perceived membership in a group" (p. 320). The bottom line of disadvantages for gay, lesbian, and bisexual persons is that their basic rights are unprotected. In most civil rights legislation, they are excluded from lists of protected categories (Byrne, 1993; R. Green, 1992; Rivera, 1991). Except for a handful of statewide laws and a few dozen municipal laws, no legal protection exists from overt discrimination in areas such as employment, housing, services, and access to public accommodations (D'Augelli & Garnets, 1995; Herek, 1995). In a national telephone survey of a probability sample of lesbians and gay men, almost half (47%) reported that they experienced discrimination because of their sexual orientation in areas such as work, housing, and health care ("Results of Poll," 1989).

Attempts to uniformly provide gay, lesbian, and bisexual persons some protections failed until groups concerned with civil liberties eventually focused on the violations of their civil rights. The struggle began in the 1970s to include same-gender and bisexual sexual orientations in the protected lists of antidiscrimination laws. This led to the passage of around 50 municipal ordinances with such guarantees (Johansson, 1990a). The larger picture continues, however, of no legal protection from discrimination throughout most of the United States. Gay, lesbian, and bisexual persons are also not a protected class in the U.S. Constitution. They do not qualify for protection under the Equal Protection Clauses of the Fifth or Fourteenth Amendments. Consequently, they generally cannot rely on the Constitution or the courts to shield them from discrimination. Only First Amendment speech and associational rights are somewhat consistently upheld by the courts (Byrne, 1993).

Sodomy laws are the historic source of all legal discrimination against gay, lesbian, and bisexual persons (Johansson, 1990b). Based on these laws, almost half of the U.S. states still criminalize (as a felony offense) private consensual same-gender sexual relations among adults. In other words, where the laws exist, gay, lesbian, and bisexual persons can be imprisoned for engaging in private, consensual, same-gender sex. Although these laws are not often invoked, they symbolically convey the message that these persons are to be punished for their same-gender involvements (D'Augelli & Garnets, 1995). For many heterosexual men and women, this message disavows the claims of gay, lesbian, and bisexual persons for fair and nondiscriminatory treatment.

A Context Example of Discrimination:
The Workplace

Job discrimination with its potential economic ruin is one of the most severe threats to lesbian, gay, bisexual, and transgenderist persons (Gonsiorek, 1993). Discrimination can result in not being hired, not being promoted, and not getting mentoring and support needed for advancement (Goldman, 1992). Employees can also be threatened with or actually lose jobs if their sexual identity is known (Kaupman, 1991; Landau, 1994; J. Lee & Brown, 1993). Hardly any federal, state, or local laws or private company policies protect them from these actions. Nor do the U.S. Constitution or the courts offer protection (*Bowers v. Hardwick, 1986;* Byrne, 1993). This situation changed to some degree in 1996 when the Supreme Court struck down a Colorado amendment prohibiting "protected status" for these employees (Mauro, 1996). In addition, the Employment Non-Discrimination Act of 1997 (ENDA) could potentially be a turning point. This bill, recently reintroduced in Congress after being defeated in the Senate by one vote in 1996, would prohibit workplace discrimination because of one's sexual orientation (National Gay and Lesbian Task Force [NGLTF], 1997).

If passed, ENDA will not apply to the armed forces or religious organizations. Lesbians, gay, and bisexual workers in those arenas therefore could still be fired (Zavos, 1995). This is the case, for example, if the military policy "don't ask, don't tell" is violated. To remain in the military, lesbians and gay men cannot participate in same-gender sexual acts or even say they are lesbian or gay (10 U.S.CA. 654) (Landau, 1994). Bohan (1996) linked this continued discrimination in the military to religious persecution of lesbians and gay men. Discrimination from both sources is based on authoritarianism or the authority to condemn. Two studies by the

Department of Defense (McDaniel, 1989; Sarbin & Karols, 1988) showed that the service records of lesbians and gay men are superior, on average, to those of heterosexual men and women. These facts, however, do not deter the discrimination against gay and lesbian persons in the military, which continues (Landau, 1994).

Legal protection from private employment discrimination is based primarily on state statutes or local ordinances. To date, however, only 11 states ban workplace discrimination against lesbian, gay, and bisexual workers (Wisconsin, Massachusetts, Connecticut, California, New Jersey, Vermont, Minnesota, Rhode Island, New Hampshire, Maine, and Hawaii), along with the District of Columbia (NGLTF, 1997). There is little consistency, however, in the extent of coverage from one state to another (Gonsiorek, 1993). With the exception of California's antidiscrimination law, the antidiscrimination laws in the other states also apply to housing and public accommodations (NGLTF, 1997). Few cities, counties, and other local municipalities provide protections (119 in 1994) (NGLTF, 1994).

Since the 1970s, various progressive private companies (as well as colleges and universities, professional organizations, and unions) developed explicit policies that prohibit discrimination on the basis of sexual orientation (Hedgpeth, 1979-1980; Kronenberger, 1991). Colleges and universities and companies associated with high technology and the entertainment industries led the way (Dodge, 1993; D. Jones & Willette, 1995). Many nonprogressive companies, however, hold explicit or implicit policies against employing lesbian, gay, or bisexual persons, or keeping them if identified (Hays, 1991). A notable example is the Cracker Barrel restaurants' 1991 policy of not employing lesbians or gay men. Under the policy, current employees identified as lesbian or gay are terminated no matter how long they have worked for the restaurant (Kaupman, 1991). As noted earlier, if gay, lesbian, and bisexual persons are not terminated from a job or career, they can still experience barriers to advancement and denials of promotion. Mentoring and support needed for advancement may not be forthcoming (Goldman, 1992).

As things stand now, only an uneven patchwork of a few state and local legal protections apply to gay, lesbian, transgenderist, and bisexual persons in the workplace. Some major regions of the country, especially the South, provide almost no protection (Landau, 1994). In many states, therefore, these workers face lawful and open discrimination by private employers, public school districts, and other public employers (Bryne, 1993).

Psychological Heterosexism

Cultural heterosexism fosters individual negative attitudes toward gay, lesbian, transgenderist, and bisexual persons by providing a system of values and stereotypes that appears to justify psychological heterosexism (Herek, 1990; Obear, 1991). This second form of heterosexism is demonstrated in both feelings and behaviors (Herek, 1995). The feelings include disgust and indignation toward lesbian, gay, bisexual, and transgenderist persons (e.g., Berrill, 1990; Herek, 1993; M. Levine, 1979; Levine & Leonard, 1984). The most well known behaviors include open hostility, which ranges from jokes and derogatory terms to verbal abuse and physical attacks. Behaviors can also include avoidance and withholding of support (McDougall, 1993).

Recent public demonstrations of psychological heterosexism include the hostile reactions to proposed legislation to make employment discrimination against lesbian, gay, and bisexual persons unlawful. When local legislatures pass nondiscrimination laws protecting these groups, other groups that oppose these laws often attempt to get

them repealed (Kirk & Madsen, 1989). In 1992, for example, Colorado voters amended the state's constitution to invalidate local antidiscrimination ordinances in several cities in the state. They also voted to prohibit "protected status" based on same-gender and bisexual orientation. As noted earlier, in 1966, the Supreme Court struck down the Colorado amendment (Mauro, 1996). Two of the latest states to pass bills extending civil rights to lesbians and gay men are Maine and New Hampshire but several far-right groups have already pledged to work on repeals of these bills (NGLTF, 1997; Quinn, 1997).

Violence

In its most severe form, psychological heterosexism results in violence or hate crimes that range from verbal harassment to murder (e.g., Berrill, 1990; Comstock, 1991; D'Augelli, 1992; Dean, Wu, & Martin, 1992; Herek, 1990, 1993; J. Hunter, 1990). Berrill reviewed 25 questionnaire studies and found that a median rate of 9% of gay and lesbian respondents had been assaulted with a weapon because of their sexual orientation. The rates for other types of violence and harassment included simple physical assault (17%), vandalism of property (19%), threats of violence (44%), throwing objects (25%), spitting (13%), and verbal harassment (80%). Results from a national telephone survey were similar ("Results of Poll," 1989).

Many lesbians and gay men do not report these kinds of incidents to the authorities. They fear that they will be subjected to further harassment at the hands of police or others who may learn of their sexual orientation (Herek, 1995; Murphy, 1994). Even with what is reported, however, the Justice Department indicates that lesbian and gay men are subjected to proportionally more physical violence than any other minority community (Reynolds, 1989). In addition, the violence is steadily growing. Between 1988 and

1991, violence in five major U.S. cities (New York, San Francisco, Chicago, Boston, and Minneapolis-St. Paul) increased 161% (Berrill, 1990). The Ku Klux Klan, Aryan Nation, and other White supremacist groups have increased in membership and stepped up activity against target groups including lesbians and gay men (Cruikshank, 1992).

Along with the escalating extent of violence, the severity of the attacks is also intensifying. Nail-studded baseball bats and switchblades are replacing drive-by slurs and egg-tossings. Individuals are sometimes picked up, tied up and beaten, and sliced with razors. After President Clinton's announced desire to lift the military's ban on openly gay and lesbian service personnel, Stengold (a gay sailor who disclosed his sexual orientation to his commanding officer) was battered to death by shipmates in a public rest room, and three marines beat a gay man while shouting "Clinton must pay" (Byrne, 1993). Even if not the direct target of violence, living with the possibility makes life more stressful; peace of mind is tenuous.

Prejudice and Stereotypes

The negative attitudes that can lead to violence result from prejudice and stereotypes. These are the core factors that produce psychological heterosexism.

Prejudice. The term *prejudice* refers to "a negative prejudgment reached before the pertinent information has been collected or examined and therefore based on insufficient or even imaginary evidence" (Johansson, 1990c, p. 1031). Herek (1995) recommended use of two constructs central to the social-psychological analysis of prejudice for understanding psychological heterosexism: *beliefs* (probabilistic statements about relationships between phenomena) and *attitudes* (evaluations of persons, issues, and objects on such dimensions as good-bad, like-dislike,

or favorable-unfavorable). Prejudice is maintained through the transmission of the beliefs and attitudes associated with stereotypes about members of a group.

Stereotypes. Some stereotypes reflect cultural ideologies about minority groups in general such as seeing the members of these groups as threatening and inferior to members of the dominant group. Other stereotypes are specific to a particular minority group such as lesbians and gay men (Herek, 1995). Instead of being based on characteristics that actually define this group (e.g., lesbians and gay men are attracted to others of their same gender), the stereotypes are based on characteristics that are unrelated to group membership (e.g., the belief that all gay men are child molesters or that lesbian and gay adults can influence the sexual orientation of children). In some instances, certain beliefs are only accurate about a few people in the group but are generalized to everyone in the group (Johansson, 1990c). For example, in research done with a sample of lesbians and gay men in bars, alcoholism may show up as a problem. It cannot be assumed, however, that all lesbians and gay men experience problems with alcohol or that alcoholism results from their sexual orientation (Herek et al., 1991). There are also many negative stereotypes specific to bisexual men and women that are held by heterosexual men and women as well as by lesbians and gay men. See Box 2.1.

Context Example of Prejudice, Stereotypes, and Harassment: The College Campus

Psychological heterosexism is pervasive in every mainstream social context. An example of one of these contexts is the college campus. Most lesbian, gay, and bisexual young adults on campus probably believe that their differentness is unacceptable there

---

Box 2.1. Stereotypes About Bisexual Men and Women

1. *Bisexual men and women are promiscuous and nonmonogamous.* The word *bisexual* implies a 50-50 split identity and the need for a lover of each gender to be satisfied. This conception leads to the stereotype that bisexual women and men are promiscuous and unable to commit themselves to long-term monogamous relationships (Ochs, 1996; Rust, 1996b). Sensational media stories perpetuate this stereotype: A woman leaves her husband for another woman, a married man participates in sex with a gay man, a woman leaves a lesbian relationship for a male lover, or a couple "swings" both ways (Ochs, 1996). These kinds of stories do not fit the lives of most bisexual men and women (Ochs, 1996). For example, only a small percentage of them are simultaneously involved with persons of both genders (Rust, 1992).

2. *Bisexual men and women are sexually indiscriminate and willing to have sex with anyone.* Like everyone else, bisexual persons are se-

lective about whom they find attractive. The main difference is that gender is not a salient requirement (Weinberg et al., 1994).

3. *Bisexual men and women are AIDS carriers.* Another media story may involve a closeted married man who contracts HIV from unsafe sex with another man and subsequently infects his wife with the virus (Ochs, 1996). In the mid-1980s, bisexual men and women gained popular and scientific attention because they were viewed as the gateway through which AIDS was spread to the heterosexual population (Rust, 1995). Bisexual men, however, are less likely than heterosexual men to engage in high-risk sexual activities (Lever, Kanouse, Rogers, Carson, & Hertz, 1992). In addition, a review of 17 studies reporting HIV prevalence rates among men who have sex with men showed higher rates of HIV infection in gay men than bisexual men (Stokes, Taywaditep, Vanable, & McKirnan, 1996). ◆

(Slater, 1993). Most likely this belief will be confirmed. The evidence is overwhelming that the college climate is hostile to these young adults. This is demonstrated in prejudice and harassment (Berrill, 1989).

Stereotypes and prejudice. Negative stereotypes and prejudice are noticeable among students, resident assistants, and instructors. Among *students,* for example, Kurdek (1988a) found that 17% agreed with each of 40 negative statements about lesbians and gay men. More than half of college student respondents surveyed by Pogrebin (1983) indicated their belief that "homosexuality" was more deviant than murder or drug addiction. D'Augelli and Rose (1990) found that more than a quarter (29%) of first-year college

students felt the campus would be a better one without lesbians and gay men. Close to half of the respondents thought same-gender sex was wrong and that gay men were disgusting. More than 80% made hostile remarks toward both lesbians and gay students; men made hostile comments more often than women. D'Augelli and Rose concluded that the students who were most hostile did not care about what problems their negative remarks caused. Males particularly viewed the harassment experienced by lesbians and gay men on campus with indifference; they also did not see it as serious.

Most first-year students live in university housing. Negative attitudes toward lesbian and gay students often appear in these settings and the *resident assistants* (especially if male) are likely to reinforce these attitudes. D'Augelli (1989b) found that two-thirds of the male candidates for resident assistant jobs in university housing admitted making negative comments about lesbians and gay men.

Lopez and Chism (1993) found that lesbian and gay students observe considerable variability among *instructors* in terms of their attitudes and behaviors. Although negative remarks in classes are rare, instructors range in their receptivity to lesbians and gay students from welcoming to negative stances. Welcoming stances include encouraging discussion of lesbian and gay issues and affirmative statements. Negative stances include deprecating remarks and humor and telling students who raise lesbian and gay issues that they are oversensitive.

A sample of gay, lesbian, and bisexual graduate students in psychology programs, studied by Cantor and Pilkington (1992), reported various negative experiences in classes. For instance, one student observed, "While discussing neurological aspects of gait impairment, the instructor walked in front of the class with a limp wrist and side-to-side motion, demonstrating what the instructor called the 'stereotypical fag walk' " (p. 5). Lopez and Chism found that the most frequent response by instructors was avoidance. They discussed families, couples, and other subjects only in relation to heterosexual persons. Some instructors did not want to deal with "messy issues" such as same-gender sexual orientation.

Harassment. The NGLTF Policy Institute (1991) collected data on the campus climate from 40 colleges and universities. Between 40% and 54% of the lesbian, gay, and bisexual respondents reported that they had been verbally harassed or threatened. Examples of this kind of harassment included demeaning jokes, jeers, and threatening notes, signs, and phone calls (Slater, 1993). Lopez and Chism

(1993) reported that lesbians and gay students may overhear or be addressed with hostile remarks such as "faggot" or "bash them back into the closet." D'Augelli (1989a) found that about two-thirds (64%) of gay and lesbian college students felt their safety on campus was in jeopardy due to their experience with threats, verbal abuse, property damage, or being chased. Hostile behaviors occur even in liberal colleges. Norris (1992) reported the results of two studies at Oberlin College, a selective liberal arts college. One of the surprises as well as paradoxes was the high attitudinal support of students for lesbians and gay men but also widespread harassment such as hostile graffiti and verbal insults.

Factors Associated With Negative Beliefs and Attitudes

Stereotypes are developed through learning. They are not present in young children prior to acculturation (Johansson, 1990c). Increasingly, however, as children get older, they show adultlike negative reactions toward same-gender sexual orientation (Bozett, 1987). Once learned, stereotypes are continually reinforced through popular culture such as the media (Herek, 1995). Adults, however, hold varying attitudes toward gay and lesbian persons, which range from acceptance to disdain. Individuals who hold the most negative attitudes consistently display certain psychological, social, and demographic characteristics (e.g., Eliason, 1995; Herek, 1988, 1991, 1995; Herek & Glunt, 1993; Kite, 1984, 1994; Logan, 1996). Although most research studies used lesbian and gay samples, the same characteristics are also likely to be associated with negative attitudes toward bisexual and transgenderist women and men.

Male gender. Overall, men (most often White) hold more heterosexist beliefs and attitudes, especially toward gay men (Laner & Laner, 1980; Page & Yee, 1985). Within the family context, males, including fathers, brothers, and sons, react more harshly than females to a family member's disclosure of a gay or lesbian identity (Herek, 1988; Kite, 1984). In contrast to female college students, male students hold more negative attitudes toward gay men but they also perceive lesbians as a threat to society's basic institutions (D'Augelli & Rose, 1990). Although Kite (1984) also found that men, compared with women, are likely to rate both gay men and lesbians more negatively, the gender difference disappeared when the magnitude of the sample size increased.

Conservatism, authoritarianism, and traditionalism. D'Augelli and Rose (1990) found that college students from conservative families were more negative about gay men than students from moderate or liberal families. Both men and women with negative attitudes express conservative political views (e.g., D'Augelli & Rose, 1990; Seltzer, 1992), display high levels of sexual conservatism (Ficarrotto, 1990), and exhibit authoritarian thinking (e.g., "I'm right, you are wrong") and intolerance for ambiguity (e.g., Herek, 1988; Obear, 1991). They are also more likely to subscribe to a conservative or fundamentalist religious ideology (S. Green, Dixon, & Gold-Neil, 1993; Herek, 1988; Seltzer, 1992). According to Johansson (1990a), when men and women feel no scruples about expressing bigotry against gay, lesbian, transgenderist, and bisexual persons, they are likely to believe that religious authority backs their negative beliefs and supports their expressions of bigotry as an obligation. Heterosexual women and men with negative attitudes and beliefs about lesbians and gay men are also likely to subscribe to traditional gender role beliefs (Herek, 1988; Kurdek, 1988a; Newman, 1989; Stark, 1991). Negative attitudes are

directed (especially by men) toward gender nonconformity. Lesbians, for example, are rated more negatively when they appear less traditionally feminine (Laner & Laner, 1980).

Older, less well educated, and bigoted residential area, and bigoted peers. Persons high on negative attitudes and beliefs tend to be older (e.g., Eliason, 1995; Marsiglio, 1993; Simoni, 1996) and less well educated (Jensen, Gambles, & Olsen, 1988; Kurdek, 1988a; Seltzer, 1992; Serovich, Skeen, Walters, & Robinson, 1993; Simoni, 1996) than those who are less negative. They are also more likely to live in areas where negative attitudes toward same-gender sexual orientation are the norm (e.g., the midwestern and southern United States, rural areas, or small towns). Families living in suburbs and other urban areas are more tolerant, followed closely by those from large cities (Hong, 1984; Irwin & Thompson, 1977). Those with negative beliefs and attitudes, especially males, are also more likely to perceive that their peers likewise manifest negative attitudes (Kite & Deaux, 1986; Nyberg & Alston, 1976; Seltzer, 1992).

Fears that others can be converted. Golden (1996) pointed out that conceptualizing sexuality as fluid or as subject to personal choice helps explain the hatred of gay, lesbian, and bisexual persons. If sexuality is not fixed, this means that exclusive heterosexuality is in danger. The fear is that young persons and adults, when exposed to a range of possible sexual identities, may choose to act given the the idea of having a choice. Sexuality as fixed and set at birth is a less threatening idea.

No contact. Negative attitudes and beliefs are associated with no personal contact with gay or lesbian persons (D'Augelli & Rose, 1990; Green et al., 1993; Herek & Glunt,

1993). D'Augelli and Rose (1990) found in a study of college students that most of them did not know a lesbian (94%) or gay man (92%) well, and more than half did not know a lesbian or gay man casually. Herek and Glunt (1993) found that in the general population, only about one-third of American adults personally know a lesbian or gay man.

Eliason (1995) indicated that many of the factors related to psychological heterosexism are interactive and overlapping. Some factors are stronger or weaker depending on whether other factors are present or not. The factor of older age, for example, may represent a cohort factor. Eventually, older people who grew up with the "sexual revolution" and in the post-Stonewall era may hold more positive attitudes than the current population of older persons.

Psychological Functions of Negative Beliefs and Attitudes

Although there are unique factors that contribute to negative beliefs and attitudes in racial and ethnic communities toward divergences in sexual orientation (see Chapter 5), in these and other communities there are psychological functions fulfilled by holding negative views. Following Herek (1995), there are three principal psychological functions or benefits: experiential, social identity, and ego-defensive.

The *experiential function* assists individuals in making sense of their previous interactions with lesbians and gay men. If they experience pleasant interactions, heterosexual persons tend to generalize from them and generally accept these men and women. Unpleasant experiences, on the other hand, generally tend to lead to negative attitudes. As indicated above, however, most heterosexual men and women do not personally know a lesbian or gay person. This leads to several possible consequences. First, their negative attitudes probably do not serve an experien-

tial function. Second, they probably view a lesbian or gay man as a symbol, generally representing the sort of person one is not, does not want to be, and does not want in one's family. This phenomenon often results in distancing oneself from "this sort of person" or attacking the person.

A second psychological function, *social identity,* increases self-esteem through two interrelated components: value-expressive and social-expressive. Through the *value-expressive component,* important values are expressed that are tied to and affirm self-concept. A fundamentalist Christian, for example, may express hostile attitudes toward lesbians and gay men to affirm her or his self-concept as a good Christian. Through the *social-expressive component,* values are expressed that strengthen one's sense of belonging to an important reference group. The expression of certain values gains acceptance, approval, and love from the group. Depending on which values the group supports, approval can be gained by regarding lesbians and gay persons either favorably or unfavorably. Violence toward lesbians and gay men is value-expressive when it conveys values central to the self-concepts of the perpetrators such as upholding moral authority. It is social-expressive when it helps perpetrators maintain status and affiliation with their peers.

The third psychological function is *ego-defensive.* Hostility toward lesbians and gay men represents an unconscious defensive strategy that helps some individuals avoid internal conflict about unacceptable parts of themselves. They perhaps fear that they too are attracted to persons of their gender. Violence is ego-defensive when perpetrators attack or punish someone who symbolizes the unacceptable part of themselves. They are probably unaware of their motivations.

Perpetrators of violence may simultaneously play out several or all of the functions. In other words, their attacks may result from multiple motives. For example, most of the reported attacks on lesbians and gay men are carried out by males and typically juveniles or young adults in groups. The victim is usually a stranger (Berrill, 1990) and usually a gay man (e.g., Kite & Deaux, 1986). Herek (1992b) explained that violent behavior in these situations is often a gender display and assertion of heterosexual orientation. Attacks on gay men particularly show antagonism toward their sexual orientation and gender violation while at the same time affirming the attacker's own heterosexual orientation and masculine gender identity (ego-defensive function). The social identity function is also in play because of benefits to the cohesiveness among group members.

◆ Mental Health Consequences of Heterosexism for Lesbian, Gay, and Bisexual Persons

There are two ways to look at the mental health of lesbian, gay, and bisexual persons. First, their sexual orientation does not cause mental health problems. Herek (1991) concluded from a review of research on the mental health of lesbians and gay men that overall they do not display difficulties such as depression, alcohol abuse, or suicide risk out of the normal range (e.g., Bell & Weinberg, 1978; Crocker & Major, 1989; Freedman, 1971; Gonsiorek, 1982; Hammersmith & Weinberg, 1973; Hart et al., 1978; Hooker, 1957; Reiss, 1980). There are exceptions to this conclusion, however, including data suggesting a high risk for suicide among bisexual, gay, and lesbian adolescents (see Chapter 8) and higher levels of alcohol and drug use by lesbians and gay men in comparison with the general population (e.g., McKirnan & Peterson, 1989). Ross, Paulsen, and Stalstrom (1988), on the other hand, concluded that the link is not between any particular minority status and mental health but be-

tween stigmatization and mental health. This is the second way to view the mental health of gay, bisexual, and lesbian persons.

Stigmatization and Internalized Oppression

Society's expectations for sex and gender, and the stigmatization of noncompliance, are internalized early in life. Consequently, gay, lesbian, and bisexual persons usually experience negative feeling about themselves when they first recognize their same-gender attractions (Goffman, 1963; Gonsiorek, 1993; Hetrick & Martin, 1984; I. Meyer, 1995; J. Smith, 1988; Stein & Cohen, 1984). This is what is meant by *internalized homophobia* (Herek, 1995). Card (1996) emphasized that *homophobia* (or *biphobia*) is an appropriate term for the fear that many lesbian, gay, and bisexual persons have of being outcasts. Neisen (1990) suggested applying the stronger concept of *shame* for the self-hatred that is internalized. A. Smith (1997) used the term *internalized oppression,* which is used here also.

Gonsiorek (1993) explained that internalized oppression is expressed in both overt and covert ways by lesbian, gay, and bisexual persons. Overt expressions include conscious self-deprecation of themselves as inferior or deviant because of their sexual orientation. They may view themselves as not deserving of support from others. Covert expressions of internalized oppression are more common. Individuals may appear to accept themselves and their same-gender sexual orientation but subtly sabotage themselves. For example, they may set themselves up for rejection by unplanned and impulsive disclosures in environments where people are likely to react with hostility, may tolerate abusive behavior from bigoted people, or may abandon educational or career plans.

For most gay, lesbian, and bisexual persons, internalized oppression, and overcom-

ing it, is the challenge of coming out (Garnets, Herek, & Levy, 1992; Gonsiorek, 1993;
Herek, 1992a; Malyon, 1981-1982). In part,
coming out is the process of reconstructing
devalued parts of the self (Malyon, 1981-
1982; Stein & Cohen, 1984). Most lesbian,
gay, and bisexual persons manage to develop
a positive identity. They may not, however,
disclose their sexual orientation for some
time, if ever (Herek, 1995) (see Chapters 4
and 5).

Minority Stress

I. Meyer (1995) used the concept of *minority stress* to look at the mental health of
741 gay men in a community sample in New
York City, none of whom was diagnosed with
HIV. *Minority stress* was defined as the
chronic stress that results from living in a
heterosexist society that stigmatizes same-
gender sexual orientation. Three types of *minority stressors* were measured: (a) *internalized homophobia* (societal negative attitudes
directed toward the self), (b) *stigma* (expectations of rejection and discrimination), and
(c) *actual confrontations with discrimination
and violence.* Meyer found that gay men who
experienced high levels of minority stress
were two to three times more likely to experience high levels of the three measured minority stressors. The experience of each minority stressor was also significantly
associated with a variety of mental health
measures (e.g., demoralization, guilt, sex
problems, suicide, and distress related to the
HIV epidemic).

Other studies showed findings similar to
those of I. Meyer (1995). Garnets et al.
(1992), for example, described numerous
mental health consequences from discrimination, assaults, and self-blame: (a) *Discrimination* can result in feelings of sadness
and anxiety (Dion, 1986) and the feeling that
life is difficult and unfair (Birt & Dion,
1987); (b) *assaults* or other overt victimiza-

tion, including threats of physical assaults
and verbal abuse, can result in feelings of
personal loss, rejection, humiliation, and depression; and (c) *self-blame* can result in
feeling justifiably punished because of one's
sexual orientation (Bard & Sangrey, 1979),
which can lead to depression and feelings of
helplessness (Janoff-Bulmam, 1979). Other
reported distress reactions include agitation,
restlessness, sleep disturbances, headaches,
and diarrhea. Deterioration of personal relationships is also common (Bard & Sangrey,
1979; Frieze, Hymer, & Greenberg, 1984).

Garnets et al. (1992) proposed that hate
crimes, which involve attacking a person's
identity in addition to his or her person or
property, can cause psychological harm beyond that associated with nonbias crimes.
Results of a recent study on hate crimes
among lesbian, gay, and bisexual persons in
Sacramento, California, reached a similar
conclusion (Herek, Gillis, Cogan, & Glunt,
1997). Psychological harm can also occur
when there are no direct assaults or violence.
This happened, for example, with the passage of Colorado's Amendment 2, which
took away the protection of rights of gay,
lesbian, and bisexual persons. Russell (1995)
found that many gay, lesbian, and bisexual
persons in the state were traumatized by the
relentless and negative process and the shock
of the outcome. The amendment was not
expected to pass but did. It was also a shock
to discover that some friends, coworkers, and
family members voted for its passage. The
psychological costs included increases in
self-reported depression and anxiety, symptoms of post-traumatic disorder, reinforced
internalized oppression, and increased fears
for one's safety.

Mediating Factors

Most bisexual, gay, and lesbian persons
clearly face numerous challenges due to society's prejudice and discrimination toward

them. Some of them experience so much psychological distress that they try to suppress their same-gender sexual orientation, wish they were heterosexual, and isolate themselves from the lesbian and gay community (Herek, 1991). Greene (1996) cautioned, however, that heterosexism is not likely to be experienced in the same way by all persons or to have the same meaning or impact for them. It will vary with social, racial, ethnic, and cultural contexts. Various other researchers also emphasized that intervening variables mediate distress (Lazarus & Folkman, 1984; I. Meyer, 1995). How one perceives an assault, for example, can be affected by one's stage in the coming out process. If in the later stages, the person may be able to balance the victimization against the past positive experiences of his or her same-gender or bisexual identity (e.g., Miranda & Storms, 1989; S. Schneider, Farberow, & Kruks, 1989). In addition, a sense of connection to the lesbian, gay, or bisexual community is often important in protecting one from minority stress or alleviating it (Garnets et al., 1992; I. Meyer, 1995). The community provides resources such as social support, affirmation and validation of one's sexual orientation, and encouragement to reappraise and devalue the dominant culture's stigmatization of one's sexual orientation (e.g., Crocker & Major, 1989; Garnets & Kimmel, 1993a; Jones et al., 1984; Thoits, 1985) (see Chapter 3). In reaction to Colorado's Amendment 2, some gay, lesbian, and bisexual persons were stimulated by the experience to increase their political involvement to fight against the discrimination of the dominant culture (Russell, 1995).

Combating Heterosexism

Reduction in heterosexism requires changes at both the institutional and the individual levels. Reforms at the institutional level are difficult to achieve although some progress has been noted (see above). Rubenstein (1996) emphasized that the law is the primary arena for the struggle toward greater institutional reforms. Change at the individual level is even more difficult to attain because it requires a transformation in the consciousness of heterosexual persons. As important as changes in laws are, gay, lesbian, and bisexual persons will not be liberated from heterosexism until they are viewed by mainstream society as full and equal citizens. This goal, however, seems remote if not unreachable. The resistance to giving up negative stereotypes is solid. Even when stereotypes are confronted with facts, they are resistant to change. Kite (1994) found that prejudices do not change with new information.

Herek (1995) explained that people use cognitive strategies to assist them to perceive their environment as generally stable, predictable, and manageable (e.g., Snyder, 1981). These strategies, however, are what also make stereotypes about gay, lesbian, and bisexual persons so hard to change. Stereotypes are used to judge the importance of information in the environment and integrate it with past experiences. In other words, people view the world selectively. Prejudiced men and women, for example, usually *only notice the characteristics that match their stereotypes* of lesbian, gay, and bisexual persons, and they ignore information that contradicts the match. In addition to distorted perceptions of current observations, stereotypes can also affect memory of past events. For example, prejudiced men and women tend to *remember only the past information that fits with their stereotypes* of same-gender or bisexual sexual orientation. Their *stereotypes also contain illusory correlations* (e.g., believing that a particular characteristic such as maladjustment occurs frequently among gay, lesbian, and bisexual persons when, in actuality, no such correlation exists).

*Strategies for Change at
the Individual Level*

Although the barriers are strong, there are strategies that focus on attempting to change prejudicial attitudes toward gay, lesbian, bisexual, and transgenderist persons. No single strategy is universally effective, but *personal contact* appears to be the most consistently influential factor in reducing prejudice (Herek & Glunt, 1993). Contact refutes misconceptions and thereby changes cognitions. Disclosure of one's identity to family members, friends, and coworkers, then, is an important way to challenge psychological heterosexism. This strategy also points to the importance of institutional changes such as passage of antidiscrimination laws so that lesbian, gay, transgenderist, and bisexual persons can disclose their identities with fewer risks (Herek, 1992a).

Herek (1995) pointed out that it is necessary that change strategies match the functions served by holding prejudicial attitudes. The contact strategy, for example, fits with the knowledge that heterosexist attitudes for some people serve an *experiential* function, meaning that their attitudes are shaped by actual experience. Attitudes that serve a *value-expressive* function, however, may not change with positive contact. Dissonance between the person's prejudices and another important value such as personal freedom may have an influence. In addition, attitudes may change if a respected authority such as a minister presents a more positive view of same-gender or bisexual sexual orientation that is grounded in religious teachings. Close contact is also not likely to have any positive influence on attitudes that serve an *ego-defensive* function. Because fears exist about one's own sexual identity, close contact may arouse anxiety and heighten defensiveness. Attitudes expressing a *social-expressive* function may change if one's reference groups change (e.g, from conservative to more liberal-thinking groups). As cultural norms shift, the attitudes of reference groups and individuals may shift accordingly. As noted throughout this chapter, however, there is not much evidence of a shift in norms as there is little condemnation of heterosexism (Herek, 1995).

*Strategies for Change at
the Institutional Level*

Two context examples are presented here: the college campus and the workplace. The purpose is to demonstrate the kinds of institutional changes that are necessary to create an affirmative environment for gay, lesbian, bisexual, and transgenderist students and workers.

The college campus. Although there are nondiscrimination policies and codes of student conduct on most campuses, only a few include specific applications to gay, lesbian, bisexual, and transgenderist students (Obear, 1991). Consequently, the personal and civil rights of these students may be violated throughout their academic careers, and they will have little or no recourse (D'Augelli & Rose, 1990).

Colleges and universities should take action in a variety of ways to ensure that bisexual, gay, and lesbian students are able to accomplish their educational goals within the context of healthy social and individual development. First, the institution should include sexual orientation in its mission and nondiscrimination policy statements. The institution should make sure the whole campus is aware of such policies through statements by the president or provost, student organizations, and handbooks (D'Augelli, 1989d). The basic goal is for lesbian, gay, transgenderist, and bisexual students to be able to participate in their campus activities without fear, harassment, or violence. It should be made clear to every person employed by or

attending a college or university which behaviors will not be tolerated (Schoenberg,
1989). Second, when hate-motivated attacks
happen to these students, the highest officers
of the institution should condemn the incidents and work to correct the underlying
problems that led to them. In addition, organizations that discriminate against bisexual,
transgenderist, gay, and lesbian students
should not be allowed to operate on campus
(D'Emilio, 1990).

Third, the president, other administrators,
and faculty should provide intellectual
leadership in learning more about diversity.
One example would be for the president to
attend a seminar on lesbian, gay, bisexual,
and transgenderist issues (Tierney, 1992).
Students should be challenged to develop the
building blocks for valuing diversity, such as
relativistic thinking, openness to new ideas,
and a belief in civil rights for all individuals
(Obear, 1991). Fourth, institutions should increase their library materials related to gay,
lesbian, transgenderist, and bisexual persons
and the issues that are relevant to them
(Schoenberg, 1989). Fifth, a gay, lesbian,
transgenderist, and bisexual student organization should be clearly recognized by the
university. The institution should help these
students with resources to obtain speakers
and sponsor dances and other programs
(Slater, 1993). Sixth, the institution should
support faculty and students who want to
pursue research on gay, lesbian, transgenderist, and bisexual persons and ensure that
there are no negative repercussions for these
areas of inquiry (D'Augelli, 1989d). Last,
one or more counselors who specialize in the
problems of gay, lesbian, transgenderist, and
bisexual persons should be on the staff of the
campus counseling center and health center
(D'Augelli, 1989d).

The workplace. Byrne (1993) described
affirmative workplaces as free of discrimination and harassment against bisexual, gay,

lesbian, and transgenderist workers and conducive to disclosure of their identities. A
pragmatic affirmative action model for moving toward these kinds of workplaces is
based on goals and timetables. The goals
involve numerical targets for hiring or promotion of qualified workers and timetables
with deadlines for achieving the goals. This
strategy sends a powerful message that an
organization is striving to ensure equality of
opportunity for lesbian, gay, bisexual, and
transgenderist workers.

While a goals-and-timetables plan is the
most effective way to ensure the hiring,
maintenance, and promotion of these workers, employers who seek to ensure equal opportunity as well as increased workplace diversity can also pursue various other
affirmative actions (Shallenberger, 1994).
Examples are listed in Box 2.2.

The success of these actions as well as a
goals-and-timetables plan depends on top
managements' commitment to the planned
changes (Ankeny, 1991) and the attitudes
of supervisors, managers, and coworkers
(J. Lee & Brown, 1993). Affirmative actions
in the workplace preferably are also backed
up by federal, state, and local civil rights
laws and ordinances. Whatever the endorse-
ments of equal treatment, however, bigoted
forces in the United States try to counter any
advances toward equality. For example, a
coalition of conservative religious groups
plans to protest and boycott corporations believed to promote "homosexuality." They
point to actions such as diversity training
programs, domestic partnership provisions,
and marketing of products and services to
lesbians and gay men. The first targeted company, American Airlines, was declared by the
coalition as among the "worst offenders"
(Caldwell, 1997a). In June 1997, the Southern Baptist Convention passed a resolution
calling on Southern Baptists to give up their
patronage of the Walt Disney Company and
its subsidiaries. The reason given was the

Box 2.2. Affirmative Actions in the Workplace

▶ Hire openly lesbian, gay, bisexual, and trans-genderist employees (Byrne, 1993).

▶ Include lesbian and gay domestic partner-ships and nonbiological children in employee benefit packages and family leave policies (Byrne, 1993; H. Jacobs, 1994).

▶ Implement strong employment policies and practices that encourage closeted employees to be open while also respecting privacy rights (Byrne, 1993).

▶ Develop an explicit policy prohibiting dis-crimination based on sexual orientation (Bryne, 1993; J. Lee & Brown, 1993).

▶ Establish zero tolerance for heterosexism in the workplace such as derogatory jokes, comments, and assumptions (Kitzinger, 1991).

▶ Intervene when problems arise; prejudice and harassment from heterosexual workers may, for example, increase in reaction to their per-ception that lesbian, gay, bisexual, and trans-genderist workers are treated in special ways (Byrne, 1993).

▶ Conduct and participate in diversity training programs and workshops that use techniques such as role-playing and videos to change attitudes and sensitize employees to others' perspectives and concerns (Byrne, 1993; J. Lee & Brown, 1993; Mickens, 1994).

▶ Foster contact between lesbian, gay, bisex-ual, transgenderist, and heterosexual co-workers (Byrne, 1993).

▶ Provide gay, lesbian, and bisexual affirmative contacts in the organization (Bryne, 1993).

▶ Talk with and learn the concerns of lesbian, gay, transgenderist, and bisexual workers (J. Lee, 1993).

▶ Actively encourage support groups for these workers (Bryne, 1993; Kronenberger, 1991; J. Lee & Brown, 1993; M. Levine & Leonard, 1984; Woolsey, 1991).

▶ Provide information on helpful organizations (e.g., Gay Teachers Association, Lesbian and Gay People in Medicine, High Tech Gays) (Brooks, 1991). ◆

"immoral ideologies" of Disney, which sup-port actions such as offering medical benefits to partners of lesbian and gay employees (Caldwell, 1997b).

◆ Summary

Heterosexism is a unique source of preju-dice, discrimination, and other rejecting ac-tions toward lesbian, gay, transgenderist, and bisexual persons. In all life arenas, their basic rights are either denied or violated. In addi-tion, there is an increase in both the incidence and the severity of violence perpetrated against these persons. The consequences of these actions or the threats of such actions can be severe in terms of mental health al-though the disturbances relate to stigmatiza-tion, not sexual orientation. Strategies to change the negative beliefs and stereotypes underlying bigoted actions face enormous barriers both on the individual and the insti-tutional levels. Nevertheless, certain inter-ventions at both levels may help to modify negative beliefs and stereotypes.

3

DEVELOPMENT

OF COMMUNITY

AND

CULTURE

◆ THE LESBIAN AND GAY COMMUNITY is represented by a national culture. This is symbolized by Pride Day parades held throughout the country every June to celebrate the Stonewall Rebellion. Globalization of the lesbian and gay community is also occurring (Likosky, 1992; N. Miller, 1992). Several international lesbian and gay organizations now exist (D'Augelli & Garnets, 1995) as well as Internet lists. These devel-

opments are leading to a sense of a worldwide community.

In previous decades, conditions were considerably different. Before World War I, for example, most lesbians and gay men in the United States did not view themselves as part of a community. They were largely isolated from each other. The few opportunities for interacting with other lesbians and gay men included small, secret friendship networks

(Berger & Mallon, 1993) and the rare clubs and bars in large cities that catered to them (D'Augelli & Garnets, 1995). The participants in friendship networks trusted each other not to disclose their identities. Outside of these groups, there was total anonymity including use of fictitious names in some locations for protection (Henry, 1941). In the decades after World War II, this closed world began to open up. Beginning community development and activism provided the early groundwork for the social, political, and cultural collectives that represent the lesbian and gay communities of contemporary America (Adam, 1987; Bérubé, 1990; D'Augelli & Garnets, 1995; D'Emilio, 1983). The objective of this chapter is to describe the circumstances leading to this dramatic transformation from hidden small groups to visible, flourishing communities. Other topics include community experiences of bisexual persons and racial and ethnic lesbian and gay persons, both in terms of the White gay and lesbian community and community developments of their own.

◆ History of Community Development

This review of the history of lesbian and gay community development in the United States barely outlines the extensive literature now available on this topic (e.g., Bérubé, 1990; D'Emilio, 1983; Duberman, 1993; Faderman, 1991). It begins with the pre-World War II period and ends with the current decade.

The World War II Impetus for Linking Up

Before World War II, there was no community like that known today to provide contacts, support, resources, role models, or a visible label for one's same-gender attractions (Bohan, 1996). The war experience,

however, fostered connections that were the foundation for the development of community (D'Augelli & Garnets, 1995). Men and women interested in same-gender sexuality often met like-minded persons in the gender-segregated military units. Many of them experienced fulfilling same-gender linkups for the first time, and a number of couples remained together following the war (Bérubé, 1990; D'Emilio, 1983). Upon their return to the United States, many of these couples and single lesbians and gay men remained in the cities in which they disembarked. This resulted in concentrations of lesbians and gay men in several large cities, especially on both U.S. coasts (Bohan, 1996). Although there were beginnings of community among lesbians and gay men, the climate was starkly repressive.

The 1950s: Seeds of National Organizations

Prior to and during the 1950s, "homosexuality" was illegal in every state (D'Augelli & Garnets, 1995; D'Emilio, 1983). If their sexual orientation was found out, lesbians and gay men were subject to reprisals across all areas of their lives. Their parents often disowned them and they often lost jobs, residences, their children, and in some cases visitation rights (D'Augelli & Garnets, 1995; D'Emilio, 1983; D. Martin & Lyon, 1995). Police raided lesbian and gay bars; subjected patrons to verbal, physical, and sexual abuse; arrested them; and gave lists of names of those arrested to newspapers. Notification to employers of arrests usually resulted in lost jobs. Periodic purges of "homosexuals" occurred on military bases, with resultant court martials and dishonorable discharges (Bohan, 1996; D. Martin & Lyon, 1995). As a result of the McCarthy hearings, any persons suspected of being a communist or "homosexual" were also purged from jobs in the federal government. "Homosexuals" also could not work in many state and local governments as well as in many institutions and businesses in the private sector (Bohan, 1996; Esterberg, 1996). There were no legal protections against any of these discriminatory actions.

Even though the repressive events provoked greater group identity among lesbians and gay men, public identity clearly was dangerous (D'Augelli & Garnets, 1995; D'Emilio, 1983). Most lesbians and gay men therefore were still isolated and afraid (D. Martin & Lyon, 1995). Nevertheless, the early seeds of what were to become national organizations were sown in this decade. Following the war, some of the individuals who met other lesbians and gay men in the military organized various social and political groups (D'Emilio, 1983). These groups, under the general title "Homophile Rights," were the beginning of the lesbian and gay community. They sought out members and evoked a sense of public group identity.

In 1951, the first formal "gay rights" group in the United States, the Mattachine Society, was founded in Los Angeles. Groups (of men) were formed in some large urban areas. In 1955, lesbians could also join or identify with a similar group, the Daughters of Bilitis, which was formed in San Francisco. The name was a disguise to make the club sound like any other women's lodge. Members could say it was a Greek poetry club even though the name Bilitis came from *The Songs of Bilitis* by Pierre Louys. This was a narrative love poem about Bilitis, who was a contemporary of Sappho on the Isle of Lesbos. When renting the first office for the club, the building manager was told that it was concerned with the sociological problems of single women. This secret club later became the first national lesbian organization (D. Martin & Lyon, 1995).

The objectives of both the Mattachine Society and the Daughters of Bilitis were to help the members, through social, educational, and consciousness-raising efforts, develop a positive self-image and adjust to society. Both groups represented accommodationist politics (D'Augelli & Garnets, 1995). They urged their members to dress and act according to mainstream standards and to avoid overt displays of their sexual identities (Bohan, 1996). For example, the Daughters of Bilitis and its newspaper, *The Ladder,* urged its members to match the "feminine" behavior acceptable to mainstream society (Esterberg, 1996). Both groups, however, encouraged their members to educate others about the mistreatment of lesbians and gay men (D'Augelli & Garnets, 1995). Given the political climate, these beginnings of support for lesbian and gay men were courageous ones. Even the attempts to fit in with mainstream society, however, did not achieve acceptance for them (Bohan, 1996).

The 1960s: The Decade of Stonewall

Much of the 1960s was not much different from the preceding decade. "Homosexuality" was still viewed as something to be socially controlled—through correction, treatment, or punishment. "Homosexual" contact in most states was still a criminal offense. Police harassment, entrapment, imprisonment, and blackmail continued. Gay men particularly were taunted, ostracized, and sometimes violently attacked (M. Levine, 1992). Many lesbian and gay groups at the time still disguised both their purpose and their membership (Cruikshank, 1992).

Social life for most lesbians and gay men was still mainly in bars, located mostly in large cities. This continued to be a dangerous risk as bars were still routinely raided by police, and arrests and overnight jail stays were still common. This largely involved working-class lesbians and gay men as those of higher social status did not tend to risk rest. Except for friendship circles and homophile organizations, they remained invisible (Bohan, 1996).

Given the continued social oppression of lesbians and gay men in the United States, it seems impossible to imagine what was to happen at the end of this decade. A routine police raid on the Stonewall Inn, a gay male bar in Greenwich Village, began on the night of June 27, 1969. Local gay men, drag queens, and "butch" lesbians, many of whom were people of color, rebelled and participated in confrontations with the police over several days. They put up a resistance to harassment and marginalization (Herdt & Boxer, 1993) and refused to get into police vans for transport to jail. A full-scale riot developed with other lesbians and gay men showing up to battle the police. Slogans were painted on walls such as "Gay Pride" (Bohan, 1996).

1970s: Major Growth of Culture and Community

Stonewall inaugurated a qualitatively different phase of politics for lesbians and gay men. There was a mass exit out of the closet with public demands for change (D'Augelli & Garnets, 1995). Although it seemed as if this mass liberation movement began almost overnight (D'Emilio, 1993), Stonewall was a watershed for the political activism that had begun to develop in the 1950s (Herdt & Boxer, 1992). Other mass movements also laid the foundation and provided models for both the Stonewall Rebellion and the Gay Liberation Front. Black militants were a model for transforming stigma into pride and strength. Movements such as the New Left provided critiques of American society and models of confrontational political action. The women's liberation movement supplied political analysis of sexism and sex roles (D'Emilio, 1993).

The key to building a mass movement for lesbians and gay men was public disclosure of their identities. As more and more of them became visible, others were drawn to do the same (D'Emilio, 1993). In early liberation publications, disclosure and being closeted were viewed as the struggle between liberation and oppression (e.g., Jay & Young, 1972). The guiding post-Stonewall philosophy in lesbian and gay communities was that invisibility reinforced stereotypes and thereby oppression (D'Augelli & Garnets, 1995). In addition to being a political strategy, disclosure was also driven by personal and social goals. On a personal level, disclosure was a giant step toward "shedding the self-hatred and internalized oppression imposed by a . . . [heterosexist] society" (D'Emilio, 1993, p. 70). Socially, it helped lesbians and gay men find each other and provided more positive identities and role models (Bohan, 1996).

In the wake of Stonewall, lesbian and gay culture was transformed from basically isolated and fragmented elements to the birth of group consciousness and more prominent cohesiveness (Cruikshank, 1992). Strong community spirit developed in neighborhoods and across the country. At the time of Stonewall, fewer than 50 gay and lesbian organizations existed and the largest demonstrations included only a few dozen participants. By 1973, more than 700 lesbian and gay groups existed. In June 1970, a march in New York to commemorate Stonewall drew about 5,000 participants (D'Emilio, 1993).

Particularly in New York and other urban areas, concentrations of lesbian and gay groups and activities developed. These included civil rights organizations, social clubs and community centers, businesses, newspapers and magazines, social service organizations, and more visible and vocal political activism (D'Augelli & Garnets, 1995; Longres, 1995). This new visibility, however,

DEVELOPMENT OF COMMUNITY AND CULTURE

made lesbians and gay men a target of attacks. In the second half of the 1970s, community development was disrupted by conservative political and religious trends. Setbacks were quite public, including, for example, Anita Brynt's 1977 "Save the Children" campaign in Florida, attempts to ban lesbian and gay teachers in California, and the assassination of an openly gay member of the Board of Supervisors in San Francisco, Harvey Milk (D'Augelli & Garnets, 1995).

The 1980s: The HIV Crisis

Political solidification continued to escalate in the face of the ongoing threats to livelihood and life itself (D'Augelli & Garnets, 1995). However, not all lesbians and gay men connected with the politically aware identity. Some people connected more with the new community-oriented identity. To them, "gay liberation" meant personal, social, and sexual freedom instead of political activism (Bohan, 1996). Unexpectedly, however, personal, social, and sexual life, as well as the political focus, changed dramatically in the 1980s. The HIV epidemic, and its accompanying social, medical, and legal crises, quickly consumed the lives of urban gay men. It affected every aspect of their lives. Illness, death, loss of friends and partners, and the fear of diagnosis for oneself were predominant themes (Arriola, 1993; Paul, Hays, & Coates, 1995). The impact of the epidemic was so strong that a distinction is now made between the "pre-AIDS" and the "post-AIDS" community. The gay and lesbian community, however, met the challenge of HIV with energetic volunteerism and by adapting existing programs to meet the needs of persons with the disease (Paul et al., 1995).

Formal social service organizations as well as an array of informal social services such as self-help and support groups were developed (D'Augelli, 1989e). In some of the large cities such as New York, gay men and lesbians created comprehensive systems of care (D'Augelli & Garnets, 1995). Many other communities, however, were not well served. For example, few HIV/AIDS programs in White lesbian and gay communities addressed the cultural needs of racial and ethnic groups (Choi, Salazar, Lew, & Coates, 1995; González & Espin, 1996; Peterson, 1995). Nor were these needs sufficiently addressed in racial and ethnic communities. Even today, HIV/AIDS education and support programs are minimal in these communities due in part to the belief that AIDS is a "White disease." González and Espin reported that in Latino communities, other barriers to effectively dealing with HIV/AIDS include a less powerful gay community and fewer economic resources. Degree of acculturation can also be a barrier. For example, less acculturated Latino gay men are not as likely to to disclose an HIV-positive status to relatives and lovers than are White gay men (Marks, Bundek, Richardson, Ruiz, & Maldonado, 1992). Latino gay men who speak English, however, are more likely to disclose both their sexual orientation and HIV-positive status to their families than those who are Spanish speakers (Mason, Marks, Simoni, Ruiz, & Richardson, 1995).

Although in White communities the community-based groups and organizations that existed in the 1980s were numerous and effective, they could not meet all of the demands created by the immense scope of the HIV epidemic. Assistance on a larger scale and across all communities, however, was slight. This was due to the lack of leadership and governmental response at the national level and intensified discrimination because of the association of HIV with gay men. In the face of vehement attacks on same-gender sexuality and a renewed focus on "homosexuality" as sin, however, the political strength of the gay and lesbian community intensified. The "common enemy" strategy promoted group solidarity throughout the 1980s and into the 1990s. Political organizing was directed at increased funding for research on HIV/AIDS and more services (Arriola, 1993; D'Augelli & Garnets, 1995; Paul et al., 1995).

The 1990s: Political Coming of Age

In the current decade, HIV/AIDS still consumes much of the energy of lesbian and gay communities. In addition, there is broadened awareness of the lack of legal protections across many areas. There are pushes now to attain civil rights at all levels of government and in businesses, universities, and other institutions (Paul et al., 1995) (see Chapter 2 for several examples). There are also ongoing debates over what political strategies to use to gain civil rights and resources for people with HIV. One group, ACT-UP (AIDS Coalition to Unleash Power), revitalized activism and increased the use of militant strategies (Altman, 1986; D'Augelli & Garnets, 1995; Paul et al., 1995). Its confrontational political tactics energized and politicized many gay men. These tactics are used in another group, Queer Nation, which was started in 1990 in New York City. Whisman (1991) observed that many young lesbian feminists are also connected with direct action groups such as ACT-UP and Lesbian Avengers. Other less militant organizations include the Lamda Legal Defense and Education Fund and the National Gay and Lesbian Task Force (NGLTF) (Herdt & Boxer, 1992). NGLTF is the oldest national group for lesbians and gay men and since 1973 has supported grassroots organizing and national advocacy (NGLTF, 1997).

◆ The Personal Story of HIV/AIDS

At the heart of the development of community resources to address HIV/AIDS, and targeting the federal government with activist strategies aimed at attaining more resources, are the people who contract the disease. The emotional impact of the discovery that one is HIV-positive oneself is usually an intense shock (Ostrow, 1996). It is a personal confrontation that is no different now than it was in the 1980s, although there are some advances in treatment. When a person first learns of an HIV-positive status, there is often extreme anxiety and/or depression (Ostrow, 1996). P. Meyer, Tapley, and Bazargan (1996) reported a rate of depression of about 70% in a sample of gay and bisexual male clients of an AIDS service organization. Dew, Ragni, and Nimorwica (1990) reported that bisexual men may experience more extensive depression and isolation because they may not have support networks in either the heterosexual or the lesbian and gay communities.

Ostrow (1996) identified four phases of psychosocial issues that HIV-positive gay and bisexual men usually traverse. They include, at *phase 1 (testing HIV-positive),* "crisis reaction, shock, denial, depression, suicidal thoughts, guilt, withdrawal, anger, relief"; at *phase 2 (symptom-free period),* "reestablish equilibrium, search for meaning, restore self-esteem, try to gain control, uncertainty"; at *phase 3 (signs and symptoms),* "loss of control and independence, guilt, anger, depression, suicidal thoughts, support, reciprocity, disfigurement, treatment decisions, bargaining"; and at *phase 4 (AIDS),* "grief, possible relief at diagnosis, depression." During this terminal phase, reactions and issues can include "preparation for death, depression, acceptance, final treatment decisions, assisted suicide" (p. 861).

Several other tasks associated with an HIV-positive status can include (a) dealing with multiple losses in addition to health such as work, financial stability, and social roles; (b) management of the stigma associated with this status, plus the internal feeling of shame or that one is being punished; (c) development of strategies to maintain optimal physical and emotional health; and (d) dealing with the decision of who is to be told about the illness (Siegel & Krauss, 1991).

The HIV epidemic also strongly affects persons who are not ill, such as by elevating their stress levels. Most lesbian, gay, and bisexual persons know others who are HIV-positive and have experienced the deaths of persons with AIDS. Many care for friends or lovers with this illness (Dworkin & Kaufer, 1995). The more people one knows who died of AIDS, the greater the risk of experiencing distress oneself such as anxiety, depression, and sleep problems. Use of drugs and sedatives may increase (J. L. Martin, 1988). Some gay and bisexual men experience "survivor guilt" because they are still healthy (Dworkin & Kaufer, 1995).

As a result of the HIV crisis, dramatic modifications of unsafe sex practices occurred among gay men. Support increased for monogamy in couples as well as celibacy. Particularly in large cities, community education programs and social services supported these changes (Paul et al., 1995). The sexual relations of both bisexual men and women were also affected. Some bisexual men stopped their sexual relations with gay men. Many bisexual women ended their sexual relations with men and adopted a lesbian identity. The value placed on sexual fidelity or monogamy also increased (Weinberg et al., 1994).

◆ **Community: Different for Women**

Most of the prior discussion of community development addressed lesbians and gay men together. This is defensible as they share basic characteristics such as variance in choice of partners and the consequent rejection and stigmatization by the dominant heterosexual community (Hanley-Hackenbruck, 1993).

There are, however, substantial distinctions between lesbians and gay men due to gender role differences as well as sexism.

One's gender is a powerful influence on how one is socialized and, consequently, on one's identity, relationship patterns, and sexual behavior (Garnets & Kimmel, 1993a). Because of the power of gender socialization, lesbians are generally more similar to heterosexual women than to gay men, who are more similar to heterosexual men (Blumstein & Schwartz, 1983). Lesbians also share with other women the institutional oppression of sexism (Eldridge, 1987b; Zimmerman, 1984). During the almost 20 years of the small, pre-Stonewall homophile movement, for example, lesbians played only a marginal part or participated in largely secondary roles (Cruikshank, 1992; D'Emilio, 1993). Bisexual women and men do not fully engage in mutual cooperation either. Rust (1995) suggested that if the gender dichotomy between men and women breaks down, hierarchies based on gender (as well as compulsory heterosexuality) will weaken. The bisexual movement is dedicated to reducing the significance of gender, but socialization differences between men and women are a barrier to the creation of a truly nongendered movement.

The Lesbian-Feminist Movement

Because of the minimal role allowed for women in the gay liberation movement and the lack of gay men's interest in women's issues, a lesbian feminist movement emerged (Abbott & Love, 1972; Jay, 1995; Jay & Young, 1972; Johnston, 1973; Myron & Bunch, 1975). The simultaneous development of the lesbian-feminist movement and the male-dominated gay liberation movement heightened the differences between the two groups (D'Augelli & Patterson, 1995). They pursued different goals that were difficult to join together. Liberation for gay men meant various unharassed freedoms such as sexual expression. For lesbian-feminists, it meant developing forms of intimacy and community that were not patriarchal (Pearlman, 1987; Raymond, 1986).

The feminist movement swayed many lesbian women to get involved in feminist organizations (D'Emilio, 1993). These organizations, however, were not always hospitable to lesbians. The association between lesbian feminists and heterosexual feminists was more conflictual than collaborative. Some chapters of the National Organization for Women (NOW) even attempted to exclude lesbians (Adler & Brenner, 1992; D'Emilio, 1993), who were considered to be a barrier to winning women's rights and to heighten stereotypes of feminists as man-haters (Ochs, 1996). Many lesbians, however, felt more comfortable working alongside women than gay men (Cruikshank, 1992) and they eventually helped modify the prejudicial attitudes toward them among heterosexual feminists (Adler & Brenner, 1992).

Participation in the feminist movement led to more radical political tendencies within the lesbian community. Not all lesbians were feminists, however, and others were not as doctrinaire in their views of feminism. Some lesbians maintained their association with male-dominated community organizations. Others worked for both feminist and gay liberation causes. For women whose main political cause was feminism, however, the gay liberation movement continued as a peripheral involvement (Cruikshank, 1992; Esterberg, 1996; Golden, 1996; Pearlman, 1987; Weston, 1991).

The Lesbian/Gay Alignment in the 1990s

In the 1990s, the power alignment between lesbians and gay men began to change. Lesbians are now in many more positions of power in lesbian and gay organizations and at all levels—local, state, and national. Even with these gains, however, many lesbian feminists want an autonomous group and movement (Cruikshank, 1992). Without separate focus on their issues such as abortion, child care facilities, custody issues, economic discrimination, and sexism, they foresee that gay and lesbian politics will be dominated by gay issues. Men outnumber lesbians in almost all gay and lesbian organizations. For this reason, if for no other, male-oriented issues tend to prevail in terms of attention and effort (Cruikshank, 1992; Paul et al., 1995).

Although lesbians and gay men see each other as lacking interest in issues pertinent to each group, an exception is HIV/AIDS. This epidemic, and the accompanying challenges of health care, discrimination, and violence, led many lesbians to become involved. Some lesbians, however, still feel antagonistic about linking up with gay groups. They are also concerned about the gender-typed caregiver role that many lesbians take with HIV-positive men. They doubt that this caregiving would be reciprocated if needed by lesbians. Others resent the attention and resources focused on HIV, a disease mainly of men. Women's health issues, such as breast cancer, fall far behind in attention (Winnow, 1989).

◆ Contemporary Lesbian and Gay Communities

Although some lesbian and gay communities are evident because of residential areas or territories, they are essentially identificational or based on a shared sense of identity (Bernard, 1973). The members do not live in the same vicinity but share "the functions, structures, activities, solidarity sentiments, and reciprocal support that other communities do" (Germain, 1991, p. 39).

Culture

The community's solidarity in part thrives through its culture. More specifically, lesbians and gay men are associated with a subculture, as distinguished from the larger culture of society. The lesbian and gay culture contains elements from the main culture, such as many of its values. Some elements, however, are indigenous to the lesbian and gay subculture, and include artifacts such as art, literature, and jewelry; groups and organizations such as political associations, baseball teams, and choruses; and special events such as music festivals (Cruikshank, 1992; D'Augelli & Garnets, 1995; Donaldson, 1990; M. Levine, 1992; Murray, 1992; Paul et al., 1995).

The culture also includes various representations of shared oppression and liberation. Some of them are symbols such as the pink triangle that gay men were required to wear in concentration camps during World War II and the rainbow flag. The "Names Project and Memorial Quilt" is a central representation of the HIV/AIDS crisis. Other representations include rituals such as the Pride Day parades that commemorate Stonewall and National Coming Out Day in October, which marks the anniversary of the 1987 National March for Gay and Lesbian Rights (Altman, 1982; Arriola 1993; Blumenfeld & Raymond, 1993; Cruikshank, 1992; D'Emilio, 1995; Herdt & Boxer, 1993). Representations of lesbian and gay culture were once images of secrecy, fear, and shame. Most of them are now positive. Pride Day parades signify this change with full, open participation of lesbians and gay men throughout the country.

Locations and Places

In recent years, lesbians and gay men created neighborhoods in many cities (Longres, 1995). Especially in large cities, lesbian and gay communities may be close to place-associated units. Although there are no distinct boundaries to lesbian and gay geographical communities, people tend to know where they are (Murray, 1992). The most notable place-associated communities are urban, but they also exist in suburbs, small towns, and rural areas (D'Augelli & Garnets, 1995).

Rural areas, small towns and cities, and suburbs. Some lesbians and gay men prefer to live in open space and on rural land (D'Augelli, 1987, 1989c; D'Augelli & Hart, 1987). There are also lesbian and gay satellite communities and other less dense populations in suburbs (F. Lynch, 1992). Lesbians and gay men who live outside big cities, however, especially those in small towns, cities, and rural areas, are often isolated and lonely (N. Miller, 1989). There are few or no facilities and services specifically for lesbians and gay men. In rural areas, often a small lesbian and/or gay bar provides the only meeting place (D'Augelli & Garnets, 1995). In addition, if lesbians and gay men want a private life, rural areas are problematic because everyone knows everyone else (D'Augelli & Garnets, 1995; Germain, 1991). If one's sexual orientation is known, therefore, prejudice and discrimination (such as in employment and housing) may be more extensive. The situation is not much different in suburbs (F. Lynch, 1992).

Large cities. For the reasons enumerated above, most lesbians and gay men tend to avoid or leave small towns, cities, and rural areas and migrate to large cities. Now, many urban cities contain identifiable, visible *concentrations* of lesbians and gay men such as Dallas, Houston, San Francisco, San Diego, Seattle, Minneapolis, New York, Chicago, Los Angeles, Miami, Boston, and Sante Fe. Concentrations of lesbians and gay men sometimes occur in one or more residential areas of some large cities (D'Emilio, 1993) and are sometimes referred to as *ghettos* (Donaldson, 1990). Such locations include the Castro in San Francisco (D'Emilio, 1993), West Hollywood, New Town in Chicago, Coconut Grove in Miami, and Greenwich Village in New York (Pope, 1995). Even in smaller cities, there is a tendency for lesbians and gay men to live close to each other. There are also *regions* such as northern California and western Massachusetts (D'Emilio, 1993) and some *resort areas* such as Provincetown, Massachusetts, and Key West, Florida, that now encompass large concentrations of lesbians and gay men (Nakayama & Corey, 1993). In other areas, a cluster of lesbian- and gay-oriented facilities foster the perception of a lesbian and gay *territory* (Murray, 1992).

◆ Diversity of Communities

Although many lesbians and gay men may not realize how diverse their community is, there are many different ways of living as a lesbian or gay person. The cultural meaning of Pride Day is not only to communicate political power but also to recognize the diversity of the gay and lesbian community. Herdt (1992) observed that in the Pride Day parades, lesbian and gay "solidarity" is in full force at least in rhetoric, but there is also considerable diversity and pluralism among the participants such as those representing "gay businesses, churches, AA, persons with HIV, gays in drag, lesbians on motorcycles, . . . [Parents, Friends, and Families of Lesbians and Gays (PFLAG)], and other factions" (p. 55). Many other factors contributing to diversity were identified in Chapter 1.

The many differences reflect the wide range of persons in the lesbian and gay community (Herrell, 1992). With so many differences, however, there are often conflicts between the varied segments of the community (e.g., D'Emilio, 1993; Franzen, 1993) and

there is not full acceptance of everyone in the various segments. The primarily Euro-American lesbian and gay communities, for example, reflect the prejudices of the larger society regarding racial and ethnic minority lesbian, gay, and bisexual persons (Garnets & Kimmel, 1993b; Greene, 1997b; Icard, 1985-1986; E. S. Morales, 1990; Rust, 1996a; Tremble, Schneider, & Apparthurai, 1989). The lesbian and gay community is also not fully welcoming of White bisexual men and women.

The Divergent Communities of Racial and Ethnic Lesbians and Gay Men

Racial and ethnic lesbians and gay men frequently experience the dilemma of managing conflicting allegiances among different communities (Cazenave, 1979, 1984; Gock, 1985; Mays, 1985). They participate in divergent social worlds such as the lesbian and gay community, the majority community, their racial or ethnic community, and, for women, perhaps a feminist community (Kanuha, 1990; Mays & Cochran, 1986; Swigonski, 1995). It requires constant effort for people to maintain themselves in these different worlds (E. S. Morales, 1990). In addition, none of these communities supports all significant parts of their lives, and often there is a dissonant choice of which community to identify with most. The biggest dilemma is the lesbian and gay community versus a person's racial or ethnic community. One provides cultural groundedness and the other intimacy with peers (Gock, 1985). Racial and ethnic persons want the intimacy, but if their primary identification is with the lesbian and gay community, they may feel that they betrayed their cultural group (Sears, 1989).

Allegiances among different racial and ethnic groups. The primary allegiance of ethnic and racial lesbians and gay men varies among groups. *Asian American* lesbians and gay men, for example, generally identify more strongly with their lesbian and gay identity than with their Asian American identity (Chan, 1989). Their Asian American self-awareness is often low and they may avoid other lesbian and gay Asian Americans in preference for White lesbians and gay persons (Nakajima, Chan, & Lee, 1996). The primary allegiance, however, can shift depending on need or stage of identity formation (Chan, 1989). For example, a crisis such as a diagnosis of HIV or a breakup of a primary linkup may precipitate seeking support from other Asian Americans (e.g., Hom, 1992).

The primary allegiance for *Latino* lesbians and gay men usually remains with their families (Espin, 1984). The family, or "familism," is a core cultural value among Latinos. It transcends the nation of origin and to some extent acculturation (Espin, 1984, 1987; González & Espin, 1996; Hidalgo, 1984; E. S. Morales, 1990, 1992). Latino families tend to be extended, with strong ties to grandparents, aunts, uncles, and cousins (Marín & Marín, 1991). These families provide a protective structure and buffer against the socioeconomic and political pressures of immigration, acculturation, and racism (González & Espin, 1996). Identification with the lesbian and gay community can be a costly move away from family and the underpinnings of a variety of supports (Espin, 1984).

Many Latino lesbians and gay men feel pulled toward allegiance to their families. Within each racial or ethnic culture, however, there are also different groups and subgroups of lesbian, gay, and bisexual persons with different allegiances (Conerly, 1996). For example, Carrillo and Maiorana (1989) found a range of participation in gay subcultures and allegiances among Latino gay men living in San Francisco: (a) working-class men who are effeminate in self-presentation,

frequent Latino gay bars, and are often "drag queens"; (b) primarily working-class men who view themselves as heterosexual or bisexual experience discreet sex with other men, frequent Latino gay bars in search of sexual encounters, and strongly identify with their ethnic group; (c) men who self-identify as gay but more so as Latino and do not participate in the Latino gay subculture; (d) men who openly self-identify as gay and participate in the Latino gay subculture; and (e) men who are marginal in Latino identity and are fully assimilated into the White gay community.

Within *African American* groups, there are Black-identified lesbian, gay, and bisexual persons and lesbian, gay, and bisexual-identified Black persons (Conerly, 1996). J. Johnson (1982) found that 60% of a sample of gay Black men were "Black identified," that is, identified primarily with their racial or ethnic community. The other respondents were "gay identified" and primarily affirmed their gay reference group identity. Both groups experienced comparable levels of mental health—self-acceptance, happiness, loneliness, and depression—but differed on social behavioral measures. The Black-identified gay men were more likely to have Black lovers and friends, live in and celebrate the Black community, and prefer traditional, subtle modes of expressing affection among gay men. The gay-identified Black men were more likely to have White lovers, live in the gay community, and favor public displays of affection among gay men. Men in each group, however, felt estranged from a central aspect of who they were in either the gay or the Black communities. According to Conerly, subgroups within these groups also exist such as Black-identified Afrocentrists who identify with African American cultural traditions, values, and practices and gay-identified interracialists who experience sexual linkups with Whites as well as other kinds of interracial linkups.

Rejection in White lesbian and gay communities. Although many racial and ethnic lesbians and gay men desire to maintain a strong allegiance to their families and communities, they generally experience a highly negative stance toward their same-gender sexual orientation in these contexts (see Chapters 2 and 5). Consequently, many of them separate from their culture to connect with lesbian and gay peers. Support, however, may not be easy to acquire in the White lesbian and gay community. They are often unacknowledged, not accepted, and discriminated against (Chan, 1989; de Monteflores, 1981; Greene, 1994a; Hom, 1992; Icard, 1985-1986; Kanuha, 1990; Loiacano, 1989; Mays & Cochran, 1986; E. S. Morales, 1990; Rust, 1996a; Tremble et al., 1989; Wooden, Kawasaki, & Mayeda, 1983). Many report hindrances to full participation in lesbian and gay bars, social groups, political organizations, and social service agencies (e.g., Chan, 1992; Greene, 1994a, 1994b, 1997b; Gutiérrez & Dworkin, 1992; Icard, 1985-1986; Loiacano, 1989; Mays & Cochran, 1988; E. S. Morales, 1992).

Another barrier is the stereotypes that White lesbians and gay men tend to hold about racial and ethnic lesbian and gay persons. For example, Asian American lesbians and gay men are often seen as "exotic, non-American, or foreign" (Nakajima et al., 1996, p. 571). White gay men often view Japanese American gay men as feminine, passive, and easy pickups (Wooden et al., 1983). In addition to these stereotypes, there can be insensitivity to the importance of families of origin to many ethnic and racial lesbian and gay persons. They may respond negatively to pressure to be activists or make public disclosures, for example, because they do not want to embarrass or disgrace their families (Savin-Williams, 1996).

Racial and ethnic gay and lesbian community developments. Partly in reaction to isolation from others in their racial or ethnic groups and in the mainstream lesbian and gay communities, ethnic and racial minorities are establishing their own support groups and social groups (Greene, 1997b; Hidalgo, 1984; Icard, 1985-1986). Organizations and services in large urban cities cater to particular ethnic groups. They also provide a place for racial and ethnic lesbians and gay men to form friendships (Icard, Longres, & Williams, 1996).

Similar to the *Black* gay and lesbian community of the 1920s (Graber, 1989) (see Chapter 5, this volume), today's Black lesbian and gay community is a subculture that integrates aspects of White lesbian and gay communities and Black communities. Today's Black lesbian and gay community provides resources not only for social contacts but also for health and mental health needs, political needs, and economic needs. Self-help groups now address HIV/AIDS, mostly in large urban cities such as New York and Los Angeles. Black gay and lesbian churches are emerging across the country. Magazines are published such as *B & G: A different point of view.* These resources, plus Black gay and lesbian writers, moviemakers, politicians, and scholars, are contributing to a new sense of community for Black lesbians and gay men (Icard, 1996).

Most urban centers with a substantial *Latino* population also now have gay Latino subcultures. The National Latino/a Lesbian and Gay Organization (LLEGO) was formed in 1987 (González & Espin, 1996). Lesbian and gay *Asian American* political and social organizations are also developing across the country (Nakajima et al., 1996). Gay Indian Americans (GAI) recently organized yearly meetings for building solidarity among Indian North American lesbians and gay men and to explore Indian American culture and spirituality (L. B. Brown, 1997). Native American AIDS activists are also working to meet the special needs of Native Americans with HIV/AIDS both in urban and rural areas (Rowell, 1997).

Politicalization of Bisexual Sexual Orientation and Community Development

Until recently, bisexual men and women did not organize around a bisexual identity or develop bisexual communities. Even in the 1990s, many bisexual men and women feel isolated (Esterberg, 1996, 1997; Hutchins & Káahumanu, 1991). They are not fully accepted in either the heterosexual or the lesbian and gay communities. Now, however, there is access to bisexual communities, at least in large cities (Fox, 1996; Rust, 1996a).

Social movement. Condemnation of the bisexual sexual orientation resulted in the ironic effect of making it a recognizable form of sexuality and spurring the rapid growth of the bisexual movement (Rust, 1995). Beginning slowly in the 1970s and picking up speed in the late 1980s and early 1990s, the bisexual community and culture developed from backyards to big-city community centers. Isolated support groups formed, sometimes associated with larger lesbian and gay groups. In the 1970s, most of these groups were made up of White, middle-class, married men. They became more open to women in the 1980s with the rise of women's organizing efforts. Women are now, in the 1990s, in many leadership positions in the national bisexual movement (Hutchins, 1996).

While early groups for bisexual men, women, or both developed largely in Boston and Seattle (Hutchins, 1996), groups now exist in almost every state in the United States and in 19 other countries (Ochs, 1995). In the larger cities, groups exist for bisexual women and men with specific areas of interest such as artists, children of alcoholics, and women of color. In addition, there are now increasing numbers of publica-

tions, cable shows, college courses, and computer lists on bisexual topics. There is a national bisexual organization, BiNet USA (Hutchins, 1996), and an international network of various bisexual groups including, for example, support groups and political action groups (Rust, 1995). The *Bisexual Resource Guide* (Ochs, 1995) provides updated lists of bisexual organizations throughout the world as well as lists of books and films. According to Hutchins, through these various developments, bisexual men and women are now visible in the popular culture. With an increasing sense of community, support, and role models, they are also more comfortable in their identities.

Political movement. The early bisexual groups were generally not politically focused. Similar to the gay and lesbian homophile groups in the 1950s, however, a supportive framework for a political movement began with the few isolated support groups and local resource centers that developed in the 1970s and 1980s (Hutchins, 1996; Rust, 1995). Eventually, increased awareness that a bisexual identity characterizes large numbers of people activated bisexual women and men to build their own political movement (Bohan, 1996). In the late 1980s, activists in newly formed bisexual political groups focused on bisexual visibility and bisexual persons' inclusion in gay and lesbian groups, their inclusion in titles of national marches, and the distribution of AIDS information packets to them (Káahumanu, 1992; Udis-Kessler, 1996). The political activists now meet each other at national and international conferences (Rust, 1995).

The AIDS epidemic further mobilized the growing bisexual movement when bisexual men were identified by the Centers for Disease Control as a major risk group and carrier of HIV to the general population. Although this was considered scapegoating, many bisexual men were infected with HIV and dying of AIDS. This situation increased the militancy of bisexual men and women and bisexual political organizations (Hutchins, 1996).

The bisexual political movement advanced rapidly because many of its activists knew how to build the framework for such a movement. They were veterans of earlier movements of the Left, feminism, and lesbian and gay communities. What the ideology of the movement should be, however, is only in a preliminary stage of development. An identifiable bisexual press and forum for debates on bisexual political ideology include newsletters of bisexual organizations and a magazine called *Anything That Moves: Beyond the Myths of Bisexuality* published by the Bay Area Bisexual Network (BARN). An ideological focus in these publications is especially evident in the 1990s (Rust, 1995). Still, according to Rust, there is not yet an extensive movement toward developing an ideological response to what it means to be bisexual or even a sense of bisexual identity, community, and history.

In contrast to the issue of what a bisexual sexual orientation is, there is more headway on the question of what bisexual men and women stand for. Rust (1995) identified three dominant themes that are current tenets of the bisexual ideology: (a) diversity, including sexual, racial/ethnic, and cultural; (b) conceptualization of bisexuality as a challenge to dichotomous categorical classification systems such as "homosexuals" versus heterosexuals or men versus women; and (c) an understanding of the nature and source of bisexual oppression, and the development of responses to it.

Gender differences. Some bisexual women complain that often the interest of bisexual men in mixed-gender groups is finding women for sexual partners. Bisexual women are less interested in this objective. Instead, they are more interested in develop-

ing a bisexual community and discussing ideological issues. Where bisexual men and women create separate groups, the women's groups are often more successful in meeting and publishing; many men's groups fold (Rust, 1995).

Activist bisexual women outnumber activist bisexual men, in contrast to most other political movements. The women's greater political training as part of feminist groups may contribute to this as well as to the greater stability of their groups. On the other hand, the combination of feminism with bisexual ideology by many activist bisexual women counters the bisexual celebration of diversity. For example, in the bisexual movement as a whole, transsexual persons are accepted as part of the diversity of the movement and also because they do not fit well into dichotomous categories. During the 1980s when many bisexual groups were forming, however, feminists were generally hostile toward and distrustful of male-to-female transsexual persons, whom they perceived to be male intruders in women's space (Rust, 1995).

◆ Hostility of Lesbians and Gay Men Toward Bisexual Women and Men

Before there was access to a bisexual community, bisexual men and women often participated in lesbian and gay communities for support and understanding (Fox, 1996). It was not unusual, however, for them to be confronted by hostility and exclusion from lesbian and gay activities and social circles (Bohan, 1996). Openly expressed attractions to both genders are met with resistance in gay and lesbian communities (Esterberg, 1996). Bisexual men and women are viewed as fence-sitters or undecided, or as in transition to a "true" lesbian or gay identity (Esterberg, 1996; Rust 1993b) (see Chapter 2), or as having adopted the label *bisexual* because they fear the stigma associated with the labels of *gay* or *lesbian* (Ochs, 1996; Weinberg et al., 1994), or as holding on to their heterosexual, mainstream privileges (Golden, 1996; Ochs, 1996).

The lesbian and gay community is not uniformly hostile to bisexual women and men (Rust, 1995). Certain segments among lesbians, however, are distinctly hostile to them. Some of these segments reject the legitimacy of bisexual identification altogether (Weinberg et al., 1994). Other segments feel threatened by the emergence of a strong bisexual women's contingent because they may be staking a claim to the same territory (Rust, 1992). Ochs (1996) suggested that lesbians are also more possessive about their label whereas more fluidity exists between the labels of *gay* and *bisexual.* Consequently, bisexual women who also identify as lesbian face more hostility among lesbians than bisexual men who also identify as gay face from gay men. Lesbians can also feel threatened by the bisexual community's challenge to the heterosexual-"homosexual" dichotomy (Byrne, 1993). Rust (1995) found that this challenge threatens to undermine the distinction between them and heterosexual persons. If there is no distinction, how can they claim to want liberation from the oppression of heterosexual persons?

Many lesbians also perceive bisexual women as untrustworthy or disloyal, both politically and personally. They are not trusted as political allies because under pressure they are likely to desert lesbian political struggles (Golden, 1996). Because of the fluidity of their identification, bisexual women are also viewed as too free-floating to be reliable allies or friends (Esterberg, 1997). When threatened with the rejection of their lesbian identity, for example, they can always assimilate into the more comfortable dominant culture or pass as heterosexual (Byrne, 1993; Golden, 1996; Rust, 1993b; Weinberg et al., 1994).

Certain lesbian communities also resent women who are sexually involved with women but not exclusively (Golden, 1996). They also tend to view these women as spreading sexually transmitted diseases to the lesbian community (Weinberg et al., 1994). The biggest threat is the transmittal of AIDS. Bisexual women are seen as the conduit through which AIDS is spread to lesbians from the heterosexual mainstream (Ochs, 1996), although the risk of HIV infection is greater for bisexual men than for bisexual women (Paul, 1996).

Rust (1993b) indicated that many lesbians (and gay men) also experience sexual relationships with a person of the other gender. Although some lesbians never experience heterosexual attractions or sexual behavior, others experience significant sexual or affectional relations with men at some point in time. Rust (1992) found that 43% of a sample of lesbians experienced sexual relations with a man since they first identified as lesbian. Lesbians who experience some heterosexual attractions were found by Rust (1993b) as less likely to hold negative beliefs about bisexual women than those who report that their feelings are exclusively directed toward women.

Gay men do not seem to experience the intensity of betrayal or discomfort regarding bisexual men and women as experienced by lesbians. Especially if they think it might fit them, however, some gay men may feel discomfort with the existence of a bisexual sexual orientation. They do not want to go through another difficult process of self-reidentification (Ochs, 1996). Political gay men also join political lesbians in attacking bisexual men and women because of their refusal to fight the enemy of heterosexism, which they perceive as resulting in political fragmentation (Weinberg et al., 1994). Both gay men and lesbians also dislike the implicit loyalty of bisexual persons to the heterosexual sexual orientation because of the absence of a singular commitment to their own gender. Many lesbians and gay men define their identities not just by whom they love but by their explicit abdication of heterosexual relationships (Bohan, 1996). In the 1970s, the lesbian label came to embody the concept of resistance to sexism and patriarchy. Whether heterosexual or bisexual, women who did not sever ties with men were seen as colluding with the patriarchy (Ochs, 1996). Lesbian feminists particularly see any women who align themselves with heterosexuals as "sleeping with the enemy" (Bohan, 1996).

Alignments and Divergences Among Lesbian, Gay, and Bisexual Persons

Because of these various hostile reactions in their interactions with lesbian and gay communities, bisexual men and women may hide the heterosexual part of their identities, label themselves publicly as lesbian or gay, denigrate heterosexual persons, and devalue their own heterosexual feelings. The cost of these strategies, however, is feeling like impostors and outsiders in both communities (Bohan, 1996; Ochs, 1996).

Bisexual men and women feel dismay and anger about their rejection in lesbian and gay communities. One way they respond to this intolerance is to criticize the political narrow-mindedness of lesbian and gay men, in contrast to the emphasis on diversity that marks the developing bisexual ideology (Roberts, 1997; Rust, 1995; Weinberg et al., 1994). Some men and women join groups such as Queer Nation that are more inclusive of a wide range of sexual identities (D'Augelli & Garnets, 1995; Esterberg, 1996; Klein, 1993). Others, however, continue to push for an open and accepted bisexual presence in mainstream lesbian and gay communities. Although they are often not welcome, they continue to feel that the lesbian and gay movement represents their interests also. They feel linked with gay men and lesbians because of the HIV/AIDS crisis and right-wing hate groups (Hutchins, 1996). These bisexual persons argue that they should be acknowledged and accepted as part of the lesbian and gay movement because bisexual men and women were part of this movement all along. They want *bi* added to the names of lesbian and gay organizations and events (Rust, 1995).

After a hard-fought battle for acceptance, a national contingent of bisexual men and women marched in the second national March on Washington for lesbian and gay rights in 1987. At the 1993 march, *bisexual* was included in the name of the march, and bisexual men and women were represented by a speaker on the main stage of the rally (Hutchins, 1996). Not all lesbians and gay men, however, accept these moves toward inclusion. They do not want bisexual women and men to reap the benefits of gay liberation because they are perceived as having done none of the work on its behalf (Rust, 1995).

Some bisexual men and women do not desire inclusion in gay and lesbian communities. They argue that their culture is diluted when mixed with the gay and lesbian culture. They perceive that the interests of bisexual men and women are different and that they should organize a separate movement with independent organizations and communities (D'Augelli & Garnets, 1995; Esterberg, 1996; Klein, 1993). This is a minority view, however, and seen by many bisexual persons as separating and divisive (Rust, 1995). Inclusion in the lesbian and gay community is largely seen as beneficial by most bisexual men and women because their community is much smaller and less politically powerful (Rust, 1996a). Still, it is uncertain at this point where things will end up. Will there be more autonomous communities or will the boundaries between lesbian, gay, and bisexual communities dissipate (Esterberg, 1996)?

The movement for transgenderist liberation is even more recent than the bisexual movement (Feinberg, 1993; Hemmings, 1996). Transgenderist persons also claim that although they contribute energy and activism to the lesbian and gay liberation movement, their name is not included in parades and other events (Denny, 1994). Increasingly, however, this is also changing.

◆ Summary

Lesbian, gay, and bisexual community and culture rose from oppression, stigma, and rejection by the majority culture. Separate groups of White bisexual persons and racial and ethnic lesbian, gay, and bisexual persons rose from rejection by segments of the White lesbian and gay community. Both White bisexual persons and racial and ethnic lesbian, gay, and bisexual persons experience conflicts between their allegiances to their own communities and to the mainstream lesbian and gay community. Heterosexism in the heterosexual community and the HIV/ AIDS crisis are major common links among all of these groups. Transgenderist men and women are also vying for inclusion.

PART II

IDENTITY DEVELOPMENT AND DISCLOSURE

COMING

OUT

◆ INCREASINGLY, MORE THEORISTS and researchers focus not on why individuals become lesbian, gay, or bisexual but on how they develop these sexual identities. A number of models of identity development or coming out now exist. This chapter addresses various issues regarding these models, and describes the coming out stages of one of the models. How lesbian, gay, and bisexual persons adjust to the coming out process is also addressed. Although individuals come out to themselves as gay, bisexual, or lesbian, they may or may not disclose their sexual identity to others, or they may disclose only to selected audiences. The dilemmas and issues regarding disclosure are examined in the next chapter.

◆ Coming Out: Models, Critiques, and Missing Pieces

The meaning of the expression *coming out* for lesbians and gay men evolved historically in three stages: (a) experiencing one's first same-gender sexual experience in the 1930s, (b) finding lesbians and gay friends and discovering gay and lesbian culture during World War II, and (c) accepting one's sexual orientation and conscious identification with the lesbian and gay culture and political movement after Stonewall (Herdt, 1992; Laumann et al., 1994; M. Levine, 1979; Weinberg & Williams, 1974). For the most part, developmental models of *coming out* focus on the psychological rather than the political meaning of the term. Political implications are more often associated with public disclosure of one's sexual identity.

Developmental Models of Coming Out

Early researchers and theorists typically defined coming out as a single or discrete event that was usually the first acknowledgment of oneself as lesbian or gay (e.g., Cronin, 1974; Dank, 1971; Gagnon & Simon, 1967; Hooker, 1967) or the recognition of one's true self (Dank, 1971; Simon & Gagnon, 1967). In contrast to this single event notion, coming out appeared to other theorists and researchers to follow a developmental process of redefining one's sexual identity. Much of the scholarship on lesbians and gay men in the 1970s and 1980s focused on developing models to describe this process (Gonsiorek, 1993; H. Levine & Evans, 1991). These models closely reflect the coming out stories told by lesbians and gay men. Typically, their stories described a linear process of discovery of true essential selves, including various milestone events along the way (Rust, 1996a).

The scholarship on the developmental process of coming out primarily occurred in the fields of *psychology* (e.g., Cass, 1979, 1983-1984, 1984; McDonald, 1982 ; Minton & McDonald, 1983-1984) and *sociology* (e.g., Coleman, 1981-1982b; Dank, 1971; DuBay, 1987; Hencken & O'Dowd, 1977; Humphreys, 1973; J. Lee, 1977; Troiden, 1979, 1989; Troiden & Goode, 1980; Warren, 1974). The developmental models fit loosely into these two groupings although some models incorporate both psychological and social factors (e.g., Cass, 1979, 1984). Some models are based on particular theories such Hanley-Hackenbruck's (1989) superego modification/ego development model and Gonsiorek's (1995) application of self psychology to the coming out process. Other

versions of coming out models also continue to develop (e.g., D'Augelli, 1994; Fassinger & Miller, 1996; Grace, 1992; H. Martin, 1991). Because of the number of models that now exist and because of space limitations, the stages of most models are not identified here. Readers are referred to the original sources for the details of each model.

Example of a Developmental Model of Coming Out

The psychosocial model developed by Cass (1979, 1984, 1996) is probably the best known developmental model of coming out. It is also the most extensively studied model, and it has both theoretical and empirical validity (Eliason, 1996). This model, called Sexual Identity Formation (SIF), integrates both psychological and social factors. It is a particularly comprehensive description of lesbian and gay identity development and addresses cognitive, emotional, and behavioral changes through six stages.

Cass based the SIF model on interpersonal congruence theory, which submits that stability and change in a person's life are influenced by the congruence or incongruence that exists in his or her interpersonal environment. Progression from one developmental stage to another is propelled by the tension of incongruities within an "interpersonal matrix." The components that make up this matrix include (a) *self-perceptions* (e.g., "I am lesbian or gay"); (b) *perceptions of one's behavior* (e.g., "My behavior may represent same-gender sexual orientation"); and (c) *perceptions of others' response* (e.g., "Others think I am lesbian or gay"). At each stage, conflict occurs within or between areas of the interpersonal matrix. Resolution of the conflict in each stage comes about either through advancement to a new stage, with increased congruence (between perceptions of one's behavior, self-identity, and other's responses), or no stage advancement, which

Cass referred to as "identity foreclosure." See Box 4.1 for a summary of the stages in the SIF model.

Cass (1984) tested the SIF model and concluded that individuals will display the cognitive, behavioral, and affective dimensions that are identified at different stages in the model. Brady and Busse (1994) also studied whether or not this model predicts stages of coming out. They found some support for the validity of the model's predictions and an association between stage progression and greater perceived psychological well-being. The data also suggested, however, that identity formation may be a two-stage rather than a six-stage process. The first stage combines the SIF stages 1 through 3 and the second stage combines stages 4 through 6. The distinction between the two stages is whether or not one achieves a coherent self-identity as a lesbian or gay person and experiences a sense of belonging in society.

Timing of the Coming Out Process

During several decades of research, the coming out process was usually found to occur in the transition to adulthood. This includes the periods of late adolescence or the early twenties (Harry, 1993). Individual differences, however, occur in both the absolute time, or ages when various stages are reached, and the relative time, or how long the whole process takes (Savin-Williams, 1990a). In McDonald's (1982) study of 199 gay men, for example, the respondents' average age of self-labeling as gay was 19, but the elapsed time (or relative time) between awareness of same-gender feelings and self-labeling extended from 1 to 33 years. In another study of gay men, D'Augelli (1991) found variability in relative timing on various milestones of identity development. For example, self-labeling as gay occurred between the ages of 11 and 21. The projected

average ages associated with various events in coming out models, then, may have no relation to the actual age at which an individual experiences the events (Rust, 1996a).

Critiques of the Coming Out Models

As a whole, the early models of coming out were largely descriptive and atheoretical explorations of the coming out process while others based on research used small samples and weak designs (Brady & Busse, 1994; Cox & Gallois, 1996; Eliason, 1996). As a group, the early models may not be generalizable beyond the cohorts that entered adolescence in the 1960s and 1970s. In the 1990s, the coming out process may occur earlier and be condensed in certain situations such as in urban, collegiate, and media-saturated communities. In large urban cities, for example, self-awareness of a lesbian or gay identity occurs for many persons in their middle and late teen years (D'Augelli & Hershberger, 1993; Herdt, 1989, 1992; Herdt & Boxer, 1993; Hetrick & Martin, 1987; Murray, 1992). Harry (1993) claimed, however, that not enough data are available to substantiate a lowering age trend. Harry and DeVall (1978) found that many youths in earlier decades also came out in their early or midteens.

Perhaps more significant critiques of most of the coming out models include their assumption of linear stages, including an end state to the coming out process, and various missing pieces, including diversity, social constructs and contexts, and political differences.

Assumption of Linear Stages and an End State

The disorder of coming out. Although researchers and theorists typically noted that

◆◆◆

Box 4.1. The Cass Model of Coming Out

Stage 1: Identity Confusion (Who am I?): Following a preliminary stage when concepts of lesbian or gay are of no personal relevance, a person begins to attend to information about same-gender sexual orientation as personally relevant. The person observes that there is something about his or her acts, thoughts, and feelings that can be viewed as lesbian or gay. If this interpretation persists, the person starts asking questions such as these: "Who am I?" Am I heterosexual? Am I lesbian or gay? At this stage, there are three alternative pathways:

▶ *Accept the relevance and desirability* of the meaning of lesbian or gay in one's life.

▶ *Accept the relevance but not the desirability* of the meaning. Try to remove all undesirable elements from one's life *(foreclosure).*

▶ *Refuse to accept one's behavior as relevant or desirable.* Try to redefine the meaning of one's behavior as not lesbian or gay, psychologically deny personal relevance, monitor behavior to remove any indications of being "homosexual," and prevent further access to information about "homosexuality." If the relevance of lesbian or gay identity is successfully suppressed, heterosexual identity is reclaimed *(foreclosure).* If suppression is unsuccessful, the person is forced to accept the applicability of the meaning of lesbian or gay for his or her life and will move to stage two.

Stage 2: Identity Comparison (I am different): In this stage, a person begins to think that he or she may be lesbian or gay but continues to present a heterosexual identity to others. Internally, the person tries to cope with a loss of direction and manage feelings of alienation or being different from others. There is also the feeling of being disconnected from one's past because one is no longer who one used to be. The person may confide in a few trusted friends or a counselor. Essentially at this stage, however, there is only internal consideration of the implications of a lesbian or gay identity and the information is not presented to others. This stage includes four possible pathways:

▶ *Self-image is positively evaluated and rewards are expected to be high* versus costs. The personal value of lesbians and gay men is contrasted with the lack of personal value of heterosexual women and men.

▶ *Positive evaluation but perceived low rewards* leads to rejection of the relevance of a lesbian or gay self-image. If successful, *foreclosure* occurs, but if unsuccessful, the person will likely conclude that he or she is probably lesbian or gay and try to lessen personal responsibility for this turn of events.

▶ The personal conflict of *negative evaluation and perceived high rewards* leads to finding ways to assess oneself as heterosexual, and not lesbian or gay. This can be done in one of four ways: *special case,* that is, "I love just this one person, that does not mean I am lesbian or gay"; *bisexual,* that is, "I can also enjoy heterosexuals"; *temporary,* that is, "This is just a phase"; and *personal innocence,* that is, "It is not my fault that I was made this way." Success with any of these strategies may lead to partial commitment to the relevance of a lesbian or gay self-image. If unsuccessful, the person is forced to move toward acceptance that he or she is probably lesbian or gay and probably not heterosexual. At this point, however, the person does not feel good about this assessment.

▶ *Negative evaluation and perceived low rewards* leads to devaluation of a lesbian or gay self-image and a positive evaluation of a heterosexual sexual orientation. If successful, *foreclosure* occurs; if not, it becomes necessary to accept the probable self-image of lesbian or gay but with increased negative self-evaluation. Self-hatred can be so extreme in this pathway that suicide or self-mutilation can occur.

Stage 3: Identity Tolerance (I am probably lesbian or gay): One moves toward greater commitment to a lesbian or gay identity at this stage. The person is likely to seek out a lesbian or gay community. Six pathways are possible:

▶ A *positive view of self as probably lesbian or gay and positive contacts* with other lesbian and gay persons leads to increasing acceptance of self-image.

▶ A *positive view of self but negative contacts* with other lesbians and gay men heightens the personal costs of adopting a self-image as lesbian or gay. Strategies are directed toward reducing contact with and devaluing lesbians and gay men. If successful, *foreclosure* occurs; if unsuccessful, one's self-understanding as lesbian or gay is reevaluated as less positive.

▶ A *negative view of self but positive contacts* with lesbians and gay men can result in the positive contacts lessening the negative self-image as probably lesbian or gay. This leads to an acceptance of a more positive evaluation of one's self-view.

▶ A *negative self-image and negative contacts* with lesbians and gay men leads to strategies to further avoid contacts. If successful, this strategy leads to *foreclosure*; if unsuccessful, a negative understanding of self emerges (but is modifiable if future positive contacts occur).

▶ A *positive self-image and positive contacts* with lesbians and gay men leads to greater commitment as lesbian or gay, with no qualifiers.

▶ *Positive self-image as partly lesbian or gay and negative contacts* with lesbians and gay men leads to a devaluation of lesbians and gay men. If this strategy is successful, *fore-closure* occurs; if not, a somewhat negative self-image as lesbian or gay is adopted.

Stage 4: Identity Acceptance (I am lesbian or gay): A person at this stage begins to feel that being gay or lesbian is a valid self-identity. One may prefer being around other gay men and lesbians. To decrease the inconsistency between the perception of oneself and others' perceptions, the person begins to disclose the new identity to more people. This often leads to another inconsistency, however, between one's concept of oneself as acceptable and views of others of oneself as unacceptable. The person still continues to "pass" as heterosexual in most contexts. If a basic strategy of "passing" continues, this is also considered a form of identity *foreclosure.*

Stage 5: Identity Pride (My sexual orientation is part of me): In this stage, one may resolve the inconsistency between thinking of oneself as acceptable and others' intolerance by devaluing the opinions and everything else that is heterosexual. At the same time, the person strongly values all that is lesbian or gay. Another strategy is to become a political activist against heterosexism. The person is likely to disclose in all or most areas of his or her life, although negative reactions may be anticipated. Such reactions, when encountered, tend to reinforce one's negative perceptions of heterosexuals. Some persons will react to the negative responses of heterosexuals by retreating to "passing" and thereby to a *foreclosed* state.

Stage 6: Identity Synthesis (I am lesbian or gay!): During this final stage of identity development, the ultimate goal is to attain psychological integration or consistency between perceptions of oneself and one's behavior and between one's private and public identities. The person also gradually modifies the "us against them" stance of the previous stage. Contact may increase with supportive heterosexual men and women. ◆

not all persons proceed through every stage or in the predicted order (e.g., Cass, 1979, 1990; Coleman, 1981-1982b; Kahn, 1991; McDonald, 1982), these variations were not viewed as negating the underlying linear process (Rust, 1993a). Other researchers and theorists, however, disagreed and claimed that coming out is not a linear process. Individuals can skip steps, experience steps in different orders, repeat steps, get stuck in steps, backtrack, or abort the process and return to a heterosexual identity (e.g., Coleman, 1981-1982b; Faderman, 1984-1985; Gonsiorek, 1993; McDonald, 1982; Rust, 1993a; Sophie, 1985-1986). In addition, some lesbians and gay men report no memory of a coming out process whereas others report a sudden revelation of their sexual orientation and comfort with it overnight (Savin-Williams, 1990a). Other persons may suspect someone is gay or lesbian before the person in question attains the same awareness (Cohen & Savin-Williams, 1996). Each individual's coming out process, then, is unique (T. Stein, 1993). What has yet to be determined, however, is whether there is one essential process, and each individual varies from that, or if there are a variety of paths.

Prescription versus description. The expectation in linear stage models is that individuals move one step at a time, in sequence, until they reach the final "mature" stage. A presumption is that all prior activity is directed toward this ultimate goal (Rust, 1993a). One of the issues with linear or developmental models, however, is that description becomes prescription. It then is expected that everyone will follow the same path and attain the same end state of "maturity." Individuals who do not reach the prescribed end state, who are unfinished in the process, or who adopt a bisexual identity are characterized as "immature." Coming out models then become moral models defining progress, arrested progress, or regression (Rust, 1996a). Therapy may be recommended for persons in "immature" states to help facilitate their advancement to the final

stage of identity integration (Kitzinger & Perkins, 1993).

A process with an end or a lifelong process? An end stage also implies that once reached, the developmental process ends. Rust (1996a), however, emphasized that the coming out process is never finished. It is a lifelong process, something not acknowledged by linear models. Even if an individual comes out as a certain identity and feels comfortable with it, she or he may go through other identity changes as available identity concepts change (see Chapter 1). Discovery of a "true" sexual identity, then, is not an accurate fit for the many individuals who experience changes in their sexual feelings and behaviors through their lives (e.g., Blumstein & Schwartz, 1977; Dixon, 1985; Esterberg, 1997). Rust found, for example, that 20% of men and women identified themselves as heterosexual again after coming out as lesbian, gay, or bisexual. A majority of women (91%) and men (68%) who initially identified as lesbian, gay, or "homosexual" later identified themselves as bisexual. Of those who identified as bisexual, 39% of women and 35% of men later identified as lesbian or gay. Some researchers described identity development as a repeating spiral pattern (e.g., Ponse, 1978), or more like a spiral staircase than a linear process. At each turn of the spiral, identity is reworked and reframed from the vantage point of new perspectives (Olson & King, 1995) and perhaps new identity concepts (Rust, 1996a). A fluid conceptualization of identity development, then, seems to fit many men and women rather than a single linear process of reaching an end point and stopping there.

Missing Pieces

Women. It was noted in Chapter 3 that gender socialization is a more powerful influence on men and women than their sexual orientation. Generic coming out models therefore are not likely to fit both genders in all aspects. For example, the identity process appears to be more fluid and ambiguous for lesbians in contrast to a more abrupt process for gay men (Gonsiorek, 1993, 1995; T. Stein, 1993). Women are also less unidirectional in the identity process than men. A sequence of stages therefore may fit men better than women (e.g., Troiden, 1989). Although several stage models for lesbians exist (e.g., Faderman, 1984-1985; Fassinger, 1995; Lewis, 1979; Sophie, 1985-1986), they do not fit the variation in women's identity development (Esterberg, 1997).

Additional differences between men and women include findings that women often become aware of same-gender sexual attractions later than gay men (Sohier, 1985-1986; Troiden, 1989). The awareness of same-gender attractions for women (both lesbian and bisexual) usually occurs before sexual involvement, in an affectionate linkup with another woman (Esterberg, 1994; Gramick, 1984; Sears, 1989; Weinberg et al., 1994). For men, this awareness more often occurs after sexual experiences (and not necessarily in the context of a close linkup). Women also self-identify as lesbians and disclose this identity later than gay men (Sohier, 1985-1986; Troiden, 1989). Women may delay identifying as lesbian because expressions of affection between women are not unusual whereas men may interpret a single same-gender sexual experience as clear evidence of a gay identity (Blumstein & Schwartz, 1977). Because lesbians become aware of their identity at later ages, they may be able to manage the coming out process more easily than gay men (Paul, 1984). In addition, acceptance of a same-gender sexual orientation may be easier for women because their sexual linkups are less stigmatized than those between men (Blumstein & Schwartz, 1977; Marmor, 1980; Paul, 1984; Sohier, 1985-1986).

Racial and ethnic diversity. In addition to gender differences, lesbians, gay, and bisexual persons experience variations in the coming out process according to their racial and ethnic backgrounds (Gonsiorek, 1993). Some work is now addressing this diversity. E. S. Morales (1992, 1996), for example, identified some of the issues confronted by Latino gay men and lesbians as they work out their same-gender identities. These include (a) *denial of conflicts* (e.g., denial of the reality of heterosexism and the extent to which one may have to hide one's sexual orientation); (b) *bisexual versus gay or lesbian* (e.g., thinking of oneself as bisexual but seeing that one's behavior is not different from the behavior that characterizes individuals who identify as gay or lesbian); (c) *conflicts in allegiances* (e.g., how to remain connected to family but also to partners and the lesbian and gay community); (d) *establishing priorities in allegiance* (e.g., assessment of links with persons with similar allegiances and how they fit in with other links); and (e) *integrating various communities* (e.g., attempts to link the Latino community and the gay and lesbian community). Espin (1987) found similar issues in her studies of Latino lesbians.

Issues of immigration. Immigration creates issues in coming out which are rarely considered in coming out models. In studies of immigrant lesbians, Espin (1997) noted, for example, that even if a woman was a lesbian prior to migration, she must learn how to be a lesbian in the new cultural context. In addition, if she is from a background other than European, acculturation as a "minority" person is necessary. The process of acculturation and identity re-formation is simultaneous.

Social contexts and constructs. H. Levine and Evans (1991) proposed that although most aspects of identity development may not be different from 10 or 15 years ago, the models need to be reconsidered in terms of new and more diverse social contexts. According to Hollander and Haber (1992), the process of coming out is mediated by environmental or contextual factors. D'Augelli (1994) pointed out, for example, that coming out in rural central Pennsylvania is quite different from coming out in Berkeley, California. Perspectives that address the social context include symbolic interactionist (B. Schneider, 1986), interactionist (Plummer, 1975), life span (D'Augelli, 1994), ecological (Hollander & Haber, 1992), sociological (Harry, 1993), and social constructionist (Kitzinger & Wilkinson, 1995; Rust, 1993a).

Approaches to identity development that consider the social context in which it occurs distinctly contrast with most coming out models that are essentialist or assume that a same-gender sexual orientation is established early and is waiting to be discovered by an individual (Eliason, 1996). Cass (1996) explained that practitioners usually work with clients who display the essentialist view, believing that their same-gender attractions are a fixed part of their inner biological/psychological self. These psychological realities are genuine and significant for clients and must be accepted as that. They do not recognize, however, that they "translate the everyday understanding of lesbian, gay, or bisexual identity provided by Western indigenous psychologies into knowledge, behaviors, beliefs, and experiences . . . via the process of reciprocal interaction" (p. 230). The identity formation process is not just one of "finding an inner sense of self" (p. 230) but the interaction between the individual and the environment. This reciprocal interaction includes individual factors such as needs and desires, biological factors such as level of sexual desire, and environmental factors such as social location, social class, and race.

The *social constructionist* approach gives attention to the social context as well as the social creation and fluidity of identities. This approach proposes that the meaning of lesbian, gay, and bisexual identities varies in different people and cultures. The meaning also changes in different time periods. In other words, sexual identity is a social category and as such is not static but is constantly changing and evolving (Eliason, 1996). It is not a quality of individuals but a venture that is socially constructed or an interpretation of personal experience developed in terms of available social constructs. Examples of possible social constructs include sociopolitical factors (e.g., the lesbian and gay rights movement) or new romantic or sexual relationships with people whose gender was unanticipated, or the appearance of a bisexual person in one's life that initiates awareness of a bisexual option (Rust, 1996c). Individuals may also believe that they introduce their own goals in a coming out process. Social constructionists, however, claim that the goals themselves are constructed (Rust, 1993a).

It was noted earlier that fluctuations in self-identity are viewed in developmental-stage models of coming out as signs of immaturity or an unfinished identity process. Maturity is the achievement of a consolidated lesbian or gay identity that, once attained, is expected to be permanent. In contrast, the social constructionist approach views fluctuations in self-identity as a socially and psychologically mature response to one's changing social contexts. Mature individuals respond to changes in the current social constructs, the sociopolitical context, and their position within the sociopolitical context (Rust, 1993a). In line with these views, Kitzinger and Wilkinson (1995) found that a "lesbian identity" is not a fixed state. Instead, a woman will continue to discover answers to the questions of what being a lesbian means to her and how she wants to live as a lesbian.

Political differences. Another critique of coming out models is that they are apolitical.

They do not acknowledge that lesbian, gay, and bisexual identities often have political meanings (Rust, 1996a). The models ignore, for example, radical lesbian feminist theories of lesbian identity. These theories include identities such as the "political lesbian" who views the patriarchy as controlling and oppressing women (Kitzinger, 1987). Radical lesbian feminism also emphasizes continued immersion in lesbian and gay political activism. In Cass's model of coming out, however, this could be viewed as interfering with growth and maturity. Reintegration with heterosexual men and women does not occur or is delayed (Esterberg, 1997).

Coming Out as Bisexual

Bisexual identity development is also missing from most coming out models. Similar to identity development for lesbians and gay men, there is no typical process or pattern of identity development for all bisexual persons (Fox, 1995; Rust, 1992, 1993a). What stands out for them is that they acknowledge and seek validation for both the heterosexual and the lesbian or gay components of their identities (Fox, 1996). Most studies report that coming out as bisexual also tends to happen later than it does for lesbians and gay men (Fox, 1995; Rust, 1993a; Weinberg et al., 1994). Rust (1996a), however, found that although lesbians were twice as likely to question their heterosexual orientation before feeling attracted to women, when these behaviors were reversed in order, that pattern occurred sooner for bisexual women.

Coming Out Process

Based on longitudinal data from a sample of bisexual men and women in San Francisco, Weinberg et al. (1994) proposed four broad stages of bisexual identity development based on the most common experiences of the respondents: (a) initial confusion, (b) finding and applying the label, (c) settling into the identity, and (d) continued uncertainty. The *initial confusion* may last for years until something leads to the second stage of *application of the label* of bisexual to one's attractions. Fox (1995) and Rust (1995) reported that before settling on a bisexual identity, women and men may first identify as lesbian or gay and move back and forth between that identity and a heterosexual identity several times. Some men and women are self-identified as gay or lesbian for years before they realize that they are bisexual. Weinberg found that following labeling and self-identification as bisexual, and perhaps years from the time of the first sexual attractions to or involvements with both genders, the third stage, *settling into the identity,* is reached. Many women and men, however, remain *uncertain* of the permanency of their bisexual identity, especially when they are not sexually involved with both genders.

Barriers to Bisexual Identification

Part of the difficulty in settling into a bisexual identity is that individuals trying to come to terms with their attractions to both men and women often do not have accurate role models for a bisexual identity. The media portray bisexual men and women as experiencing sex with both genders and usually in short-term liaisons. Men and women who are coming out as bisexual, then, may think that this pattern is necessary to complete the process of developing a bisexual identity. No particular pattern of behaviors, however, is necessary for this identity. It does not have to be defined only by behavior. It can also be defined by attractions to both genders or to people, with gender not necessarily relevant to the attraction (Ochs, 1996; Rust, 1996a).

Bisexual men and women may also feel pressure to fulfill the hybrid conceptualization of bisexual identity to qualify as bisexual: equal parts of same-gender and other-gender attraction. How can they be expected, however, to assess whether or not their sexual and emotional feelings for men and women are equal? Bisexual men and women rarely (less than one in four) report feeling equal attraction to men and women. Their attractions range across a full spectrum of proportions of attractions to men and women. In addition, emotional feelings and sexual feelings can differ toward men and women. One may, for example, feel emotionally closer to women and sexually more attracted to men. It is helpful for bisexual men and women to know that hardly anyone fits narrow definitions of a bisexual sexual orientation (Rust, 1996a). Useful books presenting more realistic views of coming out as bisexual are now available (e.g., Hutchins & Káahumanu, 1991).

Confrontation With
Social Realities

Fox (1996) identified some of the issues men and women face when they identify as bisexual: feeling different from heterosexual men and women and from lesbians and gay men, isolation and feeling a lack of community, dealing with prejudice and discrimination, and apprehension about disclosing attractions to both women and men (e.g., Coleman, 1981/1982a, 1985a, 1985b; Nichols, 1989). Matteson (1996) added that coming out as bisexual, with attractions to both genders, is also a more ambiguous status to heterosexual men and women, or harder to understand, than is coming out as gay or lesbian. Another social reality is that lesbian and gay communities often put pressure on bisexual men and women to adopt a

lesbian or gay identity (Weinberg et al., 1994). Because many bisexual persons report that they are confused themselves and are trying to figure out what they really are—lesbian, gay, heterosexual, or bisexual (Rust, 1996a)—they may accede to the pressure. They "make a choice" to be gay or lesbian, but at the cost of denying the full range of their sexual identity (Rust, 1992).

◆ Psychological Adjustment to Coming Out

Exiting from a heterosexual identity and establishing a positive gay, lesbian, or bisexual identity can result in considerable distress (D'Augelli, 1994; Gonsiorek, 1995). Coping resources can be overwhelmed (Reid, 1995) and for some there are suicide attempts (S. Schneider et al., 1989). Most lesbian, gay, and bisexual persons, however, eventually get through the coming out process with minimal or no serious troubles (e.g., Morin & Schultz, 1978; Nurius, 1983). A number of studies investigated the factors associated with positive and less positive psychological and social adjustments to coming out. These findings are summarized in Box 4.2.

Gonsiorek (1993) reported that a person's level of functioning prior to coming out best predicts long-term adjustment. Other researchers found that positive adjustment was related to delay of self-designation as lesbian or gay until after a period of experimentation. This allows internal readjustment and further acceptance (Adelman, 1991; Dank, 1971; de Monteflores & Schultz, 1978; Kahn, 1991). Because the lesbian, gay, and bisexual populations are still largely hidden, full knowledge about adjustment to the coming out process is not available. This process may be easier, however, in the contemporary context of lesbian, gay, and bisexual communities and cultures than in previous times.

Box 4.2. Factors Associated With Adverse Versus Positive Psychological and Social Adjustments to Coming Out

Adverse Psychological and Social Adjustment

▶ *Strong internalization of negative stereotypes* about one's sexual orientation (Morin & Schultz, 1978)

▶ *Denial or suppression of same-gender sexual desires* and *wishing one were heterosexual* (Bell & Weinberg, 1978; Hammersmith & Weinberg, 1973; Malyon, 1981-1982; Ochs, 1996; Weinberg & Williams, 1974)

▶ *Isolation* from other lesbian, gay, and bisexual persons (Bell & Weinberg, 1978; Hammersmith & Weinberg, 1973; Hodges & Hutter, 1979)

Positive Psychological and Social Adjustment

▶ *Low internalization of negative stereotypes* associated with one's sexual orientation (Morin & Schultz, 1978); rejection of the idea that same-gender attraction is an illness (Weinberg & Williams, 1974)

▶ *Perception of advantages* of one's sexual orientation (Adelman, 1991)

▶ *Full acceptance* of one's sexual orientation, attractions, feelings, and behaviors (Savin-Williams, 1990a); *commitment* to one's sexual orientation (Bell & Weinberg, 1978; Hammersmith & Weinberg, 1973); *no desire to change* one's sexual orientation (Weinberg & Williams, 1974)

▶ *Integration into the larger lesbian, gay, and bisexual communities* (Crocker & Major, 1989); high social contact or involvement with other lesbian, gay, and bisexual persons (Berger, 1996)

▶ *Linkage to gay, bisexual, and lesbian support systems* (Kurdek, 1988b; Leavy & Adams, 1986; Peplau & Cochran, 1981; Sophie, 1985-1986; Weinberg & Williams, 1974) ◆

◆ Summary

Almost everything known about the coming out process is in question, such as how it happens (e.g., a discovered essential lesbian, gay, or bisexual identity or a socially constructed identity), when it happens, its order or disorder, and whether there is an end state to the process or whether it is always open-ended. Another issue is that the established models of coming out do not fit the diversity of gender, culture, politics, race, ethnicity, and social and historical contexts. Even if new and more comprehensive models are developed, they cannot be looked at as static or as fitting the events unique to any given individual's life.

5

DISCLOSURE
CHALLENGES

◆ MOST COMING OUT MODELS include disclosure of sexual orientation as a necessary step to finalizing the identity process. The phrase *in the closet* is applied when lesbian, gay, and bisexual persons actively conceal their sexual orientation or when the assumption of a heterosexual sexual orientation is not challenged. *Coming out* is a shortened term for *coming out of the closet,* which implies that sexual identity is disclosed to others (Dynes, 1990a; Garnets et al., 1992). As noted in Chapter 1, the term *disclosure* is used to designate this step to avoid confusion with the internal process of coming out to oneself.

Secrecy regarding one's sexual orientation is viewed in lesbian, gay, and bisexual communities as a central cause of continued social oppression as well as in psychological adjustment and well-being (Bell & Weinberg, 1978; Byrne, 1993; Cain, 1991b; Crocker & Major, 1989; Healy, 1993; Herek, 1991; Malyon, 1981-1982; Wolfson, 1991). Although pressure is applied to make public disclosures, many lesbian, gay, and bisexual persons do not comply. Instead, they remain "in the closet" and "pass" as heterosexual.

One's circumstances may not be conducive to disclosure. Harry (1993) noted, for example, that disclosure is more a product of income level, occupation, residential location, and the sexual orientation of one's friends. Cohen and Savin-Williams (1996) concluded that lesbians and gay men who are most likely to disclose their sexual orientation are politically liberal and/or feminist, older, urban, exclusively lesbian or gay, strongly involved in lesbian and gay communities, and have supportive and accepting families and friends. In deciding whether to disclose, lesbian, gay, and bisexual persons weigh the social realities and risks (Bradford & Ryan, 1987). There are incentives against as well as for disclosure.

◆ Dilemmas of Disclosure

Incentives Against Disclosure

Some lesbian, gay, and bisexual persons no doubt hide their sexual orientation because of self-doubt, insecurity, and negative self-concept. By focusing on personal characteristics, however, the issues of nondisclosure are depoliticized and separated from their social context (Cain, 1991a). There is also an emphasis on personal change rather than social change (Kitzinger, 1987). Individuals most often conceal their sexual orientation not because of some type of emotional maladjustment but as an attempt to cope with a hostile and unaccepting social context (Cain, 1991a, 1991b). No one makes the disclosure of being lesbian, gay, or bisexual without dealing with a permeation of stereotypes, prejudices, hostility, and discrimination in his or her life (Kitzinger, 1991).

Rust (1996a) explained that self-acknowledgment as lesbian, gay, or bisexual means replacing the default identity (heterosexual), with which one grew up, with an identity that is stigmatized. Disclosure of the stigmatized identity usually results in changes in one's relationships with others and with society as a whole. It can result in rejection by friends and family. Social institutions will also treat one differently. For example, just as in earlier decades, lesbians and gay men can lose child custody (e.g., Falk, 1989), jobs, or promotions (e.g., Hall, 1989; M. Levine & Leonard, 1984). Violence is also possible (Garnets et al., 1992; Herek, 1989, 1990). Racial and ethnic lesbian and gay men who disclose their sexual orientation are also vulnerable to rejection and loneliness in their families and communities (Espin, 1987; Loiacano, 1989; Tremble et al., 1989). Bisexual persons who acknowledge same-gender attractions risk negative responses and loss of support in the heterosexual as well as in lesbian and gay communities (Bohan, 1996). In small towns or rural areas, even more negative attitudes and reprisals can occur than in larger cities (Hanley-Hackenbruck, 1989). (See Chapters 2 and 3.)

Because of one's own experiences and knowledge of what happens to others, negative reactions to disclosure of one's sexual identity are anticipated (Gartrell, 1981). When not anticipated, the "wild-card" effect can occur when those to whom one discloses react or use the information in unexpected, negative ways (Gonsiorek, 1993).

Incentives for Disclosure

Several studies report no harmful consequences to individuals who do not disclose their sexual orientation. For example, Brady and Busse (1994) found no significant differences in terms of psychological well-being and adjustment among open or closeted respondents in the last three stages of Cass's coming out model. A sample of "hidden" lesbian couples was described by Eldridge and Gilbert (1990) as high on self-esteem and overall life satisfaction. Several studies on older lesbians and gay men reported that they are not open but nevertheless are satisfied with their lives (Berger, 1982; J. Lee, 1987). Other studies, however, indicate negative social/political and personal consequences from passing as heterosexual.

Negative Results
From Nondisclosure

The negative consequences of passing or hiding one's identity are frequently noted in the disclosure literature (e.g., Cohen & Stein, 1986; de Monteflores, 1986; Gartrell, 1984; Hetrick & A. Martin, 1987; A. Martin & Hetrick, 1988; Sophie, 1987). There are risks of not disclosing for the lesbian and gay community such as continued stereotyping, isolation, and individual solutions (Pharr, 1988). Unless the community is open, it is difficult to organize politically (Dynes, 1990a). Hidden lesbians and gay men, not wanting to bring attention to themselves, are not likely to push for fair and just treatment for themselves or others. They may even openly support prejudice and discrimination so as to protect themselves (Shilts, 1987). Even if they simply say nothing when faced with bigotry and oppression, they tacitly agree that a same-gender sexual orientation is deviant (Hodges & Hutter, 1979).

Although bisexual, lesbian, and gay persons who pass are spared negative reactions, in exchange for this they must lie or mislead others, remain at a distance in social linkups, or compartmentalize their lives (H. Martin, 1991). These actions, however, create for them the stress and tension of not being able to fully reveal themselves (Weinberg et al., 1994). It is also harder to affirm their lesbian, bisexual, or gay interests if they keep them in the closet (Matteson, 1996). In addition, the fear of discovery is relentless (Bell & Weinberg, 1978; Harry, 1982b; Pope, 1995; Rofes, 1983). Passing takes considerable energy focused on making sure leaks about one's sexual orientation do not occur (Cain,

1991b; Rust, 1993a). Other negatives of nondisclosure at the personal level are summarized in Box 5.1.

Positive Results
From Disclosure

The other side of the negatives of nondisclosure is the benefits that result from disclosure. Benefits of disclosure at the social and personal levels are summarized in Box 5.2. The political benefits were noted in other chapters as well as implied above.

Cain (1991b) identified five kinds of disclosures. With the possible exception of the last one listed, the intent is to realize social and/or personal benefits: (a) *relationship-building disclosures* (e.g., trying to improve linkups with others, especially closeness); (b) *problem-solving disclosures* (e.g., trying to end constant questioning about one's private life or why one is not married); (c) *preventative disclosures* (e.g., avoiding anticipated problems with friends and employers such as telling them before they find out from someone else); (d) *political or ideological disclosures* (e.g., making disclosures because of the political benefits of larger numbers of visible lesbian, gay, and bisexual persons); and (e) *spontaneous disclosures* (e.g., an on-the-spot decision or "slip of the tongue").

◆ Dilemmas of Disclosure to Specific Audiences

Hollander and Haber (1992) suggested that disclosure can best be conceptualized as an ecological transition that brings about multiple alterations in one's position in one's social environment. Possible changes include (a) *interruptions in linkups* (e.g., marital partner, children, parents, extended family, close friends, work colleagues, and medical,

◆◆◆

Box 5.1. Negatives of Nondisclosure at the Personal Level

Negatives at the personal level include:

a. *isolation and loneliness* (e.g., Berger, 1982; Cain, 1991b; Malyon, 1981-1982);

b. *impairment of self-esteem, feelings of inferiority, and the internalization of negative self-concept* (Weinberg & Williams, 1974);

c. *guilt, shame, anxiety, and depression* (J. Smith, 1988; Weinberg & Williams, 1974);

d. *feeling unauthentic* (Goffman, 1963; I. Jones et al., 1984);

e. *feeling distressed by the discrepancy between public and private identity* (Goffman, 1963; I. Jones et al., 1984; Matteson, 1996);

f. *feeling valued for what others want one to be rather than what one wants to be* (H. Martin, 1991); and

g. *experiencing a fragmented and marginal status without full allegiance to any worl* (Bohan, 1996). ◆

---

legal, and religious representatives); (b) *creation of new linkups* (e.g., lesbian, gay, and bisexual friendships and development of linkups with accepting heterosexual persons); (c) *disruptions in settings* (e.g., changing residence and places for social events); (d) *development of new activities* (e.g., changing church, job, and leisure-time activities); and (e) *changes in sources of social support* (e.g., lesbian and gay friends versus family of origin).

In the remainder of this chapter, the issues related to interrupted or altered linkups in different audiences are addressed. These alterations may in turn lead to the other kinds of alterations listed above. First, the family of origin is addressed followed by other potential audiences including marriage partners, children, friends, college students and instructors, and work associates.

Disclosure to One's Family of Origin

Generally, lesbians and gay men disclose more often to close heterosexual friends and to siblings than to parents (or coworkers and employers) (Garnets & Kimmel, 1993a). There is probably no event that evokes as much fear and anxiety as disclosure to par-

ents (Cohen & Savin-Williams, 1996). When lesbian or gay family members become aware of their identity change, they usually experience an internal debate about whether or not to disclose this turn of events to parents.

Reasons Not to Disclose to the Family of Origin

An important reason for deciding against disclosure includes the desire not to hurt or disappoint parents (Cramer & Roach, 1988). The most important reason, however, is probably the fear of negative reactions from them. These reactions can include scorn, ridicule, alienation (Wells & Kline, 1987), disillusionment (Myers, 1981-1982), and withdrawal of emotional support (Kurdek & Schmitt, 1987). Lesbian and gay youths studied by Savin-Williams (1989) reported some of their fears about disclosure to their parents: " 'My parents won't understand'; 'My Dad will reject me, not speak to me, or throw me out of the house'; 'My mother will send me to a shrink'; 'I'll feel like I let them down' " (p. 41). Fears of these kinds of consequences can work to delay disclosure or close all possibility of it. The parents, however, may find out indirectly through some-

Box 5.2. Personal and Social Benefits of Disclosure

Benefits at the social level include (a) increased chance for *contact with others* who share similar concerns (Garnets et al., 1992); (b) *integration with the lesbian and gay community* and development of *support systems* (Gonsiorek, 1993); (c) *decreased feelings of isolation* (Murphy, 1989); (d) acquisition of *same-gender friends and partners* (Harry, 1993); (e) increased *intimacy in linkups* (Cramer & Roach, 1988; Sophie, 1987; Wells & Kline, 1987); (f) increased sense of *public affirmation of sexual identity* (B. Schneider, 1986); (g) *greater acceptance from others* (Bradford & Ryan, 1987; Miranda & Storms, 1989; Olsen, 1987); (h) disclosure as bisexual *counters the myth that bisexual sexual orientation does not exist* (Rust, 1995).

Benefits at the personal level include (a) *freedom from concealment and anticipation of rejection* (Cramer & Roach, 1988; Weinberg & Williams, 1974); (b) improved *self-esteem* (Hammersmith & Weinberg, 1973; Nemeyer, 1980); (c) higher *self-concept* (Schmitt & Kurdek, 1987); (d) *positive identity* formation (Bell & Weinberg, 1978; Coleman, 1981-1982b); (e) *identity integration* or integration of all aspects of the self (Cramer & Roach, 1988; Murphy, 1989; Pope, 1995; Rand, Graham, & Rawlings, 1982; Wells & Kline, 1987); (f) *increased self-affirmation or validation* as lesbian or gay (Harry, 1993; Wells & Kline, 1987); and (g) *lower social anxiety and depression* (Schmitt & Kurdek, 1987). ◆

one else who knows. Sometimes love letters are found or a child is observed in close physical contact with someone of the same gender (Bohan, 1996).

Racial and ethnic lesbian and gay men find it especially difficult to disclose their sexual orientation to their families (Carmen, 1991). They often feel intense pressure to remain closeted to avoid outcast status in their families (Almaguer, 1991; Blackwood, 1984; Chan, 1992; Espin, 1984, 1987; Greene, 1996; Hidalgo, 1984; E. S. Morales, 1992; Nakajima et al., 1996; Whitehead, 1981; Williams, 1986). Communities and extended families are often the primary reference groups and provide the main social and support networks for most racial and ethnic persons throughout their lives (Kanuha, 1990). To maintain these ties, they feel they must conform to acceptable outward roles (e.g., Chan, 1992; Wooden et al., 1983). In addition, because the family in most racial and ethnic communities provides the basic

means of survival for the culture, its expectations take precedence over individual desires (Garnets & Kimmel, 1993b). Disclosure of same-gender or bisexual sexual orientation by children in the family is equivalent to their putting their individual lives before their allegiance to their racial or ethnic groups and thereby threatening the survival of the culture (Kanuha, 1990).

Although there are similar themes in all strongly family-centered cultures, there are also unique issues for individuals belonging to different racial and ethnic groups (Rust, 1996a). See Box 5.3 for examples of these issues.

Patterns of Juggling the Closet

Lesbian, gay, and bisexual children use various strategies to keep their their families from discovering their sexual orientation. L. S. Brown (1989a) referred to attempts to hide sexual orientation from the family as

(text continued on p. 76)

◆◆◆

Box 5.3. Pressures Against Disclosure to Families of Origin Among Racial and Ethnic Groups

African Americans

The *African American* community is viewed by gay and lesbian members as extremely heterosexist. Both the community and families put considerable pressure on lesbian and gay family members not to divulge their sexual identities (Clarke, 1983; Gomez & Smith, 1990; Greene, 1994b, 1997b; Icard, 1985-1986; Loiacano, 1989; Mays & Cochran, 1988; Poussaint, 1990; B. Smith, 1992). Various factors underlie this pressure. First, conservative Christian religiosity is a dominant presence in African American culture (Bonilla & Porter, 1990; Greene, 1996). Churches (often referred to as "the Black church") instill the religious belief that same-gender sexual orientation is sinful and forbidden by the Bible (Icard, 1985-1986; J. Peterson, 1992). Certain interpretations of biblical scripture reinforce individual prejudice (Greene, 1996; Icard, 1985-1986). Second, gay men and lesbians may be an embarrassment to African American heterosexual men and women who perceive themselves as inferior and strongly desire "normalcy" in their communities (Poussaint, 1990). Third, strong pressures also exist in African American communities for gender role conformity (Icard, 1985-1986). In particular, young African American males may apply the label "sissy" to a male who does not conform to expected gender role behaviors, mannerisms, and gestures (B. Jones & Hill, 1996). Fourth, the negative reactions toward gay men may also result from the perceived shortage of marriageable men in the African American community and the implications of that for the continuation of the race (Dyne, 1980). Fifth, African American women may reject the whole idea of a lesbian sexual orientation because it negates heterosexual privilege. Heterosexual sexual orientation provides a higher status than a lesbian sexual orientation (Greene, 1997b). Sixth, African American lesbian, gay, and bisexual persons are also strongly attached to their cultural heritage, their

communities, and their ethnic identities. They usually claim their ethnic identity as their primary identity (Mays, Cochran, & Rhue, 1993). They also do not want to threaten their bonds with their families because of the protective barrier they provide against the racism of the dominant culture (Greene, 1997b)

African American gay men and lesbians were not always disparaged in their families and community. Networks of gay men and lesbians flourished during a brief interlude during the 1920s and 1930s (Manalansan, 1996). This was a period for tolerance of same-gender sexual experience within the African American community. The social gatherings of African American gay men and lesbians were also often viewed by Whites—heterosexual and lesbian and gay—as fashionably chic. Cultural activities included songs, cruising in speakeasies, and the Harlem costume balls where most men and women cross-dressed. This highly visible lesbian and gay community, however, disappeared with the advent of the Depression years (Graber, 1989).

Latinos

Latinos are lower on moral disapproval of same-gender sexual orientation than are African Americans (Bonilla & Porter, 1990) but still hold strongly conservative attitudes. For example, a child who pursues a lesbian or gay identity instead of a traditional identity and role is looked on as abdicating his or her responsibility to the family and community. This attitude is strongly bolstered by Catholic beliefs (Carballo-Diéguez, 1989; Rodriguez, 1996). The prescriptions of the church include clearly defined family and gender roles. Men, for example, are to provide for, protect, and defend the family (E. S. Morales, 1992). Gay men are viewed as disloyal to these prescriptions or as abandoning their family, community, and customs.

A number of other negative characterizations are attributed to gay men in Latino communities. E. Morales (1996, pp. 284-285) described these as (a) "gays as alien," "odd," "of another way," and "broken," which fosters ostracism; (b) "gays as inferior" or *joto* (meaning of no significance or worth), which signifies a degraded position in the community; and (c) "gays as feminine" or "butterflies," which perpetuates a common perception that gay men signify the opposite of manhood and machismo. Moraga and Hollibaugh (1985) reported that some Latino families think gay men are nonmen or may think that they are all feminine-identified drag queens.

Unless openly "butch," lesbians are relatively more invisible than are gay men in Latino communities. Friendships between single women may be encouraged, and even if emotionally and physically close, these relationships are not presumed by the family to involve lesbians (Espin, 1984, 1987; Hidalgo, 1984). Once the same-gender sexual orientation of Latinos is known, however, they may pay an even higher price than gay men. Women's gender roles are usually rigidly controlled as a means of preserving cultural continuity (Espin, 1997). *Etiquela,* the proper gender role for Latino women, prescribes patience, nurturance, passivity, and subservience (e.g., Ramos, 1994). Women are expected to be submissive to and respectful of elders and men. They are also expected to be virtuous and may be expected to continue to live with their parents until marriage (E. S. Morales, 1992). Because Latino lesbians violate these role expectations, they are viewed as trying to overthrow men or threaten their dominance and the masculine Latino cultural heritage. They may be called macho or man-haters (e.g., Ramos, 1994).

Lesbian Latino women are also seen as threatening the cultural norms because they may provoke other Latino women to question their status in their families and to see possibilities for their independence (Trujillo, 1991). Latina lesbians also force a culture that denies or is silent about the sexuality of women to confront it (Espin, 1987; González & Espin, 1996). Good Latino women are not supposed to be sexual. Single lesbians are more acceptable than those with sexual partners (Espin, 1984, 1987; Hidalgo, 1984). Sexual lesbians are thought to be promiscuous and unchaste (e.g., Ramos, 1994).

It is not unexpected that Latino lesbian and gay children will decide against disclosure, given the family's expectations of their children. This decision may result more from wanting to protect their parents and extended family from pain and embarrassment rather than from anxiety and anger about being rejected (González & Espin, 1996).

Asian Americans

Lesbian and gay *Asian Americans* also experience rejection because of heterosexism and their violation of family expectations in their community (Nakajima et al., 1996). Same-gender sexual orientation is a source of shame to the Asian American family (Chan, 1992), or, in stronger terms, disclosure may be experienced as an act of treason against the culture and family (Greene, 1997b). The most notable characteristic of Asian American families is their expectation of unquestioned obedience from children and the demand for conformity (Chan, 1992). The obedience is to be shown through respect and loyalty to parents and other elders (Chan, 1987, 1989, 1992, 1995; Garnets & Kimmel, 1993b; Gock, 1985, 1986; Liu & Chan, 1996; Pamela H., 1989). In East Asian families, there is a hierarchy of expected loyalty. The primary loyalty is to one's parents, followed by one's siblings, and then one's marital partner (Liu & Chan, 1996).

The demand for conformity centers on expected gender roles. Rejection of one's appropriate roles threatens the continuation of the family line (Chan, 1992; Garnets & Kimmel, 1993b; Wooden et al., 1983). Asian men are the carriers of the family name, linkage, and heritage. Consequently, they are expected to marry and provide heirs (Chan, 1989; D. Lee & Saul, 1987; Tremble et al., 1989). Women are expected to carry out the roles of dutiful daughter, wife, and mother (Chan, 1992; Pamela H., 1989). A lesbian shames the family honor by rejecting these roles (Chan, 1987; Pamela H., 1989; Shon & Ja, 1982). To neglect the family role obligations, or focus on one's own pleasure rather than the community good, is viewed as selfish (Savin-Williams, 1996).

Liu and Chan (1996) explained that the tight bond of the Asian family can seem oppressive but it also gives support, caring, and security. Gay and lesbians children therefore may not be willing to risk losing their family bond by disclosure, especially to their parents. Chan (1989) found in a sample of Asian American lesbians and gay men that they disclosed to most of their friends, and 77% disclosed to a family member, usually a sister. In the 6.2 years since coming out, however, only about a quarter (27%) had disclosed to a parent.

Asian American parents may suspect a child is lesbian, gay, or bisexual but not bring up the issue because they fear embarrassing their relatives and community (Savin-Williams, 1996). Sex is also viewed as a shameful topic. It is not to be openly discussed (Chan, 1992; Pamela H., 1989; Wooden et al., 1983). Chan (1997) added that East Asian cultures make a clear distinction between public and private selves. The public self conforms to gender and family role expectations. Any actions that would shame the family are to be avoided. This includes discussion of sex in the context of the public self. For women, particularly, the private self is never viewed outside of one's most intimate family and friends, if even with them.

Because of the pressure to maintain privacy within their cultures, many Asian American men and women will never disclose their gay or lesbian identity. Others, however, will more openly claim their identity. These men and women are probably more assimilated into Western culture. Because they still want affirmation of their ethnic identities, however, they may be open only in non-Asian contexts, and they may disclose only to non-Asians (Chan, 1997; Nakajima et al., 1996).

Native Americans

Native American lesbians and gay men do not often anticipate rejection by the traditional Native community (L. B. Brown, 1997). The attitudes of those who are more acculturated (e.g., third and fourth generations), however, are often more negative. This is attributed in large part to their adoption of Western Christian religions (Walters, 1997). The HIV/AIDS epidemic also constrains open expression of any form of sexuality on reservations and in Native American gatherings elsewhere (M. Jacobs & Brown, 1997). Native American lesbian and gay men living on rural reservations may particularly feel pressure to remain closeted (Owlfeather, 1988). As a result of this pressure, many of them move to larger urban areas. They do this with the costs, however, of losing traditional culture and family support (Greene, 1997b; Williams, 1986). ◆

"juggling the closet." One juggling pattern is to keep steadfast geographical distance from the family by living far away or in some other way reducing contact to a minimum. In some juggling patterns, other family members cooperate. For example, in the "I know you know" pattern, the family knows about a member's sexual orientation, but everyone agrees not to talk about it. In another pattern, such as "Don't tell your father," family secrets, such as a child's same-gender sexual orientation, are known by one or more family members who agree not to tell the others. Often it is the father who is not told.

Reasons to Disclose to the Family

While many lesbian, gay, and bisexual persons never disclose their sexual orientation to their families, it is important to others to make this disclosure. They are unhappy with the impersonal distance between themselves and their families (L. S. Brown, 1989a; Cramer & Roach, 1988). They are

outwardly accepted but feel inwardly isolated (Bell, Weinberg, & Hammersmith,
1981; Harry, 1982b). They may also disclose
their sexual identity because of their discomfort and guilt over concealment and the feeling that they are deliberately misleading their
families (Strommen, 1990). Increased honesty was the greatest benefit of disclosure
found by Ben-Ari (1995) in a study of lesbians and gay family members and their parents. L. S. Brown (1989a) found that many
lesbian and gay family members do not want
to misrepresent their partners either as, for
example, just a roommate.

Although many racial and ethnic lesbians
and gay men incorporated their sexual identity and same-gender partners into their lives
through invisibility and silence, Liu and
Chan (1996) found that for others, the only
acceptable option was to be open. They dealt
with parental expectations over time while
maintaining close contact. In a study of 25
Black lesbians, Jackson and Brown (1996)
found that most of them were honest and
open with their families. They also wanted to
remain close to their families.

Instantaneous Reactions of the Family to Disclosure

Parents frequently react negatively when
their children first disclose their same-gender or bisexual sexual orientation. The foundation of this reaction is the social stigma
associated with lesbian, gay, and bisexual
persons. This stigma forms the family's attitudes in general and its initial reactions to the
disclosure (Strommen, 1990).

Visceral Reactions

Upon first learning of their child's same-
gender or bisexual sexual attractions and behaviors, only a few parents are unaffected.
Even most of the liberal and well-educated

parents studied by B. Robinson, Walters, and
Skeen (1989) reported negative initial reactions when learning about their child's sexual
orientation. Parents often must deal with
conflicts between their love for their child
and the thoughts and feelings they have about
lesbian, gay, and bisexual persons (Holtzen
& Agresti, 1990). Most parents studied by
Robinson et al. did not want to know what
they had already suspected. Only a few (2%)
felt relieved to confirm what they suspected.
Most expressed regret and confusion. Reactions of parents studied by Bernstein (1990)
included shock, devastation, humiliation,
and denial. Some parents experienced grief
as if their child were dead (B. Robinson
et al., 1989).

Parents are often angry with their
child and ask why he or she did this to them
(Griffin, Wirth, & Wirth, 1986; B. Robinson
et al., 1989). If the reactions are extremely
severe, parents may physically abuse their
child or put him or her out on the street
(Bales, 1985; Hersch, 1988; A. Martin &
Hetrick, 1988). If the child is an adult and financially independent, the situation is an
emotional tragedy. If an adolescent, the situation is much worse. Bales, for example,
attributed teenage male prostitution in the
United States at least in part to the casting
out of male adolescents by parents (see
Chapter 8).

When they react with anger and shame,
some parents lose an image of themselves as
good parents or as accepting and understanding of their child (Bernstein, 1990). Rejecting and offending parents may later
blame themselves for family rifts, which may
take years to repair, if they can be repaired at
all (Mattison & McWhirter, 1995). Other
parents deny feeling shame or embarrassment. They fear these feelings may alienate
their child. Some do not question anything
about their child's sexual orientation (Bernstein, 1990).

Felt Isolation From the Child

Immediately upon disclosure, parents may feel isolated from their child or as if a wall exists between themselves and their child. They no longer feel that they know their child. Some parents believe that there is no family role for this now estranged and alien child (L. Collins & Zimmerman, 1983; DeVine, 1983-1984).

Family Realignments

It is not unusual for stress in the whole family system to occur. Other family members who also probably see the lesbian, gay, or bisexual member in terms of negative stereotypes often redefine their relationship with this individual (Strommen, 1989). Often the previous family roles and relationships break apart (DeVine, 1983-1984; Strommen, 1989). Divisions occur among some family members in how they respond to the disclosure. Old divisions, coalitions, or triangulations can reemerge and new or different alliances can emerge (L. S. Brown, 1989a).

Progression of Parent's Reactions

If the parents are initially rejecting of their child's gay, lesbian, or bisexual sexual orientation, the effects of disclosure are usually not quickly resolved. The process the family goes through to reach a more positive resolution can be as difficult and lengthy as the child's own coming out (L. S. Brown, 1989a; L. Collins & Zimmerman, 1983; DeVine, 1983-1984). Even so, improvements usually occur over time with both parents (Ben-Ari, 1995; Cramer & Roach, 1988; B. Robinson et al., 1989). Several theorists (e.g., DeVine, 1983-1984; Neisen, 1987; B. Robinson et al., 1989) categorized into stages the various challenges parents are likely to confront. See Box 5.4 for a description of one stage ap-

proach and issues regarding timing of the stages.

Typical of any stage theory, the parents' progression through stages is not always as smooth as the theories suggest. Some parents get stuck in one stage, others move back to earlier stages, and stages occur out of order (DeVine, 1983-1984; Sauerman, 1984). Although the timing of the progression through the stages is variable, the longer parents know about their child, the less negative they may feel (Holtzen & Agresti, 1990; Holtzen, Kenny, & Mahalik, 1995). Sauerman (1984) reported that the time required for some degree of acceptance varies from months to more than two years; B. Robinson et al. (1989) reported that it takes approximately two years. Serovich et al. (1993) found, however, that the length of time parents knew about their child's sexual orientation (from 1 to more than 37 years) was not associated with any indicator of attitude or acceptance. These researchers nevertheless agreed with the premise that, with time, adjustment can often occur and, with that step, acceptance is more possible. They suggested the need for further research.

Ben-Ari (1995) found that parents who feel their son or daughter disclosed their lesbian or gay identity because of a desire to be more honest are significantly more likely to later acknowledge and accept their child's sexual orientation. They are also less likely to experience shock, denial, and anger following disclosure. In addition, when lesbian or gay children use positive information in the initial disclosure (e.g, "I am lesbian and happy"), both they and their parents adjust more easily. Adjustment is more difficult when the first disclosure contains negative information (e.g., "I have a problem because I am gay") or even neutral information (e.g., "I am gay").

Parents who make a positive adaptation accept the new identity of their lesbian, gay, or bisexual child. They reject the negative

◆◆◆

Box 5.4. Stages Toward Family Acceptance

DeVine (1983-1984) described the family, especially parents, as progressing through a series of five stages from awareness to acceptance of their child's lesbian or gay sexual orientation. In the first stage, *subliminal awareness,* the family may suspect that a family member is lesbian or gay. The person in question may, for example, avoid talking about certain topics or show no interest in heterosexual dating and instead befriend many same-gender individuals. The second stage is *impact,* when there is explicit discovery or revelation of the fact of same-gender sexual orientation. Third, *adjustment* begins, but not until after the family applies pressure on the child to change or at least to hide "the truth" from others. The family's goal is to maintain respectability. The fourth phase, *resolution,* occurs when the family members grieve the loss of the heterosexual child and examine and modify their stigmatizing values about same-gender sexual orientation. In the last phase, *integration,* the family changes its values and accepts the lesbian or gay member's identity. Three characteristics of the family system influence movement through the stages: closeness of the members, rules that govern the family, and family themes including values and behaviors related to themselves and their link to the larger community. ◆

---

stereotypes associated with their child's sexual orientation and develop values that do not stigmatize their child. Accepting parents also gain the perspective that sexuality is only one part of their child's already loved characteristics. The happiness and well-being of their child is the main concern, not his or her sexual orientation. Awareness of their expectations for their child and mourning their loss also seem to help parents to create a new role for their child (Ben-Ari, 1995; Bernstein, 1990; Strommen, 1990).

Failure of parents to reach acceptance results in part from their poor crisis management. Ineffective strategies are used such as scapegoating and avoidance (L. Collins & Zimmerman, 1983; DeVine, 1983-1984). These parents get stuck at the initial point of conflict and do not move away from stereotypical, negative thinking. Their rejection of the lesbian, gay, and bisexual family member persists as do their feelings of "anger, disappointment, and guilt over the 'pervert' in the family" (Strommen, 1990, p. 28). Rejecting families idealize and long for their child's old family role. Feeling estranged, they are not able to identify with their child's feelings, as accepting families are able to do. Because they cannot overcome the negative stereotypes and respond in more positive ways, a hostile and strained family situation continues.

Adjustments to Disclosures in Racial and Ethnic Families

Following the typical response of rejection when children in racial and ethnic families first disclose their same-gender sexual identity, opposition may eventually lessen. New and open linkups with parents are possible (Jackson & Brown, 1996)—but more in some groups than in others. If, for example, children make disclosures in *Asian American* families, parents may refuse to discuss their new identity (Liu & Chan, 1996) and build a wall of silence around the family (Savin-Williams, 1996). In a sample of Chinese, Japanese, and Korean lesbian and gay young adults, Chan (1989) found that more than half of the respondents indicated that there is a denial of lesbians and gay men in their families.

In *Latino* families, rather than behavior, it is the overt acknowledgment and disclosure of a gay or lesbian identity that is likely to meet with the most disapproval (Espin, 1984, 1987; Hidalgo, 1984; E. S. Morales, 1992). Following disclosure, some Latino lesbian and gay family members maintain a place in the family and are quietly tolerated. This does not mean, however, that the parents accept their sexual orientation. Instead, it means that they too deny it (Espin, 1984, 1987; Hidalgo, 1984).

In discussing family reactions to disclosure in *Greek American* families, Fygetakis (1997) noted that families avoided talking about same-gender sexual orientation before disclosure and were not likely to modify that stance after disclosure. Gay or lesbian children whether, adolescents or adults, often collude with parents by not talking about their feelings or concerns. Although the parent-child link will generally remain intact because it is bonded with love and loyalty, it is more superficial than deep. There may be some variation in this scenario associated with the degree of assimilation into the dominant American culture; however, many Greek Americans who are several generations removed from immigration continue to strongly identify with their Greek heritage.

Although rejection following disclosure is also common in *African American* families, there is some movement toward greater ambivalence, tolerance, and acceptance. Gay African American men, for example, are tolerated by some African American families who overlook their sexual activities or identity and focus on what they do within the African American community (Hawkeswood, 1990). A. Smith (1997) suggested that a family norm of "Don't ask so they won't tell" may also allow the family to accept a

lesbian or gay family member without having to directly deal with the reality of their sexual orientation and the conflicts associated with it. Other studies found that gay African American men in some families are tolerated as long as they are silent and invisible (B. Jones & Hill, 1996; Manalansan, 1996).

African American gay men and lesbians are fighting for more openness and acceptance in their community. HIV/AIDS also forced the community to confront their existence more directly. The African American media now discuss this disease. In addition, political leaders include openly lesbian and gay persons in political coalitions. Most civil rights organizations oppose discrimination against these persons through their bylaws and support their civil rights. Open groups now also exist in a few African American churches (B. Jones & Hill, 1996).

Few *Native American* families reject a family member because of a disclosure of "difference" (L. B. Brown, 1997), and gay and lesbian children experience less pressure from their families to be other than what they are (M. Jacobs & Brown, 1997). According to Tofoya (1996), regardless of sexual orientation, the membership of many Native Americans in a clan, extended family, tribe, or nation never changes. Gay and lesbian Indian Americans living in urban areas in California reported that following disclosure, open discussion of sexuality and their sexual orientation does not occur in some of their families. Nevertheless, they generally gain acceptance by both their families and their communities and are provided a place in American Indian culture (M. Jacobs & Brown, 1997).

Some of the more acculturated Indian Americans who are not as accepting of lesbian and gay family members may deny their existence or tease and criticize them. In a culture that generally believes that people are not to be controlled, these are accepted ways to show disapproval. In part, the disapproval results from the disclosure of their sexual orientation and association with the gay and lesbian community. This brings forth various clashes between the Indian American culture and the lesbian and gay culture: (a) the value of loyalty to family and kin networks versus the move into the gay and lesbian community; (b) the value of not being singled out versus disclosure or being openly lesbian or gay; and (c) the values of cooperation and continued participation in fighting against oppression of the group versus individualism and placing one's needs above the group (K. Walters, 1997).

Diversity in Family Reactions

Although a child's disclosure usually upsets family members, there is no uniform way in which they respond. Responses vary from acceptance to rejection. For example, as indicated in prior discussions, reactions to lesbian, gay, and bisexual children among and within racial and ethnic families (Greene, 1997b) can vary according to generation, the importance of continuation of the family line, degree of assimilation into the dominant culture, and the meaning of sexuality (Greene, 1997b). There are also variations associated with social class, religions, and the magnitude of family bonding and love. Clarke (1983) reported, for example, that tolerance for a same-gender sexual orientation may be greater among poor and working-class African Americans than the more conservative middle class. This contrasts with White families in which the higher the level of income of parents, the more accepting their attitudes (Serovich et al., 1993). Also, among African Americans, Catholics may respond differently to same-gender sexual orientation than do Baptists. Even among Baptists, there will be differences of opinion. Some conservative Black parents, for example, ignore church dictates.

Love for and bonds with a child supersede them (A. Smith, 1997).

Reactions of Family-of-Origin Members Other Than Parents

In the family of origin, parental reactions to a child's disclosure of a same-gender sexual orientation are the most well documented. Even though siblings are often the first family members told, there is little information on their reactions (e.g., Chan, 1989; DeVine, 1983-1984; Weinberg et al., 1994). Strommen (1990) suggested the possibility that sibling reactions may affect overall family reactions to lesbian and gay children, either strengthening or modifying them. Siblings can also be the ones who disclose the information to the parents, rather than the lesbian or gay family members themselves.

Disclosure to Marriage Partners and Children

Marriage Partners

Most people assume their marriage partner is heterosexual so they are understandably shocked when the partner discloses a same-gender or bisexual sexual orientation. Given the huge pressures in our society for individuals to marry, however, and the fact that a same-gender or bisexual sexual orientation is so negatively stigmatized, it is not surprising that some lesbian, gay, and bisexual persons marry. Some persons marry without awareness of same-gender feelings. They can also be so embedded in heterosexual expectations that there is no concept of lesbian, gay, or bisexual linkups, and same-gender desires are not recognized (Elliot, 1985; Gramick, 1984; Lewis, 1979). No recognition of same-gender desires is probably not as common, however, as prior awareness. Most lesbians and gay men who marry, for example, are active in same-gender sexual relations before marriage. They marry because they "want to do the right thing," want a family life, or are fond of their partner (Coleman, 1981-1982a; Kirkpatrick, 1988; Turner, Scadden, & Harris, 1990; Wyers, 1987). Women may also marry for the economic benefits of heterosexual marriage (D. Green & Clunis, 1989). Some lesbians and gay men marry because they hope that it will change their sexual orientation, a notion advanced by many church and political spokespersons (see Chapter 11).

There is little information available on disclosure by lesbian, gay, or bisexual persons to marital partners. What does exist largely focuses on the partners' reactions (e.g., Hanscombe & Forster, 1982; Kirkpatrick, Smith, & Roy, 1981; Saghir & Robins, 1980). Their reactions are similar to those of parents when their children make disclosures such as shock, sense of estrangement, confusion, and guilt. The resulting stigma and sense of loss is worsened if there is no support from others (Gochros, 1985).

Wives and mothers. Lesbian wives do not often disclose to marital partners, but when they do, husbands may react in a severe and angry manner. Physical abuse by some husbands is a possibility. When ex-husbands feel extreme animosity toward them, lesbian mothers fear custody battles (Hanscome & Forster, 1982).

Husbands and fathers. Married gay men are often engaged in casual sexual encounters with men and sometimes a long-term linkup with another man (Bozett, 1980, 1981a, 1981b). They rarely disclose their sexual orientation to their families, however, due to fears of the reaction of their wives and children as well as concerns about job security and social status (Strommen, 1989, 1990). Men who decide to disclose to their families are often motivated by anxiety and guilt about living a double life (Bozett, 1980,

1981a, 1981b, 1982; Strommen, 1989). Indirect and anecdotal findings indicate that wives of disclosing husbands feel estranged and guilty. They feel that they somehow failed as wives (Gochros, 1985; Ross, 1983; Strommen, 1989).

Stokes, Taywaditep, et al. (1996) reported that bisexual men did not often disclose their sexual behavior with other men to their female partners. More than half (55%) of the bisexual men studied by Stokes, McKirnan, et al. (1996) reported that none of their female partners knew about their same-gender sexual activity prior to participating in sex with them. Similarly, they did not think that 59% of their steady female partners knew of their bisexual orientation. The men also reported that during the last six months, 71% of their female partners were not aware of their same-gender sexual behavior prior to participating in sex with them. The rates of nondisclosure were higher for Black men than White men. Weinberg et al. (1994) found, however, that most men who identified as bisexual following marriage told their partners shortly thereafter. Quick and voluntary disclosures generally helped keep the marriage intact.

A forced or unwanted disclosure, such as in the case of a bisexual husband who is HIV positive, no doubt can cause an explosive crisis. A wife is not simply confronted with a partner's bisexual sexual orientation but with marital infidelity and the possibility of being HIV-positive as well. This situation can result in feelings of loss, betrayal, vulnerability, and uncertainty about the future (Paul, 1996). (See Chapter 11.)

Divorce. Once the disclosure is made by a lesbian, gay, or bisexual marriage partner, the most common final resolution is divorce (Bozett, 1981a, 1981b; Coleman, 1985a, 1985b; L. Collins & Zimmerman, 1983; Gochros, 1985). Wyers (1987) found that a high rate of lesbian wives (97%) were divorced compared with 78% of gay husbands. Lesbians and bisexual women end marriages more quickly because of lack of sexual desire for the heterosexual partner, the partner's lack of tolerance, and dislike of open marriages or secret extramarital linkups (Coleman, 1985a; Matteson, 1987).

A husband's revelation of a gay or bisexual sexual orientation also tends to result in separation or divorce, although not as often as in the case of a wife's disclosure (Bozett, 1982; B. Miller, 1978, 1979a). Sometimes the same-gender or bisexual sexual orientation is integrated into a restructured arrangement such as an open, semi-open, or asexual friendship (Brownfain, 1985; Coleman, 1985b, Gochros, 1989; Whitney, 1990; T. Wolf, 1985). The chance for the relationship to remain intact is greater when the husband is bisexual instead of gay (Coleman, 1981-1982a, 1985a, 1985b; Gochros, 1985, 1989).

To increase the chances of remaining married when a partner discloses a bisexual identity, it is necessary for the nonbisexual partner to reach acceptance of his or her partner's same-gender attractions. If this happens, usually following confusion and possibly feelings of shame, certain other factors are necessary to help the marriage remain intact. First, it is essential that each partner is committed to the marriage. Second, it is necessary for the heterosexual partner to seek outside sources of support. Third, necessary actions between the partners include consensus about how, when, and if others are told; open communication; and mutual agreement on ground rules (Brownfain, 1985; Coleman, 1981-1982a, 1985a, 1985b; Dixon, 1985; Paul, 1996). Even though there are ground rules regarding outside partners, however, Paul emphasized that the HIV/AIDS threat is ever present as a potential source of anxiety and conflict.

When separations and divorces occur, they are complicated and painful for the part-ners, children, extended family, and friends (Myers, 1989). Long-term hostility and bitterness, however, is uncommon (Bozett, 1981a, 1981b; Gochros, 1985; B. Miller, 1979b; Ross, 1983). On the other hand, when lesbian mothers and gay fathers are divorced without disclosure, they often do not reveal their sexual orientation to former marital partners because of the fear of custody fights (see Chapter 7).

Children

The literature is sparse in the area of children's reactions to their parent's same-gender or bisexual sexual orientation. Some data indicate that a majority of children of lesbians and gay men also initially react negatively to parental disclosure (Harris & Turner, 1985-1986). Age is a factor, however, as younger children who are not aware of the stigma do not react in a negative way (Moses & Hawkins, 1986). Older children, especially adolescents, are aware of the stigma, and some express resentment and fears of abuse by others (Bozett, 1987). Researchers found that most lesbian and gay parents, however, report that openness with their children improves their relationships in the long term (Bozett, 1980; Hanscombe & Forster, 1982; Hoeffer, 1981; B. Miller, 1979a). Lesbian mothers are more open than gay fathers (Hanscombe & Forster, 1982; Hoeffer, 1981).

In Weinberg's et al. (1994) study of bisexual men and women, disclosure by parents resulted in positive as well as uncomfortable reactions from their children. Potential positive results included improved communication and increased closeness between parents and children. Some children, however, never talk about the disclosed knowledge with the parent. Others find the bisexual sexual orientation difficult to explain to their friends.

Disclosure to Friends

Lesbians and gay men usually disclose their sexual orientation to close friends first (e.g., Herdt & Boxer, 1993; Savin-Williams, 1990b). Bisexual men and women disclose more to friends (and to partners, including the marital partner) than to others (e.g., Weinberg et al., 1994). Little research exists, however, on the process of disclosure to friends or their reactions. An exception is Cain's (1991a) study of the disclosure of gay men to friends. The findings indicated that although close friends generally do not withhold important personal information from each other, it is difficult for gay men to disclose to their friends. They avoid the issue as long as possible even when it results in a sense of betrayal in friends who find out from another source. Often, just as with other audiences, an assessment is made of the benefits (e.g., honesty) versus costs (e.g., distrust). The major reason given for disclosure is closeness. Weinberg et al. (1994) found that for bisexual persons, the response from their best heterosexual friend and about 90% of their other heterosexual friends to their disclosure was benign. Similar responses occurred from their best lesbian and gay friend and other lesbians and gay friends.

Disclosure at College

Even though many gay, lesbian, and bisexual college students know of their same-gender sexual orientation long before their undergraduate days, their identity may still be in transition and disclosure of their sexual orientation on hold (D'Augelli, 1991). For students whose sexual identity is still hidden, not much is known about when during these years they decide to disclose to someone else (D'Augelli, 1993). They are at a point in their lives, however, when disclosure of their sexual orientation is a paramount issue (Lopez & Chism, 1993; Rhoads, 1994a,

1994b, 1995). Seeing or interacting with openly lesbian, gay, and bisexual students on campus is an additional push to self-disclose (Rhoads, 1995).

Some students want to disclose their sexual orientation in their classes, and they make daily assessments about whether or not to do it (Lopez & Chism, 1993). They are likely to be less open in large classrooms because of too many unknowns about the other students. The power difference between them and the instructor in any class makes it difficult to disclose even if the instructor is lesbian or gay (Lopez & Chism, 1993). Students are also less open if they fear verbal or physical harassment. In a two-year study of 40 gay and bisexual college men, Rhoads (1995) found that it is common for negative consequences to follow initial disclosure; students' stories of assault, harassment, and discrimination are endless. Firsthand knowledge of abuse, as well as threats of it, are warnings for others to stay hidden. There are many American campuses where no lesbian, gay, or bisexual student feels safe to disclose.

Disclosure at Work

Because of the discrimination in the workplace (see Chapter 2, this volume) as well as potential harassment and other abuse (Goldman, 1992; Kitzinger, 1991; Woods & Lucas, 1993), it is not surprising that the thought of disclosure at work typically creates considerable anxiety (M. Levine & Leonard, 1984). Most (more than two-thirds) of lesbians and gay men think that disclosure in a variety of work settings will create problems for them (M. Levine & Leonard, 1984; Winkelpleck & Westfeld, 1982). No matter what policies are in effect in their workplaces or how competent and skilled they are, they anticipate that they could still be devalued by their coworkers and employer if their sexual orientation became known. They could lose credibility and influence, if not worse (M. Levine & Leonard, 1984).

Some lesbians and gay men reveal their sexual orientation in every area of their lives except work. Nondisclosure at work is apparently as adaptive for some of these workers as high disclosure is for others (Hetherington & Orzek, 1989). Secrecy creates fewer problems through avoidance of stigma, discreditability, and discrimination (D'Emilio, 1983). Still, the separation between the private (sexual orientation) and the public (employee) is often a source of strain and conflict. For example, partners are not brought to social functions and their pictures are not seen on office desks (Byrne, 1993). While heterosexual coworkers talk about home life, it is unmentionable for closeted workers. There is no public celebration of positive events in their lives such as engagements or anniversaries. Even painful breakups cannot not be shared (Kitzinger, 1991). Studies of workers who "pass" at work find that this strategy is associated with feelings of depression and hostility, anxiety, low self-esteem, high rates of substance abuse, and ill health (Brooks, 1991; Hall, 1986; Triandis, Kurowski, & Gelfand, 1994).

Internally, living a double life at work and the need to lie to protect oneself are often so intolerable that they create ethical conflict (M. Levine & Leonard, 1984). For example, how acceptable can it feel to say nothing when one hears anti-lesbian-or-gay jokes (Croteau & Hedstrom, 1993)? Even when nondisclosure seems right or rational, sometimes disclosure becomes more of a heart than a head issue. Values and meaning can become more important than "objective success" (Gonsiorek, 1993). For some workers, honesty is so important that even negative reactions do not deter their commitment to be open (Shallenberger, 1994).

For other lesbians and gay men, disclosure at work varies in terms of factors such as type of occupation and position, cohort,

and geographical location. The closet is less closed, for example, in certain occupations including art, acting, and service positions such as cook, waiter, and hairdresser. Another category that is also fairly open includes largely clerical and lower white-collar occupations (Harry, 1993). Self-employed lesbians and gay men may also not be as closeted (McKirnan & Peterson, 1986). In certain other occupations, however, a strong pattern of being closeted is evident. This includes the professions of law, medicine, dentistry, ministry, science, and technology (Harry, 1993). Lesbians and gay men working with children are also less likely to reveal their sexual orientation (B. Schneider, 1986). Teachers in primary and secondary education are the most closeted occupational group. If they are open, complaints from parents and firings are possible (Byrne, 1993; Harry, 1993; Rubenstein, 1991). The stereotypes of the child-molesting or corrupting teacher still persist even though no evidence exists that children are at any greater risk of being molested by lesbians and gay men than by heterosexual adults (e.g., Jenny, Roesler, & Poyer, 1994).

Lesbians and gay men in higher-status occupations are also less likely to make disclosures at work (Bradford & Ryan, 1987; Hall, 1986; B. Schneider, 1986). Shallenberger (1994) found few gay male managers who are open. Lesbians in high-paying jobs and supervisory positions are also less likely to risk disclosure. Because, like most lesbians and gay men, they usually rely solely on their own income, the potential costs of losing their jobs are too great (B. Schneider, 1986).

Facing the possibility of disclosure to coworkers can also be quite stressful for older lesbian or gay workers (Elliott, 1993). Especially if their work is "very important," Adelman (1991) found that high satisfaction in older workers is associated with low disclosure at work. In part, low disclosure may represent a cohort effect. Regardless of sex-

---

Box 5.5. General Disclosure Management Strategies

1. *Assimilation:* This is the strategy of passing or attempting to appear as a member of the dominant group rather than one's denigrated group.

2. *Ghettoization:* Here one segregates one's denigrated life from the dominant society

such as working with the dominant group in one city and socializing with lesbian, gay, or bisexual friends in another city.

3. *Confrontation:* In this strategy, identity is disclosed and one lives and works openly in the face of stigma (de Monteflores, 1986). ◆

---

ual orientation, older workers rarely discuss their personal lives at work.

A. Ellis and Riggle (1996) found that geographical location makes a difference in the motivation to disclose at work. For example, lesbians and gay men in San Francisco who are less open at work are less satisfied with their lives than those who are less open in Indianapolis. Those in San Francisco may be more bothered by their lack of disclosure in light of greater tolerance and acceptance in that location. There are different expectations for openness than in Indianapolis. Weinberg et al (1994) found that close to 40% of bisexual persons in their San Francisco sample disclosed their sexual orientation to a boss and about half to other persons at work.

◆ Disclosure Management

Although disclosure is the "end stage" of many coming out models, it is an often-repeated action (Rust, 1996a). Instead of the misconception of disclosure as a one-time, all-or-nothing event, the risks and possible consequences of disclosure in each and every situation are often weighed. This endeavor is complex, grueling, and never finished (Garnets et al., 1992; Gonsiorek, 1993; Healy, 1993; Kitzinger, 1991; A. Walters & Phillips,

1994). In some instances, for example, lesbian, gay, and bisexual persons may decide to disclose to parents but it is probably of no benefit to anyone to disclose to the mail delivery person or the person bagging groceries (Barbone & Rice, 1994). Some individuals may disclose to coworkers on a particular job. If they change jobs, however, they may return to the closet. This may also happen when moving from a large city to a small town (Cruikshank, 1992). In late life, individuals may decide to close the door on the closet if, for example, they must enter a predominantly heterosexual nursing home. Gonsiorek (1993) recommended that lesbians and gay men should be as open as possible because it feels better to be honest but closed if necessary to defend against discrimination. A. Smith (1997) emphasized that strategies such as passing can be "adaptive" as a way to avoid: "exile, isolation, exclusion, or extermination, physically, politically, economically, and socially" (p. 289).

Throughout their lives, then, lesbian, gay, and bisexual persons are accustomed to disclosure management. Three general disclosure management strategies, identified by de Monteflores (1986), are listed in Box 5.5.

When lesbian, gay, and bisexual persons decide against disclosure in the workplace, they usually try to fit in or "assimilate" by

---

Box 5.6. Subterfuges at Work

▶ *Stringent boundaries between personal and work lives* are maintained (Hall, 1986, 1989; Kitzinger, 1991; M. Levine & Leonard, 1984; Shachar & Gilbert, 1983). Associations with coworkers (sometimes including known lesbians and gay men) are superficial and restricted to work; leisure time with them is avoided (B. Schneider, 1984).

▶ *Conformity to "appropriate" gender-role* is displayed through dresses, makeup, and long hair for women and a masculine appearance for men. The purpose is to resemble everyone else (Kitzinger, 1991).

▶ *Avoidance* is a pattern of staying away from situations where hints of one's sexual orientation may occur. Personal situations are particularly avoided such as casual conversations about leisure time and home life (M. Levine & Leonard, 1984; Shachar & Gilbert, 1983).

▶ *Monitoring* involves watching one's reactions to heterosexist comments and jokes (Byrne, 1993) so as not to let discomfort show.

▶ *Distraction* involves directing information away from oneself (Hall, 1989; M. Levine & Leonard, 1984). Images are purposively developed to convey other kinds of differentness such as "feminist" or "liberal" to distract attention away from a lesbian, gay, or bisexual identification (Hall, 1989).

▶ *Inventions* of heterosexual dates, fiancées, and marital partners are used as a "heterosexual" front. At social functions, for example, gay men are "dates" for lesbian workers and the reverse if gay workers. Same-gender partners or dates are *reinvented* as friends and introduced as such. Some partners who never appear at any work function are reinvented in conversations with coworkers as of the other gender; this is done by changing pronouns when they are discussed (Byrne, 1993; Peters & Cantrell, 1993). ◆

---

presenting a heterosexual front or "act" (Byrne, 1993). Various studies of lesbians and gay men showed that about three-quarters of the samples put a significant amount of energy into creating various forms of subterfuge to manage and monitor information about themselves at work (e.g., Hall, 1989; Kitzinger, 1991; Kronenberger, 1991; B. Schneider; 1984; Shachar & Gilbert, 1983; Stewart, 1991). See Box 5.6.

Sometimes disclosure decisions get so complicated that disclosure management becomes less efficient. For example, individuals who decide to disclose to some audiences but not to others must try to assure that no one who knows their sexual orientation knows anyone who does not. Or they can use the tactic of collusion by telling only a selected group of persons and asking them to agree to keep the information secret (Davies, 1992). There are, however, problems with these strategies. Once one or more people are told, maintaining control over what is known and by whom is difficult (B. Schneider, 1986). Some audiences overlap and members may talk with each other (Harry, 1993). As the new confidants do not have the same investment in secrecy, accidental disclosure is possible (B. Schneider, 1986). Also, the more audiences individuals are out to, the harder it may be to alter behavior in situations where they are not out. They can feel pressured to go ahead and disclose to all of the audiences (Harry, 1993).

◆ Summary

Although lesbian, gay, and bisexual communities pressure their members to make public disclosures of their sexual orientations, many only disclose to selected audiences or not at all. Although there are positive personal, social, and political reasons to disclose, there are always risks of negative reactions. Both sides of this dilemma are weighed many times in the never-completed process of disclosure management.

PART III

FAMILY

6

COUPLES

◆ LESBIANS, GAY, AND BISEXUAL PERSONS are involved in various family relationships "as partners, as parents and stepparents, and as extended and chosen kin" (Allen & Demo, 1995, p. 111). This chapter reviews the current social science research on lesbian, gay, and bisexual adults in couples. Chapter 7 addresses lesbian and gay men who are parents and stepparents. Family-of-origin involvements are discussed in this and various other chapters.

Weston (1991) referred to the partners and friends of lesbians and gay men as "chosen families." Instead of blood ties, these families are based primarily on voluntary choice and love. They are fluid and change in composition over time and with geographical moves. Not all lesbian, gay, and bisexual persons place as much value on others outside of their biological families. This is more the case among racial and ethnic group members (see Chapter 5). For most lesbian, gay, and bisexual persons, however, their major support system includes their friends and partners—or family of choice (D'Augelli & Garnets, 1995; Kurdek, 1988b; Kurdek & Schmitt, 1987; Nardi, 1992a, 1992b; Nardi & Sherrod, 1994; Weston, 1991). Many lesbians and gay men obtain more support from their primary partner and close friends than from their families of origin. For persons with AIDS, the family of choice is often the sole or major support throughout the progression of the illness (Dworkin & Kaufer, 1995; Paul et al., 1995).

When in a couple, one's primary partner is usually the most important part of one's chosen family. In this chapter, many topics related to gay, lesbian, and bisexual couples are explored: terminology, desires for a partner, meeting and dating, values, linkup arrangements and scripts, couple themes, satisfaction, commitment and duration, obstacles to satisfaction and duration, and breakups. Peplau and Cochran (1990) identified many of these topics as issues of concern in a linkup perspective on same-gender adult pairs. To date, there are considerably more research findings on these topics related to lesbians and gay men than to bisexual women and men. Among both of these groups, little is known about the effects of racial, ethnic, and other diversity on couples.

◆ Couple Criteria and Terminology

Close or primary linkups are the focus of this chapter. According to Kelley et al. (1983), close linkups include four necessary components: relatively long duration, frequent interaction, strong and intense influence on each other, and mutual influence on each other over a range of issues. Although this definition could fit close friendships and work associations, it is used here to refer to couples. It is a given, however, that lesbian and gay couples may have various other definitions for a close or primary linkup. For example, while some couples may insist that living together is a criterion, many other couples consider themselves close but do not live together. Kitzinger and Coyle (1995) suggested several reasons that lesbian and gay couples may choose not to live with each other. Those who are closeted may think that living together will increase visibility. Those with children from an earlier marriage may have concerns about the effects of cohabiting on pending custody hearings or effects on the children. Other reasons include the desire for more flexibility and autonomy than cohabitation may allow or, in the event of a breakup,

not wanting the complications of dividing joint property.

Bryant and Demian (1994) did a national survey of 1,729 self-selected lesbians and gay men including 560 lesbian couples and 706 gay couples, most of whom (95%) were White. The main focus of the study was close linkups, which averaged six years in duration. One of the topics was the terms that lesbians and gay men use to refer to their close linkups. Two terms were most often and about equally used: *lover* and *partner* or *life partner.* More men (40%) than women (30%) preferred the term *lover* whereas more women (37%) than men (27%) preferred the terms *partner* or *life partner.* Various problems are associated with all of these terms. The term *partner,* for example, can imply a business association (Murphy, 1994). The term *lover* can be objectionable because of its association with sex (R. Berger, 1990a; Murphy, 1994). It seems best to ask the individual couple what term they prefer (R. Berger, 1990a).

◆ Desire for a Partner

There are many similarities among lesbian, gay, bisexual, and heterosexual couples. They all, for example, value close linkups and desire a partner (Kurdek, 1995b; Peplau & Gordon, 1983; Weinberg et al., 1994). Most lesbians (75%) and gay men (83%) report that they and their partners are in love (Peplau, 1981), and about three-quarters (74%) of African American lesbians and 61% of African American gay men report that they are in love (Peplau, Cochran, & Mays, 1997). Bryant and Demian (1994) found that most lesbians (92%) and gay men (96%) in couples also committed themselves to be together for life or "a long time." Peplau et al. (1997) found, however, that although both African American lesbians and gay men were on average relatively certain they would be

COUPLES   93

with their current partner for one year, they
were less confident when looking at a five-
year or longer period. Weinberg et al. (1994)
found that about one-third of unmarried bisexual men and women in their sample said
yes when asked if they wanted to marry in
the future, about a third said no, and another
third were undecided. Love, heterosexual
sex, and children were the main reasons marriage was desired.

A major contrast between lesbians and
gay men and bisexual women and men centers on the lower desire of most bisexual men
and women for a committed monogamous
linkup with one person. Most of Weinberg et
al.'s (1994) sample indicated that a marriage
would have to be with another bisexual person or someone who could accept bisexual
activity and nonmonogamy. Rust (1996b)
found that close to half of lesbians (48%) and
more gay men (80%) indicated that they want
a lifetime monogamous linkup with one partner compared with 30% of bisexual women
and 15% of bisexual men. The higher desire
for monogamy among gay men is likely attributable to the fear of HIV/AIDS. The low
percentage of bisexual men desiring monogamy is puzzling because, as found by Weinberg, they also fear HIV/AIDS.

◆ Meeting and Dating

After self-identification as lesbian, gay, or
bisexual, individuals usually begin involvement in same-gender or bisexual linkups. In
a study of more than 300 lesbian, gay, and
bisexual youths between the ages of 14 and
23, Savin-Williams (1990b) found that more
than half of their romantic linkups during
adolescence and young adulthood were with
same-gender partners. This reflects not just
the desire to be linked up with someone but
also further commitment to their new identity (Coleman, 1981-1982b; Troiden, 1979;
Weinberg et al., 1994).

Venues of First Meetings

One stage everyone passes through on the
way to being part of a couple is meeting a
partner. Both underground and mainstream
venues provide opportunities for potential
meetings (Weinberg et al., 1994). Gay and
bisexual men tend to meet partners more in
underground venues than do lesbian and bisexual women (Berger, 1990a; McWhirter &
Mattison, 1984; Weinberg et al., 1994). Gay
couples are more likely than lesbian couples
to meet at bars (22% versus 7%) or through
anonymous or sexually identified situations
such as parks and classified ads (39% versus
9%) (Bryant & Demian, 1994). Bisexual men
also meet anonymous sex partners in bars
and in cruising areas such as parks (Weinberg
et al., 1994). J. Peterson (1992) found that
gay Black men also look for partners in bars
and through classified sections of gay newspapers and magazines. They also use dating
and matching services.

Today, more mainstream organizations
and meeting places are designed to bring
people together. Especially in large urban
areas, there are diverse locations in which to
meet people (Huston & Schwartz, 1995). A
third of the Weinberg et al. (1994) lesbian
and gay sample mentioned mainstream
means for meeting partners such as friends
or conventional parties. Other meeting
places include work, organizations (Berger,
1990a), bookstores, churches, schools, jog-
ging trails, theater lobbies (Weinberg et al.,
1994), personals ads, dating services
(Nakayama & Corey, 1993), vacation tours,
and organized sports (Murphy, 1994). Black
gay men look for partners in mainstream
venues such as private house parties and
friendship networks (J. Peterson, 1992). Bisexual women and men in San Francisco are
most likely to meet their second and third
significant partners and casual sex partners
in support groups, rap groups, and workshops on nontraditional sexual patterns. The

most significant partner is more often met in conventional settings such as school, recreational groups, or work. This partner is most likely heterosexual and may become a marriage partner (Weinberg et al., 1994).

Dating

Klinkenberg and Rose (1994) studied courtship scripts in a sample of 51 gay men (aged 21-51) and 44 lesbians (aged 19-55). Sexual scripts, a version of script theory (Ginsburg, 1988; Simon & Gagnon, 1986), were used to understand the courtship and dating behavior of lesbians and gay men. The researchers discovered that cultural and interpersonal scripts for same-gender dating parallel heterosexual scripts during all stages of a first date. This finding indicates the strength of the first date script no matter what the sexual orientation of the participants is. The strength of gender influences is also clear. For example, gay men are similar to heterosexual men who follow traditional roles in orchestrating a date and other actions. Behaviors on first dates for lesbians are more often negotiated by both partners. Nearly half (48%) of the men also indicated they had sex on their most recent first date, compared with only 12% of women.

Peplau et al. (1997) reported that African American lesbians (17.5%) were also significantly less likely to have sex on the first date than African American gay men (30%). Other dating practices by racial and ethnic lesbians and gay men are essentially unknown. Only a few studies addressed their dating and partner preferences. J. Johnson (1982), for example, found that Black-identified gay men more often preferred other Black men as ideal lovers whereas gay-identified Black men more often preferred White men. More Black-identified men reported that they would not date White men in the future. J. Peterson (1992) reported, however, that more gay Black men preferred interracial linkups than gay White men.

In the absence of visible, positive portrayals of Asian American men as masculine and desirable, many Asian gay men do not desire to link up with other Asian gay men. A pejorative term, *sticky rice,* is used by Asian gay men to refer to Asian Americans attracted to other Asian Americans. Non-Asian men who have an exclusive interest in Asian American men are called *rice queens.* Asian American men involved with a rice queen are likely to encounter disapproval from the Asian American gay community and from non-Asian peers (Nakajima et al., 1996).

◆ Linkup Arrangements for Bisexual Men and Women

Meeting and dating are more complicated for bisexual men and women. Those who reject the monogamous model seek a number of different linkups to fulfill sexual, romantic, and emotional needs (Rust, 1996a). Women desire a person of each gender because they fulfill different emotional needs (Blumstein & Schwartz, 1977; Nichols, 1988a) whereas men desire both genders primarily for meeting sexual needs (Matteson, 1987).

Most Desired Linkup Patterns

Rust (1996b) found various arrangements of partners associated with bisexual men and women: (a) a partner who fulfills multiple needs but is not solely responsible for all of one's needs; (b) different people who each fulfill one particular need; (c) sexual friendships or people regarded both as friends and as sexual partners, but not romantic partners; and (d) purely sexual encounters with acquaintances and strangers. For bisexual men and women who divide their needs among multiple linkups, some of their lovers live in other cities, states, and countries and are seen only rarely.

Rust (1996b) identified several linkup patterns preferred by bisexual men and women involving multiple partners. The most common preference was *a primary linkup or marriage with one person and secondary sexual encounters or romantic linkups with other persons.* The primary linkup was an "open" one and the partners agreed that each can form secondary sexual, romantic, or emotional (or any combination of) links with other persons. Women preferred secondary romantic linkups (17.4%) somewhat more than sexual linkups (14.5%) while men preferred secondary sexual linkups (28.2%) to romantic linkups (19.2%). Many respondents had *two primary linkups,* one with a man and the other with a woman. These linkups may be separated from each other or integrated into a single triadic arrangement.

The next most common preferences for linkup arrangements that Rust (1996b) found for bisexual women was *serial monogamy* (11%) followed by *lifetime polyfidelity* (7.5%) (including three or more people who agreed that sexual, emotional, and romantic linkups can occur within the group). Bisexual men were more likely to prefer lifetime polyfidelity (14.1%) or multiple linkups in which none is primary (9%). Few bisexual men or women desired a *swinging* type of linkup (when two or more primary couples exchange partners).

Weinberg et al. (1994) also found that the dual primary and simultaneous primary and secondary linkups were the most popular ideal relational forms for bisexual men and women. The most frequent ideal arrangement involved two core linkups, one heterosexual and one same-gender. This ideal arrangement was constructed in different ways. From the most common to least common, the variations included (a) a linkup open and free of boundaries regarding other possible sexual partners; (b) a primary het-

erosexual linkup (often but not always a marriage), with secondary same-gender linkups on the outside; and (c) a primary same-gender linkup with one or more secondary heterosexual linkups .

Actual Linkup Patterns

In an American sample of romantically involved bisexual, gay, and lesbian couples, Rust (1996b) found that lesbians and gay men are more likely to be involved in monogamous linkups and not looking for additional sexual or romantic partners. Bisexual women and men were twice as likely (33%) as lesbians and gay men (16%) to indicate that they were involved with more than one person (ranging from dating to serious involvement) and that they were open to additional linkups or sexual encounters. Rust found that the most preferred linkup pattern *(a primary linkup or marriage with one person and secondary sexual encounters or romantic linkups with other people)* was the most common actual linkup arrangement.

About half of the Weinberg et al. (1994) sample who reported a significant primary link also reported a secondary one. A tenth of the sample also reported more than two significant secondary links. Many were also involved in nonsignificant casual sexual relationships. About half were involved in anonymous sex. The initial interviews in this study were, however, concluded in 1983 when the AIDS epidemic was emerging. In a follow-up study in 1988, Weinberg found the subject of sex was hardly ever discussed without being tied to the fear of AIDS.

The primary or most significant linkup for the bisexual men and women studied by Weinberg et al. (1994) was most likely a heterosexual one and the second significant relationship a same-gender one. Once a bisexual person connected to a primary partner, the other partner usually took a secondary position. This could result from the primary partner thinking that the secondary partner takes up too much time or the secondary partner feeling there is not enough time available. The secondary linkup (present for about half of those reporting a "significant linkup") was less emotionally intense, less involved, and more casual than the primary linkup. It was also less stable and enduring, even though about two-thirds of the respondents with a secondary linkup thought it would last about 10 years.

Ideal Arrangements Are Not Easy to Accomplish

Many bisexual men and women never achieve their ideal linkup arrangement. Only one-third of the Weinberg et al. (1994) sample reported that they actually attained their ideal arrangement at some point in their lives. When attained, it typically only lasted six months or less. Other researchers (e.g., Fox, 1995; Rust, 1992) found that less than 20% of bisexual men and women were in linkups with both genders at the time of their studies. In a study of bisexual women, Rust (1992) found that most of them (five out of six) were involved with one or more people of only one gender, usually in serious or marriagelike linkups. Only one of six were simultaneously involved with members of both genders. Weinberg et al. (1994) found that women were equally involved with men or women or more with men. Overall, however, the overwhelming majority of significant partners were of the other gender, with about a fifth being marriage partners.

Constraints in a primary partnership, such as restrictions on outside sexual activities, can interfere with achieving the ideal of non-monogamy or multiple partners (Fox, 1995). Weinberg et al. (1994) found that although a high majority of bisexual men and women were in a primary partnership that was "open," only about a quarter of them thought their partners were free from jeal-

ousy. "Ground rules" were used to try to reduce jealousy such as boundaries regarding what a partner could do.

◆ Linkup Scripts for Lesbians and Gay Men

Harry (1982a) identified three scripts or patterns that are used by gay men and, as Peplau and Cochran (1990) reported, also exist among lesbian couples: (a) mentor, (b) traditional, and (c) friendship. The first two patterns are not common among contemporary lesbian and gay couples. The *mentor, or apprentice, pattern* usually involves an age difference of five to ten years. The older partner takes on the role of mentor or leader and holds more power in decision making. In studies of gay men, this pattern describes only a small minority of couples (Harry, 1982a, 1984). Lesbians are even less likely to follow this pattern (Blumstein & Schwartz, 1983; Reilly & Lynch, 1990).

A common belief is still prevalent that partners in same-gender couples mimic heterosexual couples. In this *traditional pattern,* they do this by adopting the role of either "husband" or "wife," or one plays a masculine dominant role and the other a feminine submissive role (Peplau, 1982-1983; Weitz, 1989). Although now rare, this "butch-fem" pattern was once dominant in the United States, particularly from the 1920s to the early 1960s (Davis & Kennedy, 1986; Faderman, 1992; Nestle, 1992; D. Wolf, 1979). In the 1950s, it was notably prevalent among lesbians (Nestle, 1992). D. Wolf (1979) observed that butches were tough, masculine looking, and assumed the traditional male role of protecting partners. Fems were feminine looking and took care of their partners through traditional feminine behaviors such as cooking and cleaning.

The popularity of the traditional role dichotomy began to diminish in the late 1960s, especially among lesbians (Marecek, Finn, & Cardell, 1982-1983; Risman & Schwartz, 1988; Ross, 1983). A more androgynous "lesbian-feminist chic" is now favored (Walker, 1993, p. 875). Contemporary lesbians typically do not desire either to be or to look like a man (Unger & Crawford, 1992). Neither do gay men tend to portray effeminate mannerisms, a pattern that was common several decades ago. Today, they appear almost stereotypically masculine (Silverstein, 1981). Faderman (1992) described a renewed butch-fem interest observed in the 1980s and 1990s but in versions that seem mostly unrelated to earlier patterns. In some pairs, for example, "butch" is reduced to the one who makes the first sexual move.

This is not to say that no one in lesbian and gay communities plays traditional roles. Peplau (1981) reported that a few individuals may be comfortable with these roles. This preference is more likely to occur among gay men, older lesbians and gay men, and those at lower socioeconomic levels. Most contemporary lesbian and gay couples, however, dislike the dichotomous roles such as wife-husband, butch-fem, dominant-submissive, or active-passive (e.g., Kurdek, 1987; J. Lynch & Reilly, 1986; Murphy, 1994; Peplau, 1991, 1993; Risman & Schwartz, 1988; M. Schneider, 1986).

The third pattern identified by Harry (1982a) is based on peer relations where partners emphasize the norms of friendship. Most lesbians and gay men in the United States follow a *best friend pattern* (Blumstein & Schwartz, 1983; Caldwell & Peplau, 1984; Harry, 1983; Peplau, 1981, 1993). This pattern, in contrast to the other two patterns, assumes relative similarity in age, status, power, interests, resources, and skills (Peplau, 1993). It promotes equality, sharing, reciprocity, companionship, and role flexibility (e.g., Blumstein & Schwartz, 1983; Harry, 1982a, 1983; Kurdek & Schmitt, 1986b; Larson, 1982; J. Lynch & Reilly,

1986; Marecek et al., 1983-1983; Peplau, 1983). Innovative rules, expectations, and divisions of labor are developed (Peplau & Cochran, 1990).

Studies of how lesbians and gay men who live together allocate household labor found most of the qualities of the friendship pattern in the division of the work. Lesbians and gay men tend to equally distribute the number of household tasks so that one partner does not do it all (McWhirter & Mattison, 1984). Although one partner may do more of some household jobs and fewer of others, partners do not tend to specialize in either "feminine" or "masculine" activities (Peplau, 1993). The division of labor is worked out through a process of trial and error in finding out each other's interests and talents (Blumstein & Schwartz, 1983). Lesbian couples tend to follow this ethic of equality in household tasks more than gay men (Blumstein & Schwartz, 1983; Kurdek, 1993; Peplau, 1993; Peplau & Cochran, 1990).

Without the clear behavioral guidelines available in heterosexual marriage, the innovation required in working out nontraditional linkup patterns can cause stress and conflicts. Issues and roles that married couples may take for granted must be negotiated in lesbian and gay couples (D. Patterson & Schwartz, 1994). The heterosexual model developed largely because of male and female gender role expectations. Lesbian and gay couples have more to work out as each partner was socialized for the same kind of gender role (Decker, 1984).

Other notable forms of best friend linkups also exist. For example, as noted in Chapter 1, some women are in what are termed *Boston marriages*. This is a best friend linkup that does not involve sexuality (Rothblum & Brehony, 1993). Rose (1996) identified several other alternative love scripts among lesbians and gay men such as race relevant and gender blended. A *race-relevant* script includes the issue of racism and how it affects both own-race and cross-race linkups. A *gender-blended* script integrates romance and adventure into each partner's roles. Alternative love scripts are increasingly created in lesbian and gay communities.

◆ Linkup Themes

Two themes characterize most close linkups: (a) power and influence and (b) attachment versus autonomy. Two areas of research that focus on power and influence include the balance of power in close linkups and the kinds of strategies partners use to influence each other.

Power and Influence

The Balance of Power

All groups, whether gay, lesbian, heterosexual, or bisexual, value equal-power linkups (Peplau & Cochran, 1990). Following the principles of exchange theory (Burgess & Huston, 1979; Kelley & Thibaut, 1978), power tends to be equal for partners who are evenly interested, committed, or in love, and when their resources are equivalent. When there are inequities, Caldwell and Peplau (1984) found that (a) the most dependent, involved, and committed partner is at a power disadvantage whereas the less involved partner is at a power advantage and (b) the partner with the most resources (e.g., education and income) is at a power advantage and vice versa.

Other findings are not always consistent with the results just described (e.g., Reilly & Lynch, 1990). For example, findings that participants in gay male couples who are older, wealthier, or more physically attractive hold the power advantage (Harry, 1982a, 1984) are not fully applicable to lesbians. Blumstein and Schwartz (1983) showed that although money is "an extremely important

force" in determining who is dominant in gay couples, this is not usually the case in lesbian couples. Lynch and Reilly (1986) proposed that the different findings for lesbians may relate to factors such as gender socialization, not having much money, and rejection of the heterosexual model that aligns power with income. The most important view of money by lesbians is as a means to avoid dependency on their partners. Another factor, however, can influence the power balance in lesbian couples with children: the biological mother holds more power (Huston & Schwartz, 1995).

Effects of Power on Influence Strategies

A basic definition of power is the ability to attain what one wants through interpersonal influence (Huston & Schwartz, 1995). Falbo and Peplau (1980) found that individuals, regardless of gender or sexual orientation, who perceived themselves as relatively powerful in their linkups tended to use strategies of persuasion and bargaining. Those low in power tended to use strategies of withdrawal and emotion. In another study that also compared influence tactics in close linkups of lesbians, gay men, and heterosexual men and women, Howard, Blumstein, and Schwartz (1986) discovered different kinds of strategies than those found by Falbo and Peplau. Lower power partners in all three types of couples tended to use "weak" strategies such as supplication and manipulation whereas the more powerful partners tended to use "strong tactics" such as autocratic and bullying behaviors.

Dyadic Attachment and Personal Autonomy

A fundamental task for partners in a close linkup is to try to balance dyadic attachment and personal autonomy, which Peplau (1993) defined as value orientations. *Dyadic attachment* (or intimacy or closeness) reflects the value given to an emotionally close, sharing, exclusive, committed, and secure linkup with another person. *Personal autonomy* (or independence or separation) reflects the boundaries between the partners. Some partners desire minimal boundaries and do everything together. They exclude outside interests and activities. Other partners desire to maintain personal independence and separate interests and friends. Independence is guarded within the linkup through equal division of finances and equal participation in making decisions. Although independent, the two value orientations are not polar opposites. Some partners, for example, prefer a combination of both high togetherness with high independence. For other partners, the variables are distinctly independent so that one is emphasized and the other is not.

A common perception about lesbians is that they emphasize togetherness to the exclusion of autonomy. They are so prone to become excessively attached to their partners that they lose their personal boundaries (Kirkpatrick, 1989). Although not found in nonclinical samples (Kurdek, 1991c), some clinicians (e.g., Burch, 1982; Kaufman, Harrison, & Hyde, 1984; Pearlman, 1989; Roth, 1985) and researchers (e.g., Clunis & Green, 1993; Kirkpatrick, 1989; Krestan & Bepko, 1980; Toder, 1992) associate fusion, merger, or enmeshment with lesbian couples. Merger or excessive mutual dependency may be an obstacle for individuals in some lesbian couples to assert their own needs (Roth, 1989) or act with autonomy (Schreurs & Buunk, 1996). Merger as a general "problem," however, is important to question because it locates the problem within the individual (Kitzinger & Perkins, 1993). It can also be viewed in an alternate way as a healthy adaptation in a hostile heterosexual world (Browning, Reynolds, & Dworkin, 1991; Zacks, Green, & Marrow, 1988).

◆ Satisfaction With One's Primary Linkup

The idea that there can be happy lesbian and gay couples is a new one (J. Lee, 1991). Yet lesbians and gay men create linkups that are as satisfying and close as they are for heterosexual women and men (Peplau & Cochran, 1990). The overall picture shows no differences between lesbians and gay couples and heterosexual couples in quality (Kurdek, 1994b, 1995a), adjustment (Cardell, Finn, & Marecek, 1981; Kurdek, 1995b; Kurdek & Schmitt, 1986c), or satisfaction (e.g., Adler, Hendrick, & Hendrick, 1986; Duffy & Rusbult, 1986; Kurdek, 1994b, 1995b; Kurdek & Schmitt, 1986b, 1986d; Peplau & Cochran, 1990; Peplau, Cochran, & Mays, 1986).

Factors Associated With Satisfaction and Stability

Factors that promote satisfaction in lesbians and gay couples are also presumed to promote stability. A number of studies looked at variables that may correlate with satisfaction or dissatisfaction in lesbian and gay couples (e.g., Blumstein & Schwartz, 1983; Bryant & Demian, 1994; Eldridge & Gilbert, 1990; Kurdek, 1995b; Kurdek & Schmitt, 1986d; Peplau & Cochran, 1990; Peplau, Padesky, & Hamilton, 1982). Several of these factors are discussed below: areas of conflict, conflict resolution strategies, abuse and violence, the interpersonal factor, and equal involvement, commitment, and power. In addition, Kurdek's (1991a, 1992, 1995b) extensive work on various models related to couple satisfaction is briefly reviewed.

Areas of Conflict

Kurdek (1994a) identified six areas of conflict in a comparison study of 51 lesbian, 75 gay, and 108 heterosexual couples who lived together without children during a one-year period. They included *power* (e.g., overly critical), *social issues* (e.g., politics), *personal flaws* (e.g., smoking), *distrust* (e.g., lying), *intimacy* (e.g., sex), and *personal distance* (e.g., job commitments). The couples reported equal frequency of conflict in four of the areas: power, personal flaws, intimacy, and personal distance. When there was frequent arguing over power, satisfaction with one's linkup decreased during the one-year period. Areas of conflict identified in other studies included, among others, identity management, work, and interracial differences.

Identity management issues. It is not unusual for couples to experience conflicts about identity management issues (Roth, 1989; A. Smith, 1997). One or both partners may be in the process of negotiating a new identity as a lesbian or a gay man. If this is the central focus of the linkup, it can produce considerable stress. Partners can also be at different stages in disclosure (Decker, 1984; Roth & Murphy, 1986). Strain can result between one partner who is vigilant about hiding his or her identity and the other who is not. The conflict can intensify if one partner feels that the other partner's disclosure threatens his or her employment and friendships (Germain, 1991; Gonsiorek, 1993). Either partner may feel that the other devalues the linkup (Roth, 1989).

Work. Conflicts regarding work are central in several studies of lesbian and gay couples. Most of these couples experience the same dual-career issues faced by many heterosexual couples (e.g., Eldridge, 1987a; Hall & Gregory, 1991; Hetherington & Orzek, 1989; Shachar & Gilbert, 1983). The basic problem centers on the allocation of time and energy (D. Patterson & Schwartz, 1994; Shachar & Gilbert, 1983). Because there is no full-time homemaker and neither working partner is likely to take over household tasks, conflicts can occur over distribu-

tion of these tasks. These conflicts are more consequential for linkup stability than are conflicts over the demands of paid work. Because the conflicts are centered in the home, they require quick resolution for reduction of tension (Kurdek, 1993).

Gay couples can experience more conflict about work than lesbian couples. Berger (1990a) found that it is difficult for gay men to be successful at work, where aggression and competitiveness are required, and at home, where nurturing is required. It is also difficult to accept the partners' achievements. Each partner matches his career success with that of his partner. Gay men also experience power struggles associated with income. Although the income of two-male households is higher than incomes of the other types of couples (U.S. Bureau of the Census, 1990), money conflicts are frequent (Berger, 1990a; Blumstein & Schwartz, 1983). Typically, the underlying struggle is about dominance. Income equals power such as in decision making. Especially when the income difference is extensive and the power differences clear, the inequality can cause hard feelings. Even though one partner may earn less, he will not likely easily give up independence and influence in decisions (Blumstein & Schwartz, 1983; Huston & Schwartz, 1995). Gay couples can also experience problems due to differences in values and background factors such as socioeconomic level, religion, and racial or ethnic group (McWhirter & Mattison, 1994).

Interracial issues. A few studies looked at conflict in interracial lesbian and gay couples. In general, lesbians of color are in a greater number of linkups with women who are not members of their racial or ethnic group (Greene, 1995; Mays & Cochran, 1988). The resolution of issues in these linkups is often more complicated because of mixed loyalties. Both partners may be perceived as lacking loyalty to their own ethnic or racial group and may feel ashamed of their involvement with a person of a different group (Clunis & Green, 1993; Falco, 1991; Greene, 1994a, 1995). One way some lesbians respond to accusations of betrayal by other lesbians in their racial or ethnic groups is to not acknowledge them (Leslie & Mac Neill, 1995).

Lesbians in interracial linkups also challenge and confront racism in a more active, overt way than partners in same-race or ethnic linkups. A White partner, for example, may not be prepared to deal with racial incidents or comments or may not perceive a situation as racist. This partner may also not realize the different risks involved for the other person in disclosing to her family of origin (Leslie & Mac Neill, 1995). In addition, lesbians in interracial couples are likely to confront differences in culture and values regarding their roles in a linkup, food, religion, child-rearing behaviors, maintaining a household, and the role of other family members in their lives (Greene, 1994a, 1995; Leslie & Mac Neill, 1995). Dworkin (1997) pointed out that in an interracial couple (e.g., African American and Jewish), there can also be an insufficient understanding of historical issues in each person's culture. In addition, present conflicts between the two communities can affect the couple.

As indicated above, few Asian gay men are coupled with other Asian gay men. The Asian American gay partner in an interracial linkup with a White gay male, however, may feel that he has less power and that his partner can easily link up with someone else. Jealousy and frustration may result (Nakajima et al., 1996).

Conflict Resolution

All couples deal with conflict. Frequent conflict between partners is usually viewed as a cost in continuing the linkup (Duffy & Rusbult, 1986), so it is important to use pro-

ductive strategies to resolve conflict. Compared with happy couples, unhappy couples appear to differ in their approach to resolving conflicts (Kurdek, 1991a). Only a few studies so far, however, have looked at conflict resolution in lesbian and gay couples (Blumstein & Schwartz, 1983; Falbo & Peplau, 1980; Kurdek, 1991a, 1994a; Metz, Rosser, & Strapko, 1994). Kurdek (1991a) found that satisfied gay and lesbian partners were more likely to use positive problem-solving methods such as focusing on the specific problem at hand. They were less likely to use negative approaches such as personal attacks, defensiveness, or withdrawal from the interaction. Metz et al. (1994) compared conflict resolution patterns in lesbian, gay, and heterosexual couples. Lesbian couples were different from gay or heterosexual couples in some important ways such as feeling greater optimism about conflict resolution, making a greater effort to resolve conflict, and engaging in assertion more than physical aggression. These and other differences indicate a more positive pattern of conflict management among lesbians.

Unless they are resolved in a positive way, conflicts can get out of hand and can sometimes result in partner abuse and violence. Other factors that contribute to violence and other abusive behaviors in both same-gender and other-gender couples include jealousy, dependency, dominance, and misuse of alcohol and drugs (Peplau, Veniegas, & Campbell, 1996; Renzetti, 1992; Schilit, Lie, & Montagne, 1990). Abusive behaviors can include verbal abuse (e.g., making fun of a partner in front of others), destructive actions (e.g., destroying a partner's property), sexual coercion, and physical violence (Renzetti, 1992).

Lesbians and gay men do not often report partner violence or seek outside help (Renzetti, 1992). Lesbians may presume that women are not physically abusive and that it is only men who perpetuate violence against women. When it happens to them, therefore, they may not label it as battering or abuse (Kanuha, 1990; Renzetti, 1992). Even if they recognize it for what it is, they may remain in abusive linkups because of dependence on the partner or because of the high value they place on making their linkups work (D. Patterson & Schwartz, 1994). In addition, they may be socially isolated and have no one to turn to (Renzetti, 1992).

The literature on violence in lesbian linkups is growing (e.g., Coleman, 1994; Hammond, 1988; Kanuha, 1990; Lie & Gentlewarrier, 1991; Lie, Schilit, Bush, Montagne, & Reyes, 1991; Lockhart, White, Causby, & Isaac, 1994; Lundy, 1993; Morrow & Hawxhurst, 1989; Renzetti, 1992; Schilit et al., 1990). Much less research is focused on abuse and violence in gay male couples. Aggression and violence between men is often believed to be acceptable or at least sometimes unavoidable. This may provide a justification for men to abuse a partner or accept it from a partner (Island & Letellier, 1991). Reporting it may be seen as a sign of weakness (Waterman, Dawson, & Bologna, 1989). Which partner is the batterer and which one the victim appears to relate to power imbalances between the partners. Battering itself sometimes shifts the power in favor of the batterer. For gay men, AIDS can complicate the picture of abuse. Abuse from a batterer with AIDS may be be excused because of the disease. On the other side, if a partner with AIDS is abused, his physical condition and dependency on the abusing partner for support may be a justification for not leaving (D. Patterson & Schwartz, 1994).

The Interpersonal Factor

Couples in which both partners are linkup centered are the happiest and most committed (Blumstein & Schwartz, 1983). More than any other type of couple, lesbian couples are linkup centered, caring, nurturant,

and expressive of feelings (Kurdek, 1989). Happy lesbian couples also experience a high degree of closeness (Schreurs & Buunk, 1996). Eldridge and Gilbert (1990) found that emotional intimacy was the strongest contributor to linkup satisfaction for lesbians. In their sample of African American lesbians and gay men, Peplau et al. (1997) found that subjective evaluations of being in love and feeling emotionally close were significant correlates with satisfaction. Both African American gay men and lesbians reported high levels of closeness although the level was somewhat higher for lesbians.

As noted earlier, gay men are likely to experience too much individuation and not enough intimacy (D. Patterson & Schwartz, 1994). Kurdek (1991a) concluded, however, that on the whole lesbians and gay couples are more similar than different from each other in their desire for intimacy (e.g., Blumstein & Schwartz, 1983; Deenen, Gijs, & van Naerssen, 1994; Duffy & Rusbult, 1986; Peplau & Cochran, 1990). Some gay couples may even be in the situation of experiencing too much processing of feelings (Mattison & McWhirter, 1990).

Equal Involvement, Commitment, and Shared Power

When both partners are equally involved in their linkup and are committed (Peplau & Cochran, 1990; Peplau et al., 1982), satisfaction tends to be high. Equal involvement also refers to the extent to which partners share power in the linkup (Kurdek, 1995b). High satisfaction is related to perceptions by lesbians and gay men that they share power and decision making equally with their partners (Harry, 1984; Kurdek & Schmitt, 1986d; Peplau et al., 1982). When Peplau and Cochran questioned lesbians and gay men about their ideal for the balance of power in their current linkup, 97% of lesbians and 92% of gay men said it should be exactly equal. Neither group, however, thought that their partnership was "exactly equal" (59% of lesbians, 38% of gay men).

Individual Differences, Investment, Problem Solving, and Discrepancy Models of Linkup Functioning

Kurdek's (1991a, 1992, 1995b) work advanced the use of theoretical models to identify social-psychological processes that regulate how linkups function. He identified four interrelated propositions or models of linkup functioning derived from theoretical work on dating and married heterosexual couples. The propositions included (a) appraisals of linkup satisfaction through individual difference variables (such as beliefs about the linkup and traits associated with general interpersonal competence) that filter linkup information (*individual differences model*) (Bradbury & Fincham, 1988); (b) interdependence of appraisals of rewards and costs of being in the linkup and the match between the linkup and an internal standard of a "good" linkup (*investment or interdependence model*) (Rusbult, 1983); (c) problem-solving styles used to resolve conflict (*problem-solving model*) (J. M. Gottman & Krokoff, 1989); and (d) partner discrepancy or incompatible vantage points regarding linkup needs, importance placed on linkup values, and differences in interpersonal competence (*discrepancy model*) (Cowan & Cowan, 1990). Kurdek found that all four of the tested propositions are reasonably good in explaining variability in linkup satisfaction and linkup stability in lesbian and gay couples. Overall, the partners did not differ in terms of both the strength of association between satisfaction and variables in each model of linkup functioning and the mean level of variables in the models. In specific areas, however, such as the value of the linkup or rewards attained, lesbians tended to report higher satisfaction than gay men

(Blumstein & Schwartz, 1983; Kurdek, 1988c, 1991a).

Who Has the Edge on Satisfaction Factors?

According to Kurdek (1988c), lesbian couples, compared with gay couples, report stronger liking for their partner; greater satisfaction, trust, and shared decision making; stronger intrinsic and instrumental desire for involvement in their linkup; and less external motivations for involvement in their linkup. Kurdek suggested that these findings might partly be accounted for by lesbians' high ratings on interpersonal factors such as caring and sensitivity to the needs and feelings of their partners. Bryant and Demian (1994) reported that more lesbians (47%) than gay men (36%) rated the quality of their linkup at the highest level.

Satisfaction Through Time

Across all couples, satisfaction is likely to change through time, up or down (Kurdek, 1995b). Same-gender couples are no more or less troubled than mixed-gender couples. Longitudinal studies on lesbians and gay couples are extremely rare but, fortunately, Kurdek's (1989, 1992, 1995b) work assessed satisfaction in these couples over time.

Ecological Variables

In a one-year study, Kurdek (1989) found that satisfaction and love for one's partner decreased for gay couples but not for lesbian couples. The findings of the study were grouped into contexts representing variables in an ecological model: personal, psychological, interpersonal, and social/cultural. At the one-year follow-up, positive linkup quality was related to the presence of variables from each of the contexts at the outset of the year. Considered together, they predicted well over half of the difference in linkup quality at the end of a year. The predictive variables included (a) *personal* (low education); (b) *psychological* (strong intrinsic and instrumental motivations for being in the linkup, low values regarding autonomy, and few beliefs regarding both the destructiveness of disagreements and the expectation of mind-reading and expressiveness); (c) *interpersonal* (frequent shared decision making and strong trust); and (d) *social/cultural* (high satisfaction with social support).

Cost-Reward Variables

Kurdek (1992, 1995a) also found that linkup satisfaction increased through time as perceived costs decreased and perceived rewards and emotional investment increased. In other words, satisfaction was higher if there were relatively more personal rewards and fewer personal costs. More specifically, contentment with one's partner grew in conjunction with (a) increases in satisfaction with the partner as a source of support and comfort and the partner's willingness to express warmth and nurturance and (b) smaller differences with the partner regarding satisfaction with social support and expressiveness.

Stage Models

Findings that gay and lesbian couples experience changes in satisfaction over time suggest that stages in linkups occur. A few stage models were developed for gay couples (e.g., Harry & Lovely, 1979; McWhirter & Mattison, 1984) and lesbian couples (e.g., Clunis & Green, 1993). These theorists acknowledged that not all couples fit the stages in their models such as blending, nesting, maintaining, building, releasing, and renewing for men (McWhirter & Mattison, 1984) or prerelationship, romance, conflict, accep-

tance, commitment, and collaboration for women (Clunis & Green, 1993). For example, some couples skip stages or start out in some stage other than the first one. HIV/AIDS can also accelerate stage progression. In a study of male couples in which a partner was diagnosed as HIV-positive, McWhirter and Mattison (1990) found that an early response to the diagnosis is for the couple members to draw closer together. Whatever the length of the linkup, couples facing AIDS act like those in the renewing stage of couple development. This is a stage usually reached by couples who are together for many years and may be facing death from natural causes.

◆ Commitment and Duration

Commitment means to stay the course. What factors contribute to lesbians and gay men staying the course in their linkups? What is the duration of their linkups and of the linkups of bisexual persons?

Threats to Commitment

Two main theoretical approaches help define what maintains or threatens commitment in couples: exchange theory and interdependence theory. Each theory is briefly described here.

Exchange Theory: Attractions and Barriers

Exchange theory analysis proposes that in any type of linkup, the level of commitment relates to two factors: (a) *positive attractions* associated with the partner and the linkup and (b) *barriers* (psychological and/or material) that make termination costly. Positive attractions, such as love or satisfaction, motivate partners to stay in a linkup. These attractions, however, may decline in strength over time, leading to a breakup. On the other hand, many factors can act as barriers to termination such as investments in the linkup or financial costs of termination. Even non-positive factors such as the lack of alternatives can act as barriers (Levinger, 1979).

In general, lesbian and gay couples and married heterosexual couples do not differ in *positive attractions*. They report similar levels of satisfaction and love for their partners. Heterosexual men and women, however, perceive more *barriers* than do lesbians or gay men because of multiple ties between them. Heterosexual marriage creates barriers such as joint investments, the cost of divorce, possible negative effects on children, and lower earning power of wives making it difficult to leave an unhappy marriage (Kurdek & Schmitt, 1986d). In contrast, lesbian and gay couples start out and end up in an unequal position regarding barriers. They do not experience socially sanctioned public events such as an engagement or a wedding to mark their union. Although they use other symbols and behaviors for confirmation (e.g., moving in, commitment ceremonies, wearing rings), these do not provide barriers as strong as the ones available for heterosexual couples (Berger, 1990a; J. Meyer, 1990; Murphy, 1994). Because there are no legal ties and rarely any legal formalities to negotiate (Decker, 1984; Harry, 1984; Peplau, 1993), lesbians and gay men can end their linkups just by packing their suitcases (Fajer, 1992).

Perceived barriers may motivate married couples to work to improve an unhappy linkup (Huston & Schwartz, 1995; Kurdek & Schmitt, 1986d). Metz et al. (1994) suggested, however, that because same-gender couples are without equivalent barriers or the same degree of social supports, they may put extra effort into trying to make their linkups work. Also, these couples share a common "coming out" experience that can bond them together. On the other hand, lesbians and gay

men may leave unsatisfying linkups if they perceive alternatives that are more attractive than their current linkup (Kurdek, 1991c). This is likely to occur more for gay men as they tend to perceive the availability of more alternative partners (Kurdek & Schmitt, 1986d). The HIV/AIDS crisis, however, influenced both the desire to make their linkup work and a decrease in attention to alternatives.

Interdependence Theory:
Pulls and Pushes

According to interdependence theory (Kelley, 1983), developmental changes in commitment are linked to changes in the conditions that pull one toward or push one away from a linkup (Kelley, 1983). Kurdek (1995a) proposed that these pulls and pushes are tied to personal needs in the areas of dyadic attachment, personal autonomy, and equality. Consistent with predictions associated with interdependence theory (Kelley, 1983; Rusbult, 1983), a decrease in commitment is explained by changes in ideal versus current levels of equality (equality falls below the ideal level) and changes in the balance between current levels of attachment and current levels of autonomy (the importance of autonomy over attachment increases). This is the same in lesbian or gay couples.

Duration: How Long Do Same-Gender and Bisexual Couples Last?

It is not easy to assess how long lesbian and gay linkups last without marriage and divorce records (Peplau, 1993). The best comparisons of breakup rates among different groups are based on the findings of Blumstein and Schwartz's (1983) landmark study that included 3,574 married couples, 642 cohabiting couples, 957 gay couples, and 772 lesbian couples. The study provided rare longitudinal data on the longevity of these groups, which were followed for 18 months. In the beginning of the survey period, all of the groups were about equal in predicting expectations of staying together. At the end of this period, most couples were still together. Fewer than one in five couples broke up. The proportions of breakups by group were lesbian (22%), gay (16%), cohabiting (17%), and married (4%).

The higher rate of breakup for lesbians in the Blumstein and Schwartz (1983) study was also found in several other studies. The Teichner poll ("Results of Poll," 1989), for example, reported a median length of 2.5 years for gay couples and 1.8 years for lesbian couples. Weinberg et al. (1994) also found that lesbian linkups were shorter in duration than other linkups (heterosexual, bisexual, and gay). The instability of lesbian couples is attributed in part to the participants being too quick to commit and move in together. Commitment and quick decisions are based on initial attraction and emotional connection. Lesbians may not be comfortable with initiating and managing a long dating period, and they tend not to like casual sex (Fowlkes, 1994). Berger (1990a) cautioned that couples who move in together too soon may find they are incompatible later.

Huston and Schwartz (1995) suggested that endurance or "lifetime" marriage, which indicates "success" in heterosexual couples, may not apply to lesbian and gay couples. These couples may use other criteria for success such as equity and happiness. How many lesbian and gay couples these conceptions describe, however, is not known. Many of these couples appear to desire longevity given that they are together for long periods of time. Several studies found lesbian and gay couples together 10 years or longer (e.g., R. Berger, 1996; Bryant & Demian, 1994; B. Johnson, 1990; McWhirter & Mattison,

1984). In anecdotal accounts, older lesbian and gay men report that linkups of 20 years' duration or longer are not unusual (e.g., Adelman, 1986; Clunis & Green, 1993; McWhirter & Mattison; 1984; Silverstein, 1981). Kehoe (1989) found linkups in a study of older lesbians that were 30 years or longer in duration. When couples stay together for a long period, this in itself may play a role in the continued longevity of their linkups. For couples already together for more than 10 years in the Blumstein and Schwartz (1983) study, for example, breakups were rare.

Many bisexual men and women studied by Weinberg et al. (1994) indicated that bisexual activity (e.g., nonmonogamy) had a negative effect on the stability of their linkups over time. Often a partner is unable to handle the nonmonogamy. About a third of the Weinberg et al. sample reported that their bisexual behaviors contributed directly to the breakup of their marriages. Often, heterosexual partners struggle more with the issue of monogamy than with the issue of same-gender sex.

About a third of the bisexual women and about a quarter of the bisexual men in Weinberg's et al. (1994) study reported that the longest linkup in their lives lasted four years or less (compared with a quarter of heterosexual women and men and about half of lesbians and gay men). About a third of the bisexual women and 40% of the bisexual men, however, reported a linkup that lasted for 10 or more years (compared with nearly half of heterosexual women and men, 20% of gay men, and 12% of lesbians). Overall, the longevity rates for bisexual linkups were in the middle range, between the longest linkups (heterosexual women) and the shortest linkups (lesbians). Weinberg concluded, therefore, that bisexual men and women experience moderately long-term involvements, a finding that contradicts popular images of only short-term involvements.

◆ Breakups: Contributions of Individual, Interpersonal, and External Factors

No couple, whether lesbian, gay, bisexual, or heterosexual, is safe from the possibility of an eventual breakup. Certain individual, interpersonal, and external factors may play a role.

Individual Factors

Most of the lesbians and gay men in Weinberg's et al. (1994) study assessed individual factors such as *personality, self-esteem,* and *maturity* as important contributors to breakups. Kurdek (1991a, 1992) also identified individual characteristics of partners that contributed to breakups: *younger age, lower satisfaction with the linkup, negative affectivity* (e.g., depression, anxiety), *less investment in the linkup, lack of love, nonresponsiveness* (e.g., no communication or support), *emotional distance,* and *higher value placed on personal autonomy.* In a study of lesbians, Peplau et al. (1982) found that one-half of the sample rated their *desire to be independent* as the major factor that contributed to the breakup of a past linkup and one-third indicated that their partner's desire to be independent was the major factor.

Individual factors identified in other studies included the *expectation of perfection in sexual relations* (Blumstein & Schwartz, 1983), *dissatisfaction with sex* (Blumstein & Schwartz, 1983; Kurdek, 1991b), *sexual nonexclusivity* (Bell & Weinberg, 1978), *work ambitions,* and *time spent at work* (Blumstein & Schwartz, 1983). Personal problems of a partner were also contributors such as *drug or alcohol addiction, mental cruelty,* and *frequent absences* (Kurdek, 1991c). In a recent report, Kurdek (1997) also found that due to behaviors

such as *unrealistic standards* and *destructive problem-solving methods,* a neurotic partner wears down the other partner's positive evaluation of the linkup. Eventually, this partner's personal dedication to the linkup declines.

Interpersonal Factors

Some lesbians and gay men in Weinberg's et al. (1994) study referred to the importance of missing interpersonal factors as contributors to their breakups such as *"shared values, common interests, communication, emotional compatibility, mutual determination, trust,* the *desire to share, the amount of love, basic respect, finding time for each other, and the willingness to make adjustments"* (p. 183). In Peplau's et al. (1982) study of lesbians, the importance of differences was highlighted in areas such as *interests* (36%), *attitudes about sex* (24%), *background* (17%), and *political views* (7%). Interpersonal factors found in other studies as contributors to breakups include *not spending time together* (Blumstein & Schwartz, 1983); *sexual incompatibility* (Kurdek, 1991c); *arguments about sex* (Blumstein & Schwartz, 1983; Kurdek, 1991b); *arguments about money; financial management problems,* and *not pooling incomes* (Blumstein & Schwartz, 1983).

External Factors

Lesbian and gay couples, as all couples, are embedded in a wider social context beyond the traditional focus on individual and interpersonal processes (Kitzinger & Coyle, 1995). The social environment affects the formation and maintenance of their linkups. Along with external factors that may negatively affect any couple such as the intrusion of work responsibilities, lesbians and gay couples also face extraordinary and unique challenges that may play a part in breakups. These challenges are external to couples but can create internal difficulties that interfere with, if not destroy, satisfaction.

Climate of Cultural Heterosexism

Peplau et al. (1982) found that only 15% of a lesbian sample cited "societal attitudes toward lesbian linkups" as a reason for a breakup. The other couples, however, may not acknowledge the power of cultural heterosexism in their lives. Lesbians and gay men link up with partners in a climate of anti-"homosexuality" (Murphy, 1994) or cultural heterosexism (Herek, 1995). They must cope with the societal message that their linkups are fundamentally wrong. Society "condemns their sexuality, penalizes their partnership and derides their love for each other" (Kitzinger & Coyle, 1995, p. 67). Couples also can be the target of harassment, ranging from minor but humiliating insults such as name-calling to threats of death (Huston & Schwartz, 1995; Murphy, 1994).

Fewer Binding Social Arrangements

In addition to the legal oppression regarding private sexual interactions, lesbian and gay couples are denied other recognitions and rights that are provided heterosexual couples (Bryant & Demian, 1994; Fajer, 1992; Huston & Schwartz, 1995). Except in a few locales in which domestic partnerships can be registered, they have no legal status (D'Augelli & Garnets, 1995). Without legal status, institutional policies that are available for heterosexual couples are closed to lesbian and gay couples such as insurance regulations, inheritance laws, tax regulations, and hospital visitation rules (D'Augelli & Garnets, 1995; Greene, 1997b).

In December 1996, a Hawaii court ruled that denying same-gender couples a marriage license is unconstitutional under the state's Equal Rights Amendment. A final ruling is expected in about two years from the date of the December ruling, following completion of the appeals process (Ward, 1997). Not a surprise, opposition to the ruling is fierce, and various states have already developed legislation to block its legality in the event the final court ruling is favorable to same-gender marriage. Among lesbians and gay men themselves, while some desire legally sanctioned marriage (Trosino, 1993; Zicklin, 1995), others want to pursue an alternate course of legal changes that ensure all committed couples the same rights and privileges as those who legalize their commitment (e.g., Bryant & Demian, 1994; Curry & Clifford, 1986; Zicklin, 1995). Various writings exist on the pros and cons of legal marriage (e.g., Bradley, 1994; Huston & Schwartz, 1995; Trosino, 1993; Tully, 1994).

Lack of Support From Families of Origin and Heterosexual Friends

Intimate linkups are human creations and thereby tenuous. Support from society, friends, and family fortifies them (P. Berger & Kellner, 1975). Support for lesbian and gay couples, however, does not come from all the sources typically available to heterosexual couples. Married heterosexual couples, for example, usually can count on congratulations, blessings, presents, and additional tangible and intangible support from the time they declare themselves to be a serious couple. Lesbians and gay men rarely receive anything close to this degree of support when they are in couples (Bryant & Demian, 1994).

Many families of lesbians and gay men may not know when their relative's primary linkup began, how long the involvement existed, or anything else about it. They may never meet the primary partner (Kurdek & Schmitt, 1987). Even when lesbian and gay couples announce their partnership to their families, the reaction from parents, siblings, and other relatives is more often one of overt hostility rather than support (Bryant & Demian, 1990). If they plan a ceremonial "marriage" and invite their families, few attend (Serovich et al., 1993). Rather than celebrate the linkup, families may deny or trivialize it. In addition to its beginning, they often do not acknowledge any other important marker events such as house purchases, anniversaries, or retirement (Kurdek & Schmitt, 1987).

According to A. Smith (1997), the "taking in" of partners as new members of the family is more critical for some African American lesbians and gay men than "coming out" or disclosure to their families. In a study of African American lesbian couples, however, Greene and Boyd-Franklin (1996) found that, similar to same-gender couples in most racial and ethnic communities, they are largely unsupported in their families of origin. There is often a collusion of silence, ambivalence, and denial related to these couples.

If one's lesbian or gay partnership is in trouble, there is not likely to be much encouragement from family or heterosexual friends to work out the problems. They do not give the same attention as they would to a troubled heterosexual couple (Greene, 1997b). For example, African American families were found not to provide support or empathy when distress in their lesbian child's primary linkup occurred (Greene & Boyd-Franklin, 1996). When a couple ends their linkup, heterosexual friends and family members often do not realize the emotional impact of the loss. Instead of attention to the loss, families may pressure their member to develop a heterosexual linkup, marry, and bear children (Zastrow & Kirst-Ashman, 1990).

The Paradox of Lesbian and Gay Communities

When help is needed with their linkups, lesbian and gay couples most likely turn to lesbian and gay friends (Bryant & Demian, 1994). Kurdek (1988b) found that the most frequent sources of social support for couples is friends first, then partners, family, and coworkers. Friends are the bulk of the support (43%). Friendships and support provided by the lesbian and gay community, then, are highly valuable resources for couples. The community can also, however, be a threat to couples because of the opportunities to meet other lesbians and gay men (Huston & Schwartz, 1995). Weinberg et al. (1994) reported that couples in their San Francisco sample did not view the lesbian and gay community as promoting long-term linkups.

Consequences for Couples From External Obstacles

The external obstacles confronted by lesbian and gay couples can create damaging consequences within their linkups. They include hiding and passing and self-fulfilling prophecies.

Hiding and Passing

Because of hostile responses, many lesbian and gay couples attempt to be invisible. They make no public disclosures. They also engage in various subterfuges such as introducing partners as "friends," sleeping in different rooms when parents visit, going on "heterosexual dates," not participating in conversations about personal life, changing pronouns when talking about whom one did things with over the weekend, and inventing (if not even acquiring) a fiancé or spouse (Kitzinger & Coyle, 1995; M. Levine & Leonard, 1984; Murphy, 1994; B. Schneider, 1984). Although lack of disclosure may not affect couple satisfaction directly (e.g., Eldridge & Gilbert, 1990), trying to hide one's couple status is an added pressure.

The couple may tighten its boundaries against a threatening world (Krestan & Bepko, 1980). Dependency on one another is likely to increase (D. Patterson & Schwartz, 1994) and any move toward individuation on the part of one of the partners can be threatening to the other partner (Roth, 1989; Roth & Murphy, 1986). Because they are isolated from other lesbians and gay men, few models are observed for alternate couple behaviors and maintenance. Partners can also experience a sense of unreality about their couple status when no one else knows about them (D. Patterson & Schwartz, 1994).

Negative self-fulfilling prophecies. Same-gender couples may play out negative self-fulfilling prophecies (Bryant & Demian, 1994; Goffman, 1963). Stereotypes persist that lesbian and gay men experience low feelings of love and unsatisfactory linkups. Couples presented in the media are often negative representations with painful endings or deaths from AIDS (Murphy, 1994). These cultural beliefs and images saturate the lives of lesbians and gay men possibly to the point of their believing that they cannot form enduring happy linkups or that their linkups do not compare favorably with heterosexual linkups (Bryant & Demian, 1994). Acceptance and internalization of society's negative attitudes can also result in guilt, fear, and even self-hatred or hatred of the partner (Murphy, 1994).

◆ Dissolutions and the Emotional Effects

Whether or not the various individual, interpersonal, and external factors identified above will actually result in breakups is not known. If, however, some of these challenges are a source of conflict for a given couple, this may at the least lower satisfaction if the conflict is not resolved. At this point, if not earlier, and perhaps helping to prevent a breakup, counseling is often sought. Lesbians (45%) are more likely to seek this assistance than gay men (27%) (Bryant & Demian, 1994).

The challenges will most likely be more troublesome in the second and third years of the linkup. During the first year together when couples are much in love, issues that can be problems later may be overlooked. Couples in Kurdek and Schmitt's (1986a) study on stage development experienced higher satisfaction in the first and after the third year. In the second and third years, or the "nesting stage," couples were not as much in love, differences were more in the foreground, and adjustments and compromises were required. If the partners were comfortable with resolutions, the following years could be ones of regained satisfaction. Many couples, however, do not make it this far. Lesbian and gay linkups that begin with high hopes for a lifetime of love and closeness often dissolve. Murphy (1994) suggested that because these couples do not separate legally or sign divorce papers, sometimes the end of therapy officially marks the end of their linkups.

In the event of possessions to be divided or legal issues, mediation can be useful (Bryant, 1992; Engelhardt & Triantafillou, 1987). Other frequent practical problems include managing contact with the former partner and financial stress (Kurdek, 1991c; Kurdek & Blisk, 1983). Otherwise, the major problems are the emotional ones that usually accompany the breakups of any close couple, whether gay, lesbian, bisexual, or heterosexual (Bloom & Hodges, 1981; Kurdek, 1991c; Marcus, 1988; McWhirter & Mattison, 1984; D. Wolf, 1979).

Blumstein and Schwartz (1983) observed that individuals in their sample of gay, lesbian, and heterosexual couples talked about their breakups with *sadness, regrets, and/or anger.* In a study that compared lesbian and heterosexual women when their close linkups ended, *depression* was a common experience for both groups. For lesbians, this was especially likely if the partner was the only confidant and the person was not connected to a lesbian network (Rothblum, 1990). In addition, the loss of a partnership may threaten lesbians' sense of who they are as many came out in the context of a linkup with another woman (Browning et al., 1991). Kurdek (1991c) found that certain factors were related to more severe emotional reactions for both lesbians and gay men: a linkup of long duration, pooled finances, strong emphasis on attachment, and greater love for the partner.

As noted earlier, when lesbian and gay men experience sadness and loneliness from a breakup, they may not receive support and sympathy from their families of origin or from heterosexual friends. If these persons never supported the linkup, they may be happy about the breakup, which adds to the stress of the situation (Becker, 1988). If closeted, lesbians and gay men may feel pressure to disclose their sexual orientation to receive support from others in their community (Browning et al., 1991). Many times, however, they suffer and grieve alone (Becker, 1988).

Some partners experience the relief of an end to conflict, personal growth, and desired independence at the time of the dissolution of their linkups instead of the severe negative emotions experienced by others (Kurdek, 1991c). Kurdek found that certain factors predict the emotional impact of separation. Lesbians and gay men who adjust well generally had *many years of education, knew and lived with the partner for only a short time,* reported *low love for the partner, did not join finances* with the partner, and placed a *low value on attachment.* They also reported *frequent psychological distress* during the course of the linkup. Lazarus and Folkman (1984) found that *expecting and being prepared for a separation* is also positively related to postseparation adjustment. When one feels a *sense of self-efficacy and in control,* it is possible to contain the stress of separation. Over time, other lesbian, gay, and heterosexual persons who experienced severe emotional reactions to dissolution are also likely to experience relief from the conflict as well as personal growth, in addition to loneliness (Kurdek, 1991c; Kurdek & Blisk, 1983).

◆ Summary

Human services professionals will often encounter lesbians and gay men in couples or after a breakup. Knowledge about these couples, and bisexual couples, is therefore essential especially because there are many misconceptions and stereotypes about them. First, it should not be assumed that same-gender couples are completely different from heterosexual couples. Findings on linkup development, issues, conflicts, satisfaction, and dissolution show similar patterns for all couples. Nevertheless, there are unique differences in the types of problems faced by same-gender and bisexual couples such as coming out, lack of support from families, and the effects of discrimination and stigmatization. It should also be remembered that just like in the heterosexual population, there is no typical lesbian, gay, or bisexual couple. Each couple is unique and may be affected by numerous personal, social, and cultural factors.

7

MOTHERS, FATHERS, AND CHILDREN

◆ IN THIS CHAPTER, gay and lesbian families with children are examined including their diverse structures, their similarities to and differences from heterosexual families, their challenges, and their strengths. Gay and lesbian parents do not represent a new phenomenon. What is new is that, increasingly, these parents are openly identifying their sexual orientation (Casper, Schultz, & Wickens, 1992).

◆ The Varieties of Lesbian and Gay Families With Children

Rohrbaugh (1992) described several varieties of lesbian families with children, including blended families, single-parent families, shared-parenting families, and extended families. *Blended lesbian* families are stepfamilies that include a lesbian partnership and children from the previous linkups (often heterosexual marriages) of both women. The blended family may be the most common structure for lesbian families with children. *Single-parent* lesbian families typically consist of a lesbian adult raising a child from a previous linkup. *Shared-parenting* lesbian families consist of a lesbian partnership and at least one child being raised by both women. *Extended families* can consist of any of the above structures with the added linkups of the families of origin. Similar structures exist for gay male-headed families.

◆ How and Why Lesbians and Gay Men Become Parents

Lesbians and gay men may become parents in the context of either a heterosexual or a same-gender linkup. Those who bear children in the former context were married for a variety of reasons, as noted in Chapter 5. An unknown percentage of these marriages, many with children, end in divorce. Gay men and lesbians also become parents in the context of a same-gender linkup. Lesbians can give birth to children following donor insemination by a friend, relative, acquaintance, or an unknown donor through a sperm bank. A lesbian can also conceive a child through planned sexual intercourse with a consenting man who may or may not play a part in the child's upbringing. Finally, lesbians can become parents through adoption or foster care (Pies, 1990). Like lesbians, gay men can adopt or provide foster care to children. They can also become fathers to children through donor insemination or sexual intercourse with a woman with whom they agree to share a parenting role (C. Patterson, 1992).

The reasons that lesbians and gay men have when they choose to become parents are not necessarily different from anyone else's reasons. They were usually socialized to be-

lieve that raising children is an important thing to do. They may feel compelled to carry on the family name or leave their legacy to the next generation (Bigner & Bozett, 1990). Both lesbians and gay men may also truly enjoy children and feel they would be good parents (Bigner & Bozett, 1990). Some may wish to share the joys and struggles of parenthood to enrich their love relationship (Pies, 1990). Lesbians may also wish to experience pregnancy and childbirth (Harvey, Carr, & Bernheine, 1989).

◆ Interactions With Other Systems

While their motivations for parenthood may not be unique, actual and potential discrimination against lesbian and gay parents interacting with various social systems can place unique burdens on them. These systems include health care, especially for lesbians experiencing pregnancy and childbirth; the courts, especially in child custody cases; the child welfare system, especially foster care and adoption; and the schools attended by their children.

Health Care System

Harvey et al. (1989) found that 17% of the lesbians in their sample were less than comfortable with their obstetrical providers, and that 11% felt their providers were less than supportive. In general, 14% were less than satisfied with their providers. Ratings were somewhat lower for physicians than midwives. The relatively high level of comfort and satisfaction experienced by these women was perhaps partially due to their openness about their sexual orientation because 90% of them were out to their providers. When lesbians keep their sexual orientation secret, providers may make a variety of erroneous assumptions about them, which can create an atmosphere of mistrust and nonsupport. Also problematic are heterosexist obstetrical literature and childbirth classes that do not welcome single women or lesbian couples.

The Courts

While many lesbian and gay adults may have children, they are often in danger of having them removed. Most frequently, a lesbian mother's child custody is contested by a former husband upon learning of her sexual orientation, especially if a same-gender partner moves in with her. The custody of a mother's children is always precarious because many American states allow for contesting child custody at any time. In many cases in which mothers do not have custody of their children, their former husbands also seek to terminate the mothers' visitation rights (C. Meyer, 1992). Custody or visitation can also be challenged by grandparents or other relatives. The courts often exhibit bias against lesbian or gay parents, awarding child custody to the challengers. These parents may be at greatest risk outside of the major cities.

Court decisions regarding child custody are typically based upon the "best interests of the child" standard, which is usually open to a judge's interpretation. This standard requires that the judge consider the child's emotional and physical needs, the stability of the home, and the fitness for parenthood of those persons seeking custody. In weighing the fitness for parenthood, judges using the *per se approach* often presume that being lesbian or gay automatically makes one unfit, or that children with a gay or lesbian parent are harmed. In other cases, judges use a *nexus approach* in which decisions regarding parental fitness are based upon evidence brought to the court. When the per se approach is used, the courts voice concerns about the possible harmful effects of having lesbian or gay parents upon a child's sexual

orientation or identity and also about the effects of stigma associated with having gay or lesbian parents. Some judges also express concerns about sexual abuse of children by lesbian or gay parents or their partners and friends. All of these concerns are based on myths that have been refuted by considerable scientific research. Since 1987, many courts have been using the nexus approach and more custody cases are won by lesbian mothers. In these cases, there is no per se assumption that a gay or lesbian sexual orientation makes one unfit to be a parent. Instead, the court examines evidence related to the actual effect of the parent's sexual orientation on the child. If there is not sufficiently convincing evidence that it adversely affects the child, then custody may be awarded to that parent (C. Meyer, 1992).

Because the linkups of lesbians and gay men are not legally sanctioned, the courts do not tend to view nonbiological coparents as having parenting rights. For example, the nonbiological comother of a child conceived through artificial insemination methods may lose all contact with that child if her linkup with her partner, the biological mother, terminates. In a few states a same-gender partner may gain parental rights through a process of second parent adoption. In this process the biological parent consents to giving up parental rights in favor of the coparent. The courts are most likely to uphold this kind of transfer of rights in cases of artificial insemination, especially when there is no known donor. In some states a sperm donor can sue for custody at any time, even if he had previously signed an agreement that he would not do so, and the courts may uphold his parental rights, especially if he is heterosexual. One other method by which a same-gender coparent may gain some parental rights is through informal legal guardianship, which requires documentation of the custodial parent's consent but not court intervention. These coparents are less likely to win formal legal guardianship, which does require court sanction of their rights (C. Meyer, 1992).

Ettebrick (1993) stated that lesbians face problems with the courts such as those described above because the family law system is "resolutely heterosexual in its structure and presumptions" (p. 514). Laws having to do with families tend to assume that families with children have two parents, both heterosexual. The courts must then try to fit the experiences of families with one parent, or with lesbian or gay parents, into this model. At their base, the problems described above revolve around the determination of who is a parent, with the courts emphasizing biological contributions to the child's conception and birth. Considerably less emphasis is given to the idea of a functional, or psychological, parent.

Attorneys representing gay or lesbian parents in custody disputes commonly devote considerable effort to dispelling myths and overcoming prejudices held by judges about their client's sexual orientation and its presumed effects on children. Although such efforts may help individual cases, they do not significantly affect the legal system as a whole. Rubenfeld (1994) argued that judicial training programs should be developed to decrease the likelihood of prejudicial treatment of these cases. Polikoff (1991) described a judicial education program on gay and lesbian parenting that was implemented at the 1988 Judicial Conference of the District of Columbia. This program involved the use of a case simulation. Rubenfeld noted that only two such programs are documented, both occurring in 1988. Nevertheless, the American Bar Association (ABA; 1990) adopted a Model Code of Judicial Conduct that blocks judges from manifesting bias or prejudice on the basis of sexual orientation in the performance of their duties (Canon 3 [B] [5]). Rubenfeld stated that this provision of the code may lay the

groundwork for more comprehensive judicial education programs so that lesbian and gay parents are more likely to encounter fair treatment by the courts. The states, however, are not compelled to follow ABA recommendations.

Child Welfare System

Lesbian and gay families with children are most likely to come in contact with the child welfare system through foster care, adoption, or family preservation programs. Some states use openly gay or lesbian homes for foster placement of children (Kirkpatrick, 1990). Such placements tend to occur quietly and without publicity. In 1976, the California Department of Social Services was the first state child welfare agency to adopt a formal policy allowing the licensure of lesbian and gay foster parents. Only a handful of state agencies now prohibit the licensing of gay men or lesbians as foster parents: Massachusetts, New Hampshire, and South Dakota. The absence of such rules in most states means that foster placement with gay and lesbian families is theoretically possible but not necessarily implemented (Ricketts & Achtenberg, 1990).

The Massachusetts regulations arose from a sensationalized story in a major Boston newspaper about the placement of two young boys with a gay male foster family in 1984. The family was a stable, financially secure couple who were favorably evaluated by the Massachusetts Department of Social Services during the course of more than a year. The boys were placed with the written consent of their mother. Nevertheless, shortly after the placement was implemented, the newspaper made it a front page story and instigated a media circus that pressured the Department of Social Services to remove the children from the foster home. One newspaper editorial accused the department of allowing its foster care policy to be used by childless gay or lesbian families to "acquire the trappings of traditional families" ("A Model," 1985). In addition to terminating the foster placement, the department also wrote new regulations for licensing foster families that in effect, although it was not explicitly stated, prohibited gay and lesbian foster placements. In writing these regulations, the department ignored the expert opinions of the National Association of Social Workers, the Massachusetts Psychiatric Society, the Society for the Prevention of Cruelty to Children, and many other organizations who publicly opposed the new regulations (Ricketts & Achtenberg, 1990). This incident highlights how vulnerable lesbian and gay families are to the whims of public opinion and their consequences in child welfare policy.

Like children who are members of other minorities, lesbian and gay children are often difficult to place. Kirkpatrick (1990) noted, however, that many homeless gay and lesbian youths need foster placements. According to Ricketts and Achtenberg (1990), there are programs in a few cities that focus on seeking foster placements and adoptions for lesbian and gay youth. Some youths believe that their interests may be best served in an appropriate placement with gay or lesbian adults given that other foster parents may treat them in a discriminatory manner.

Lesbian and gay adults who wish to adopt a child face obstacles in some state laws, the courts, and formal and informal agency policies (Evall, 1991). Only Florida and New Hampshire statutorily prohibit adoptions by lesbians and gay men. Colorado, Kentucky, Montana, and Oklahoma, however, prohibit all unmarried couples from adopting children (Pierce, 1995). Many judges in state courts disallow adoptions by lesbians and gay men for a variety of reasons including the existence of sodomy legislation as well as judges' discriminatory personal attitudes regarding sexual orientation (Evall, 1991). Adoption agencies in most states, however,

may not have formal policies prohibiting gay men and lesbians from adopting, with Florida the notable exception. Agencies in many states, including California, Indiana, Montana, Minnesota, Nevada, and New Jersey, have informal policies that allow such adoptions. In many more states, including Kansas, Louisiana, Michigan, New York, and Pennsylvania, the decision on whether to allow adoptions is left up to the individual caseworker. In Michigan and New Jersey, adoption by gay men or lesbians is allowed only when no eligible heterosexual adopters are available. Agencies in other states claim that gay men and lesbians receive equal consideration (Pierce, 1995). Although caseworkers who are members of the National Association of Social Workers (NASW) must uphold its Code of Ethics (NASW, 1996), which prohibits discrimination on the basis of sexual orientation, many agency caseworkers may not be social workers or members of NASW.

Children of lesbian and gay parents are less likely to be sexually or physically abused (Gold, Perrin, Futterman, & Friedman, 1994). Like other parents, however, some lesbian or gay parents may be referred for family preservation services if there is some danger of their neglecting or abusing their children (Faria, 1994). Family preservation curricula do not tend to include information about lesbian and gay families, which increases the likelihood that personal biases and misconceptions could affect the handling of these cases (e.g., Faria, 1994). As with adoption, not all family preservation caseworkers are social workers bound by a code of professional ethics. In addition, social workers who received their professional education some time ago were probably not exposed to curricula about lesbians and gay men, which is now mandated in accredited schools of social work. Personal bias could lead some caseworkers to recommend removal of a child from a lesbian or gay home when supportive services might allow the family to remain together.

Schools

Sears (1994) reported that "every major professional educational association has adopted resolutions calling upon schools to address" the topic of gay and lesbian sexual orientation (p. 148). The National Educational Association, the American Federation of Teachers, and the American School Health Association are some of the organizations that affirm the rights of gay and lesbian students. A few states have adopted sexual orientation nondiscrimination statutes. When it implemented one of these statutes, Wisconsin also issued guidelines for the adoption of school curricula that reflect ethnic and sexual orientation diversity. At the local level, some school districts, including Cambridge, Massachusetts; St. Paul, Minnesota; San Francisco; and Los Angeles adopted policies prohibiting discrimination against gay and lesbian students. Several cities developed specialized programs for gay and lesbian students: New York (Harvey Milk School) and Los Angeles (Project 10). Nevertheless, most school districts do not provide these students with protection from harassment nor do they encourage the development of gay- and lesbian-inclusive curricula. They apparently prefer to ignore the presence of gay and lesbian students, and gay and lesbian parents of students, in their schools.

According to Casper et al. (1992), lesbian and gay parents hold a variety of ideas regarding disclosure of their sexual orientation to the schools their children attend. Some parents keep their sexual orientation hidden for fear of personal rejection while others fear discrimination by public agencies, fueled by a belief that school officials may share information with other agencies. In light of the lack of protections against discrimination in most cities and towns, parents

may fear losing their job or home, or being victimized by anti-lesbian-and-gay violence. They may also fear that their children will be treated in a discriminatory manner by teachers or victimized by their peers. On the other hand, some parents feel that by not disclosing to the school, they are communicating shame about their family.

Some parents may disclose their sexual orientation in indirect ways such as when both partners are visible in dropping off or picking up their child or in volunteering for school activities. Others are more direct and cross out "father" on school forms and write in "comother." Casper et al. (1992) stressed the importance of open disclosure in these settings and encouraged lesbian and gay parents to engage teachers and school administrators in discussions about their situations, needs, and experiences.

Sears (1994) encouraged educators to reach out to lesbian and gay parents in their districts through several strategies. First, parent-teacher organizations should explicitly welcome them, possibly developing a support network for them. Second, informal faculty meetings should be held with these parents to identify any unmet needs and to come up with possible ways of meeting them. Third, schools should develop more inclusive, nonbiased curricula and adopt nondiscrimination and antiharassment policies. These kinds of strategies convey that lesbian and gay parents are equal and accepted members of the school community.

◆ Research on Lesbian and Gay Families

Health care professionals, judges and attorneys, social welfare agency workers and administrators, and educators and other school personnel who hold negative biases and misconceptions regarding lesbian and gay families cannot claim that there is an absence of research-based knowledge about them. Several authors (e.g., Falk, 1994; G. Green & Bozett, 1991; C. Patterson, 1995) demonstrated that there is now a considerable body of empirical research on this population. There are limitations, however, on the research accomplished to date. According to G. Green and Bozett (1991), most of the available data are from research using relatively small, nonrandom samples that are predominantly White, well educated, and urban. The majority of subjects in these studies also felt relatively positive about their sexual orientation. C. Patterson (1995) added that the samples were also largely middle to upper-middle class. Generalizations from the available data to the population of all lesbian and gay families therefore must be made with caution.

Research on Lesbian Mothers

Extensive summaries of the body of research on lesbian mothers are provided by Falk (1989), G. Green and Bozett (1991), and C. Patterson (1995). G. Green and Bozett reported that previous research on lesbian mothers frequently addressed the question of whether they are different from other mothers because of their sexual orientation. Within this larger question, research explored whether lesbian mothers demonstrate pathology that is unique to them, are less maternal in their interactions with their children, or deny their children access to male role models. In general, researchers did not find lesbian mothers different from other mothers in their behavior toward their children or in their *general functioning*. Kirkpatrick (1990) noted that research on lesbian mothers found that they are "remarkably similar to their heterosexual counterparts" (p. 209). Rand et al. (1982) found lesbian mothers to exhibit normal psychological well-being, especially those who are open

about their sexual orientation. Flaks, Ficher, Masterpasqua, and Joseph (1995) examined the *relationship quality* of lesbian and heterosexual couples with children. There was no difference between the two groups. Patterson noted that lesbian mothers who conceived within a previous heterosexual relationship are generally found to be as warm to their children and as interested in child rearing as heterosexual mothers.

Addressing the question of whether lesbian mothers restrict their children's *access to male role models,* Hare and Richards (1993) interviewed 28 lesbian couples with children, 70% of whom were conceived in the context of a previous heterosexual relationship. Most (90%) of the children, especially the boys, maintained regular contact with their fathers. These data are consistent with those found by Kirkpatrick et al. (1981). Divorced lesbian mothers may in fact maintain better relationships with their former male partners, and include men in their lives more often, than divorced heterosexual mothers. Hare and Richards found that children conceived within the context of a lesbian relationship experience less contact with their fathers than those conceived within the context of a previous heterosexual relationship. All of these mothers, however, believe that male role models are important for their children.

Increasingly, researchers are examining other issues regarding lesbian mothers such as their parenting skills, their experience with stress, their coping patterns, and their particular strengths (e.g., Ainsley & Feltey, 1991; Flaks et al., 1995; Hare, 1994; Levy, 1992; Lott-Whitehead & Tully, 1993). Flaks et al., for example, compared the *parenting skills* of a sample of lesbian couples (all of whom conceived through donor insemination) with a sample of matched heterosexual couples. The lesbian couples measured higher on parenting awareness skills than the comparison heterosexual couples. More specifically, lesbian parents were better at identification of hypothetical child care problems and solutions to them. They had the same level of awareness of the skills needed to implement the solutions as the heterosexual parents.

Slater and Mencher (1991) described a variety of *stressors* in the life course of lesbian families. They explained that lesbian families must continually face challenges to their viability, regardless of the family's duration. Both society at large and families of origin may continue to see them as "temporary, platonic, and largely incidental" (p. 376). Although married heterosexual couples are assisted in the confirmation of their viability through social rituals and legal status, lesbian couples must frequently shoulder this burden alone.

Lott-Whitehead and Tully (1993) described a sample of lesbian-headed families that experienced high levels of stress derived largely from the prejudice and discriminatory treatment perceived or experienced within society. The stress levels may also be partially explained by the high percentage of single parents in this sample given that previous research has associated stress with single parenthood (Compas & Williams, 1990). A few women in the sample stated that they also feel unsupported by some segments of the lesbian community. Other sources of stress included intrafamily conflicts and concerns about money. In Hare's (1994) sample of lesbian couples, nearly half of them related that antilesbian prejudice and stigma prevented them from being seen by others as a family, and that being seen as part of an unconventional family structure was stressful for them. One of their major concerns was that their children may experience stigma because of being raised in a lesbian-headed family. According to Kirkpatrick (1990), some lesbian mothers also experience intimidation from ex-husbands who threaten them with loss of child custody.

In a study of the *coping behaviors* of lesbian mothers (Levy, 1992), at least 90% of the sample endorsed four behaviors as helpful in "coping with life in a . . . [heterosexist] environment" (p. 25). These behaviors were engaging in satisfying relationships (97%), building close relationships with people (93%), socializing with women friends (93%), talking with someone about how I feel (90%), and socializing with lesbian friends (90%). Levy noted that for most of these women, support came from interactions with others who validated their dual identities of mother and lesbian. Slater and Mencher (1991) reported that some lesbian couples respond to the stress of living in a hostile environment by creating a "two against the world" (p. 378) stance and a relationship marked by fusion. Those who become active in lesbian communities, however, may learn ways of coping that are less isolating. According to Ainsley and Feltey (1991), lesbian mothers who identify themselves as feminists are likely to engage in extended support networks that provide "a supportive social context in which to be a lesbian feminist and to raise children according to feminist values" (p. 81).

Lesbian-headed families may demonstrate particular *strengths*. Lott-Whitehead and Tully's (1993) sample of lesbian mothers hold deep commitments to their children, devoting significant efforts toward maintaining a nurturant and safe family environment. Locating themselves in socially liberal communities and monitoring media images of lesbian and gay families are two strategies they employ so as to protect their children. According to Ainsley and Feltey (1991), some families headed by feminist lesbian mothers are organized into extended networks consisting of other lesbians and their families, serving to provide "a supportive social context" (p. 81) for raising children. These networks function much the same as extended family networks based on biological kinship and marriage.

Levy (1992) recommended that professionals assist lesbian-headed families. They can encourage lesbian mothers to be open about their sexual orientation and also advise them about the risks they may realistically face. They can support such mothers who face conflict with former husbands and other systems such as those described earlier in this chapter. Perhaps most important, professionals should identify the important supports and strengths that lesbian mothers already have so they can bolster them and help their clients to use them more effectively.

Research on Gay Fathers

There are only a handful of studies examining gay men who are fathers. They focus primarily on their integration of fatherhood with a gay identity, their parenting styles, their family relationships including their partnership, and disclosure of their sexual orientation to their children. Most studies examined divorced gay fathers. Unlike lesbian mothers, most of these men are noncustodial parents (Crosbie-Burnett & Helmbrecht, 1993) given that the courts are much less likely to grant custody to fathers than to mothers (C. Patterson, 1995). According to Bigner and Jacobson (1989), however, research so far provides no support for the notion that being gay makes a man unsuitable for parenthood.

According to Bozett (1989), research indicates that married gay men tend to become aware of their sexual orientation later than gay men who do not marry. Having children makes it more difficult for them to come out. Perhaps because many people consider being a gay man and being a father mutually exclusive categories, both Bozett (1981a) and B. Miller (1986) studied the process by which married gay fathers gradually accept their sexual orientation and *integrate their*

identities as both gay men and fathers. Bozett reported that gay fathers are able to attain this integration by accepting their sexual orientation, considering being gay an important part of their identity, and disclosing their identity to heterosexual men and women. Miller noted that gay fathers are most likely to begin the movement toward accepting and valuing the gay dimension of their identity when they fall in love with another man. A variety of obstacles may impede their progress, however, including the disbelief that being gay is a viable alternative, a lack of perceived support from other gay men or lesbians, and perceived hostility and opposition from their family or community. Fathers who are integrated in a gay community, however, gain an improved sense of well-being.

A few studies examined the *parenting styles* of gay fathers. Bigner and Jacobson (1992) found that a sample of gay fathers expressed parenting attitudes and styles that are not significantly different from those of similar samples of nongay fathers. In an earlier study, Bigner and Jacobson (1989) found that gay and nongay fathers do not differ significantly on their level of involvement or intimacy with their children. Compared with nongay fathers, gay fathers are more responsive to the needs of their children while also being more strict with them. They use more reasoning, however, in explaining appropriate behavior to their children. Another study (Scallen, 1981) reported that more gay fathers than nongay fathers endorsed nurturer, as opposed to economic provider, as central to their role as a father. They also assessed their performance in the father role more positively than did nongay fathers.

Several studies examined the *family relationships* of gay fathers. Crosbie-Burnett and Helmbrecht (1993) described the association of family happiness with family dynamics in a sample of gay stepfamilies. Findings showed that integrating the stepfather into the family and developing a good relationship between the stepfather and stepchild were the most important keys to family happiness. Unresolved emotions about the prior family and relations with the child's mother were not significantly associated with happiness. Problems with child visitation, however, were associated with lower happiness. In another study, McPherson (1993) reported that *gay couples* choosing parenthood after becoming a couple divided their household and child care responsibilities more evenly than did heterosexual couples. They reported a higher level of satisfaction with their division of child care tasks and in their relationship with each other.

Bigner and Bozett (1990) reported that gay fathers who *disclose* their sexual orientation to their children experience closer relationships with them than those who keep it secret. Although Bigner and Bozett stated that children are never too young to be told about their father's sexual orientation, they recommended that fathers come to terms with it themselves before discussing it with their children. Waiting too long, however, risks the undesirable possibility that children will hear this information from another source. Fathers should keep the discussion positive and sincere, and avoid treating it like a confession. Perhaps most important, a father should provide reassurance that his children's link with him will not change because of his sexual orientation.

Research on Children of Lesbian and Gay Parents

Several extensive reviews of the literature are available on the outcome of children of lesbian and gay parents. In summarizing the findings of this research, Flaks et al. (1995) stated, "There is no empirical support for the proposition that the children of divorced lesbian and gay parents are different from other children" (p. 106). They added that successful child development cannot be predicted by

a custodial parent's sexual orientation. Likewise, C. Patterson (1995) noted that currently published research does not indicate any significant problems with sexual identity, social relationships, or any other areas of personal development in children of lesbian or gay parents. In another review of this literature, G. Green and Bozett (1991) concluded that the sexual orientation of parents does not determine a child's health status or well-being. Similarly, Falk (1994) found that research evidence points to the quality of the parent-child relationship, not the parent's sexual orientation, as most significant for determining child outcome.

Gold et al. (1994) observed that much of the previous research examining the children of lesbian and gay parents focused on whether they experience "pathology" in their sexual orientation or their social, behavioral, and psychological development as a result of their parent's sexual orientation. Far fewer studies examined whether these children derive particular strengths from having gay or lesbian parents.

Bailey, Bobrow, Wolfe, and Mikach (1995) examined the sexual orientation of 82 adult sons (17 years of age or older) of 55 gay fathers. The fathers reported what they believed to be their son's *sexual orientation* as well as their level of certainty about it. Among 68 sons whose sexual orientation was reported with "virtual certainty," the data indicated a high concordance between the fathers' report of their sons' sexual orientation and the sons' self-report. Of the sons whose sexual orientation could be rated, more than 90% were rated heterosexual. Whether heterosexual or gay, a son's sexual orientation was not significantly correlated with the length of time the father and son lived together, the quality of their relationship, or the level of the son's acceptance of the father's sexual orientation.

Tasker and Golombok (1995) compared the sexual orientations of adult children of lesbian and heterosexual single-mother families. The sample consisted of 8 men and 17 women raised by a lesbian mother, and 12 men and 9 women raised by a heterosexual mother. There was no significant difference between the two groups of adult children in the proportion reporting same-gender sexual attraction. Among those children who did report same-gender sexual attraction, however, significantly more of the children of lesbian-headed families actually engaged in some form of same-gender sexual behavior or were involved in a same-gender sexual linkup.

In light of the two studies reported here, parents' sexual orientation may not have any bearing on their children's sexual orientation, but having a lesbian or gay parent may make it easier for those children who are gay or lesbian to act on their sexual attractions. Similar findings were reported from several earlier studies (J. S. Gottman, 1990; Huggins, 1989; B. Miller, 1979a).

Flaks et al. (1995) compared the *social relationships* and *behavioral adjustment* of 15 children of lesbian-headed two-parent families and 15 children of similar heterosexual two-parent families. They found no significant differences between the groups for internalizing (overcontrolled), externalizing (undercontrolled), or total problems. Similarly, levels of social competence and adaptive functioning were not found to differ significantly for the two groups of children.

In their study of adult children of lesbian and heterosexual single-mother families, Tasker and Golombok (1995) found no significant differences between the quality of current relationships between the children and their parents or of the amount of teasing or bullying experienced by peers during their childhood or adolescence. J. S. Gottman (1990) compared social adjustment in 35 adult daughters of divorced lesbian mothers and 35 adult daughters of divorced heterosexual mothers using the California Psycho-

logical Inventory (CPI) (Gough, 1960). No significant differences were found on 17 of the 18 CPI subscales. On the Well-Being subscale there were differences associated with the presence or absence of older brothers in the home. Daughters of lesbian mothers scored lower on Well-Being when older brothers were present, while daughters of heterosexual mothers scored higher. Other studies (R. Green, Mandel, Hotvedt, Gray, & Smith, 1986; Harris & Turner, 1985-1986) also failed to find parents' gay or lesbian sexual orientation associated with social or behavioral problems in their children.

Some studies examined the self-esteem and levels of anxiety in children of lesbian and gay parents. Huggins (1989) was unable to find significant differences between 18 adolescent offspring of divorced lesbian mothers and 18 similar offspring of divorced heterosexual mothers on any dimension of *self-esteem.* Tasker and Golonbok (1995) found no significant differences between adult children of lesbian and heterosexual mothers on their level of *anxiety.*

Children of gay or lesbian parents may exhibit particular *strengths.* Gold et al. (1994) noted that they tend to hold more tolerant views of diverse populations, and they are more likely to have open discussions about sexuality than children of heterosexual parents.

◆ Services for Lesbian and Gay Families

Increasingly, there is support for lesbian and gay families, should they need it. The Gay & Lesbian Parents Coalition International (GLPCI) is an international advocacy and support organization for gay, lesbian, and bisexual parents, their partners, and their children. Founded in 1979, there are more than 100 local chapters of GLPCI across the United States and in several other countries.

Some major cities have more than one member group. This organization provides information and referrals on a variety of issues including custody, adoption, surrogacy, artificial insemination, and coparent rights. It sponsors an annual conference and a quarterly newsletter. Local chapters provide ongoing support for their members.

Children of Lesbians and Gays Everywhere (COLAGE) is a project of GLPCI that offers support groups, newsletters, pen pals, and an annual conference for children of lesbian and gay parents. In addition, this organization provides myth-challenging information to the courts, the media, and the general public concerning these children and their families. It also prints a newsletter for its members and sponsors support groups in many cities.

◆ **Summary**

Lesbian and gay couples often face systematic discrimination that affects their ability to maintain healthy relationships and raise well-adjusted children. Nevertheless, a review of research on lesbian mothers, gay fathers, and their children shows that they manage to do so at least as well as heterosexual women and men. Family processes, not particular family structures, seem to be the key to successful child rearing.

PART IV

LIFE

COURSE

YOUTH

little research

◆ RESEARCH ON DEVELOPMENT across the life course is almost exclusively based on heterosexual populations (Fertitta, 1984; Garnets & Kimmel, 1993a; Kimmel, 1978; J. Lee, 1987; Sang, Warshow, & Smith, 1991). Therefore, few developmental models exist for lesbian, gay, and bisexual persons to conceptualize the normative events in their lives (Kimmel & Sang, 1995). Because they share many of the same developmental tasks that face heterosexual persons, traditional theories of life course development are applicable in many ways (e.g., Cornett & Hudson, 1987). These groups, however, also experience unique challenges. According to Erik Erikson (1985), heterosexual individuals work to resolve four adolescent and adult stages: (a) identity versus diffusion, (b) intimacy versus isolation, (c) generativity versus stagnation, and (d) integrity versus despair.

Although these stages present similar challenges for gay, lesbian, and bisexual persons, there are differences. In the area of generativity, for example, lesbians and gay men may be generative in ways other than the bearing and raising of children. They may instead express generativity in their friendships, intergenerational commitments, creativity, and work. Even more unique for bisexual, gay, and lesbian persons is the ongoing struggle for social and legal rights, additional life events such as coming out and disclosure of their sexual orientation, the struggles of integration of their sexual orientation into various life arenas such as their families of origin and work, and the difficulties associated with HIV/AIDS.

A major limitation of studies on the life course as a whole is their homogenous samples. Members of all groups take a variety of

similar life dev as hets but unique too

paths in life. Much of the research, however, does not address this diversity. The few life course studies of gay and lesbian persons also include mainly White, well-educated, middle- to upper-class, and urban samples. Christian and Keefe (1997) pointed out that studies on different segments of the life course are also problematic because of the lack of comparison between differences attributable to aging versus particular cohorts and inconsistencies in definitions of *adolescent, youth, middle age,* and *older.* In addition, persons in different age groups are often not addressed separately. Men and women from their forties to eighties, for example, may be grouped together with no distinctions made between differences in life experiences. There are also few research efforts on the lesbian and gay population that define subgroupings within different age groups.

Keeping in mind the research issues noted here and in Chapter 1, this chapter addresses some of the unique challenges for lesbians, gay, and bisexual adolescents and, in addition, young adults on college campuses. The life periods of middle adulthood and older adulthood are addressed in the next two chapters. Research on bisexual men and women in these two periods, however, is practically nonexistent.

◆ Adolescence

During adolescence, individuals begin the transition from childhood to adulthood. They face two major developmental challenges: adapting to pubertal changes, which transform their bodies from being children to adults, and developing an independent identity. The first challenge occurs primarily during early adolescence and the second one in mid- to late adolescence. Although this period of life may be tumultuous for some, there are indications that the majority of adolescents successfully make the transition to

young adulthood without the catastrophic distress and conflict that are often attributed to them (Boxer & Cohler, 1989; Turner & Helms, 1991). Nevertheless, because adolescence involves so many physical, psychological, and social changes, numerous hazards can arise before its end.

Gay, lesbian, and bisexual adolescents share the same developmental concerns and processes of other adolescents (Savin-Williams, 1995). Being lesbian, gay, or bisexual, however, may affect every aspect of this important developmental period. Because puberty is an inherently sexual process, the nature of one's sexual strivings often becomes self-evident during its course. Because peer groups are so important during adolescence, and the pressure for conformity so intense, lesbian, gay, or bisexual teens who feel fundamentally different may experience alienation and marginalization. Because adolescence in American society focuses on developing an independent identity in which youths come to understand both who they are and what they want to accomplish, incorporating an identity as a young gay, lesbian, or bisexual person is central to this task.

Although this chapter examines many of the problems encountered by lesbian, gay, and bisexual adolescents, one should not assume that all, or even a majority, of members of this population are troubled and in need of professional intervention. According to Savin-Williams (1994), "The vast majority of gay, bisexual, and lesbian youths cope with their daily, chronic stressors to become healthy individuals who make significant contributions to their culture" (p. 262). Likewise, M. Schneider (1989) described several young women who developed positive lesbian identities "through a combination of personal resources and external supports" (p. 121). As pointed out in studies of other populations, people are resilient and able to cope reasonably well with many stressors and obstacles if they have sufficient resources on which to draw (Clair & Genest, 1987; Crocker & Major, 1989; Halpern, 1993). Consistent with this view, Savin-Williams (1990b) called for the investment of adult attention, commitment, and money toward the future of bisexual, gay, and lesbian adolescents.

Problems Encountered by Lesbian, Gay, and Bisexual Adolescents

Claims notwithstanding that most gay, lesbian, and bisexual adolescents do not develop severe problems, these youths may be uniquely at risk for problems such as suicide, prostitution, homelessness, chemical dependency, HIV, and violence. They may be rejected by their families and assaulted by their schoolmates. Their presence may be denied in their schools, and their needs may be minimized or ignored by social services (Savin-Williams, 1990b). Rotheram-Borus, Rosario, Van Rossem, Reid, and Gillis (1995) found that the greater the number of stressful life events that gay and bisexual male adolescents experience, the more likely they are to use alcohol and engage in delinquent behaviors. The more personal resources they have, however, such as higher self-esteem and positive life events, the less likely they are to feel distressed and to use alcohol. Thus sufficient personal resources may buffer the effects of stressful life events, with fewer problematic outcomes as a result. Without such resources, gay, lesbian, and bisexual youths are at risk for the kinds of problematic outcomes mentioned above.

Suicide risk. Several studies reported that gay, lesbian, and bisexual adolescents are at high risk for suicide. Proctor and Groze (1994) found that 40% of a sample of 276 American and Canadian gay, lesbian, and bisexual youth group members attempted suicide at least once, and another 26% seriously thought about it at least once. Remafedi, Farrow, and Deisher (1993) reported that 30% of a sample of 137 gay and bisexual males in Minneapolis and Seattle attempted suicide at least once, and nearly half of this group made more than a single attempt. D'Augelli and Hershberger (1993) reported that 42% of a sample of 194 youths obtaining the services of gay, lesbian, and bisexual community centers across the United States attempted suicide at least once. Attempters made an average of three suicide attempts, and 8% thought about suicide frequently. The suicide attempt rate for males and females was not significantly different.

There is some controversy surrounding findings such as these. Durby (1994) noted that researchers have not yet shown that lesbian, gay, and bisexual male adolescents in general are at high risk for suicide because the research often used convenience samples (e.g., support groups). It is possible that youths who participate in support groups are at higher risk than most lesbian, gay, or bisexual youths. Likewise, it is not clear what differences may exist in suicide attempt rates between gay, lesbian, and bisexual youths and heterosexual youths. Nevertheless, these findings do indicate that many bisexual, gay, and lesbian adolescents think about and attempt suicide, perhaps at a higher rate than their heterosexual counterparts.

Proctor and Groze (1994) examined differences between suicide attempters and nonattempters in their mixed-gender sample. Attempters rated their parental relations, school performance, self-esteem, and level of depression as significantly worse than did nonattempters. There were no reported differences between males and females. Suicide attempters were thought to possess fewer coping resources, both external (e.g., support system) and internal (e.g., self-esteem).

Remafedi et al. (1993) examined a variety of characteristics of gay and bisexual male suicide attempters and nonattempters to determine any differences between these two groups. Those youths who attempted suicide were significantly more likely to have experienced parental divorce and sexual abuse. They scored significantly higher on depression as measured by the Beck Depression Inventory (BD) (Beck, Ward, Mendelson, Mock, & Erbaugh, 1961); however, both groups scored low on depression when compared with norms. Attempters scored lower on a measure of male sex role identification. They tended to self-identify as gay or bisexual, engage in same-gender sexual behavior, and disclose their sexual orientation to others at an earlier age. Attempters were also more likely to use illegal drugs and be arrested. They may use drugs to cope with their distress, although this strategy apparently does not help.

D'Augelli and Hershberger (1993) found that low self-esteem, alcohol abuse, and loss of friends due to their sexual orientation were significant predictors of suicide attempts among males. Among females, alcohol abuse and loss of friends due to their sexual orientation were significant predictors. Both male and female attempters self-identified as gay, lesbian, or bisexual earlier than nonattempters.

Prostitution. An unknown number of gay, lesbian, and bisexual adolescents turn to prostitution to meet a variety of needs. Coleman (1989) estimated that the majority of adolescent male prostitutes are gay or bisexual. He found that many of them either run away from home or are thrown out of their homes. Their families are often chaotic, with chemically dependent parents, and the adolescents are often physically and/or sexually abused. They often enter prostitution during early adolescence to make money for survival, or for excitement. They also seek caring and affection, and a sense of belonging, which they sometimes receive from fellow prostitutes. Coleman also reported that as

many as 40% of adolescent male prostitutes abuse drugs and alcohol, and they are likely to use the money they make to support these habits.

Prostitutes who work the streets are at high risk for rape, violence, and sexually transmitted diseases as well as other forms of exploitation. They are likely to come from lower-class families and they may experience significant conflict regarding their sexual orientation. There are higher-status prostitutes, however, who do not work the streets and who command higher prices for their services based on their physical attractiveness. These boys may come from middle-class families and are more likely to accept their gay sexual orientation (Coleman, 1989).

Durby (1994) noted that there is less research on adolescent female prostitutes. Unlike their gay counterparts, lesbian prostitutes tend not to have same-gender clients (Schaffer & DeBlassie, 1984). In other words, regardless of the prostitute's gender, the clients are usually men. Durby stated that young lesbian prostitutes are likely to come from the same kinds of family backgrounds as those described for young male prostitutes. They are also vulnerable to the same risks as the males, including violence, rape, and sexually transmitted diseases.

Homelessness. Like other youths, gay, lesbian, and bisexual adolescents may be homeless either temporarily or on a long-term basis. Some of them leave home without their parents' knowledge to escape family problems, often returning home after one night but sometimes doing this repeatedly. Some of them are told by their parents to leave home, even though they have nowhere else to go. Other homeless youths run away from unsuccessful foster homes. Still others may be long-term homeless youths who engage in prostitution or sell drugs for survival (Rotheram-Borus, Rosario, & Koopman,

1991). Savin-Williams (1994) claimed that several reports grossly underestimated the numbers of runaway and homeless youths who are lesbian, gay, or bisexual. Many of these youths are unlikely to volunteer information to researchers or other authorities about their sexual orientation. Some may be unclear about their sexual orientation. While several of these studies found that lesbian, gay, or bisexual youths were approximately 6% of their samples of runaway and homeless youths, other studies found them to constitute as much as 40% of their samples (e.g., Orion Center, 1986).

Chemical abuse. Shifrin and Solis (1992) found that 17% of a sample of 75 young lesbian clients of the Hetrick-Martin Institute in New York City engaged in problematic chemical use, according to counselor assessment. The Hetrick-Martin Institute is a multiservice agency serving gay and lesbian youths. The researchers also found that 19% of a similar sample of 191 young gay male clients engaged in problematic chemical use. The most frequently used chemicals include alcohol, marijuana, and cocaine. Among 75 homeless gay and lesbian clients, 100% were addicted to crack cocaine. Based on data also collected in New York City, Rotheram et al. (1992) reported chemical use among young gay and bisexual male youths in their lifetimes: alcohol (77%), marijuana (42%), crack or cocaine (23%), and hallucinogens (15%). Among young lesbians during the three months prior to the study, the rates included alcohol (83%), drugs (56%), and crack or cocaine (11%). Shifrin and Stolls explained the chemical use as a strategy for coping with anxiety, depression, and low self-esteem. Chemicals may provide these youths with feelings of mastery, power, and wholeness. According to Durby (1994), alcohol and drugs such as crack, marijuana, crystal methamphetamine, and heroin help homeless gay, lesbian, and bisexual youths to soothe and dull feelings of rejection, loneliness, and a sense of worthlessness.

Health risks. Lesbian, gay, and bisexual adolescents are at risk for a variety of health problems including HIV and sexually transmitted diseases. These risks increase among runaway and homeless youths, youths engaged in prostitution, and in all youths when chemicals are used during sex (Durby, 1994). Cranston (1991) reported that most HIV-infected adolescents are infected through same-gender sexual behavior. Morris, Baker, and Huscroft (1992) found that gay and lesbian adolescents were among the groups at highest risk for HIV infection in their sample of incarcerated youths. Those youths who had more than 25 sex partners, prostituted, used IV drugs at least once a week, or were pregnant at least once were most likely to be infected.

Monteiro and Fuqua (1994) claimed that young African American gay males are at an even higher risk for HIV infection than similar Euro-American males, but there are only limited data to support their claim. One study of gay and bisexual men in San Francisco revealed an infection rate of 14% among the participants who were 17-19 years old. African American participants age 17-25, however, had an infection rate of 23% (Lemp, Neri, & San Francisco Department of Public Health, 1991). Grossman (1997) noted that some racial and ethnic youths who engage in same-gender sexual activities make a distinction between these sexual involvements and their sexual identity. Even though they participate in same-gender sex, they do not view themselves as gay. Consequently, they may not identify themselves as at risk for HIV/AIDS. As noted in Chapter 1, in some cultures only men who are receptive in sexual behaviors are labeled as gay. In addition, as noted in Chapter 3, HIV/AIDS in some racial and ethnic communities is viewed as a "White disease."

Young lesbians are at high risk for HIV infection primarily if they or their partners participate in sex with men. Especially if their sexual encounters involve the use of alcohol or drugs and poor judgment, they may lead to pregnancy as well as HIV and other sexually transmitted diseases. There may be no insistence on the use of condoms or other preventive measures. Young lesbians who participate in sex only with other women who likewise avoid sex with men may be at low risk for HIV infection. They are at risk for other sexually transmitted diseases, however, such as gonorrhea, syphilis, and hepatitis, as are young gay males. Other health risks for females include yeast infections and chlamydia (Durby, 1994).

Gay and bisexual male youths are at high risk for HIV infection for a variety of social and developmental reasons. First, because most of the people who were infected with HIV during the early years were adult gay men, that population was targeted for prevention efforts. Even though youths are now at risk for HIV infection, it is frequently difficult to develop educational and health programs that target adolescent sexual behavior, including both teen pregnancy and HIV prevention programs. In part this is due to the ambivalence of our society toward adolescent sexuality. An additional obstacle is that in many communities lesbians and gay men risk prosecution for child molestation when they experience any kind of contact with youths. The fear of prosecution may keep many otherwise knowledgeable and caring adults from offering their help and guidance to this population. A second reason for the high risk of HIV infection was noted by Cranston (1991), who claimed that young persons who have low self-worth are not likely to adopt and maintain healthy behaviors. Even though they may learn the mechanics of safer sex, including condom use, they may lack self-efficacy, or "the belief that one possesses the ability to use the learned skills in defense of personal well-being" (p. 250). According to Cranston, self-efficacy comes from a combination of high self-esteem and personal skill competencies.

Violence. Gay and lesbian adolescents may face physical violence both outside and within their families. In one study, J. Hunter (1990) reported that 40% of 500 gay and lesbian youths seeking services from the Institute for the Protection of Lesbian and Gay Youth (IPLGY, later the Hetrick-Martin Institute) stated that they were physically assaulted at least once. Other studies reported a similarly high prevalence of violence against this population. Frequently, the perpetrators of these attacks are other teenagers (Savin-Williams, 1994), some of whom are members of organized hate groups (Berrill, 1990). Uribe and Harbeck (1992) recounted the story of a gay male adolescent in a Los Angeles high school who was assaulted by his peers and verbally abused by his teachers, which eventually led him to drop out of school and turn to the streets. According to the authors, many gay and lesbian adolescents have these kinds of school experiences. According to A. Martin and Hetrick (1988), such violence may result from the youth's disclosure to peers. Frequently, those youths who are at highest risk for victimization also display nontraditional gender identification in their behavior or dress.

Bisexual, gay, and lesbian adolescent victims of hate-inspired violence may get little help from authorities empowered to respond to violent crime. Many of these victims are blamed for the attack (A. Martin & Hetrick, 1988; Uribe & Harbeck, 1992) while the violent behavior of the perpetrators is rationalized or excused. For example, in 1988 District Judge Jack Hampton handed down two concurrent 30-year sentences to an 18-year-old man convicted of shooting to death two Dallas gay men, which made him eligible for parole in $7\frac{1}{2}$ years. In a newspaper interview shortly after the trial, Hampton said that he rejected the maximum penalty, a life sentence, because of the murderer's "youth, his clean record, and his good home life" (Montgomery & Collins, 1989, p. A17). In addition, Hampton told the newspaper, "These two guys that got killed wouldn't have been killed if they hadn't been cruising the streets picking up teenage boys. . . . I don't much care for queers cruising the streets and picking up teenage boys" (p. A1). These comments apparently stemmed from early claims by the murderer that the victims had picked up him and his friends to have sex with them. These claims, however, were contradicted by the murderer's friends, who reported that they drove to Dallas from their suburban homes with the sole purpose of harassing gay men.

Judge Hampton was censured by the Texas Commission on Judicial Conduct for his comments about the victims. Shortly afterward, however, he ran unopposed for his bench and was reelected. More than 300 people donated a total of more than $30,000 to his reelection bid, the largest amount for any uncontested judicial race in the county (J. Collins, 1990). The judge, however, did not act alone in this miscarriage of justice. In the context of early publicity about the case regarding allegations that the victims solicited sex from the accused and his friends, the Dallas County district attorney asked the grand jury hearing this case to reject the charge of capital murder, which would have carried a sentence of death. The grand jury complied (Montgomery & Collins, 1989). Although the victims were adults, this case illustrates the prejudice that adolescent victims of violence may face if they seek redress.

According to Savin-Williams (1994), violence against gay and lesbian adolescents also often occurs in the home, perpetrated by family members. In one study of lesbian and gay adolescents seeking help from IPLGY, 49% of those who experienced physical violence were assaulted at home, either by parents or by siblings (A. Martin & Hetrick, 1988). Some young lesbians may even engage in male-female sex and become pregnant to hide their sexual orientation and thereby avoid violent family reactions. Frequently, such violence occurs when the family learns of the adolescent's sexual orientation. In A. Martin and Hetrick's study, 22% of the sample reported experiencing sexual abuse. Although not all of these instances occurred within the family, Martin and Hetrick reported that it was often perpetrated by older male relatives such as a father, an uncle, or a brother. Victims may blame themselves for the abuse, feeling either that they seduced the perpetrator or that they should have been able to stop the abuse.

Problems in schools. American schools are a microcosm of the larger society, and because prejudice, discrimination, and violence against gay, lesbian, and bisexual adolescents is tolerated by many school authorities, schools play a central role in the perpetuation of heterosexism (Herdt & Boxer, 1993). According to Durby (1994), the stresses related to self-discovery, coming out, and potential harassment and abuse interfere with many lesbian, gay, and bisexual students' educational and social learning. In one study of 168 adolescents obtaining services from several gay and lesbian community centers, 71% of the lesbian youths and 73% of the gay youths reported that they faced problems in school due to their sexual orientation. These problems included physical abuse and threats of abuse, hearing rude comments and jokes, finding profanities written on their lockers, and feeling afraid and lonely (Telljohann & Price, 1993). In another study, 32% of a sample of 500 lesbian and gay youths considered dropping out of school because of their "cognitive, social, and emotional isolation" (A. Martin & Hetrick, 1988, p. 178).

Discriminatory treatment of gay, lesbian, and bisexual youths may occur in schools because counselors, teachers, and administrators are personally uncomfortable with sexual orientation issues and because they lack training in dealing with them (A. Martin & Hetrick, 1988). Price and Telljohann (in press) reported, for example, that only one-fourth of a sample of counselors reported feeling competent in working with gay and lesbian students. In classrooms, lesbian students studied by Telljohann and Price (1993) felt that sexual orientation should be discussed more often and in a respectful manner, and that heterosexist comments should not be allowed. They also wanted lesbian support groups and better qualified school counselors. The gay male participants had similar suggestions, although they also wanted to see punishment handed down to students who made derogatory remarks.

Lesbian or gay teachers, who may be able to provide leadership for schools grappling with these issues and role modeling for students, are frequently forced to remain hidden. Because most communities allow discrimination against them, they could lose their jobs (Khayatt, 1994). Nevertheless, Khayatt's adolescent lesbian interviewees reported that they often knew which of their teachers were gay or lesbian. In general they understood why the teachers were hidden, and they seemed to be encouraged just by knowing they were there. On the other hand, they indicated that the silence in schools about same-gender sexual orientation reinforces their suspicions that the topic is taboo, and it makes them feel bad or terrified about their same-gender attractions.

Rofes (1989) noted that positive changes are happening in some school districts. For example, Project 10 in the Los Angeles Unified School District is a program offering specialized supports for lesbian, gay, and bisexual students. The Hetrick-Martin Institute, a private agency in New York, runs the Harvey Milk School, an alternative high school for bisexual, gay, and lesbian youths who have not succeeded in other New York City schools. A number of high schools allow gay or lesbian couples to openly attend their official proms. In several states, improved educational and support services to these students are recommended. Nevertheless, most schools tend to deny the presence, and ignore the needs, of their gay, lesbian, and bisexual students.

Problems in child welfare settings. In addition to schools, other traditional support structures also tend to fail lesbian, gay, and bisexual adolescents (Uribe & Harbeck, 1992). These include child welfare services such as foster family and residential treatment settings. Sullivan (1994) noted that there are not enough qualified foster family homes to serve current needs and that this deficit is even more serious for lesbian and gay youths. These youths frequently enter the child welfare system at a somewhat older age than others, which makes them harder to place. In addition, it is even more difficult to find appropriate placements for adolescents who are open about their sexual orientation. On the other hand, interested gay men and lesbians who are qualified to care for foster children are frequently denied that opportunity by child welfare agencies. Thus gay and lesbian youths in need of support and positive role models are even less likely to find them (see Chapter 7).

It is similarly difficult for lesbian and gay adolescents in need of residential treatment placements to find appropriate services. According to Mallon (1992b), "Gay and lesbian youth are in treatment in every Residential Treatment Center in [the United States]" (p. 59). Youths who are openly gay or lesbian, however, are rarely admitted into residential placement. Many of the gay and lesbian youths who are admitted to these settings experience verbal harassment, physical abuse, and rape. Lacking protection from agency staff, some may take it upon themselves to fight back, whereupon they are blamed for their victimization and sometimes ejected from the facility. Other youths run away, choosing to take their chances on the streets rather than enduring more mistreatment. In either situation these adolescents become even harder to place, because of reputations as aggressive or as runaways. Mallon noted that it is even harder to find appropriate residential services for young lesbians than for young gay males.

Services Needed by Lesbian, Gay, and Bisexual Adolescents

Several authors describe the services and supports that gay, lesbian, and bisexual youths need to successfully meet the challenges of adolescence. Noting the central importance of peer support, K. Robinson (1991) encouraged social workers to use gay and lesbian *support groups* as primary resources for them and, if there are none in the area, either to start one or to work with the local gay and lesbian community to start one. One such youth group is OutRight. Located in Durham, North Carolina, this group is run primarily by adult lesbians and gay men, who also founded it. They are in charge of the long-range planning for the group as well as programming, financial backing, and community linkage. Another group, OutYouth Austin (Texas), established a toll-free phone number intended for youth support and information. An avalanche of calls nearly bankrupted the organization (Singerline, 1994). Although this experience illustrates the need for such services, many of the phone calls this organization received were from people opposed to its existence, apparently hoping to destroy it by driving up its phone bill.

Adult support is another important resource needed by bisexual, gay, and lesbian adolescents. Parents and Friends of Lesbians and Gays (PFLAG) is a volunteer-run organization instrumental in rallying this support. It was originally formed as a support group for parents with lesbian and gay children because these parents must cope with a variety of difficult feelings after their children disclose to them (see Chapter 5). In addition to this support, PFLAG now also provides community education and advocacy for gay and lesbian issues (Federation of Parents and Friends of Lesbians and Gays, 1984). Its members often get the most rousing receptions of any group when they march in gay, lesbian, and bisexual pride parades with placards that proclaim, "We love our gay and lesbian children." There are PFLAG chapters in every state and the District of Columbia.

Taking a leadership role among helping professions, the American Psychological Association (DeLeon, 1993) adopted a Resolution on Lesbian, Gay, and Bisexual Youths in the Schools. It supports "providing a safe and secure educational atmosphere in which all youths, including gay, lesbian, and bisexual youths, may obtain an education free from discrimination, harassment, violence, and abuse, and which promotes an understanding and acceptance of self" (p. 782). Uribe (1994) called for the implementation of support for gay, lesbian, and bisexual adolescents in schools including small groups in which their issues can be discussed, libraries that maintain a collection of lesbian, gay, and bisexual-affirming books, and a list of supportive local resources that can include churches, mental health clinics, and gay, lesbian, and bisexual community organizations. Project 10, which Uribe developed in a Los Angeles high school, provides these kinds of support. It also provides training and education for school personnel and administrators, and it promotes a code of conduct for students and faculty to ensure safety for gay, lesbian, and bisexual students. Project 10 has been so successful that it is now used throughout the Los Angeles Unified School District. This district eventually formed a Gay and Lesbian Education Commission empowered to make recommendations to the Board of Education regarding gay and lesbian youth (Greeley, 1994). The Project 10 model is also now used by the San Francisco Unified School District and other schools (Uribe, 1994).

Rofes (1989) noted several challenges facing those seeking to better meet the needs of gay, lesbian, and bisexual adolescents in schools. First, all issues of sexuality are often taboo in schools, not only same-gender sexuality. Second, many teachers lack education on lesbian, gay, and bisexual issues and require significant training if they are to be helpful. Third, many schools exist within communities that are extremely heterosexist. Teachers or administrators who advocate positive changes in their schools may be open to attack from parents and other community members who disagree with them. Fourth, many educators and others still believe that all young people are heterosexual or, if they know otherwise, try to protect heterosexual youths from "corruption." These challenges illustrate how improving life for bisexual, gay, and lesbian adolescents in schools requires intervention at many different levels, some going well beyond the boundaries of the school campus.

Mallon (1992a) made a variety of suggestions for improving conditions for gay, lesbian, and bisexual adolescents in *out-of-home care settings*. First, provide accurate information about gay, lesbian, and bisexual youths to staff members and youths in these placements. Second, develop a code of conduct in which verbal slurs and other forms of harassment are not tolerated. Third, help lesbian, gay, and bisexual youths being served by the agency to deal with family and school

problems they may be experiencing due to their sexual orientation. Fourth, help them to develop coping skills for handling conflict and peer pressure. Fifth, create opportunities for all youths being served to openly discuss their sexually with each other.

To improve the effectiveness of *HIV prevention efforts* for bisexual, gay, and lesbian youths, Pederson (1994) recommended an ecological approach. Education about HIV and the methods by which youths can prevent infection is only one part of such an approach. Coping skills training, case management, and ongoing support are other important parts. Pederson warned that gay, lesbian, and bisexual adolescents infected with HIV must not be treated in the same way as adults given that they often lack the skills and experience needed to fight existing "institutional, sociocultural, logistical, and financial barriers" (p. 145) to receive appropriate treatment. They are likely to become overwhelmed by the fragmented nature of services and the staggering amount of paperwork required to apply for services. Even more problematic, many agencies deny their services to adolescents. Political action is needed to pressure these systems to be more responsive to gay, lesbian, and bisexual adolescents.

Cranston (1991) advocated using a self-empowerment model in HIV prevention efforts among lesbian, gay, and bisexual adolescents. In this model, efforts are directed toward helping them create a sense of self-worth and a community of support. To implement the model, school-based programs should provide education not only about HIV but also about lesbian, gay, and bisexual issues. Multiservice agencies working with these adolescents should develop programs that target those at highest risk. Finally, youth self-help groups should work on building a sense of personal and collective empowerment among these adolescents.

During the past 15 years, several *service organizations* were developed specifically to help bisexual, gay, and lesbian adolescents. Some of the best known of these organizations are the Hetrick-Martin Institute in New York City; Gay and Lesbian Adolescent Social Services in Los Angeles; the Sexual Minority Youth Assistance League in Washington, D.C.; and the Boston Alliance of Gay and Lesbian Youth. Although these organizations had a variety of origins, some as youth-led support groups and others as adult- or professionally led services, they all eventually developed a similar set of services for youths. These services include public and professional education, youth support groups, case management, counseling, and, in some cases, housing (Greeley, 1994). Another well-known program, the Horizons Youth Group, a program of Chicago's Horizons Community Services, is described in detail by Herdt and Boxer (1993).

Some of the programs targeted for lesbian, gay, and bisexual youths, less publicized in the Southwest, are the Teen Project, a collaborative program of the Tarrant County (Texas) Lesbian/Gay Alliance and the local PFLAG chapter; OutYouth Dallas, a special interest group of the Dallas Gay and Lesbian Alliance; and OutYouth Austin (Texas). The Teen Project provides services to gay, lesbian, and bisexual adolescents in the Fort Worth areas through a telephone support line and weekly support groups run by trained adult volunteers. OutYouth Dallas provides education and social contact for lesbians, gay, and bisexual youths age 17-25 through a weekly discussion meeting and other special activities, including an annual alternative prom. OutYouth Dallas is youth-run, although it receives financial support and occasional advice from its parent organization. OutYouth Austin provides support groups, social and educational activities, community education, telephone counseling and referrals, and a drop-in center. Both adult and youth volunteers provide these services.

◆ Young Adults on Campus

This section examines developmental issues and mental health concerns of lesbian, gay, and bisexual young adults during their college years. Young adults may move away from home for the first time to go to college and begin to make more independent decisions. Their links with peers continue to supplement and replace family ties. They may also establish their identities as gay men, lesbians, or bisexuals while at college.

Developmental Issues

The developmental processes for bisexual, gay, and lesbian college youths include, among others, individuation and establishing intimate, social, and community links. Accomplishment of these tasks, however, is complicated by a social context characterized by widespread negative attitudes toward them, harassment of them, and discrimination against them (see Chapter 2).

Individuation. Young lesbian, gay, and bisexual adults, as other young adults, are typically separating from their families of origin or moving toward further individuation of themselves. This process involves questioning parental values, including ones that denigrate a same-gender or bisexual sexual orientation. If gay, lesbian, and bisexual young adults avoid this questioning and redefinition of their relationships with parents, they may not complete the task of developing their own identities. This leaves parents with too much influence, which may interfere with their child becoming a separate adult and moving further ahead in establishing a same-gender or bisexual sexual identity (Browning, 1987; Slater, 1993).

At college, lesbian, gay, and bisexual young adults who have not already come out may feel greater freedom to acknowledge their same-gender feelings, distanced from the close watch of family and high school friends (D'Augelli & Rose, 1990). If they are just beginning to acknowledge their same-gender sexual and romantic attractions, they are likely to be intensely interested in learning all they can regarding gay, bisexual, and lesbian sexual orientations (D'Augelli, 1992). Lopez and Chism (1993) found some lesbian and gay students who were so consumed with identity issues that they spent most of their time reading literature about other lesbians and gay men. It was difficult for them to concentrate on schoolwork, and their grades deteriorated. Some even dropped out of school. Almost all who remained, however, eventually resumed their previous level of academic performance.

At this crucial time of exploration, lesbian, gay, and bisexual students need acknowledgment and affirmation. Unfortunately, on campuses where they experience considerable heterosexism, their identities may incorporate negative characteristics ranging from nonacceptance to self-hatred (Slater, 1993). In addition, much of the literature they read at college does not affirm their lives. Bisexual, gay, and lesbian issues are not likely to be discussed in courses, which results in further devaluation of their identities. An exception is a course on lesbian, gay, and bisexual persons developed and taught by D'Augelli (1992). The course provides the kind of affirmative information young lesbian, gay, and bisexual youths need for a more positive young adulthood. A central assumption of the course is the richness and exceptionality of gay, lesbian, and bisexual lives. According to J. Martin (1995), faculty who are themselves gay, lesbian, or bisexual hold a special responsibility to role-model openness about their sexual orientation, to provide mentoring, and to exert leadership in assuring the availability of resources for these students. By contrast, the existence of closeted lesbian, gay, or bisexual

faculty members may cause students to perceive that it is unsafe for them to be open about their sexuality or to discuss lesbian, gay, and bisexual issues.

Establishing intimate linkups, social networks, and community. According to Erikson (1985), a central task of young adulthood is to develop intimacy with another person. Sohier (1985-1986) reported that most lesbians and gay men establish their first serious linkup during their early twenties, although Savin-Williams (1990b) reported that this can also happen in adolescence. D'Augelli (1991) found that half of their sample of gay male college students were in their first same-gender linkup during their college years.

Another developmental task during young adulthood is to expand one's social networks and community with supportive members. Bisexual, gay, and lesbian college students may establish a new and growing network of individuals to whom they disclose (D'Augelli & Rose, 1990). This network is likely to become increasingly important to them. In D'Augelli's (1991) study of gay male college students, 54% identified gay friends as being the most important people in their lives. By contrast, only 15% considered their families to be most important. Unfortunately, the college campus may provide serious barriers to the establishment of supportive networks. While supportive peer groups are usually available to heterosexual college students, lesbian, gay, or bisexual students may find them more difficult to locate (Browning, 1987), even if they are open about their sexual orientation. Increasingly, however, either formal or informal gay, lesbian, and bisexual helping systems exist on college and university campuses such as student organizations and support or discussion groups. Some universities and colleges provide funding for these groups, often through the student government (Sherrill & Hardesty, 1994). In D'Augelli's (1991) study, 54% of surveyed gay male college students reported participation in the university's lesbian, gay, and bisexual student organization. Of these, 40% indicated that most of their social activities were related to this organization. Many of these students were also involved with the local gay community. These were settings in which close friendships with other gay men developed. Lesbian, gay, and bisexual college students who choose to remain hidden probably will not seek out the support that is available, which could result in feelings of isolation (Slater, 1993; Wall & Evans, 1991).

One problem that students encounter in seeking support is the fragile nature of many campus groups. For example, although numerous colleges and universities in the Dallas-Ft. Worth area sponsor interest groups for bisexual, gay, and lesbian students, most of the groups do not remain active for more than a year or two at a time. When student leaders graduate or become too busy with other responsibilities, such groups fold until new leaders emerge. The active participation of a faculty adviser may help to reduce these fluctuations and add continuity as student leaders come and go. Official campus offices that provide specialized services for lesbian, gay, and bisexual students are also helpful in this regard. For example, the Lesbian, Gay, and Bisexual Programs Office at the University of Michigan, in existence for more than 20 years, provides support groups, mentorship, social activities, educational events, and other services. The existence of paid staff assures that support will be available to gay, lesbian, and bisexual students on a continuous basis, and it shows that the institution has a commitment to them.

Another way that universities and colleges show their commitment to bisexual, gay, and lesbian students is by having a non-discrimination policy that includes sexual orientation. Without such policies, gay or lesbian students have no recourse if they encounter discriminatory treatment from faculty, staff, or other students (see Chapter 2).

Mental Health Concerns of Lesbian, Gay, and Bisexual Students

Few research projects have examined the mental health concerns of gay, lesbian, and bisexual youths in college (D'Augelli, 1993). In D'Augelli's (1991) study of gay male college students, 77% indicated that anxiety was a problem for them, and 63% reported that depression was a problem. In addition, many participants indicated other problems that were "very" or "extremely" troublesome for them. Three-quarters of the participants included "ending a close linkup" on this list. More than two-thirds (68%) included "disclosing to parents," and 56% included "worrying about AIDS." Other serious problems reported by Eldridge and Barnett (1991) included internalized oppression and thoughts of suicide.

◆ Summary

Like their heterosexual counterparts, the majority of gay, lesbian, and bisexual adolescents successfully negotiate the challenges of this sometimes turbulent life stage. Discrimination and isolation, however, lead some of these adolescents to the devastating consequences of homelessness, prostitution, violence, chemical abuse, serious illness, or suicide. Lesbian, gay, and bisexual adolescents need peer and adult support, which a variety of organizations are now providing in many American cities.

The developmental process of bisexual, gay, and lesbian young adults on college campuses is also complicated by discrimination and harassment. The only relief for students if harassed or discriminated against is a nondiscrimination policy that includes sexual orientation. Some colleges and universities provide specialized programs and services for lesbian, gay, and bisexual students. On a few campuses, official offices coordinate these activities.

9

MIDDLE
ADULTHOOD

◆ ADULTS OFTEN WANT TO KNOW: "When will I be middle aged?" Although the age boundaries are approximately between 30 and 64, the midlife period is not clearly definable by age (Bumpass & Aquilino, 1995). Neither are there clear-cut stages during this life period (Clausen, 1986). Given these ambiguities, there is a developing literature on the themes and issues of midlife. For lesbians and gay men, however, this literature is only in a preliminary stage of development; with the exception of the impact of HIV/AIDS, it has yet to begin for bisexual women and men. This chapter reviews the available literature on midlife lesbians and gay men across various areas.

A fact that stands out about lesbians and gay men now at midlife is that they are charting a new path. They are the first generation of this population to reach this period of life since the arrival of the modern gay liberation movement. Some of them were active participants in the social protests associated with the 1969 Stonewall Rebellion. Although many gay men and lesbians benefitted from some progress in civil rights protections and increased social acceptance, they still contend with severe stigma and discrimination, as did previous generations. In addition, as a result of the HIV disease, now in its second decade, most gay and bisexual men in midlife experience the premature illness and deaths of friends and partners their age or younger or their own illness and impending death (see Chapter 3). Because most individuals diagnosed with HIV are men, they experience the greatest impact. In this respect, the psychology of middle age for lesbians and bisexual women is markedly different than it is for many gay and bisexual men (Kimmel & Sang, 1995).

◆ Lesbians at Midlife

The most extensive data to date on midlife lesbians came from from a small set of reports primarily produced in the last decade. The samples were composed mainly of White, professional, and middle- to upper-middle-class women. For this particular group of lesbians, changes at midlife are mostly positive.

Positive Changes at Midlife

Midlife for women in the general population is not without its difficulties. On the other hand, particularly for those with an economic advantages and college educations, new and exciting opportunities, unexpected pleasures, and greater self-esteem and self-acceptance are characteristic of this period (Baruch & Brooks-Gunn, 1984; Haan, 1989; Hunter & Sundel, 1989, 1994; Mitchell & Helson, 1990). Mitchell and Helson (1990) went as far as to proclaim midlife, more specifically the early fifties, as the prime time of life for women.

Although there can be financial worries and time pressures, the midlife period also appears to be a prime time for lesbians in the samples studied. For example, Fertitta (1984) found positive changes such as gaining perspective and wisdom and increased self-acceptance. Sang (1991) found that lesbians were still growing and developing in this period of life. Based on effective coping

with the past, they felt confidence and optimism about the future. Sang (1990, 1991, 1992, 1993) identified nine themes that reflect positive changes at midlife for many lesbians in her sample. These include (a) more comfort with who one is and more self-acceptance; (b) wanting more play and fun instead of pushing oneself as much for career or work achievements; (c) more creative expression such as writing and art; (d) self-discovery or increased self-knowledge and, as a consequence, letting go of things not working in one's life; (e) reconnection with previous interests and suppressed aspects of oneself; (f) change and refocus in areas such as jobs and interests; (g) more time for meaningful activities such as contributing to one's community; (h) greater self-confidence and self-direction; (i) balancing diverse aspects of one's life such as work, linkups, interests, and community; and (j) celebration of midlife with other lesbians and feminists.

Meaning in Life and Philosophies

In Sang's (1991) survey of midlife lesbians, part of the focus was on meaning and philosophies. What gives lesbians between the ages of 40 and 59 meaning in their lives, or how do they deal with the existential issues of midlife? The women in Sang's (1991) sample attained meaning and satisfaction through the following sources: intimate relationships (47%), friendships (38%), work (37%), spirituality (20%), children (13%), hobbies and interests (10%), and personal growth and development (9%). Many of these women also identified their own personal sources of meaning such as "making a difference in the world" or "being your own person" (p. 210). Meaning was not attained just through work, primary linkups, or other interests. These activities were embedded in a larger philosophical framework that for many was connected to a spiritual quest.

Each respondent in Sang's (1991) sample was asked to describe her unique life philosophy or worldview. Responses of each woman fell into two or more of the following categories: (a) maintaining friendships, accepting people as they are, and making a difference for people (63%); (b) political involvement, promotion of peace, justice, and equality, and respect for the planet (55%); (c) being true to oneself, making the most of each day (55%); (d) appreciation of life and its offerings of joy, pleasure, and humor (28%); and (e) taking responsibility for one's life, belief in being in control of what happens to oneself (25%).

Life Areas

Education and Work

In 1991, Bradford and Ryan reported on the health concerns of midlife lesbians age 40 to 60. The data were drawn from the 1984-1985 National Lesbian Health Care Survey. Some of the data addressed education and work. Part of Sang's (1990, 1991) survey of midlife lesbians also addressed work. The findings of these researchers provide most of what is known about midlife lesbians' education, career expectations, work, and income.

Education. Many midlife lesbians are well educated. Among the Bradford and Ryan (1991) respondents, for example, 24% graduated from college or completed some graduate work, and 48% completed a graduate or professional degree. Only 15% had no college education.

Early career expectations. More than half of Sang's (1990, 1991) sample (62%) experienced a variety of interests and career possibilities as adolescents. The younger they were when they identified as lesbians, the earlier they were likely to have had expecta-

tions for a career. For example, those who identified as lesbians in their teens and twenties were more likely (79%) to indicate that they had career expectations compared with those who identified as lesbians in their thirties (59%) or over age 40 (44%). Those who came out in their teens and before age 40 were also more likely (74%) to project themselves in nontraditional careers such as scientist, doctor, or business owner than those who came out after age 40 (44%). Women who did not identify as lesbian until midlife expected to attain traditional careers such as nursing and teaching (Sang, 1990).

Actual careers. Sang (1990) pointed out that although just a little more than half of the lesbians in her sample expected to have careers as adults, almost all were in careers. More than three-fourths are professionals; the others were in business or held working-class jobs. For half of the sample, careers and jobs were nontraditional for women, such as dean, financial analyst, and truck driver. Bradford and Ryan (1991) found that almost all of their lesbian respondents were employed. In comparison with employed women in this age group in the general population, midlife lesbians are four times as likely to work in professional or technical fields. They are more likely to be employed as managers or administrators and less likely to be clerical workers. Other occupations of lesbians include craftswomen, service workers, and skilled and unskilled laborers.

Family Links

From current data, it is not known whether midlife linkups differ from those at younger ages, how being in a primary linkup affects life satisfaction, or, if single, why and whether this is a satisfactory state or not (Kimmel & Sang, 1995). It is known that linkup patterns for midlife lesbians are varied.

Partners. Many lesbians want partners and a sexual life during midlife. Bradford and Ryan (1991) found that 74% of their sample were either involved in a primary linkup or dating someone. Few (19%) described themselves as single and uninvolved. While a primary linkup is important, it also creates stress. Midlife is a busy time in life so that finding enough time for a partner, friends, and work is difficult. Trying to balance these areas is likely to be harder when children are also part of the equation. Another stressor is termination of a partnership. As observed by Kirkpatrick (1989), a psychotherapist, due to the feeling that time is running out, a woman may leave a primary lesbian linkup in midlife for the chance of greater fulfillment or excitement.

Friends. Lesbian friends around the same age are one of the most prominent sources of support for midlife lesbians (Bradford & Ryan, 1991; Fertitta, 1984; Sang, 1991). Raphael and Robinson (1984) surveyed 20 lesbians over age 50 and found that strong friendship ties provided support and correlated positively with self-esteem. Single midlife lesbians had more lesbian friends than coupled midlife lesbians. Most of the close women friends of the Bradford and Ryan (1991) respondents were also lesbians (64%) and of the same ethnicity (58%). Half of the sample also had close male friends who were all or mostly all gay. A quarter of the sample (25%) had close male friends who were not gay.

Midlife lesbians are closer to and more comfortable with their lesbian friends than their families of origin, especially if they are not open with their families (Bradford & Ryan, 1991). Fertitta (1984) found in her sample of midlife lesbians that four-fifths (81%) were more likely to receive support from friends, ex-lovers, and lovers than from their families of origin. They retained a close

link with ex-lovers, twice as much as did heterosexual women (50% versus 25%).

Mothers and children. Many lesbians have or want children (e.g., Bradford & Ryan, 1991; Kirkpatrick, 1988, 1989; Rothschild, 1991; Sang, 1992) (see Chapter 7). One-third of the Bradford and Ryan sample had children. For those who are mothers at midlife, their children are probably in adolescence. In addition to the issues common to all parents at this time, lesbian mothers often experience the additional fear that their children may become antagonistic and rejecting because of their sexual orientation. They typically conform to peer attitudes that may be hostile to a same-gender sexual orientation or they may fear embarrassment and ridicule (Kirkpatrick, 1989). Relationships with adolescent children can also be difficult for mothers just coming out as lesbians at midlife (e.g., Sang, 1992). Children leaving the home, however, does not appear to provoke a momentous change for midlife lesbian mothers. As Kimmel and Sang (1995) speculated, one reason for this could be that their identities are often derived from sources other than motherhood, such as work.

Adult daughters and mothers. Warshow (1991) reported that during midlife, negative or positive feelings about one's sexual orientation affect the mother-daughter linkup. She studied 20 lesbians between the ages of 40 and 57 in New York City. All were middle class and well educated, and all but two where White. For 15% of the respondents, the mother-daughter linkup never varied from being positive. Some daughters (10%) idealized their mothers and experienced no conscious negative feelings about them at any time. Other mother-daughter pairs exhibited negative feelings. How the daughters felt about their own sexual orientation affected whether the linkup eventually changed from negative to positive. This change occurred for 70% of the daughters with the most positive feelings about their own sexual orientation. For 80% of other daughters with the most negative feelings about their sexual orientation, the negative status of the mother-daughter linkup continued. Warshow speculated that a prerequisite for a more positive linkup between most daughters and their mothers was for the daughters to reach positive self-acceptance of their own sexual orientation.

Caregiver for elderly parents. A role for many midlife women is caregiver to elderly parents. Although the caregiving literature is extensive, hardly any of it focuses on midlife lesbians. Daughters, however, and unmarried daughters particularly, are usually the "chosen" caregivers after marital partners (Brody, 1990). Midlife lesbians, then, are likely often drafted into this role (Kimmel & Sang, 1995). Still, the actual proportion of this population who are in a caregiving role for parents is unknown.

Community Links

General community links. Fertitta (1984) found that the links of midlife lesbians to the lesbian community were important for self-acceptance and a positive lesbian identity. Almost all of the 68 participants in the study were involved in the lesbian community. Other studies, however, did not find this extent of community connection. For example, in Woodman's (1987) sample of lesbian and gay organizations, fewer midlife lesbians (34%) affiliated with community resources. Often these women felt in a bind between fearing disclosure of their sexual orientation and social isolation from others who might be potential friends.

Few midlife lesbians in the Bradford and Ryan (1991) study participated in either neighborhood or community activities except those specifically for lesbians and gay men or for women. A majority (52%) attended events for lesbians only at least once or twice a month. The most frequent activities were supportive, social, or lesbian and gay rights oriented. Those who participated in lesbian and gay rights organizations (37%) were more likely to be open about their sexual orientation. One-third of the sample also participated regularly in some type of social group. Social time was mostly spent with other lesbians or in mixed lesbian and gay activities. Close to the same proportion attends women's support groups or women's rights groups.

Involvement with religious institutions. Whereas almost everyone (95%) attended a religious institution while growing up, two-thirds of lesbians were no longer affiliated with any such institution in midlife. Half of those who currently attended a religious institution reported that their attendance was rare. The religious institutions of childhood were for the most part not kept. This was more often true for Protestant and Catholic than Jewish women. Affiliation with more liberal religious institutions (e.g., Unity, Unitarian, Quaker, Metropolitan) was five times greater during midlife than in childhood (Bradford & Ryan, 1991).

Physical Health Issues

Most midlife lesbians in the Bradford and Ryan (1991) survey study reported few if any complaints about physical health. Four out of five respondents perceived their health to be excellent or good. Sang (1993) reported, however, that a new health concern for some midlife lesbians (35%) was maintaining good health. This was not always easy, as

Bradford and Ryan (1991) acknowledged. Good health is "hard-won and accomplished with the support and help of counselors and other gay people, rather than through the social institutions which provide safety and structure for heterosexual individuals and couples" (p. 163).

Menopause. Concerns of all midlife women include menopause and sexuality following menopause. For many years, menopause and midlife were thought of as synonymous for women. Any emotional upset in a woman in her forties or fifties was typically seen to result from menopause (Clausen, 1986). Updated research, however, strongly counters the long distorted history of menopause. For most women, it results in few psychological or physical changes or problems (Schaie & Willis, 1991). The situation for midlife lesbians is no different.

Cole and Rothblum (1990, 1991) accomplished the first empirical survey of lesbian women at menopause. The sample, which included 41 women (ages 43 to 68) was non-clinical and White. These women were asked about positive changes in their lives since menopause. In addition to no menstruation, they reported

> increased sex, increased orgasms, greater self-acceptance, coming out as a lesbian, feeling more free, positive changes in body fat distribution, viewing life more seriously and wondering about the security of the future, professional security, being less driven, relishing their maturity, wonderful sex, financial security, nothing to prove, kids leaving home. (Cole & Rothblum, 1991, p. 190)

Only 22% of the sample indicated that they experienced no positive changes following menopause.

Sexuality after menopause. In the general population of midlife women, the physi-ological changes accompanying menopause do not directly affect sexual capacity or interest. Despite popular myths to the contrary, women's sexual capacity and interest continue long beyond menopause (Starr & Weiner, 1981). Close to half (46%) of Cole and Rothblum's (1991) lesbian respondents reported no change in the frequency of sexual activity, and the majority (76%) reported no sexual problems. Changes such as taking longer to reach orgasm were not viewed as problems. For more than half of the respondents (56%), there was no change in orgasms while for 20% they were less frequent and for 22% more frequent.

About three-quarters of the lesbian respondents studied by Cole and Rothblum (1991) spoke of their sex lives as being as good as or better than ever. They defined their sexual activity in terms of enjoyment, pleasure, and satisfaction. In Sang's (1993) study, 75 women answered a question specific to sex and menopause. Half (50%) indicated that their sex life was better than before. It was more open and exciting because of better communication and more emphasis on behaviors other than those leading to the pressured goal of orgasms, such as touching.

Not all midlife lesbians experience positive results in their sex lives. A decrease in the perceived quality of sex was reported by 29% of the Cole and Rothblum (1991) sample. Reported reasons included changes in physiology (orgasms not as intense), possible negative consequences of hormone replacement, losses such as not feeling passionate, and feeling guilty about situations such as lack of sexual desire when the partner wanted sexual activity.

The Worries of Midlife

The most common worry for midlife lesbians in the Bradford and Ryan (1991) survey was money (55%). Even with advanced education and professional/technical jobs, their earned income did not reflect their preparation or positions. Economic uncertainty therefore was not uncommon. More than a quarter (28%) of Sang's (1990, 1991) sample also indicated that financial security was a new issue at midlife. More than half (55%) of the respondents experienced current distress because of financial problems; they were at least five times more likely than other women their age to experience money problems.

Other worries experienced by about one-fourth of the Sang (1990, 1991) sample included problems with jobs or school, too much responsibility at work, and lovers. Worry was experienced by smaller percentages of women regarding family members and children, job dissatisfaction, illness and/or death, and discovery of one's sexual orientation. Bradford and Ryan (1991) found that for more than half of their sample, worries were common and often affected daily lives. About a quarter (24%) of the respondents were often so worried or nervous that they could not accomplish routine tasks; this happened sometimes for 40% of the sample.

Coming Out in Midlife

Midlife lesbians may be further along in the development of a strong sense of self than are heterosexual women because they are used to fighting to be themselves and not conforming to social expectations about sexual orientation. In midlife, then, they are skilled in standing up against opposition for what they believe and who they are (Sang, 1991). Consequently, developing as independent individuals with an identity separate from others is not usually a central issue for midlife lesbians (Fertitta, 1984). On the other hand, identity issues will be of considerably more concern to women who first self-identify as lesbian in midlife. A small set of studies focused on the significant life event of women coming out at midlife. Many

women who experienced this identity change at midlife had been or were currently heterosexually married.

Married Life

Sang (1991) reported that the majority of lesbians in her sample who came out in midlife were at some time heterosexually married (57%), and 44% had one or more children. In Bradford and Ryan's (1991) survey sample of midlife lesbians, 34% had been heterosexually married in the past, and 4% were still married. Findings reported by Charbonneau and Lander (1991) and Lander and Charbonneau (1990) have provided the most data so far on previously or currently married women who came out as lesbians in midlife. The sample included 30 women who ranged in age from 35 to 55 and were of varied ethnic, religious, and social class backgrounds. All of the women grew up accepting the traditional definitions of the "proper" goals for women: marriage and motherhood (see Chapter 5). With one exception (engaged three times, six children), all were married from 1 to 32 years. More than half remained in long-term marriages of 10 years or longer. At the time of the survey, none of the women was with her husband. All but six were mothers; four of the six who had no children had tried but could not conceive. While several women had large families of four to six children, most had two or three children (Charbonneau & Lander (1991).

Prior Indicators of Same-Gender Attraction or Unexpected Attraction at Midlife?

In Sang's (1991, 1992) sample, some respondents experienced same-gender attraction earlier in life but did not self-identify as lesbian until midlife. They suppressed their same-gender attractions and returned to or did not venture from pursuing a heterosexual partnership. Ponse (1980) found that some married women had no same-gender sexual experience but identified as lesbians because of fantasies. Kirkpatrick (1989) reported that for some women, suppressed same-gender desires and identification were revived during midlife.

Other women reported no indicators of same-gender attractions before midlife (Sang, 1991). Lander and Charbonneau (1990) emphasized that the women in their sample of midlife lesbians did not know of any attraction to other women in most of their prior adult lives. With few exceptions, they never considered it a possibility. They were committed heterosexual wives and mothers and never questioned their heterosexuality. Those who fell in love with a woman or experienced sexual attraction to a woman in midlife were surprised. Even more surprising was the willingness to embrace the label "lesbian." Charbonneau and Lander (1991) reported that some of the women felt they were always lesbians but did not know it. When same-gender sexual experiences happened in midlife, they felt immediately satisfying and natural.

Precipitators of Self-Identification as Lesbian

Twenty of the women studied by Charbonneau and Lander (1991) participated in previous political work, which ranged from mainstream activities such as voter registration drives to more radical activities such as antiwar demonstrations. The political context perhaps prepared these women for nonconformity in their sexual orientation in midlife. Most of the women, however, recalled more specific events that precipitated the transition to a lesbian identity. The shift was so dramatic that the events leading up to it were often remembered with dates and details. Precipitating events identified by Charbonneau and Lander are listed in Box 9.1.

No single event was viewed as the precipitator of the shift in identity. Instead, a combination of events occurred that provided a context for change. Whatever the unique combination of events that was important in each woman's transition to a lesbian identification, however, it was essential that she also reconceptualize negative stereotypes about lesbians. For some women, reconceptualization was a slow process but for others it happened as a result of a single encounter (Charbonneau & Lander, 1991).

The Upside of Coming Out at Midlife

Women who had lived a long time identified as heterosexual experienced a radical change and redirection when they reidentified as lesbian in midlife. Sometimes the consequences were profound. For example, some women felt "for the first time I am me" (Charbonneau & Lander, 1991). Others, after living with men most of their adult lives, described the intimacy with other women as at a depth they never before experienced or even imagined (McGrath, 1990). Sexual awakening with a woman usually led to redefinition not only of sexual orientation but also of gender role. Behavior that before was viewed as masculine and unacceptable for women was reinterpreted as acceptable for women too. Comfort developed with a combination of roles previously defined as male or female.

The Downside or Costs of Coming Out and Disclosure at Midlife

In addition to the upside of coming out at midlife, there is also usually a downside. Two basic kinds of costs can result from self-identifying as lesbian in midlife. First, there are the costs of no longer being in a primary linkup with a man: (a) giving up privileges associated with a male partner; (b)

◆◆◆

Box 9.1. Precipitating Events Leading to Identity Change

1. For some women, a precipitator was a *parent's death or serious illness or a serious illness of one's own* that evoked a sudden realization of the transience of life. This led to a review of one's life and reassessment of how to live the rest of it, including movement to a lesbian identification and same-gender partner.

2. Half of the women actively participated in *the women's movement,* which created a climate for asking questions and looking at themselves from a different perspective. More specific precipitating events included consciousness-raising groups, reading feminist texts, women's concerts, and all-women's weekends.

3. Many women cited *divorce* or the moment they *first thought of leaving the marriage* as turning points.

4. A *time apart from men* provided an opportunity in which at least half of the women reassessed their lives. In this independent state, they planned fulfillment of their own needs. A break from old patterns allowed them to realize that they could be happy and productive without men in their lives.

5. Many women began self-examination of their sexual orientation because of *changes in their daily lives.* These changes included moving, entering school, leaving or entering a job, joining a consciousness-raising group, and entering therapy. ◆

---

giving up fantasies of being cared for by a man; (c) losing the social support associated with a male partner; (d) relating to others on the basis of one's own merit alone; (e) linking up with women, which in most social contexts does not gain the respect and status that links with men do; and (f) harsh criticism by men intolerant of nonconforming gender role behavior (Cummerton, 1982; de Monteflores & Schultz, 1978; Groves & Ventura, 1983; Kirkpatrick, 1989).

The second basic cost involves negative reactions to disclosure as a lesbian. Although disclosure is important in connecting with lesbians and gay men and finding a partner, many of the respondents in the Bradford and Ryan (1991) survey also experienced negative reactions. A large majority of these women experienced verbal harassment such as screaming and painful comments. Many others experienced losses such as canceled invitations to family occasions (Lander &

Charbonneau, 1990). Women who felt that a lesbian sexual orientation was "natural" felt more attacked or threatened by these reactions than those who felt that they chose to self-identify as lesbian. Women in the latter group ignored negative reactions more easily and were willing to drop former acquaintances and others if their sexual orientation was not acceptable to them. Even for these women, however, the negative reactions were sobering because they too had been previously unaware of the intensity of prejudice against a same-gender sexual orientation (Lander & Charbonneau, 1990). No doubt, these kinds of reactions led many of these women to seldom or never disclose their sexual orientation. Bradford and Ryan found that many midlife lesbians were not open about their sexual orientation with most groups of people including family members, heterosexual friends, and work associates.

Counseling Issues

Although financial concerns are the most worrisome, midlife lesbians more often seek mental health services for emotional distress and relationship problems. The distress associated with disclosure is also significantly associated with long-term use of mental health counseling by midlife lesbians. Other reasons counseling is sought include feeling sad or depressed (62%), problems with lovers (62%), problems with family members (39%), feeling anxious or afraid (36%), personal growth (32%), problems with sexual orientation (27%), loneliness (24%), alcohol and drug problems (20%), work problems (20%), problems with friends (10%), and problems with racism (4%) (Bradford & Ryan, 1991).

Other issues midlife women lesbians may want to address in counseling are listed in Box 9.2. Some of the issues relate to midlife lesbians in general; others focus more specifically on women just coming out in midlife.

◆ Gay Men at Midlife

Kimmel and Sang (1995) discussed two basic patterns of adult development for gay men. In the first pattern, men do not come out as gay until midlife and may welcome a new search for identity and sexuality in this life period. Prior to this time, however, there can be a wrenching struggle, accompanied by guilt, secrecy, and traumatic crisis in the family or heterosexual marriage. In the second pattern, men recognized their desire for same-gender identification early in life and began to follow this path at that time. As noted earlier, not much else is known about midlife gay men. The exception is the HIV/AIDS literature, which is extensive. The limited knowledge in various life areas is addressed here as well as the impact of HIV.

The samples of midlife gay men are also basically White, affluent, and well educated.

Life Areas

Kimmel and Sang (1995) identified various issues pertinent to midlife gay men. These include education, income, and work; intimate linkups and social networks; sexuality; and the "midlife crisis."

Education, Income, and Work

Most studies on gay men find high levels of education and income compared with the general population of men (Adams & Kimmel, 1991; R. Berger, 1996; Lee, 1987; Quam & Whitford, 1992). In comparison with heterosexual men (e.g., Vaillant, 1977), however, the career ladder often differs for gay men because of discrimination due to sexual orientation or continual efforts to hide their sexual orientation (see Chapters 2 and 5). In addition, some midlife gay men may not pursue higher-level work positions. Instead, they try to balance career and personal linkups. In other words, the desire to maintain satisfaction in their love linkups plays a role in their career decisions (Kimmel & Sang, 1995).

*Intimate Linkups and
Social Networks*

Little is known specifically about middle-aged gay couples. A few studies exist that note the importance of friendship networks for aging gay men (Friend, 1987). As discussed below, however, one of the impacts of HIV/AIDS is that many midlife men lose friends and partners to this disease. Midlife gay men's social networks in some parts of the country are depleted because of losses to AIDS. On the other hand, AIDS-related organizations provide significant social networks for gay men, and many men who are

◆◆◆

Box 9.2. Counseling Issues of Midlife Lesbians

▶ New feelings toward another woman occurring prior to counseling or discovered in the course of counseling are often addressed. Midlife lesbians may need assistance in conceptualizing *coming out* as a life transition, which, as any transition, can be stressful and painful. Clarifying the challenges ahead may facilitate a more positive transition (Bridges & Croteau, 1994).

▶ If one's prior self-identification included heterosexual marriage, making the shift to a positive *self-identification as lesbian* can be difficult, as found in 53% of Wyers's (1987) sample of formerly married lesbians. It is important to provide once-married midlife lesbians accurate and affirming views of lesbians to counter previous negative images. The primary means is positive contact with other lesbians. Other means include affirmative books, support groups, and the therapeutic technique of cognitive restructuring (Bridges & Croteau, 1994).

▶ Counselors may need to assist once-married midlife lesbians to adapt to potential differences between heterosexual marriage with males and linking up with *a lesbian partner* (Bridges & Croteau, 1994). Several differences identified by Bridges and Croteau include lack of social validation for lesbian couples, perhaps more difficulty negotiating the balance between autonomy and connection, and differences in sexual practices such as more emphasis on kissing and hugging versus goal-oriented orgasms.

▶ *Children* of midlife lesbians may be negatively affected by their parent's divergence from the norm in sexual orientation (Sang, 1992). They also go through a coming out process with their friends, and they may also fear being stigmatized or rejected (Rothschild, 1991). A support group for children in similar situations can be useful.

▶ Although there are now many activities and institutions available, particularly in urban lesbian and gay communities, not all midlife and older lesbians take advantage of these opportunities for *social support* (Adelman, 1988; Kehoe, 1986; Raphael & Robinson, 1984). It is important to determine the reasons for low social support and look for alterations in ways of obtaining social support (Sang, 1992).

▶ In Sang's (1991) study of lesbian professionals, one of the major issues identified was the effort to *balance* various aspects of their lives—work, linkups, interests, spirituality, community, child care, and aging parents. Prioritizing and time management strategies may be helpful here.

▶ *Economic concerns* can also be an issue in counseling (Hayes, 1991). Special retirement planning is pertinent for the many midlife lesbians who are self-supporting (Sang, 1992). Once-married midlife lesbians may need services related to financial security similar to what any newly divorced woman may need (Bridges & Croteau, 1994). Knowledge about legal protection of resources is also essential. ◆

---

at midlife participate in them. Some of these men, in fact, provided leadership in the creation of services for gay men with HIV/AIDS (Kimmel & Sang, 1995).

Sexuality

Similar to studies on lesbians, Pope and Schulz (1990) found in a study of 87 gay men age 40-70 that most of them were reportedly sexually active (91%) and that there was no change in sexual enjoyment (69%). Increased sexual enjoyment was reported by 13%. Similar findings occurred in studies by Gray and Dressel (1985) and Berger (1996). Whereas Gray and Dressel (1985) found no significant difference by age group in the number of partners or amount of sexual activities, an earlier study by Weinberg and Williams (1974) found that gay men age 45 and older reported less sexual activity than younger respondents. Blumstein and Schwartz (1983) found that a decrease in sexual activity for both gay men and lesbians in couples was associated more with length of the linkup than age alone.

Midlife Crisis

Gay and heterosexual men may experience many of the same concerns that are often claimed to be associated with a midlife crisis. The classic midlife crisis symptoms include a sense of despair and frenzied pursuit of youthful ideals (S. Hunter, 1994; M. Stein, 1983). Kimmel and Sang (1995) argued that gay men may experience a midlife crisis because of their

> concerns about issues of mortality and a search for meaning and wholeness in life within a heterosexist society, fear of physical illness, occupation-related stress or being passed over for a promotion, family issues including care of aging parents, concerns about one's family lineage, and a feeling that one has lost some masculine prowess with advancing age. (p. 207)

Although the issues just cited are not unlike the issues that heterosexual men may confront, there are additional issues that

evolve from a gay identity (Linde, 1994). For example, developmental theories (e.g., Levinson, Darrow, Klein, Levinson, & McKee, 1978) indicate that heterosexual men spend time on finding a solid place in the world and fathering children. This conception, however, may need modification for gay men because their livelihood often depends on a successful pretense of being heterosexual (see Chapter 5). Also, if they desire to nurture children, they are often impeded by prejudice in the heterosexual community, the schools, and the legal system (Hopcke, 1992) (see Chapter 7).

In addition, the timing of some events may differ for heterosexual and gay men. The shakeup and transformation of a settled life pattern that is expected in the midlife period may come much earlier for many gay men. The classic midlife crisis pattern, for example, is supposed to occur for men in the late thirties or early forties. In a comfortably settled life, they experience pressures to switch from their outward orientation to inward reflection and transformation. For gay men, this switch may occur during the coming out process and when coping with heterosexism (Hopcke, 1992). They may develop competence in dealing with crises because of this unique experience (Kimmel & Sang, 1995).

Whenever this transformation process occurs, it is a time when men assess life decisions and purpose in life and develop a more authentic sense of self (Hopcke, 1992). In addition, according to Linde (1994), midlife may present a crisis of identity and social interaction for gay men. Anxiety about loss of sexual attractiveness may precipitate a crisis, for example, because gay men often attach much of their self-esteem to their physical attractiveness. In midlife, they may feel increasingly rejected and abandoned because of their perceived lack of physical attractiveness. The task, then, is "to redefine their own self-worth. They may also have to learn new ways of relating to other men that are not based primarily on an ideal of youthful sexual attractiveness" (p. 35).

The Impact of HIV

The issues identified above are often stressful. More often they probably provoke a life transition rather than a tumultuous crisis (S. Hunter, 1994). The HIV disease, however, is nothing but a crisis; the most momentous impact on midlife for contemporary gay men is the HIV disease. Nothing discussed above is as powerful an issue for them as this one. Hopcke (1992) described the gay community as "saturated with the consciousness and experiences of mortality" (p. 106). It is not uncommon for an urban gay man to experience the deaths of dozens of men he knew during the last decade or so. And he probably knows twice as many who are living with the infection (Hopcke, 1992).

As coordinator of an AIDS prevention education program in San Francisco, Hopcke (1992) observed that it is more likely for a gay man to be infected with HIV in his twenties and thirties than in his forties or fifties. Nevertheless, the men at younger ages are dealing with midlife issues. This is the effect psychologically because HIV causes a confrontation with mortality. Hopcke stated,

A man in "the first half of life" who receives a positive result on the HIV-antibody test is confronted immediately and abruptly with the possibility that he is perhaps not in the first half of life at all, but has advanced, without his knowledge, far into the second. (p. 106)

This shows how the chronological view of midlife can be limited. Midlife issues can occur not because of a chronological age but because of a confrontation with mortality. In Hopcke's observation, HIV-positive men experience an "AIDS-induced midlife" crisis (p. 108). One's first experience with a close

friend or partner who receives a positive test result or is dying from AIDS can be another equally powerful confrontation with mortality. It forces a person to undertake the processes of reflecting on his life and making changes for the better long before traditional views of when this occurs.

The psychological crisis that results from the confrontation with mortality parallels the classic midlife pattern (see Chapter 3). HIV-infected gay men may, if they can modify the sense of crisis, allow time for reflection and thought. They can thereby examine with a new consciousness elements of their lives, before HIV, when life was projected to be longer. Now with a shortened time period, what do they want to retain or discard in their lives? When learning they are infected with HIV, some men may leave everything behind including their partners, jobs, residences, families, and support system. They may move to another location such as San Francisco because of its resources for HIV-infected individuals. "Faced with the possibility of their death, they have divested themselves of their previous life to create a new one based on an awareness of their mortality" (Hopcke, 1992, p. 106). As stated in the beginning of this chapter, compared with lesbians and bisexual women, midlife is qualitatively different for gay and bisexual men, whether they are infected with HIV, threatened by infection, or know friends who are infected and dying or already dead.

Counseling Issues

For midlife gay men who are not HIV-positive, their concerns may center on the increasing effects of ageism. This stigma related to age affects both lesbians and gay men as they get older (see Chapter 10). Kooden (1997) proposed that overcoming internalized ageism and developing positive attitudes about aging is the key to successful aging for midlife men. Accomplishment

---

Box 9.3. Prerequisite Tasks for Overcoming Ageism

▶ Resolve internalized homophobia or oppression.

▶ Seek out positive role models for successful aging with which to identify.

▶ Develop new age-appropriate standards of attractiveness.

▶ Develop a unique, personal value system.

▶ Develop high self-esteem, confidence, and comfortableness in saying what one is thinking and feeling.

▶ Develop positive interpersonal linkups with peers and others in one's family of choice, and value the individuality of the members.

▶ Excuse one's family of origin for what is negative in one's life.

▶ Visualize a positive future as a mature adult; work on life planning and goal setting.

▶ Experience joy in work and play, which may be merged.

▶ Develop a sense of taking charge of one's life.

▶ Accept physical aging.

▶ Take active steps in health care.

▶ Accept mortality and eventual death; develop a sense of spirituality or meaningfulness about life. ◆

---

of several tasks is necessary to reach this outcome and is pertinent to address when counseling this population. These tasks are listed in Box 9.3.

The tasks for overcoming ageism identified for midlife gay men are pertinent for midlife lesbians as well. Those who address both internalized ageism and internalized oppression because of their sexual orientation may live a more optimal life in older adulthood.

◆ **Summary**

Lesbians and gay men at midlife are a pioneer generation. Many are positive role models and are among the people who helped create the lesbian and gay community. This generation, although not fully open, is less closeted than older generations. It will significantly affect the patterns of aging for lesbians and gay men in the future. In addition to expanding the knowledge on lesbians and gay men at midlife, research on these populations can expand the current theories of midlife. The current midlife cohorts, particularly of gay and bisexual men, are also distinctly different because of HIV/AIDS.

10

OLDER

ADULTHOOD

◆ THE CURRENT COHORT of older lesbians and gay men (approximately age 65 and beyond) grew up in the pre-Stonewall era, or before the "gay liberation" movement of the late 1960s and the 1970s. There were no concepts such as "gay pride" (Christian & Keefe, 1997) or "out is in" (Wahler & Gabbay, 1997). Described in Chapter 3, the social climate for the young adult lives of these lesbians and gay men was a harsh and constricting one. As a result, they did not conceive of being open about their identities with their families or in any type of work setting (Christian & Keefe, 1997). They continuously managed their lives so that their sexual identity was not discovered (Friend, 1987, 1990). Because they were closeted, isolation from other lesbians and gay men was prevalent (Gray & Dressel, 1985).

The current historical period is not as harsh but the social context for older lesbians and gay men is still oppressive and their sexual identities are still stigmatized (e.g., Dunker, 1987; D. Martin & Lyon, 1992; Raphael & Robinson, 1984; Reid, 1995). In addition, they are stigmatized because of their stage of life. *Ageism* in our society interacts with *heterosexism* in the construction of particularly negative stereotypes of older lesbians and gay men (Deevey, 1990; Friend, 1990; Kelly, 1977). Older lesbians, for example, are frequently described as unattractive, lonely, and alone. Older gay men are often described as sexually frustrated, lacking support of family and friends, alone, lonely, depressed, and unhappy (R. Berger, 1980, 1982, 1996; Friend, 1980; O. Martin & Lyon, 1992; Raphael & Robinson, 1984). Younger lesbians and gay men who disclose their sexual orientation to their families may be told something like the following: "Imagine how lonely you will feel when you grow old." The family may be concerned about their lesbian or gay member's happiness but heterosexist and ageist messages are imparted as well (Friend, 1990).

In the lesbian and gay community itself, there is considerable ageism. As noted in Chapter 9, the gay male subculture is particularly youth oriented. Value and status equals young and attractive (Weinberg & Williams, 1974). The notion of "premature aging" was emphasized in early writings on gay men because they defined themselves as old (and unattractive) at an earlier age than did heterosexual peers (Friend, 1980; Kelly, 1977; Laner, 1978; Minnigerode & Adelman, 1976). Whether or not these concerns reflect accelerated or premature aging, however, is not always clear (Friend, 1987); neither is it clear whether this is a permanent state. A concern about aging may occur temporarily in early midlife but subside later. Harry (1982b) found, for example, that gay men in their early forties were more concerned with growing old and not looking youthful than either younger or older gay respondents. Other studies (e.g., R. Berger, 1996; Minnigerode, 1976) also found that older gay men experience less anxiety and worry about older age than younger gay men, and that they do not perceive themselves as aging earlier than heterosexual men.

In addition to heterosexism and ageism, racial and ethnic older gay men and lesbians contend with racism, and older lesbians with sexism. For older African American gay men studied by Adams and Kimmel (1997), *racism* was more pervasive than age dis-

crimination or antigay discrimination. This is not to say that they did not experience the other forms of discrimination but that racism was more often in their everyday awareness. *Sexism* adds yet a another layer of bias and discrimination to the lives of older lesbians. In the larger culture, views of older women in general are usually more negative than those of older men (e.g., Auger, 1992; S. Green, 1981; Schoonmaker, 1993). In addition to the stereotypes mentioned above, misconceptions about older lesbians include that "there are none; that they only live on the east or west coasts; or that they are unhappy childless spinsters or mannish-looking female truck drivers" (Deevey, 1990, p. 35).

Much of the literature on older lesbians and gay men addresses the negative stereotypes associated with them. Considerable attention is focused on the criteria of *life satisfaction* as a corollary to the negative stereotypes although some researchers attempt to provide a more comprehensive understanding of the lives of older lesbians and gay men (Christian & Keefe, 1997). The research on older lesbians, for example, presents quite a different picture from the negative stereotypes. Although some older lesbians play out butch and fem roles, most of the lesbians over the age of 50 in Deevey's (1990) study rejected these roles. Kehoe (1989) also found that most older lesbians do not support or even acknowledge these roles. Older lesbians tend to be more similar to younger professional women who were influenced by the women's movement (Tully, 1983). Various studies of older lesbians (e.g., Adelman, 1980; R. Berger, 1984; Kehoe, 1986; Minnigerode & Adelman, 1978; Raphael & Robinson, 1984; Tully, 1983) found that they tend to be highly educated, professionally employed, politically liberal, not traditionally religious, sexually active, and unmarried. Kehoe (1986) studied 100 lesbians over age 60 from 23 states and

Washington, D.C. These participants experienced themselves as strong and independent. They tended to value characteristics usually associated with men such as assertiveness, courage, and determination.

The stereotypical lonely, isolated older gay man is also not supported by research (Dorfman et al., 1995; Francher & Henkin, 1973; Friend, 1980; Kelly, 1977; Kimmel, 1977, 1978; Moses & Hawkins, 1986). Only a small minority of gay men grow old in isolation (Dawson, 1982). Even so, with such negative stereotypes of old age, many gay men acquire negative attitudes and fears about aging. Saghir and Robins (1973) found, for example, that only 28% of a sample of gay men believed that they would be in a stable linkup when old. A smaller group believed they would feel afraid and lonesome in old age. These attitudes, however, are not universal. Kelly (1975) found that gay men of all ages held negative beliefs about aging, but with increasing age, negative beliefs declined.

This chapter addresses further what life is like for the current cohort of older lesbians and gay men. Although findings are sparse, some pieces of the picture of their lives are available. The topics include positive adjustment, life satisfaction, sources of strength and well-being, health concerns, and adjustment difficulties.

◆ Positive Adjustment and Life Satisfaction: Overview

Studies show that most of the older gay and lesbian participants are psychologically well adjusted, happy, and adapting well to getting older (e.g., Adelman, 1988; Almvig, 1980; Deevey, 1990; Friend, 1991; Kehoe, 1986; Raphael & Robinson, 1984). For example, Minnigerode, Adelman, and Fox (1980) compared lesbians, gay men, and

heterosexual men and women age 60 and older. Few differences occurred in psychological adjustment among the different groups. Minnigerode and Adelman (1976) also found no differences in morale among these comparison groups. Weinberg's (1970) survey of 1,100 older gay men found that they were as well adjusted as younger gay men. Other studies showed that lesbians and gay men did not experience any significant decrease in self-acceptance or increase in loneliness, anxiety, or depression as they got older (R. Berger, 1980, 1996) nor was there any difference between heterosexual men and women in rates of depression (e.g., Dorfman et al., 1995). Weinberg and Williams (1974) found that older gay men reported better self-concepts and were more psychologically stable than their younger counterparts. Other studies found that most lesbians and gay men were not anxious about their own aging. Satisfaction with their life situation was high. They recognize the positive aspects of their lesbian or gay identity and were satisfied with who they were (J. Lee, 1987; Quam & Whitford, 1992).

◆ Factors Contributing to Adjustment and Satisfaction

The positive outcomes in adjustment and satisfaction reported for older lesbians and gay men appear to be associated with various factors that are categorized here as sources of strength and sources of well-being. The *sources of strength* include crisis competence and gender role flexibility. The *sources of well-being* include a positive identity, managing conflicts about sexual orientation prior to self-identification, an ordered sequence of developmental events, disclosure, integration with the lesbian and gay community, and interpersonal supports. These sources of strength and well-being may allow lesbians and gay men to make adjustments more easily in later life.

Sources of Strength

Crisis Competence

Many researchers (e.g., R. Berger, 1980, 1982; Dawson, 1982; Francher & Henkin, 1973; Friend, 1987; Kehoe, 1985; Kimmel, 1978, 1979-1980; J. Lee, 1987; Minnigerode et al., 1980; Quam & Whitford, 1992; Weeks, 1983) proposed that successful resolution of the crises of coming out and disclosure energizes one to cope with later life crises. The notion is that lesbians and gay men are psychologically strengthened after facing the ridicule and ostracism associated with disclosure. Reid (1995) suggested, however, that the coming out and disclosure processes can either provide an opportunity for personal growth and development or overwhelm individuals and their coping resources.

Also contrary to the prediction of crisis theory, J. Lee (1987) found that gay men are better off not experiencing numerous crises. Some of the highly satisfied men experienced long periods of identity crisis and some who did not go through a crisis of this kind were unhappy. Most of the happiest participants, however, reported the fewest number of crises, whether or not related to their sexual orientation. They also reported that they attained self-acceptance more easily than other participants. R. Berger (1996), however, claimed that the research design in Lee's study did not adequately test the crisis hypothesis. Various essentials required in such a test were missing from the study: a comparison between older heterosexual and gay men, examination of stressors that are unique to each group, outcome measures of successful crisis resolution, and more measures of adjustment to aging than the single variable of life satisfaction. R. Berger

agreed, however, that multiple, difficult crises (Lee measured the number and intensity of crises), which are not quickly and effectively resolved, can deplete social and emotional resources. This can in effect jeopardize one's capacity to cope well with subsequent stressors in life.

J. Lee (1987) declared that any theory that requires the necessity of surviving suffering earlier in life so that old age can be positive is nothing more than the old Puritan ethic. The real "crisis competence" for older gay men includes, instead, "good health, social class advantage, and exchange power, often enhanced by alliance with a significant other" (p. 60). These conditions are no different from ones that benefit older men and women in any other group. Lee found that older gay men with the most income, highest education, and most prestigious occupations also experience the fewest disabling crises. Income level is also closely related to life satisfaction but it does not guarantee that outcome. For example, a respondent with one of the highest incomes produced one of the lowest scores on life satisfaction. Nevertheless, wealthy men generally tend to fare better because they can access more resources.

Gender Role Flexibility

In challenging traditional gender roles, lesbians and gay men potentially attain more freedom to behave in nontraditional ways. When they are older, therefore, lesbian and gay men are likely to feel more comfortable than heterosexual men and women in engaging in nontraditional gender role behaviors. They can care for themselves better by performing tasks typically associated with the other gender, such as financial management for women or cooking for men (Friend, 1991). They also learn to be self-reliant and independent (R. Berger & Kelly, 1986). In a sample of 100 older lesbians and gay men, D. Wolf (1982) described them as learning at an early age to fend for themselves and increase their personal autonomy. Quam and Whitford (1992) found that lesbians and gay men are also forced to plan carefully for the economic problems of aging.

Sources of Well-Being

Positive Identity

Friend (1991) developed a theory of successful aging related to lesbians and gay men. The ultimate goal is the achievement of a positive identity. This accomplishment provides an advantage for continued adaptation to the challenges of aging. Attaining a positive identity, however, is not easy because of the social stigma attached to a same-gender sexual orientation. Consequently, Friend described three different outcomes of identity formation: optimal affirmative, stereotypical, and passing.

Optimal affirmative outcome. Even though the historical period in which they grew up was hostile and oppressive, older lesbians and gay men who reached the optimal outcome were able to actively construct a positive identity. They rejected the larger culture's negative views and the assumptions of heterosexist ideology and replaced them with a new construction of meaning regarding their sexual orientation. Once they resisted external definitions of self, they constructed their identity on their own terms as positive and valuable. Some did this through personal and political activism, others through lives that reflected who they were (Friend, 1991). Affirmative lesbians and gay men were also more likely to be open with and accepted by their families of origin. They were also likely to encourage accepting family members to challenge heterosexism

through participation in groups such as PFLAG (Friend, 1990).

These older lesbians and gay men who were satisfied with their sexual orientation were the ones who attained high levels of psychological adjustment (e.g., Adelman, 1991; Almvig, 1982; R. Berger, 1980, 1982, 1996; Dawson, 1982; Dunker, 1987; Francher & Henkin, 1973; Friend, 1980, 1987; Kehoe, 1986; Kelly, 1977; Kimmel, 1977, 1978; Raphael & Robinson, 1984). They talked about self-acceptance and the advantages of their sexual orientation. A major characteristic of participants who reported lower satisfaction was their perception that their stigmatized sexual orientation resulted in failed careers and relationships with friends and partners (Adelman, 1991).

In two less optimal outcomes, individuals gave in to the negative beliefs and attitudes. They also incorporated the negativity into beliefs and feelings about themselves.

Stereotypical option. "Stereotypical" older lesbians and gay men conformed to the negative beliefs associated with heterosexism. They hid their sexual orientation and lived with self-loathing, shame, and guilt. Their current lives matched the popular images that stereotype all older lesbians and gay men as alienated, lonely, and depressed (Friend, 1991).

Secrecy was perhaps the major characteristic of this group. The members hid all or parts of themselves from families and friends, creating a wall of separation and distance. Contact with families was most likely minimal and superficial (Friend, 1991). Members of this group also maintained distance from other lesbians and gay men and were unlikely to develop social or emotional support systems with them. Separated from affirmative lesbians and gay men, opportunities to challenge their heterosexist beliefs about themselves were limited (Friend, 1990).

Icard (1996) noted that older gay Black men who were raised to view their sexual attractions as a disease or sin were also not usually part of the modern gay community. Few of them openly associated with other gay Black men either. The main component of their identity was their race, not their sexual orientation. In a study of gay Black men (with an average age of 56), Adams and Kimmel (1997) found that most of the respondents never specifically discussed their sexual orientation with their families although they reported that their families knew they were gay. Some of these men openly discussed their sexual orientation with siblings.

Passing option. This option is in the middle range of Friend's model. Although not much different from those in the stereotypical group, members in the passing group were a little less isolated and therefore not totally accepting of society's negative views of them. They believed the heterosexist assumptions but also acknowledged and marginally accepted their same-gender orientation (Friend, 1990). They cannot fully accept their sexual orientation, however, because they felt valued for what others expected them to be rather than for who they really were (Minton & McDonald, 1983-1984). For example, perhaps because they thought of heterosexuality as superior to the same-gender sexual orientation, they were often heterosexually married (Bozett, 1984; Dunker, 1987; Friend, 1991, 1990; Miller, 1979b). They often remained married and closeted so as to "pass" as heterosexual (Friend, 1991).

Many older persons in the passing group kept their distance from identifiable lesbians or gay men. Others interacted with them or were even in a long-term primary linkup with someone of the same gender. If they entered a same-gender linkup, however, they did it in such a way as to still appear as heterosexual. They basically lived in two worlds: one public and one secret. The emotional costs of this incongruent life were often high (Friend, 1991) (see Chapter 5).

The stereotypical and passing groups of older lesbians and gay men are difficult to find as they are still mostly hidden (Friend, 1990; Quam, 1993). It is rare for individuals, closeted most of their adult lives, to disclose themselves in the last stages of life (Quam, 1993). The findings reported in this chapter therefore tend to reflect the affirmative group of older lesbians and gay men because they are more likely to be open and participate in research studies.

An Ordered Sequence of Developmental Events

Adelman (1991) found that adjustment to later life is associated with the sequence of early developmental events. Individuals who experimented with being lesbian or gay prior to self-identification experienced high life satisfaction, low self-criticism, and few psychosomatic complaints. By contrast, individuals who defined themselves as lesbian or gay prior to experimenting experienced less positive patterns of adjustment. Experimentation before self-definition appears to allow adjustment to stigma prior to developing a positive lesbian or gay identity (Dank, 1971; de Monteflores & Schultz, 1978). This also allows time to develop skills to cope with stigma (Adelman, 1991). Positive identity for some, however, was not achieved until after years of struggle (Adelman, 1991; Minnigerode et al., 1980). Other researchers have also found that managing conflicts about sexual orientation earlier in life was associated with positive adjustment in later life (e.g., Kehoe, 1989; J. Lee, 1990).

Disclosure

After the Stonewall Rebellion some 30 years ago, lesbians and gay men were more willing to speak out (see Chapter 3). As noted above, however, disclosure did not occur for all of the groups identified by Friend (1991). Although Friend considered the no-disclosure groups to be less optimal than the affirmative group who did make disclosures, other studies (e.g., Adelman, 1991; Quam, 1993) found that adjustment for older lesbians and gay men was associated with no disclosure. J. Lee (1987) found that many older gay male respondents were content even after a lifetime of concealment, which in some cases involved concealment from wives and children. No association was found between concealment and self-rated life satisfaction. Lee concluded that concealment, more than disclosure, led to a happy old age for gay men. Although participants studied by Adelman (1991) felt frustration and anger about discrimination and the need for secrecy, they also tended not to disclose their sexual orientation. Disclosure for this group led to loss of children, jobs, and family support. The rejection by their families was often lifelong. Adelman found that adjustment to later life and high life satisfaction were also associated with low disclosure at work.

J. Lee (1987) suggested that the next generation of older lesbians and gay men will likely hold quite different attitudes about disclosure. In addition to the optimal affirmative outcome identified by Friend (1991), however, findings in certain other studies on the current older generation contradict the findings that associate no disclosure with adjustment and satisfaction. R. Berger (1980, 1996), for example, found in a sample of older gay men that low concealment of sexual orientation was associated with positive psychological adjustment. Weinberg and Williams (1974) also found that older gay men were less concerned about exposure of

their sexual orientation than were younger gay men. It is possible that the respondents in these studies were more "affirmative" and, consequently, also more open.

Integration into the Lesbian and Gay Community

Adelman (1991) found that adjustment to later life and high life satisfaction were also associated with low involvement with other lesbians and gay men. There are other studies, however, which contradict this finding as well. These studies found that older lesbians and gay men who were well integrated into the lesbian and gay community were less fearful of aging, more self-accepting, less depressed (R. Berger, 1982, 1996), higher in self-esteem and self-worth (R. Berger, 1980), higher in psychological well-being (Weinberg & Williams, 1974), and happier (J. Lee, 1987). Whitford (1997) found that participation in social and religious activities in the gay community were important to quality of life for older gay men.

Involvement in the lesbian and gay community also plays a key role in whether or not participants feel that their sexual orientation helps or hinders their aging process. Participants who are not active in social organizations are most likely to believe that their sexual orientation hinders their adjustment to aging. Participants who are active in service and political organizations are more likely to believe the opposite (Quam & Whitford, 1992).

Some research showed a consistent decrease of participation in social and political activities as gay men get older (e.g., R. Berger, 1996; Kelly, 1975). This pattern, however, may differ by age group. According to Quam and Whitford (1992), the current cohort of old-old (age 75 to 90) lesbians and gay men are not likely to participate in community services because they probably do not want to be distinguished from other heterosexual adults. In contrast, the young-old cohorts (age 60 to 80) seem quite interested in pertinent services and programs. Benefits of participation, however, may be associated with ages younger than 60. Whitford (1997) found that the gay men who are more integrated into the community informally and formally, and more likely to believe that their sexual orientation helps their aging process, were under age 60 (age 50-59). Participation in social organizations also contributed to life satisfaction for the younger gay men (age 50-59) but not for those age 60 and older.

Interpersonal Support

The importance of friends. Lesbian, gay, and heterosexual friendships are associated with high life satisfaction (Adelman, 1991; J. Lee, 1987). Friend (1980) found that friendships were an important source of psychological well-being for older gay men. Raphael and Robinson (1984) found that strong friendships were associated with higher self-esteem and adaptation to aging for older lesbians.

Friends provide significantly more support than families of origin (Dorfman et al., 1995). Older lesbians and gay men studied by Minnigerode and Adelman (1978) were closer to their friends than their families of origin. Friend (1980) found that even though the social networks of older gay men also included family-of-origin members, their closest emotional support came from friends. Tully (1988) asked lesbians in their fifties whom they turned to first for caregiving. All of the respondents reported that they either turned to their current partner or to women friends with whom they had an emotionally intimate link.

Intimate linkups. Several studies found that satisfaction with life for older lesbians

and gay men is generally associated with an intimate, enduring linkup. Approximately 70% of older gay men and 50% of older lesbians, however, are not involved in primary linkups (Almvig, 1982; R. Berger, 1996; Kehoe, 1986; Kelly, 1975; Kimmel, 1979-1980; Silberman & Walton, 1986). According to Kelly (1975), primary linkups reach their greatest numbers between age 45 and age 55 and decline after that to close to none. Kimmel (1978) found a decrease in the number of gay men's relationships after age 50. Quam and Whitford (1992) found that 24% of the older gay men in their sample were in same-gender linkups; 17% were separated from a same-gender linkup; and the same-gender partners of about 5% were deceased. Christian and Keefe (1997) noted that older gay men are reluctant to recommit to a primary linkup after losing a partner to death or a breakup. They suspected that this is basically age related. Peterson and McKirnan (1987), however, reported little difference in the linkup patterns between older and younger groups of gay men. Other data also indicated higher involvement of older gay men in intimate linkups. R. Berger (1996), for example, found that 43% of men over age 40 lived with a partner.

The types of linkups prevalent among older gay men vary. They include (a) short-term, same-gender sexual linkups, (b) long-term, same-gender partnerships, and (c) heterosexual marriage (R. Berger, 1996; Kimmel, 1977; J. Lee, 1987). Kimmel (1978) identified five "social-sexual" patterns: (a) heterosexual marriage with or without periodic same-gender relations following or followed by life as a gay man, (b) celibacy with same-gender affectional linkups, (c) raising children, (d) one or more long-term linkups with a gay friend/lover, and (e) bisexual life without marriage.

Several researchers (R. Berger, 1980, 1996; J. Lee, 1987) found that older gay men in long-term partnerships, whether same or cross-gender, were much more likely to be satisfied with their lives than those who chose an unattached single life. Christian and Keefe (1997), however, suggested that reports like these reflect an underlying bias toward associating happiness with linkups that resemble long-term heterosexual marriages. In Lee's study, for example, 26 of the older happy men were not in a couple. The emphasis of the report, however, was the seven happy men who were in a couple. Although satisfaction is associated with romantic linkups, other arrangements that may also be associated with satisfaction are ignored. Bell and Weinberg (1978) reported, for example, that the happiest men in their sample were in a "Close-Coupled" linkup (little outside sexual activity) but that those in another type of couple arrangement, "Functional," were almost as happy (95% versus 99%). Participants in the "Functional" type of couple were not in a partnership with each other but experienced sex several or more times a week. In addition, during the previous year, their minimum number of sexual partners was 20.

Not much is known about older lesbians' primary linkups. Each person in Kehoe's (1989) study of older lesbians experienced at least one same-gender linkup, and two-thirds of the sample experienced both same-gender and cross-gender linkups. They reported that their same-gender linkups are more caring, gentle, emotionally close, and sexually satisfying than their heterosexual linkups. They also described their current same-gender linkups as less intense, quieter, and more stable than earlier ones. Only 18% of the participants, however, were in a current committed linkup with another woman. More than half of another sample of lesbians aged 50 and older were with a current lover, and nearly half lived alone (Almvig, 1982). Raphael and Robinson (1984) found in their study of older lesbians that 55% lived alone and 45% lived in a coupled linkup with another older woman. Older lesbians in this study preferred other older women as intimate partners. Schreurs and Buunk (1996) found that the older the participants were in lesbian couples, the more satisfied they were.

Sexuality. Little research has considered the effects of aging on the sexual activities of older lesbians and gay men. It is known that they experience the same physiological changes as anyone else, and also that a decrease in frequency of sexual outlets occurs as they get older (e.g., Bell & Weinberg, 1978; J. Lee, 1990). According to Kimmel (1978), although older gay men have fewer sexual partners and lower frequency of sex than their younger counterparts, sex is still important in their lives. Their level of sexual interest does not decrease with age (Bell & Weinberg, 1978), and they continue to experience high levels of sexual activity (e.g., R. Berger, 1996; Silverstein, 1981). The majority of older gay men also rate their current sex lives as satisfactory (R. Berger, 1984, 1996; Kelly, 1977; Kimmel, 1978). Half of Kimmel's older male respondents felt that sex was more satisfactory in later life than it was when they were younger. R. Berger's (1992) older respondents indicated that sex was qualitatively different, with less focus on the sexual act and more on the total person.

Bell and Weinberg (1978) found that although older lesbians were less sexually active than younger lesbians, most of them still participate in sex. Likewise, most of Deevey's (1990) sample of older lesbians reported that they were still sexually active. Sex is still important for all of the older lesbians studied by Raphael and Robinson (1984). Although more than two-thirds (68%) of the older women in Kehoe's (1986, 1989) sample were celibate, this was not a voluntary state for most of these women.

Two-thirds of the sample considered sex (after age 60) an important aspect of a lesbian linkup, although no one thought it was the main part. For most of the respondents, friendship and intimacy were more important.

◆ Concerns and Downturns of Aging

With the exception of contending with heterosexism, concerns of older lesbians and gay men are similar to those of older heterosexual men and women (Almvig, 1982; R. Berger, 1984; Kehoe, 1989; Quam & Whitford, 1992). They include physical health, support, coping with isolation and loneliness, maintaining autonomy, difficulties protecting oneself, managing finances, and age discrimination (Quam, 1993; Reid, 1995). Quam and Whitford reported that health is the most serious concern in the present and the future, especially for lesbians. Finances are also more likely to be a problem for older lesbians, who are more likely to experience poverty (Friend, 1987).

Health Issues

As late life progresses, chronic or terminal illness becomes a greater threat. Medical and other needed services tailored for older lesbians and gay men, however, are rarely available. This is unfortunate because older lesbians and gay men suffering from chronic or terminal illnesses fear intolerance, stigma, and discrimination (Reid, 1995) across the array of social and medical services (Poor, 1982). Such fears are warranted (Schwanberg, 1996). Older lesbians and gay men are likely to confront bias and oppression in traditional settings (Anderson, 1981; Quam & Whitford, 1992; Reid, 1995). Professionals in social and medical services are often not respectful of lesbians and gay men or sensitive to their linkups (Randall, 1989). Older

lesbians and gay men also fear institutionalization in nursing homes or rehabilitation centers because these environments are also perceived to be unsupportive (Auger, 1992; Beckett & Schneider, 1992; Friend, 1987; Quam & Whitford, 1992; Tully, 1988). Deevey (1990) described the most pertinent health issue as "the wear-and-tear of living in environments (including health-care settings) that are . . . [heterosexist] or hostile to lesbian and gay people" (p. 37). Every day, lesbians and gay men negotiate environments "that range from hostile to friendly, they are acutely aware of subtleties in language and manner that suggest danger or safety" (p. 37).

Older lesbians and gay men may also be prevented from visiting their life partners in hospitals or nursing homes, excluded from decisions regarding their care, and ignored at their funeral services (Herek & Glunt, 1988; Hooyman & Lustbader, 1986; Murphy, 1994; Reid, 1995). Problems of inheritance are also frequent (Decker, 1984; Schaie & Willis, 1991).

Both the possibility of declining health and the issues surrounding older couples when a partner requires outside care or dies make it imperative that older coupled or single lesbians and gay men plan ahead for their later years. Such planning should include obtaining disability and health insurance and becoming knowledgeable about the health care and legal systems before a crisis occurs. A will and power of attorney are important legal instruments in the event of severe illness or death (Dunker, 1987; Kimmel, 1978; D. Martin & Lyon, 1992). Friend (1990) emphasized that older lesbians and gay men must plan in advance to ensure that agreements regarding living wills, funeral arrangements, and personal and joint property are honored. They must take responsibility to see that legal documents are prepared exactly according to their wishes (R. Berger, 1990a; Friend, 1987; Reid, 1995).

The Complications of HIV/AIDS

The health picture for older gay men is complicated by the HIV epidemic (e.g., Fishman & Linde, 1983; Linde, 1994; O'Neil, 1990). The largest percentage of people over age 50 with HIV (about 10%) are gay and bisexual men (Catania et al., 1989; Kooperman, 1994). HIV disease presents special problems in older people such as faster progression of the illness. In addition, older gay men who are not open about their sexual orientation may delay diagnosis or keep it a secret from family and friends (Kooperman, 1994). Kochman (1993) found that older gay men with a low sense of self-worth and an HIV-positive diagnosis can feel even greater shame about their sexual orientation. Especially men in their sixties and seventies may believe that HIV/AIDS confirms that they are as worthless as they always believed they were.

Older gay and bisexual men studied by Kooperman (1994) acknowledged the necessity to modify their sexual activity because of HIV. They were knowledgeable about transmission and used low-risk sexual activity. Most reported that they talked to their sexual partners about unsafe sexual activity they were unwilling to engage in. Linde (1994) found that the fear of HIV led some older gay men to avoid all sexual contact.

Adjustment Difficulties

Lesbians and gay men, just as heterosexual men and women, vary in their experiences with aging. As indicated above, most older lesbians and gay men are well adjusted and happy (McDougall, 1993). Other older lesbians and gay men, however, struggle with stigma, loneliness, bereavement, lack of acceptance of aging, and low income (R. Berger & Kelly, 1996; Kimmel, 1977; McDougall, 1993; Sang, 1992; Whitford, 1997).

Problems with self-esteem because of the *stigma* associated with one's sexual orientation can be modified by learning to manage cognitive thoughts and replacing negative ones with more positive and self-defensive ways of thinking about one's life (Friend, 1990). To confront stereotypical and stigmatized images of older lesbians and gay men, diverse models are helpful. Particularly useful are models that reflect older persons who are active, productive, self-motivated, and sexual (Friend, 1990). Friend (1987) also recommended affirmative books to help challenge myths and misconceptions of older lesbians and gay men with accurate information. Examples include *Gay and Gray* by Berger (1996) and *Rubyfruit Jungle* by R. M. Brown (1973). Interaction with lesbians and gay men of different ages is also helpful in providing social stimulation as well as varied role models (Friend, 1987). As suggested later, however, qualifications may be necessary regarding the benefits of connections between older and younger gay men.

Some older lesbians and gay men experience *loneliness* just as some older heterosexual women and men do. It can be useful to determine what the loneliness results from: unavailability of places to meet others, fear of rejection, or limited social skills (Friend, 1987). As noted in Chapter 3, the White lesbian and gay community is not viewed by racial and ethnic lesbians and gay men as accepting of them. Older racial and ethnic persons therefore may feel lonely because they are isolated from both their racial and ethnic communities and the gay and lesbian communities (Adams & Kimmel, 1997).

One of the loneliest times can occur when a partner dies. Lesbian and gay "widowers" and "widows" experience the same emotions as their heterosexual counterparts (B. Johnson, 1990; Kehoe, 1986; Kochman, 1997; Saunders, 1990; Silverstein, 1981). Kimmel (1977) reported that *bereavement* is one the few difficulties that motivate older gay men to seek counseling or therapy. Both lesbians and gay men may need help with the grieving process especially when there are few accepting family members (Klinger & Cabaj, 1993).

In addition to loneliness, Whitford (1997) found that a *lack of acceptance of aging* and *low income* are significant predictors of a belief that sexual orientation hinders the aging process. Informal relations in the gay community are important in increasing acceptance of aging but formal organizations are less important. Low income may restrict activity in social organizations.

When older gay men lose partners or for other reasons desire to make more social connections with other gay men, there can be formidable barriers even if they have sufficient income. Christian and Keefe (1997) clarified the obstacles. They developed a model, drawn from the work of Bell and Weinberg (1978) and Hooker (1967), to assist in defining some of the problems and hazards of aging for gay men as well as problems unique to the current cohort. It provides a way to conceptualize the link between the individual and the larger social community and to differentiate contributions of larger system dynamics from those of the individual. The model conceptualizes three dominant sociosexual interactive fields in the gay community. They include (a) the *Sexual Market Field* (short-term sexual encounters), (b) the *Primary Relation Field* (primary links between gay men), and (c) the *Social Network Field* (social interactions between gay men). Each field comprises a twofold primary function: (a) As an intermediary structure, it links a person with larger social institutions, and (b) it provides a sociopsychological buffer from the heterosexist society. Using Hooker's (1967) definition, each field is also defined "as a particular set of institutions, facilities, or areas governed by a common set of expectations, beliefs, and values" (p. 172).

According to Christian and Keefe (1997), a gay man occupies the core of a field when there is an inner sense of sociopsychological unity with other field participants and he can maintain a positive identity with no regrets. Although only one of the fields is a primary choice at any given time, the fields can be occupied simultaneously. A person can move in and out of fields or remain in a fixed pattern indefinitely. There can also be movement toward or away from fields or closer to or away from the core of the field currently occupied. It is also possible to disengage from all three fields.

Christian and Keefe (1997) used their model to identify hazards in a small sample of 15 gay men with an average age of 53. For example, men who were basically involved in the Primary Relationship Field reported feeling lonely and cut off when not involved in either of the two other fields. They were also concerned about what would happen if they lost their partner. On the other hand, men who were never involved in the Primary Relationship Field experienced frustration trying to connect with other gay men.

Movement toward the Social Network Field as a primary field can be difficult for older gay men. Many gay organizations are basically composed of younger men or, as described by Grube (1990), liberationists with a more visible and vocal political agenda. Older men feel pressured by the younger men to not accommodate to heterosexism and to quit hiding and living double (sometimes married) lives. The value differences between the two groups are often painfully clear to older gay men who grew up in secret clique societies (e.g., Hooker, 1967). Participation in the younger group requires subscription to a set of expectations, beliefs, and values that are often at odds with much of their previous experience.

The men most at risk of reporting *loneliness* in Christian and Keefe's (1997) study included those who (a) were exclusively involved in the Primary Relationship Field, (b) were recently in heterosexual marriages, or (c) were pulled away from the Sexual Market Field without moving into either of the other fields. Although they may want to move toward the core of the Social Network Field, they can experience the problems with organizations composed of younger men noted above. Finding a social setting that is not dominated by younger men, however, is difficult for most of these men. They also experience difficulty in gaining access to the private circles of other older gay men.

Whitford (1997) found that the men in his study also worried about lacking friends and linkups as they grew older. They desired more social outlets to develop more of these links. As explicated by Christian and Keefe (1997), however, trying to get older gay men to assimilate into existing gay social networks may not produce the same positive results that it does for younger gay men. Alternate services and programs specifically for older gay men are needed.

◆ Community Services

The number of organizations for older lesbians and gay men is growing in the United States and Canada. Several organizations in large urban areas provide a variety of social and support services. The most comprehensive program is Senior Action in a Gay Environment (SAGE) founded in New York City in 1977 (Friend, 1987). Other programs include the Society for Senior Gay and Lesbian Citizens/PROJECT RAINBOW in Los Angeles (Galassi, 1991) and Gay and Lesbian Outreach to Elders (GLOE) in San Francisco (Reid, 1995). Prime Timers is a self-help group that originated in Boston but now exists in other parts of the United States (McDougall, 1993). Gays and Lesbians Older and Wiser (GLOW) is a unique support

group that is part of the services provided by a university-based geriatric clinic in Ann Arbor, Michigan. Social workers on the staff help to facilitate the program (Slusher, Mayer, & Dunkle, 1996). Unfortunately, few cities offer anything equivalent to these organizations and services (R. Berger, 1990a, 1990b).

Quam and Whitford (1992) and others also studied interest in retirement communities. About 50% to 60% of respondents indicated an interest in lesbian and gay retirement communities (Almvig, 1982; Kehoe, 1989; Quam & Whitford, 1992). One study (Lucco, 1987) found that 88% of the respondents were interested.

For professionals working with older lesbians and gay men, a resource guide on lesbian and gay aging is distributed by the National Association for Lesbian and Gay Gerontology. It includes pertinent research, audiovisuals, and lists of organizations. Metz (1997) also described a seven-step process for preparing social service providers to work with older lesbian and gay men.

◆ Summary

Taken together, the available literature on older lesbians and gay men indicates that the stereotypes of this population as lonely, alienated, and depressed are incorrect, especially for those who are "affirmative." The general conclusion is that older lesbians and gay men who achieve a positive self-identity are at an advantage for psychological adjustment, continued growth, happiness, and adaptation in later life. It is important for members of this current cohort of older lesbians and gay men to tell their stories of how they managed the oppressive social context in which they grew up. All lesbians and gay men can learn from them.

PART V

HUMAN SERVICES PRACTICE WITH LESBIAN, GAY, BISEXUAL, AND TRANSGENDERIST CLIENTS

AFFIRMATIVE
PRACTICE:
OVERVIEW

◆ IN THIS CONCLUDING CHAPTER to the book, a review of the changing approaches to mental health practice with lesbian, gay, bisexual, and transgenderist clients is presented. First, there is a description of nonaffirmative practice with lesbians and gay men prior to the removal, in 1973, of "homosexuality" as a mental disorder from the American Psychiatric Association's Diagnostic Manual. Since that time, development of an affirmative approach to human services practice with lesbian, gay, bisexual, and transgenderist clients began.

◆ **Mental Health Practice Before 1973**

Prior to 1973, the American Psychiatric Association listed "homosexuality" as a mental illness. As a consequence, lesbians and gay men were viewed as in need of treatment to "cure" their illness by responsible mental health practitioners. This entailed various biological therapies such as induced seizures, nausea-inducing drugs, electric shock, lobotomy, castration, implanting "normal" testes, and increases in various hormones. Psychotherapy was perhaps the most humane treatment for these "troubled," "ill" persons (e.g., Coleman, 1978; Haldeman, 1994; Silverstein, 1991b).

Psychological Conversion: "Curing" the Sick

The sought-after outcome of the psychotherapeutic "cure" of "homosexuality" was no different than for all of the other treatments listed above: conversion or transformation to "heterosexuality." A lesbian named Harriet, who sought the "cure" from several psychiatrists in the 1950s, stated,

> Of course many of us were loaded with self-hate and wanted to change. How could it have been otherwise? All we heard and read about homosexuality, was that crap about how we were inverts, perverts, queers—a menace to children, poison to everyone else, doomed never to be happy. And so we went humbly to the doctors, and took whatever other nastiness they wanted to spew out about homosexuality, and we paid them and said thanks. (Faderman, 1991, p. 137)

Generally, two approaches to psychotherapeutic "cure" were used: psychoanalysis and behavior modification.

Freud (1935/1955) did not claim to "cure" "homosexuality" and in fact commented that the "homosexual" person should be helped to find harmony and peace of mind. Nevertheless, *psychoanalysis* in the post-World War II years quickly took on the task of attempting to "cure" "homosexual" patients. Their claims of "cure," however, are not supported by data (Gonsiorek, 1996; Haldeman, 1994). A treatment program described by Bieber et al. (1962) exemplifies the shortcomings in the analytic arena. The analysts touted a 27% success rate of converting "homosexual" persons to heterosexuality. Only 18% of the treatment group, however, was exclusively "homosexual" and about half of

the so-called successes were bisexual. The methodology, intensive long-term therapy, was used only on a clinical sample and the only assessment of outcomes was therapist impressions. Gonsiorek underscored that the analysts who did the therapy also designed the study, rated the clients, and interpreted the results. It was no surprise, therefore, when they claimed their theory was verified. In reality, their work was more of a case study in how to build researcher bias into a research experiment.

In other analytically based studies on respondents with exclusive same-gender sexual orientation, typically there was little or no reported change (e.g., Curran & Parr, 1957; Mayerson & Lief, 1965). Haldeman (1994) pointed out that when any change in analytical studies was reported, it was mostly behavior such as increased contact with heterosexual persons. Even if heterosexual sex occurred, this was not a barometer for sexual orientation change. Birk (1980) found that same-gender fantasies continued even for those who reported that they were happily married. In addition, the prevalent evaluation of the methodology in most of the analytic studies was self-report (e.g., Birk, 1980; Hadden, 1966; Mintz, 1966). This is always problematic and particularly in group treatment programs (e.g., Hadden, 1966; Mintz, 1966). The self-report of clients is susceptible to social influence by other members in the group (Haldeman, 1994).

Programs using the *behavioral* approach are based on the premise that "homosexuality" is a result of faulty learning. As an example, Freud (1977) combined aversion therapy with positive conditioning toward females as a behavioral treatment for male "homosexuality." As a result of this effort, 20% of the men married and had children. In follow-up studies, however, Freund concluded, "Virtually not one 'cure' remained a 'cure' " (p. 238). He stated further, "I am not happy about my therapeutic experiment which, if it has 'helped' at all, has helped clients to enter into marriages that later became unbearable or almost unbearable. Virtually all the marriages of these clients had become beset with grave problems ensuing from their homosexuality" (p. 239).

Other researchers (e.g., McConaghy, 1981; Rangaswami, 1982) confirmed Freund's (1977) findings. Behavioral approaches were deemed no more successful at "curing" "homosexuality" than were the analytic approaches. Rangaswami reported, for example, that behavioral conditioning may control "homosexual" behavior but it does not increase heterosexual interest. Many of the behavioral programs also used self-report to evaluate outcomes. The few studies that used external measures also did not show that change followed treatment (e.g., Conrad & Wincze, 1976).

Haldeman (1994) noted that the treatments in both the analytic and the behavioral areas attempt to cure something that is not documented to be an illness. How this was determined is discussed later, along with the effects on treatment.

Religious Conversion Programs: "Curing" the Sinful

Fundamentalist Christian therapists contend that lesbians and gay men are not only sick but immoral. They must, then, be "converted" to heterosexuality to be saved from a life of sin (Haldeman, 1994). Religious conversion therapists are church affiliated and use religious exhortation often intermingled with elements of 12-step self-help programs (Gonsiorek, 1996). These programs also publicize claims of success. Virtually no data, however, support these claims. Haldeman pointed out that religious-based programs use unspecified treatment methods such as prayer and corrective sexual experiences. Outcome measures, if they exist at all, are primarily in the form of testimonials.

Even practitioners involved in the programs admit that the most realistic outcome is celibacy rather than a heterosexual sexual orientation (Blair, 1982; Rosenberg, 1994). This is not, however, because religious conversionist therapists do not try to change the sexual orientation of their mostly male clients. At times, they even use group pressure and brainwashing to try to coerce gay men not to act on their same-gender sexual attractions. If successful, they claim that these men "chose" to stop their immoral life and live a "moral" heterosexual life. Here again, however, there are no data showing that these men are "cured" of their same-gender sexual orientation (Gonsiorek, 1996). Other religious conversion programs publish no outcome data and do not allow participants to be interviewed for follow-up studies. In addition, it was discovered that many of the workers in these programs were unsure of their own sexual orientation (Blair, 1982).

Haldeman (1994) concluded that whether in a psychotherapeutic or religious program, "individuals undergoing conversion treatment are not likely to emerge as heterosexually inclined" (pp. 224-225). Instead, destructive outcomes often occur as individuals become "shamed, conflicted, and fearful about their homoerotic feelings" (p. 224). Even when someone claims that he or she is "cured" of "homosexuality," this usually only means that sexual behavior is controlled. Sexual attraction to individuals of the same gender is almost always still reported (Gonsiorek & Weinrich, 1991). Similarly, heterosexual marriage may present a facsimile of heterosexuality but will not convert sexual orientation (Coleman, 1981-1982a). Although some individuals, most often gay men, try to change their sexual orientation through marriage (Weinberg et al., 1994), same-gender dreams, fantasies, and attractions continue (Bell & Weinberg, 1978; Pattison & Pattison, 1980).

◆ Mental Health Practice
Since 1973: Overview

In 1957, it was unquestioned among psychologists and psychiatrists that "homosexuality" was a mental illness. "Homoerotic" feelings and/or behavior equaled psychological disturbance. In that same year, however, Evelyn Hooker used a battery of psychological tests on 30 gay and 30 heterosexual men to see if there were any differences between the groups in mental health. According to Gonsiorek (1991), the only pertinent issue was whether or not any nonpathological gay man existed. A panel of psychological test experts could not differentiate the test results between the two groups. The conclusion of this and subsequent research was that "homosexuality" per se is not a sign or a symptom of psychological disturbance. This finding was the empirical basis for the depathologizing of "homosexuality." Later, other researchers (e.g., LaTorre & Wendenberg, 1983; Nurius, 1983) also demonstrated that bisexual women and men are not pathological or psychologically maladjusted.

In 1973, "homosexuality" was declassified as pathological by the American Psychiatric Association, and it was removed as a psychiatric disorder from the *Diagnostic and Statistical Manual (DSM-III)* in *1978.* All final remnants of "homosexuality" as part of any diagnostic condition were removed *in 1987.* After the major modification in 1973, the approach to treatment of lesbians and gay men began to progress toward an affirmative one. This approach is built on the premise established above that there are no differences between lesbian, gay, and heterosexual persons in the distribution of psychological health and mental illness.

In 1974, the American Psychological Association adopted a statement urging its members to exert a leadership role in removing the mental illness stigma associated with

"homosexuality" (Hunt, 1993). Every major mental health profession eventually adopted similar statements regarding the professional responsibility to offer treatment to lesbians and gay men based not on "homosexuality" as an illness but on their needs, and to offer services without bias or discrimination. Accordingly, new approaches to treatment developed. Coleman (1978) and other early advocates of new treatment models urged that the focus must be on helping lesbians and gay clients to accept and value their sexual identities while living in a heterosexist society. Gradually these new approaches become known as *affirmative practice.*

In 1980, Woodman and Lenna published the first guidebook for counseling lesbians and gay men that emphasized positive lives. Among the concepts, issues, and counseling procedures discussed, the authors recommended that problem assessment should be carried out from the person-situation perspective. In other words, the social context should be part of understanding gay and lesbian clients.

Further recognition of affirmative practice occurred in the publication of a special issue of the *Journal of Homosexuality* in 1982. In the Foreword, John De Cecco complimented the editor, John Gonsiorek, for "assembling a cadre of psychiatrists, psychologists, and clinical social workers who are among the leaders of the effort" (De Cecco, 1981-1982, p. 1). As the journal issue illustrates, the effort to identity and develop a model for affirmative practice is an interdisciplinary effort. Gonsiorek (1981-1982) recommended that emerging models of lesbian and gay affirmative practice must meet the following requirements: (a) be relevant to the life experience of gay men and lesbians in a society that is at the least unsympathetic, (b) enhance the mental health of gay men and lesbians, (c) assist gay men and lesbians in meeting the challenge of creating a healthy, ethical, and useful place in society, (d) apply to the full range of psychological adjustments of individuals, and (e) accumulate strong empirical support.

Another step in the evolution of affirmative practice occurred with the publication of Moses and Hawkin's book, *Counseling Lesbian Women and Gay Men* (1986). It addressed diverse issues confronting lesbians and gay men. The authors urged mental health professionals not simply to assist these clients to "adjust" but to help them develop satisfying lives. This includes helping them develop ways of relating and self-expression that are not based on traditional heterosexual expectations. For example, the heterosexual model for marriage conflicts with the desire of many lesbian and gay men for more equality in their linkups (see Chapter 6).

Three trends can be identified in contemporary affirmative practice. The first trend is the development of *practice more specifically for lesbians and gay men* but built on increased understanding of the differences between the two genders (e.g., Dunkle, 1994; Falco, 1991). A second practice trend is the *identification of subgroups among lesbians and gay men with special needs*. Examples of special needs groups include *adolescents* (e.g., Morrow, 1993; Teague, 1992), *adults* (e.g., Morrow, 1996), persons with *mental illness* (e.g., Helfand, 1993; Hellman, 1996), persons with *disabilities* (e.g., McAllan & Ditillo, 1994), persons with *HIV/AIDS* (e.g., O'Neil, 1990; C. Robinson, 1994), and *racial and ethnic persons* (e.g., Greene, 1994a, 1994b; Greene, & Boyd-Franklin, 1996; E. S. Morales, 1996; Nakajima et al., 1996).

The third practice trend is the *adaptation and application of various interventions and theoretical approaches* to problems as they are experienced by lesbians and gay men. Examples of types of interventions include *couple counseling* (e.g., L. S. Brown, 1995b; Burch, 1986; Butler & Clarke, 1991; Kirkpa-

trick, 1991; McWhirter & Mattison, 1988; Roth, 1989), *self-help groups* (e.g., Eller & King, 1990), *group work* (e.g., Ball, 1994), *group therapy* (e.g., Chojnacki & Gelberg, 1995), *sexual therapy* (e.g., Hammadock, 1988; Nichols, 1987, 1988b; Reece, 1987), and *family therapy* (e.g., Bernstein, 1990; Granvold & Martin, in press; Laird & Green, 1996; Weinstein, 1992).

Theoretical approaches include *psychodynamic therapy* (e.g., Forstein, 1986; Stein & Cohen, 1986), *analytic therapy* (e.g., Herron, Kinter, Sollinger, & Trubowitz, 1981-1982; Isay, 1990; MacIntosh, 1994; Sussal, 1993), *Eriksonian hypnosis* (e.g., Wolf & Klein, 1988), *self-psychology* (e.g., Cornett, 1995; Mitchell, 1988), *cognitive therapy* (e.g., Mylott, 1994; Padesky, 1989), *Adlerian therapy* (e.g., Fisher, 1993), *brief counseling* (e.g., Gluth & Kiselica, 1994), *developmental counseling* (e.g., Gumaer, 1987), and *feminist therapy* (e.g., L. S. Brown, 1988; Falco, 1991; A. Smith, 1990; Unterberger, 1993). It is notable that analytic therapy is on this list because of its notorious nonaffirmative history. Psychoanalytic models exist now, however, that do not view same-gender sexual orientation as an illness and can be useful in assisting with difficulties experienced by lesbian, gay, and bisexual persons (Gonsiorek, 1996).

Examples of *problem areas* include *alcoholism* (e.g., Nicoloff & Stigliz, 1987), *eating disorders* (e.g., L. S Brown, 1987), *sexual abuse* (e.g., E. Brady, 1992), *parenting* (e.g., Loulan, 1986), and *codependency* (e.g., Smalley, 1988).

Affirmative practice specifically focused on bisexual men and women is much less prevalent in the practice literature. In recent years, however, resources have increased (e.g., Matteson, 1996; Nichols, 1988a). Even fewer materials are available on practice with transgenderist persons (e.g., Emerson & Rosenfeld, 1996; Rosenfeld & Emerson, 1995).

Contributions of
Feminist Therapy

The development of affirmative practice is strongly influenced by feminist therapy. According to L. S. Brown (1988), "Feminist therapy was probably one of the first approaches to psychotherapy that was built on the premise that lesbians and gay men were not per se pathological" (p. 206). The influence of feminist therapy can be identified in affirmative lesbian and gay practice in a number of ways.

First, feminist therapists do not view women's lives as deviant. By *eliminating the question of deviance* from the process of therapy as well as from the client, therapy can proceed more quickly.

Second, feminist therapists recognize that people and their *problems are political.* Feminist therapy brings to affirmative practice the acknowledgment of the impact of heterosexism and internalized homophobia on clients. The reality of pervasive societal oppression, first addressed with women, is easily seen as an important therapy issue with lesbian, gay, bisexual, and transgenderist clients (e.g., Browning et al., 1991; Neisen, 1993). Practitioners operating from an affirmative practice perspective understand that whatever difficulties these clients experience, they are aggravated by ongoing cultural and individual heterosexism (see Chapter 2). Just as feminist therapists see heterosexism as leading to oppression, they also recognize that race, class, and gender all interact to produce multiple levels of discrimination. Feminist therapy influences affirmative practice to address these complex sociocultural issues (L. S. Brown, 1988).

Third, in addition to recognition of the effects of oppression on gay, lesbian, bisexual, and transgenderist persons, feminist therapy encourages *political action.* For example, a feminist therapist will discuss with clients ways to become involved in political action so that they can become personally empowered and influence political and/or social change. In fact, feminist therapists may also speak out through professional and other organizations to educate the public about the oppression experienced by their clients.

Fourth, although most schools of therapy address the need for empathy and respect for clients, feminist therapy is especially mindful of the unequal power differential found in the typical therapy relationship. Efforts are made to equalize this link by forming a *collaborative or partnership type of interaction* with negotiated goals.

Principles of
Affirmative Practice

A review of the literature on current affirmative practice indicates a number of underlying principles. They are recommended for use by human services practitioners to demonstrate care and acceptance and to assure the highest quality of service to their gay, lesbian, bisexual, and transgenderist clients. Examples of these principles are listed in in Box 11.1.

The list of affirmative principles provides general guidance for working with bisexual, transgenderist, gay, and lesbian clients either in direct services or at organizational and other system levels. Material collected by Garnets, Hancock, Cochran, Goodchilds, and Peplau (1991) is also recommended. It provides a comparison of biased versus sensitive or affirmative practice, with examples. In addition to these general guidelines, specific methods to assess problems of daily life are needed as well as guides for specific practice interventions. In the next sections, an ecological/system approach to problem assessment is reviewed followed by a case example and recommended assessment and interventions.

(text continued on p. 179)

◆◆◆

Box 11.1. Principles of Affirmative Practice

▶ *Principle 1: Understand and abide by your professional code of ethics.* As indicated above, many professional organizations passed resolutions in support of the declassification of "homosexuality" as a mental illness. These include equal treatment of lesbian, gay, bisexual, and transgenderist persons in their codes of ethics (e.g., National Association of Social Workers [NASW], 1996).

▶ *Principle 2: Value clients' sexual orientations.* Practice is not neutral. Therapists never "make ethically or politically neutral decisions" (Davidson, 1991, p. 139). Affirmative practice emphasizes active valuing of clients' sexual orientation so that the positive growth and development of clients is facilitated.

▶ *Principle 3: Humans are variable in their sexual orientation.* This is a fact of life and does not reflect a problem, sin, or illness. Sexual orientation is conceptualized as multidimensional continua. People do not fit into dichotomous categories. They tend to place themselves at various points on continua related to elements such as sexual fantasy, sexual behavior, emotional preference, and self-identification (see Chapter 1). The ideas of variability and continua are helpful to persons, no matter what their sexual orientation, when exploring sexual and emotional feelings. Hartman (1993) cautioned, however, that although we view sexual orientation as an aspect of human variability, we should not take the view that it does not matter.

▶ *Principle 4: Sexual orientation per se is not the problem.* Most lesbian, gay, or bisexual persons do not request help because of their sexual orientation. Growing up and living in a society that is heterosexist, however, does create problems for them (Krajeski, 1984) (see Chapter 2).

▶ *Principle 5: Attempting to discover the cause of sexual orientation is a waste of time and can be destructive to the client.* After years of research from dozens of theoretical perspectives, there is no definitive answer about the cause of gay, lesbian, or bisexual sexual orientations. Pursuing the causes implies that these sexual orientations are a sickness and conveys the message to the client that "if there is a cause, there is a cure" (see Chapter 1).

▶ *Principle 6: Do not engage in any attempt to convert or change a client's sexual orientation.* Since the 1973 decision to drop "homosexuality" as a mental illness from the *Diagnostic Manual of the American Psychiatric Association,* fewer gay and lesbian clients request therapeutic interventions to change their sexual orientation. Even if a client desires to change, it is our ethical responsibility not to respond to that request (Davidson, 1991; Malyon, 1981-1982; Silverstein, 1991b). As discussed above, there are also no persuasive data that show that therapy, religious experience, or heterosexual marriage can successfully result in anything other than short-term superficial changes. Often, the client who asks for change is in reality asking for acceptance (Fassinger, 1991). Facilitating a change in the client's attitude toward being a lesbian or gay man is more appropriate as well as exploring the probable reasons for his or her desire to change—heterosexism and internalized oppression (NASW, 1984).

▶ *Principle 7: It is the right of clients to decide for themselves their level of "outness."* As clients struggle with and explore issues of coming out, an important task for the practitioner is to facilitate the assessment of risks and benefits of disclosure to family and community (L. S. Brown, 1988). Although there are various political positions on this issue, there are no right or wrong positions for an individual client.

► **Principle 8: Understand the effects of heterosexism on practice and on clients.** Although open hostility toward bisexual, transgenderist, gay, and lesbian clients by practitioners is not usually reported by clients, numerous studies indicate that they are dissatisfied because of negative prejudicial attitudes and lack of understanding. Practitioners may report that they are neutral or supportive of same-gender sexual orientation, for example, but give a different subtle message to clients (Rudolph, 1988). Everyone grows up in a heterosexist society. Consequently, practitioners are influenced by negative biases, myths, and stereotypes about gay, lesbian, bisexual, and transgenderist persons. If we are to avoid doing psychological harm to these clients, we must all examine the effects of our socialization in a heterosexist society (Hartman, 1993) and we must deliberately and consciously modify our own heterosexist attitudes (Hunt, 1993). We must also familiarize ourselves with the effects of heterosexism on gay, lesbian, bisexual, and transgenderist individuals, couples, families, and communities. The coming out process of identity development, for example, is often difficult and long lasting because of the anticipated rejection (Hartman, 1993).

► **Principle 9: Create a therapeutic partnership with clients based on equality.** The practice relationship should model equality so that the traditional power disparity between practitioner and client is decreased. Practice goals are mutually negotiated and agreed upon by the client and practitioner (L. S. Brown, 1988).

► **Principle 10: Obtain training and knowledge concerning issues unique to lesbian, gay, bisexual, and transgenderist persons.** Research studies conducted with human services providers and students indicate that providers received little if any training in working with these persons as clients. They lack basic knowledge about the lives of lesbian,

gay, bisexual, and transgenderist persons and give incorrect responses to statements about them (Hunt, 1993). In a study of psychologists, social workers, and psychiatrists by Graham, Rawlings, Halpern, and Hermes (1984), 26% did not think, for example, that helping clients disclose to others would be a part of therapy or counseling. Hartman (1993) urged that we must inform ourselves with accurate information as well as listen to our clients who will tell us their own understandings of their lives.

► **Principle 11: Obtain appropriate supervision.** Given that there is so much mythology, misinformation, and unawareness about gay, lesbian, bisexual, and transgenderist persons, human services professionals may have difficulty identifying unbiased information related to their problems. Consequently, to ensure that clients receive unbiased knowledge and service, it is important to have the resource of a knowledgeable supervisor (House & Holloway, 1992).

► **Principle 12: Become knowledgeable about community resources.** Lesbian, gay, transgenderist, and bisexual clients often feel isolated. Accurate and timely information about social support groups, centers, political groups, reading material, and other resources can help modify isolation. Clients should be encouraged to establish a support system (Fassinger, 1991).

► **Principle 13: At the organizational level, we must examine our agency or organization for discriminatory policies and work to change them.** In organizations, human services managers and supervisors can disseminate information on stereotypical thinking about bisexual, transgenderist, lesbian, and gay persons and promote awareness to change overt and covert discriminatory policies and practices. Staff education on sensitive services should be a crucial part of inservice education. In our educational programs in colleges and universities, we must ask for and provide up-to-date content on these groups of men and women (Hartman, 1993).

> ► *Principle 14: At the national level, we must push our professional organizations to advocate for the civil rights of lesbian, gay, bisexual, and transgenderist persons.* Political candidates who support these rights need our support and vote. Without the protection of enforced civil rights, gay, lesbian, transgenderist, and bisexual persons are without the protections guaranteed to every American citizen (Hartman, 1993). ◆

◆ Ecosystems Model

The problems faced by gay, lesbian, bisexual, and transgenderist clients of mental health or other human services arise from multiple sources. Consequently, to develop an understanding of the complexity of their life problems, human services practitioners are encouraged to view them from a broad perspective. A model that provides this broad view is based upon ecological and system approaches.

Bronfenbrenner (1975), an early proponent of viewing children's development from an environmental context, explained that the term *ecology* implies "a fit between the organism and its environment" (p. 439). This ecological concept was later combined with concepts from systems theory and referred to as *the ecosystems model.* This model is built on the recognition that there is a high degree of interaction between the person and the environment. In practice situations, therefore, the focus of intervention can be the person, the environment, or both.

According to proponents of the ecosystems model (e.g., Compton & Galaway, 1984; Germain & Gitterman, 1996; Hepworth & Larsen, 1993; A. Morales & Sheafor, 1995; Pincus & Minahan, 1973; Siporin, 1979), a major goal of practice is to enhance or restore the social functioning of individuals. Social functioning is viewed as a dynamic and transactional process between a client and the environment (Siporin, 1979). For a person to obtain a satisfactory level of social functioning, there must be adequate resources in the environment and positive transactions between the person and the environment (Hepworth & Larsen, 1993).

Person-in-Environment Classification System

A recently developed ecosystems model, the Person-in-Environment Classification System for Social Functioning Problems (PIE), is a tool for collecting and ordering information for determining a client's level of social functioning and goals for its enhancement. A completed assessment points to multiple targets for intervention. No particular theory of human behavior or intervention is dictated by this system. PIE was developed by Karls and Wandrei (1994a) and published by the National Association of Social Workers.

The PIE system guides the collection of a large amount of information about a client but also provides a way to categorize it in a concise way. Based on the problems identified, a treatment plan is then developed and implemented.

In a PIE assessment, information about a client's problems is classified according to four factors:

Factor I: Social Functioning Problems
Factor II: Environmental Problems
Factor III: Mental Health Problems
Factor IV: Physical Health Problems

Factor I, Social Functioning Problems, considers a person's functioning in social roles, which are grouped into four categories: (a) family, (b) other interpersonal, (c) occupational, and (d) special life situations. Each of these categories is divided into subcategories. The family category, for example, contains the subcategories of parent, child, spouse, sibling, other family roles, and significant other.

Factor II, Environmental Problems, focuses on factors external to the client. This factor recognizes the ecosystems model's concerns with the interaction of the client and the environment. The assumption is that external factors affect the client's social functioning. Problems in six environmental arenas can be examined: (a) economic/basic needs systems, (b) education/training systems, (c) judicial/legal systems, (d) health, safety, and social services systems, (e) voluntary association systems, and (f) affection support systems. Each of these categories also contains subcategories of specific possible problems. A client may experience problems, for example, in the economic needs system due to employment problems, with the specific subcategory of unemployment. An additional dimension of Factor II is discrimination experienced by the client. Discrimination can be classified on the basis of 12 categories such as age, sex, race, and sexual orientation. The practitioner can also examine the impact of the environmental conditions identified in Factor II on Factor I social functioning problems.

Factor III, Mental Health Problems, allows the practitioner to identify issues regarding a client's mental health through the uses of axes I and II of the *DSM-IV.* If present, these problems are integrated into the overall picture of the client.

Factor IV, Physical Health Problems, provides a way to include current physical conditions that may be potentially pertinent for the client's management of, for example, his or her social roles or environmental problems.

Problems identified in each factor can be coded in four other ways including (a) problem type, (b) severity of the disruption caused by the problem, (c) problem duration, and (d) client ability to cope with each problem.

A Case Example

Bill (age 39) and Anne (age 38) were referred to a family service agency by the school counselor for help with their 10-year-old son Bobby. He fought with other students at school, his grades dropped, and he appeared upset most of the time.

Bill came for the appointment by himself because Anne did not want to participate. He explained that his 12-year marriage was ending as a result of his recent self-identification as gay. Two months before, Anne followed Bill after he said that he was leaving for the evening to attend a business meeting. Instead, she found him visiting a man in his apartment. After many accusations, Bill admitted that over the years he had frequented gay bars. He met John, the man he was caught visiting, at a bar. He also indicated that he always felt attracted to men but that John was the only man whom he truly loved. He was ready to stop denying his same-gender sexual orientation, accept it, and begin a process of self-disclosure to others. He also wanted to live with John.

As a result of Bill's revelations, Anne was hurt and angry. She told Bill that she did not know if he loved her in the past or if he was simply using her as a cover to gain respectability in the community. In addition, she was concerned about their son, who was asking why his dad was "throwing him away" so that he could move in with another man. He also wondered if his dad loved him.

Another area of concern for the family was reactions from the community. Bill was a well-known local businessperson and civic leader. With knowledge of his sexual orientation, however, people in the community might refuse to do business with him. Bill decided that it was best to sell his business and move to another state rather than subject himself and his family to gossip and rumors. John was moving to the new location first and Bill planned to follow him.

The families of Bill and Anne did not know the reasons the couple was getting a divorce or Bill's plan to move to another state. In fact, Bill and Anne disagreed about how to handle this situation. Bill did not want to discuss the reasons for his intended move with either of their families. Anne, on the other hand, wanted to let her family know what had happened in order to get their support. Bill believed that if the families were told, they would not understand his current actions or his long-lasting predicament regarding his sexual orientation.

Anne filed for divorce and asked for custody of Bobby. In addition, she threatened to make Bill "pay" for the hurt he had inflicted on the family by severe restrictions on his visitation rights. Bill is worried that the court will discriminate against him because he is gay.

Anne also made plans to get tested for HIV. She fears the possibility that she contracted this disease from Bill. Because of the HIV epidemic, this situation creates ethical dilemmas (Sleek, 1996). Rust (1996a) commented that if for no other reason than physical health, a married man who engages in same-gender sexual activity should both practice safe sex and inform his wife about this activity.

Assessment and Targets for Intervention

Although all three family members need help with the situation, Bill alone requested assistance. Anne does not yet know what professional support she will seek for herself and Bobby. Consequently, the PIE assessment focused on Bill. It identified concerns

in Factor I (Social Functioning) and Factor II (Environment). The Factor I concerns included Bill's roles as parent, marital partner, worker, and adult child. They can be addressed through individual or group counseling. Factor II concerns involve three systems: employment, judicial and legal, and voluntary associations. Referrals can be made for assistance with a job search and for legal advice and legal representation regarding divorce and child custody. Bill also needs information concerning supportive resources for gay men in his new location.

As a supplement to the PIE assessment method, the work of Hollander and Haber (1992), first addressed in Chapter 4, is useful in Bill's situation because it shows the multiple changes that occur in a person's life during a coming out and disclosure transition. Following Bronfenbrenner (1979), the changes are viewed in the ecological context of four nested subsystems: *microsystem* (activities, roles, and interpersonal relations), *mesosystem* (social network), *ecosystem* (larger community), and *macrosystem* (broad cultural and social issues). Changes in a person's activities, roles, and interpersonal relations may cause additional shifts in the same areas so that developmental processes are both a consequence and a precipitator of changes.

Although interventions can focus on any level of the environment, Hollander and Haber (1992) suggested that they can most easily be carried out in the micro- and mesosystems. For example, at the *microsystem* level, education can be useful for Bill that indicates what to expect in the coming out and disclosure transition as well as interventions that facilitate coping with disclosure, disrupted linkups, and the development of new linkups. At the *mesosystem* level, the social network will change in response to changes in the microsystem. People will leave Bill's network, and new people will enter it. According to Hollander (1989), assistance in developing new support, as the availability of for-mer support is modified, will help reduce the stress associated with the coming out and disclosure transition. In Bill's situation, vari-ous systems at the *ecosystem,* or larger com-munity, level are also pertinent including the legal system regarding issues such as divorce and child custody. Cultural heterosexism at the *macrosystem* level is an ongoing factor that will affect his life in multiple ways.

The ultimate goal for gay men, as well as lesbian, bisexual, and transgenderist per-sons, is a positive identity. Another important implication of ecologically based assump-tions is the clarity that a positive identity cannot be achieved and maintained all by oneself. Social linkages or, more specifi-cally, nurturing sources of social support are needed to provide psychological sustenance for its maintenance. These assumptions also emphasize that ultimately a positive identity depends on a person using social experiences and support to renounce regrets about his or her identity (Christian & Keefe, 1997).

◆ Summary

In line with professional codes of ethics as well as what should be one's personal ethics, the only acceptable practice approach for human services professionals with lesbian, gay, bisexual, and transgenderist clients is an affirmative one. In addition to abiding by affirmative practice principles, the assess-ment and intervention overview presented here offers an alternative to traditional psy-chiatric nomenclature that is ill-suited to the problems of living encountered by these clients.

REFERENCES

Abbott, S., & Love, B. (1972). *Sappho was a right-on woman.* New York: Stein & Day.

Adam, B. D. (1987). *The rise of the gay and lesbian movement.* Boston: Twayne.

Adams, C. L., & Kimmel, D. C. (1991, November). *Older African-American gay men.* Paper presented at the annual meetings of the Gerontological Society of America, San Francisco.

Adams, C. L., & Kimmel, D. C. (1997). Exploring the lives of older African American gay men. In B. Greene (Ed.), *Ethnic and cultural diversity among lesbians and gay men* (pp. 132-151). Thousand Oaks, CA: Sage.

Adelman, M. (1980). Adjustment of aging and styles of being gay: A study of elderly gay men and lesbians (Doctoral dissertation, Wright Institute, 1980). *Dissertation Abstracts International, 40.*

Adelman, M. (1986). *Long time passing.* Boston: Alyson.

Adelman, M. (1988). Quieting our fears: Lesbians and aging. *Outlook: National Lesbian and Gay Quarterly, 1,* 78-81.

Adelman, M. (1991). Stigma, gay lifestyles, and adjustment to aging: A study of later-life gay men and lesbians. In J. A. Lee (Ed.), *Gay midlife and maturity* (pp. 1-32). New York: Haworth.

Adler, N. L., Hendrick, S. S., & Hendrick, C. (1986). Male sexual preference and attitudes toward love and sexuality. *Journal of Sex Education and Therapy, 12,* 27-30.

Adler, S., & Brenner, J. (1992). Gender and space: Lesbians and gay men in the city. *International Journal of Urban and Regional Research, 16,* 24-34.

Ainsley, J., & Feltey, K. M. (1991). Definitions and dynamics of motherhood and family in lesbian communities. *Marriage and Family Review, 17,* 63-85.

Allen, K. R., & Demo, D. H. (1995). The families of lesbians and gay men: A new frontier in family research. *Journal of Marriage and the Family, 57,* 111-127.

Almaguer, T. (1991). Chicano men: A cartography of homosexual behavior. *A Journal of Feminist Culturalist Studies, 3,* 75-100.

Almvig, C. (1980). *Adjustment to aging and styles of being gay: A study of elderly gay men and lesbians.* Unpublished doctoral dissertation, Wright Institute, Boston.

Almvig, C. (1982). *The invisible minority: Aging and lesbians.* Syracuse, NY: Utica College of Syracuse.

Altman, D. (1982). *The homosexualization of America.* New York: St. Martin's.

Altman, D. (1986). *AIDS in the mind of America.* Garden City, NJ: Doubleday.

American Bar Association. (1990). *Model code of judicial conduct.* Chicago: Author.

American Psychiatric Association. (1987). *Diagnostic and statistical manual of mental disorders* (3rd ed., revised). Washington, DC: Author.

American Psychological Association, Committee on Lesbian and Gay Concerns. (1991). Avoiding heterosexist bias in language. *American Psychologist, 46,* 937-974.

American Psychological Association. (1994). *Publication manual of the American Psychological Association* (4th ed.). Washington, DC: Author.

Anderson, C. L. (1981). The effect of a workshop on attitudes of female nursing students toward male homosexuality. *Journal of Homosexuality, 7,* 57-70.

Ankeny, D. C. (1991). Creating the statistical portion of an affirmative action plan. *Tulane Law Review, 65,* 1183, 1205.

Arriola, E. R. (1993). Coming out and coming to terms with sexual identity. *Tulane Law Review, 68,* 283-309.

Auger, J. A. (1992). Living in the margins. *Canadian Woman Studies, 12,* 80-84.

Bailey, J. M. (1995). Biological perspectives on sexual orientation. In A. R. D'Augelli & C. J. Patterson (Eds.), *Lesbian, gay, and bisexual identities over the lifespan: Psychological perspectives* (pp. 102-135). New York: Oxford University Press.

Bailey, J. M. (1996). Gender identity. In R. C. Savin-Williams & K. M. Cohen (Eds.), *The lives of lesbians, gays, and bisexuals: Children to adults* (pp. 71-93). Ft. Worth, TX: Harcourt Brace.

Bailey, J. M., Bobrow, D., Wolfe, M., & Mikach, S. (1995). Sexual orientation of adult sons of gay fathers. *Developmental Psychology, 31,* 124-129.

Bailey, J. M., & Pillard, R. C. (1991). A genetic study of male sexual orientation. *Archives of General Psychiatry, 48,* 1089-1096.

Bales, J. (1985, December). Gay adolescents' pain compounded. *APA Monitor, 16,* 21.

Ball, S. (1994). A group model for gay and lesbian clients with chronic mental illness. *Social Work, 39,* 109-115.

Barbone, S., & Rice, L. (1994). Coming out, being out, and acts of virtue. *Journal of Homosexuality, 27,* 91-110.

Bard, M., & Sangrey, D. (1979). *The crime victim's book.* New York: Basic Books.

Bardis, P. D. (1980). A glossary of homosexuality. *Maledicta, 4,* 59-63.

Baruch, G., & Brooks-Gunn, J. (1984). The study of women in midlife. In G. Baruch & J. Brooks-Gunn (Eds.), *Women in midlife* (pp. 1-8). New York: Plenum.

Baumrind, D. (1995). Commentary on sexual orientation: Research and social policy implications. *Developmental Psychology, 31,* 130-136.

Beck, A. T., Ward, C. H., Mendelson, M., Mock, J., & Erbaugh, J. (1961). An inventory for measuring depression. *Archives of General Psychiatry, 4,* 561-571.

Becker, C. S. (1988). *Broken ties: Lesbian ex-lovers.* Boston: Alyson.

Beckett, J. O., & Schneider, R. L. (1992). Older women. In R. L. Schneider & N. P. Kroff (Eds.), *Gerontological social work: Knowledge, service settings and special populations* (pp. 323-338). Chicago: Nelson-Hall.

Beemyn, B., & Eliason, M. (Eds.). (1996). *Queer studies: A lesbian, gay, bisexual, and transgender anthology.* New York: New York University Press.

Bell, A. P., & Weinberg, M. S. (1978). *Homosexualities: A study of diversity among men and women.* New York: Simon & Schuster.

Bell, A. P., Weinberg, M. S., & Hammersmith, S. K. (1981). *Sexual preference: Its development in men and women.* Bloomington: Indiana University Press.

Ben-Ari, A. (1995). The discovery that an offspring is gay: Parents', gay men's, and lesbians' perspectives. *Journal of Homosexuality, 30,* 89-112.

Berger, P., & Kellner, H. (1975). Marriage and the construction of reality. In D. Brissett & C. Edgely (Eds.), *Life as theatre* (pp. 219-233). Chicago: Aldine.

Berger, R. M. (1980). Psychological adaptation of the older homosexual male. *Journal of Homosexuality, 5,* 161-175.

Berger, R. M. (1982). The unseen minority: Older gays and lesbians. *Social Work, 27,* 236-242.

Berger, R. M. (1984). Realities of gay and lesbian aging. *Social Work, 29,* 57-62.

Berger, R. M. (1990a). Men together: Understanding the gay couple. *Journal of Homosexuality, 19,* 31-49.

Berger, R. M. (1990b). Passing impact on the quality of same-sex couple relationships. *Social Work, 35,* 328-332.

Berger, R. M. (1992). Research on older gay men: What we know, what we need to know. In N. J. Woodman (Ed.), *Lesbian and gay lifestyles: A guide for counseling and education* (pp. 217-233). New York: Irvington.

Berger, R. M. (1996). *Gay and gray: The older homosexual man* (2nd ed.). Binghamtom, NY: Haworth.

Berger, R. M., & Kelly, J. J. (1986). Working with homosexuals in the older population. *Social Casework: The Journal of Contemporary Social Work, 67,* 203-210.

Berger, R. M., & Kelly, J. J. (1996). Gay men and lesbians grown older. In R. P. Cabaj & T. S. Stein (Eds.), *Textbook of homosexuality and mental health* (pp. 305-316). Washington, DC: American Psychiatric Press.

Berger, R. M., & Mallon, D. (1993). Social support networks of gay men. *Journal of Sociology & Social Welfare, 22,* 155-174.

Berkey, B. R., Perelman-Hall, T., & Kurdek, L. A. (1990). The multidimensional scale of sexuality. *Journal of Homosexuality, 19,* 67-87.

Bernard, J. (1973). *The sociology of community.* Glenview, IL: Scott, Foresman.

Bernstein, B. E. (1990). Attitudes and issues of parents of gay men and lesbians and implications for therapy. *Journal of Gay & Lesbian Psychotherapy, 1,* 37-53.

Berrill, K. (1989). *Report of the campus project of the National Gay and Lesbian Task Force.* Washington, DC: National Gay and Lesbian Task Force.

Berrill, K. T. (1990). Anti-gay violence and victimization in the United States. *Journal of Interpersonal Violence, 5,* 274-294.

Bérubé, A. (1990). *Coming out under fire: The history of gay men and women in World War II.* New York: Free Press.

Bieber, I., Dain, H. J., Dince, P. R., Drellich, M. G., Grand, H. G., Gundlach, R. H., Kremer, M. W., Rifkin, A. H., Wilbur, C. B., & Bieber, T. B. (1962). *Homosexuality: A psychoanalytic study.* New York: Basic Books.

Bigner, J. J., & Bozett, F. W. (1990). Parenting by gay fathers. *Marriage and Family Review, 14,* 155-175.

Bigner, J. J., & Jacobson, R. B. (1989). Parenting behaviors of homosexual and heterosexual fathers. *Journal of Homosexuality, 18,* 173-186.

Bigner, J. J., & Jacobson, R. B. (1992). Adult responses to child behavior and attitudes toward fathering: Gay and nongay fathers. *Journal of Homosexuality, 23,* 99-112.

Billy, J. O. G., Tanfer, K., Grady, W. R., & Klepenger, D. H. (1993). The sexual behavior of men in the United States. *Family Planning Perspectives, 25,* 52-60.

Birk, L. (1980). The myth of classic homosexuality: Views of a behavioral psychotherapist. In J. Marmor (Ed.), *Homosexual behavior: A modern reappraisal* (pp. 376-390). New York: Basic Books.

Birt, C. M., & Dion, K. L. (1987). Relative deprivation theory and responses to discrimination. *British Journal of Social Psychology, 26,*139.

Blair, R. (1982). *Ex-gay.* New York: Homosexual Counseling Center.

Blackwood, E. (1984). Sexuality and gender in certain Native American tribes: The case of the cross-gender females. *Signs, 10,* 27-42.

Blanchard, R. (1989). The classification and labeling of nonhomosexual gender dysphorias. *Archives of Sexual Behavior, 18,* 315-334.

Blanchard, R., Clemmensen, L. H., & Steiner, B. W. (1987). Heterosexual and homosexual gender dysphorias. *Archives of Sexual Behavior, 16,* 139-152.

Bloom, B. L., & Hodges, W. F. (1981). The predicament of the newly separated. *Community Mental Health Journal, 17,* 277-293.

Blumenfeld, W. J. (1992). Introduction. In W. J. Blumenfeld (Ed.), *Homophobia: How we all pay the price* (pp. 1-22). Boston: Beacon.

Blumenfeld, W. J., & Raymond, D. (1993). *Looking at gay and lesbian life.* Boston: Beacon.

Blumstein, P., & Schwartz, P. (1977). Bisexuality: Some social psychological issues. *Journal of Social Issues, 33,* 30-45.

Blumstein, P., & Schwartz, P. (1983). *American couples.* New York: William Morrow.

Bohan, J. S. (1996). *Psychology and sexual orientation: Coming to terms.* New York: Routledge.

Bonilla, J., & Porter, J. (1990). A comparison of Latino, Black, and non-Hispanic White attitudes toward homosexuality. *Hispanic Journal of Behavioral Sciences, 12,* 437-452.

Bowers v. Hardwick, 478 U.S. 186 (1986).

Boxer, A., & Cohler, B. (1989). The life course of gay and lesbian youth: An immodest proposal for the study of lives. *Journal of Homosexuality, 17,* 315-355.

Bozett, F. W. (1980). Gay fathers: How and why they disclose their homosexuality to their children. *Family Relations, 29,* 173-179.

Bozett, F. W. (1981a). Gay fathers: Evolution of the gay-father identity. *American Journal of Orthopsychiatry, 51,* 552-559.

Bozett, F. W. (1981b). Gay fathers: Identity conflict resolution through integrative sanctioning. *Alternative Lifestyles, 4,* 90-107.

Bozett, F. W. (1982). Heterogeneous couples in heterosexual marriages: Gay men and straight women. *Journal of Marital and Sexual Therapy, 8,* 81-89.

Bozett, F. W. (1984). Parenting concerns of gay fathers. *Topics in Clinical Nursing, 6,* 60-71.

Bozett, F. W. (1987). Children of gay fathers. In F. W. Bozett (Ed.), *Gay and lesbian parents* (pp. 39-57). New York: Praeger.

Bozett, F. W. (1989). Gay fathers: A review of the literature. *Journal of Homosexuality, 18,* 37-162.

Bradbury, T. N., & Fincham, F. D. (1988). Individual difference variables in close relationships: A contextual model of marriage as an integrative framework. *Journal of Personality and Social Psychology, 54,* 713-721.

Bradford, J., & Ryan, C. (1987). *National Lesbian Health Care Survey: Mental health implications.* Washington, DC: National Lesbian and Gay Health Foundation.

Bradford, J., & Ryan, C. (1991). Who we are: Health concerns of middle-aged lesbians. In B. J. Warshow & A. J. Smith (Eds.), *Lesbians at midlife: The creative transition* (pp. 147-163). San Francisco: Spinsters.

Bradley, D. (1994, May 4). Unions. *Dallas Morning News,* p. C1.

Brady, E. (1992). Psychotherapy issues in working with the lesbian incest survivor. In S. Dworkin & F. Gutiériérrez (Eds.), *Counseling gay men and lesbians: Journey to the end of the rainbow* (pp. 203-210). Alexandria: VA: American Association for Counseling & Development.

Brady, S., & Busse, W. J. (1994). The gay identity questionnaire: A brief measure of homosexual identity formation. *Journal of Homosexuality, 26,* 1-22.

Bridges, K. L., & Croteau, J. M. (1994). Once-married lesbians: Facilitating changing life patterns. *Journal of Counseling & Development, 73,* 134-140.

Brody, E. M. (1990). *Women in the middle: Their parent care years.* New York: Springer.

Bronfenbrenner, U. (1975). Reality and research in the ecology of human development. *Proceedings of the American Philosophical Society, 119,* 439-469.

Bronfenbrenner, U. (1979). *The ecology of human development: Experiments by nature and design.* Cambridge, MA: Harvard University Press.

Brooks, S. E. (1991). Resources. In N. J. Evans & V. A. Walls (Eds.), *Beyond tolerance: Gays, lesbians, and bisexuals on campus* (pp. 213-232). Alexandria, VA: American College Personnel Association.

Brown, L. B. (1997). Women and men, not-men and not-women, lesbians and gays: American Indian gender-style alternatives. *Journal of Gay & Lesbian Social Services, 6,* 5-20.

Brown, L. S. (1987). Lesbians, weight, and eating: New analyses and perspectives. In the Boston Lesbian Psychologies Collective (Eds.), *Lesbian psychologies: Explorations and challenges* (pp. 294-309). Urbana: University of Illinois.

Brown, L. S. (1988). Feminist therapy with lesbians and gay men. In M. A. Dutton-Douglas & L. E. A. Walker (Eds.), *Feminist psychotherapies: Integrating therapeutic and feminist systems* (pp. 206-227). Norwood, NJ: Ablex.

Brown, L. S. (1989a). Lesbians, gay men and their families: Common clinical issues. *Journal of Gay & Lesbian Psychotherapy, 1,* 65-77.

Brown, L. S. (1989b). New voices, new visions: Toward a lesbian/gay paradigm for psychology. *Psychology of Women Quarterly, 13,* 445-458.

Brown, L. S. (1995a). Lesbian identities: Concepts and issues. In A. R. D'Augelli & C. J. Patterson (Eds.), *Lesbian, gay, and bisexual identities over the lifespan: Psychological perspectives* (pp. 3-23). New York: Oxford University Press.

Brown, L. S. (1995b). Therapy with same-sex couples: An introduction. In N. S. Jacobson & A. S. Guttman (Eds.), *Clinical handbook of couple therapy* (pp. 274-291). New York: Guilford.

Brown, R. M. (1973). *Rubyfruit jungle.* New York: Daughters, Inc.

Brownfain, J. J. (1985). A study of the married bisexual male: Paradox and resolution. *Journal of Homosexuality, 11,* 173-188.

Browning, C. (1987). Therapeutic issues and intervention strategies with young adult lesbian clients: A developmental approach. *Journal of Homosexuality, 14,* 45-52.

Browning, C., Reynolds, A. L., & Dworkin, S. H. (1991). Affirmative psychotherapy for lesbian women. *Counseling Psychologist, 19,* 177-196.

Bryant, S. (1992). Mediation for lesbian and gay families. *Mediation Quarterly, 9,* 391-395.

Bryant, S., & Demian. (1994). Relationship characteristics of American gay and lesbian couples: Findings from a national survey. *Journal of Gay and Lesbian Social Services, 1,* 101-117.

Bullough, V. L. (1994). *Science in the bedroom: A history of sex research.* New York: Basic Books.

Bumpass, L. L., & Aquilino, W. S. (1995). *A social map of midlife: Family and work over the middle life course.* Vero Beach, FL: MacArthur Foundation Research Network on Successful Midlife Development.

Burch, B. (1982). Psychological merger in lesbian couples: A joint ego psychological and systems approach. *Family Therapy, 9,* 201-208.

Burch, B. (1986). Psychotherapy and the dynamics of merger in lesbian couples. In T. S. Stein & C. J. Cohen (Eds.),

Contemporary perspectives on psychotherapy with lesbians and gay men (pp. 57-71). New York: Plenum.

Burch, B. (1993). *On intimate terms: The psychology of difference in lesbian relationships.* Urbana: University of Illinois.

Burgess, R. L., & Huston, T. L. (Eds.). (1979). *Social exchange in developing relationships.* New York: Academic Press.

Butler, M., & Clarke, J. (1991). Couple therapy with homosexual men. In D. Hooper & W. Dryder (Eds.), *Couple therapy: A handbook* (pp. 196-216). Philadelphia: Open University Press.

Byrne, J. S. (1993). Affirmative action for lesbians and gay men: A proposal for true equality of opportunity and workforce diversity. *Yale Law & Policy Review, 11,* 47-108.

Cain, R. (1991a). Relational contexts and information management among gay men. *Families in Society, 72,* 344-352.

Cain, R. (1991b). Stigma management and gay identity development. *Social Work, 36,* 67-73.

Caldwell, D. K. (1997a, March). "Pro-gay" companies targeted: Conservatives say values compromised. *Dallas Morning News,* pp. G1, G4.

Caldwell, D. K. (1997b, June). Baptists vote to boycott Disney Co. *Dallas Morning News,* pp. A1, A16.

Caldwell, M. A., & Peplau, L. A. (1984). The balance of power in lesbian relationships. *Sex Roles, 10,* 587-600.

Cantor, J. M., & Pilkington, N. W. (1992, August). *Homophobia in psychology programs: A survey of graduate students.* Paper presented at the Centennial Convention of the American Psychological Association, Washington, DC.

Carballo-Diéguez, A. (1989). Hispanic culture, gay male culture, and AIDS: Counseling implications. *Journal of Counseling and Development, 68,* 26-30.

Card, C. (1992). Lesbianism and choice. *Journal of Homosexuality, 23,* 39-51.

Card, C. (1996). Prologue. *Journal of Homosexuality, 32,* 1-5.

Cardell, M., Finn, S., & Marecek, J. (1981). Sex-role identity, sex-role behavior, and satisfaction in heterosexual, lesbian, and gay male couples. *Psychology of Women Quarterly, 5,* 488-494.

Carmen, Gail, Neena, & Tamara. (1991). Becoming visible: Black lesbian discussions. In Feminist Review (Eds.), *Sexuality: A reader.* (pp. 216-244). London: Virago.

Carrillo, H., & Maiorana, H. (1989). *AIDS prevention among gay Latinos in San Francisco: From behavior change to social change.* Unpublished manuscript.

Casper, V., Schultz, S., & Wickens, E. (1992). Breaking the silences: Lesbian and gay parents and the schools. *Teachers College Record, 94,* 109-137.

Cass, V. C. (1979). Homosexual identity formation: A theoretical model. *Journal of Homosexuality, 4,* 219-235.

Cass, V. C. (1983-1984). Homosexual identity: A concept in need of definition. *Journal of Homosexuality, 9,* 105-126.

Cass, V. C. (1984). Homosexual identity formation: Testing a theoretical model. *Journal of Sex Research, 20,* 143-167.

Cass, V. C. (1990). The implications of homosexual identity formation for the Kinsey model and scale of sexual preference. In D. P. McWhirter, S. A. Sanders, & J. M Reinisch (Eds.), *Homosexuality/heterosexuality: Concepts of sexual orientation* (pp. 239-266). New York: Oxford University Press.

Cass, V. C. (1996). Sexual orientation identity formation: A Western phenomenon. In R. P. Cabaj & T. S. Stein (Eds.), *Textbook of homosexuality and mental health* (pp. 227-251). Washington, DC: American Psychiatric Press.

Catania, J., Turner, H., Kegeles, S., Stall, R., Pollack, L., & Coates, T. (1989). Older Americans and AIDS: Transmission risks and primary prevention research needs. *Gerontologist, 29,* 373-381.

Cazenave, N. A. (1979). Social structure and personal choice. Effects on intimacy, marriage and the family alternative lifestyle research. *Alternative Lifestyles, 2,* 331-358.

Cazenave, N. A. (1984). Race, socioeconomic status, and age: The social context of American masculinity. *Sex Roles, 11,* 639-656.

Champagne, J. (1993). Seven speculations on queers and class. *Journal of Homosexuality, 26,* 159-174.

Chan, C. S. (1987). Asian lesbians: Psychological issues in the "coming out" process. *Asian American Psychological Association Journal, 12,*16-18.

Chan, C. S. (1989). Issues of identity development among Asian-American lesbians and gay men. *Journal of Counseling and Development, 68,*16-20.

Chan, C. (1992). Cultural considerations in counseling Asian American lesbians and gay men. In S. Dworkin & F. Gutiérrez (Eds.), *Counseling gay men and lesbians* (pp. 115-124). Alexandria, VA: American Association for Counseling and Development.

Chan, C. S. (1995). Issues of sexual identity in an ethnic minority: The case of Chinese American lesbians, gay men, and bisexual people. In A. R. D'Augelli & C. J. Patterson (Eds.), *Lesbians, gay, and bisexual identities over the lifespan* (pp. 87-101). New York: Oxford University Press.

Chan, C. S. (1997). Don't ask, don't tell, don't know: The formation of a homosexual identity and sexual expression among Asian American lesbians. In B. Greene (Ed.), *Ethnic and cultural diversity among lesbians and gay men* (pp. 240-248). Thousand Oaks, CA: Sage.

Charbonneau, D., & Lander, P. (1991). Redefining sexuality: Women becoming lesbian in midlife. In B. Sang, J. Warshow, & A. Smith (Eds.), *Lesbians at midlife: The creative transition* (pp. 35-43). San Francisco: Spinsters.

Choi, K., Salazar, N., Lew, S., & Coates, T. J. (1995). AIDS risk, dual identity, and community among gay Asian and Pacific Islander men in San Francisco. In B. Greene & M. Herek (Eds.), *AIDS, identity and community* (pp. 115-134). Thousand Oaks, CA: Sage.

Chojnacki, J. T., & Gelberg, S. (1995). The facilitation of a gay/lesbian/bisexual support-therapy group by heterosexual counselors. *Journal of Counseling & Development, 73,* 352-354.

Christian, D. V., & Keefe, D. A. (1997). Maturing gay men: A framework for social service: Assessment and intervention. *Journal of Gay and Lesbian Social Services, 6,* 47-78.

Chung, Y. B., & Katayama, M. (1996). Assessment of sexual orientation in lesbian/gay/bisexual studies. *Journal of Homosexuality, 30,* 49-62.

Clair, D., & Genest, M. (1987). Variables associated with the adjustment of offspring of alcoholic fathers. *Journal of Studies of Alcohol, 48,* 345-355.

Clarke, C. (1983). The failure to transform: Homophobia in the Black community. In B. Smith (Ed.), *Home girls: A Black feminist anthology* (pp. 197-208). New York: Kitchen Table—Women of Color.

Clausen, J. A. (1986). *The life course: A sociological perspective.* Englewood Cliffs, NJ: Prentice Hall.

Clunis, D. M., & Green, G. D. (1993). *Lesbian couples: Creating healthy relationships for the 90's.* Seattle, WA: Seal.

Cohen, C. J., & Stein, T. S. (1986). Reconceptualizing individual psychotherapy with gay men and lesbians. In T. S. Stein & C. J. Cohen (Eds.), *Contemporary perspectives on psychotherapy with lesbians and gay men* (pp. 27-54). New York: Plenum.

Cohen, K. M., & Savin-Williams, R. C. (1996). Developmental perspectives on coming out to self and others. In R. C. Savin-Williams & K. M. Cohen (Eds.), *The lives of lesbians, gays, and bisexuals: Children to adults* (pp. 113-151). Ft. Worth, TX: Harcourt Brace.

Cole, E., & Rothblum, E. D. (1990). Commentary on "Sexuality and the midlife woman." *Psychology of Women Quarterly, 14,* 509-512.

Cole, E., & Rothblum, E. D. (1991). Lesbian sex at menopause: As good as or better than ever. In B. Sang, J. Warshow, & A. Smith (Eds.), *Lesbians at midlife: The creative transition* (pp. 184-193). San Francisco: Spinsters.

Coleman, E. (1978). Toward a new model of treatment of homosexuality: A review. *Journal of Homosexuality, 3,* 345-359.

Coleman, E. (1981-1982a). Bisexual and gay men in heterosexual marriage: Conflicts and resolutions in therapy. *Journal of Homosexuality, 7,* 93-101.

Coleman, E. (1981-1982b). Developmental stages of the coming-out process. *Journal of Homosexuality, 7,* 31-43.

Coleman, E. (1985a). Bisexual women in marriages: Conflicts and resolutions in therapy. *Journal of Homosexuality, 11,* 87-99.

Coleman, E. (1985b). Integration of male bisexuality and marriage. *Journal of Homosexuality, 11,*189-207.

Coleman, E. (1987). Assessment of sexual orientation. *Journal of Homosexuality, 14,* 9-24.

Coleman, E. (1989). The development of male prostitution activity among gay and bisexual adolescents. *Journal of Homosexuality, 17,* 131-149.

Coleman, V. (1994). Lesbian battering: The relationship between personality and the perpetration of violence. *Violence and Victims, 9,* 139-152.

Collins, J. (1990, February 14). Despite furor, Hampton gets $30,000 for unopposed race. *Dallas Times Herald,* pp. A1, A7.

Collins, L. E., & Zimmerman, N. (1983). Homosexual and bisexual issues. In J. C. Hansen, J. D. Woody, & R. H. Woody (Eds.), *Sexual issues in family therapy* (pp. 82-100). Rockville: Aspen.

Compas, B. E., & Williams, R. A. (1990). Stress, coping, and adjustment in mothers and young adolescents in single- and two-parent families. *American Journal of Community Psychology, 18,* 525-545.

Compton, B. R., & Galaway, B. (1984). *Social work processes.* Homewood, IL: Dorsey.

Comstock, G. D. (1991). *Violence against lesbians and gay men.* New York: Columbia University Press.

Conerly, G. (1996). The politics of Black lesbian, gay, and bisexual identity. In B. Beemyn & M. Eliason (Ed.), *Queer studies: A lesbian, gay, bisexual, and transgender anthology* (pp. 133-145). New York: New York University Press.

Conrad, S., & Wincze, J. (1976). Orgasmic reconditioning: A controlled study of the effects upon the sexual arousal and behavior of male homosexuals. *Behavior Therapy, 7,* 155-166.

Cornett, C. (1995). *Reclaiming the authentic self: Dynamic psychotherapy with gay men.* Northvale, NJ: Jason Aronson.

Cornett, C. W., & Hudson, R. A. (1987). Middle adulthood and the theories of Erikson, Gould, and Vaillant: Where does the gay man fit? *Journal of Gerontological Social Work, 10,* 61-73.

Cowan, P. A., & Cowan, C. P. (1990). Becoming a family: Research and intervention. In I. E. Sigel & G. H. Brody (Eds.), *Methods of family research: Biographies of research projects: Vol. 1. Normal families* (pp. 1-51). Hillsdale, NJ: Lawrence Erlbaum.

Cox, S., & Gallois, C. (1996). Gay and lesbian identity development: A social identity perspective. *Journal of Homosexuality, 30,* 1-30.

Cramer, D. W., & Roach, A. J. (1988). Coming out to mom and dad: A study of gay males and their relationships with their parents. *Journal of Homosexuality, 15,* 79-91.

Cranston, K. (1991). HIV education for gay, lesbian, and bisexual youth: Personal risk, personal power, and the community of conscience. *Journal of Homosexuality, 22,* 247-259.

Crocker, J., & Major, B. (1989). Social stigma and self-esteem: The self-protective properties of stigma. *Psychological Review, 96,* 608-630.

Cronin, D. M. (1974). Coming out among lesbians. In E. Goode & R. R. Troiden (Eds.), *Sexual deviance and sexual deviants* (pp. 268-277). New York: William Morrow.

Crosbie-Burnett, M., & Helmbrecht, L. (1993). A descriptive empirical study of gay male stepfamilies. *Family Relations, 42,* 256-262.

Croteau, J. M., & Hedstrom, S. M. (1993). Integrating commonality and difference: The key to career counseling with lesbian women and gay men. *Career Development Quarterly, 41,* 201-209.

Croteau, J. M., & Kusek, M. T. (1992). Gay and lesbian speaker panels: Implementation and research. *Journal of Counseling and Development, 70,* 396-401.

Cruikshank, M. (1992). *The gay and lesbian liberation movement.* New York: Routledge & Kegan Paul.

Cummerton, J. (1982). Homophobia and social work practice with lesbians. In A. Weick & S. T. Vandiver (Eds.), *Women, power and change* (pp. 104-113). Washington, DC: National Association of Social Workers.

Curran, D., & Parr, D. (1957). Homosexuality: An analysis of 100 male cases. *British Medical Journal, 1,* 797-801.

Curry, H., & Clifford, A. (1986). *A legal guide for lesbian and gay couples* (4th ed.). Berkeley, CA: Nolo.

Dank, B. (1971). Coming out in the gay world. *Psychiatry, 34,* 180-197.

D'Augelli, A. R. (1987). Social support patterns of lesbian women in a rural helping network. *Journal of Rural Community Psychology, 8,* 12-21.

D'Augelli, A. R. (1989a). Gay men's and lesbians' experiences of discrimination, harassment, and indifference in a university community. *American Journal of Community Psychology, 17,* 317-321.

D'Augelli, A. R. (1989b). Homophobia in a university community: Views of prospective resident assistants. *Journal of College Student Development, 30,* 546-552.

D'Augelli, A. R. (1989c). Lesbian women in a rural helping network. *Women and Therapy, 8,* 119-130.

D'Augelli, A. R. (1989d). Lesbians and gay men on campus: Visibility, empowerment, and educational leadership. *Peabody Journal of Education, 66,* 124-142.

D'Augelli, A. R. (1989e). The development of a helping community for lesbians and gay men: A case study in community psychology. *Journal of Community Psychology, 17,* 18-29.

D'Augelli, A. R. (1991). Gay men in college: Identity processes and adaptations. *Journal of College Student Development, 32,* 140-146.

D'Augelli, A. R. (1992). Lesbian and gay male undergraduates' experiences of harassment and fear on campus. *Journal of Interpersonal Violence, 7,* 18-29.

D'Augelli, A. R. (1993). Preventing mental health problems among lesbian and gay college students. *Journal of Primary Prevention, 13,* 1-17.

D'Augelli, A. R. (1994). Identity development and sexual orientation: Toward a model of lesbian, gay, and bisexual development. In E. J. Trickett, R. J. Watts, & D. Birman (Eds.), *Human diversity* (pp. 312-333). San Francisco: Jossey-Bass.

D'Augelli, A. R., & Garnets, L. D. (1995). Lesbian, gay, and bisexual communities. In A. R. D'Augelli & C. J. Patterson (Eds.), *Lesbians, gay, and bisexual identities over the lifespan* (pp. 293-320). New York: Oxford University Press.

D'Augelli, A. R., & Hart, M. (1987). Gay women, men and families in rural settings: Toward the development of helping communities. *American Journal of Community Psychology, 15,* 79-93.

D'Augelli, A. R., & Hershberger, S. L. (1993). Lesbian, gay, and bisexual youth in community settings: Personal challenges and mental health problems. *American Journal of Community Psychology, 21,* 421-448.

D'Augelli, A. R., & Patterson, C. J. (Eds.). (1995). *Lesbians, gay, and bisexual identities over the lifespan.* New York: Oxford University Press.

D'Augelli, A. R., & Rose, M. L. (1990). Homophobia in a university community: Attitudes and experiences of heterosexual freshmen. *Journal of College Student Development, 31,* 484-491.

Davidson, G. C. (1991). Constructionism and morality for homosexuality. In J. C. Gonsiorek & J. Weinrich (Eds.), *Homosexuality: Research for public policy* (pp. 137-160). Newbury Park, CA: Sage.

Davies, P. (1992). The role of disclosure in coming out among gay men. In K. Plummer (Ed.), *Modern homosexualities: Fragments of lesbian and gay experience* (pp. 75-83). London: Routledge & Kegan Paul.

Davis, D., & Kennedy, E. L. (1986). Oral history and the study of sexuality in the lesbian community: Buffalo, New York, 1940-1960. *Feminist Studies, 12,* 7-26.

Dawson, K. (1982, November). Serving the older gay community. *SIECUS Report, 17,* 5-6.

Dean, L., Wu, S., & Martin, J. L. (1992). Trends in violence and discrimination against gay men in New York City: 1984-1990. In G. M. Herek & K. T. Berrill (Eds.), *Hate crimes: Confronting violence against lesbians and gay men* (pp. 46-64). Newbury Park, CA: Sage.

De Cecco, J. P. (1981-1982). Foreword. *Journal of Homosexuality, 7,* 1-12.

De Cecco, J. P., & Elia, J. P. (Eds.). (1993). *If you seduce a straight person can you make them gay? Issues in biological essentialism vs. social constructionism in gay and lesbian identities.* Binghamton, NY: Haworth.

De Cecco, J. P., & Shively, M. G. (1983-1984). From sexual identity to sexual relationships: A contextual shift. *Journal of Homosexuality, 9,* 1-26.

Decker, B. (1984). Counseling gay and lesbian couples. *Journal of Social Work and Human Sexuality, 2,* 39-52.

Deenen, A. A., Gijs, L., & van Naerssen, A. X. (1994). Intimacy and sexuality in gay male couples. *Archives of Sexual Behavior, 23,* 421-431.

Deevey, S. (1990). Older lesbian women: An invisible minority. *Journal of Gerontological Nursing, 16,* 35-37, 39.

DeLeon, P. H. (1993). Proceedings of the American Psychological Association Incorporated for the year 1992: Minutes of the annual meeting of the Council of Representatives, August 13 and 16, 1992 and February 26-28, 1993. *American Psychologist, 48,* 745-788.

D'Emilio, J. (1983). *Sexual politics, sexual communities: The making of a homosexual minority in the United States, 1940-1970.* Chicago: University of Chicago.

D'Emilio, J. (1990). The campus environment for gay and lesbian life. *Academe, 76,* 16-19.

D'Emilio, J. (1993). Gay politics and community in San Francisco since World War II. In L. D. Garnets & D. C. Kimmel (Eds.), *Psychological perspectives on lesbian & gay male experiences* (pp. 59-79). New York: Columbia University Press.

D'Emilio, J. (1995). Homophobia and the trajectory of postwar American radicalism: The career of Bayard Rustin. *Radical History Review, 62,* 80-103.

de Monteflores, C. (1981). Conflicting allegiances: Therapy issues with Hispanic lesbians. *Catalyst, 12,* 31-36.

de Monteflores, C. (1986). Notes on the management of difference. In T. Stein & C. Cohen (Eds.), *Contemporary perspectives in psychotherapy with lesbians and gay men* (pp. 73-101). New York: Plenum.

de Monteflores, C., & Schultz, S. (1978). Coming out: Similarities and differences for lesbians and gay men. *Journal of Social Issues, 34,* 59-72.

Denny, D. (1994). You're strange and we're wonderful: The relationship between the gay, lesbian, and transgender communities. *TransSisters: The Journal of Transsexual Feminism, 6,* 21-23.

Denny, D., & Green, J. (1996). Gender identity and bisexuality. In B. A. Firestein (Ed.), *Bisexuality: The psychology and politics of an invisible minority* (pp. 84-102). Thousand Oaks, CA: Sage.

DeVine, J. L. (1983-1984). A systematic inspection of affectional preference orientation and the family of origin. *Journal of Social Work and Human Sexuality, 2,* 9-17.

Devor, H. (1993). Toward a taxonomy of gendered sexuality. *Journal of Psychology & Human Sexuality, 61,* 23-55.

Dew, M. A., Ragni, M. V., & Nimorwica, P. (1990). Infection with human immunodeficiency virus and vulnerability to psychiatric distress. *Archives of General Psychiatry, 47,* 734-744.

Diggs, M. (1995). Romantic friends or a "different race of creatures"? The representation of lesbian pathology in nineteenth-century America. *Feminist Studies, 21,* 317-340.

Dion, K. L. (1986). Relative deprivation theory and responses to discrimination and relative deprivation. In J. M. Olson, C. P. Herman, & M. P. Zanna (Eds.), *The Ontario Symposium* (Vol. 159). Hillsdale, NJ: Lawrence Erlbaum.

Dixon, J. K. (1985). Sexuality and relationship changes in married females following the commencement of bisexual activity. *Journal of Homosexuality, 11,* 115-134.

Dodge, R. (1993, December). Fed accused of bias in job promotions. *Dallas Morning News,* pp. D1-D2.

Donaldson, S. (1990). Subculture, gay. In W. R. Dynes (Ed.), *Encyclopedia of homosexuality* (pp. 1257-1261). New York: Garland.

Donovan, J. M. (1992). Homosexual, gay, and lesbian: Defining the words and sampling the populations. In H. L. Minton (Ed.), *Gay and lesbian studies* (pp. 27-47). New York: Haworth.

Dorfman, R., Walters, K., Burke, P., Hardin, L., Karanik, T., Raphael, J., & Silverstein, E. (1995). Old, sad and alone:

The myth of the aging homosexual. *Journal of Geronto-logical Social Work, 24,* 29-44.

DuBay, W. H. (1987). *Gay identity: The self under ban.* Jefferson, NC: McFarland.

Duberman, M. B. (1993). *Stonewall.* New York: Dutton.

Duffy, S. M., & Rusbult, C. E. (1986). Satisfaction and commitment in homosexual and heterosexual relationships. *Journal of Homosexuality, 12,* 1-24.

Dunker, B. (1987). Aging lesbians: Observations and speculations. In the Boston Lesbian Psychologies Collective (Eds.), *Lesbian psychologies: Explorations and challenges* (pp. 72- 82). Urbana: University of Illinois.

Dunkle, J. H. (1994). Counseling gay male clients: A review of treatment efficacy research: 1975-present. *Journal of Gay and Lesbian Psychotherapy, 2,* 1-19.

Durby, D. D. (1994). Gay, lesbian, and bisexual youth. *Journal of Gay and Lesbian Social Services, 1,* 1-37.

Dworkin, J., & Kaufer, D. (1995). Social services and bereavement in the lesbian and gay community. *Journal of Gay and Lesbian Social Services, 2,* 41-60.

Dworkin, S. H. (1997). Female, lesbian, and Jewish: Complex and invisible. In B. Greene (Ed.), *Ethnic and cultural diversity among lesbians and gay men* (pp. 63-87). Thousand Oaks, CA: Sage.

Dyne, L. (1980, September). Is DC becoming the gay capitol of America? *Washingtonian,* pp. 96-101, 133-141.

Dynes, W. R. (1990a). Closet. In W. R. Dynes (Ed.), *Encyclopedia of homosexuality* (pp. 244-246). New York: Garland.

Dynes, W. R. (1990b). Gay. In W. R. Dynes (Ed.), *Encyclopedia of homosexuality* (pp. 455-456). New York: Garland.

Dynes, W. R. (1990c). Heterosexuality. In W. R. Dynes (Ed.), *Encyclopedia of homosexuality* (pp. 532-535). New York: Garland.

Dynes, W. R. (1990d). Homophile. In W. R. Dynes (Ed.), *Encyclopedia of homosexuality* (p. 552). New York: Garland.

Dynes, W. R., & Donaldson, S. (1992). General introduction. In W. R. Dynes & S. Donaldson (Eds.), *Homosexuality and psychology, psychiatry, and counseling* (pp. v-xx). New York: Garland.

Eldridge, N. S. (1987a). Correlates of relation satisfaction and role conflict in dual-career lesbian couples. *Professional Psychology: Research and Practice, 18,* 567-572.

Eldridge, N. S. (1987b). Gender issues in counseling same-sex couples. *Professional Psychology: Research and Practice, 18,* 567-572.

Eldridge, N., & Barnett, D. C. (1991). Counseling gay and lesbian students. In N. J. Evans & V. A. Walls (Eds.), *Beyond tolerance: Gays, lesbians, and bisexuals on campus* (pp. 147-178). Alexandria, VA: American College Personnel Association.

Eldridge, N. S., & Gilbert, L. A. (1990). Correlates of relationship satisfaction in lesbian couples. *Psychology of Women Quarterly, 14,* 43-62.

Eliason, M. J. (1995). Attitudes about lesbian and gay men: A review and implications for social service training. *Journal of Gay & Lesbian Social Services, 2,* 73-90.

Eliason, M. J. (1996). Identity formulation for lesbian, bisexual, and gay persons: Beyond a "minoritizing" view. *Journal of Homosexuality, 30,* 31-58.

Eller, M., & King, D. J. (1990). Self-help groups for gays, lesbians, and their loved ones. In R. J. Kus (Ed.), *Keys to caring: Assisting your gay and lesbian clients* (pp. 330-339). Boston: Alyson.

Elliott, J. E. (1993). Career development with lesbian and gay clients. *Career Development Quarterly, 41,* 210-226.

Elliot, P. E. (1985). Theory and research on lesbian identity formation. *International Journal of Women's Studies, 8,* 64-71.

Ellis, A. L., & Riggle, E. D. B. (1996). The relation of job satisfaction and degree of openness about one's sexual orientation for lesbians and gay men. *Journal of Homosexuality, 30,* 75-85.

Ellis, H. (1942). *Studies in the psychology of sex* (Vols. 1-2). New York: Random House.

Elton, L. (1990, October 23). A word to the wise [Letter to the editor]. *Advocate,* p. 11.

Emerson, S., & Rosenfeld, C. (1996). Stages of adjustment in family members of transgender individuals. *Journal of Family Psychotherapy, 7,* 1-12.

Engelhardt, B. J., & Triantafillou, K. (1987). Mediation for lesbians. In the Boston Lesbian Psychologies Collective (Eds.), *Lesbian psychologies: Explorations and challenges* (pp. 327-343). Urbana: University of Illinois.

Erikson, E. H. (1985). *Childhood and society* (2nd ed.). New York: Norton.

Espin, O. M. (1984). Cultural and historical influences on sexuality in Hispanic/Latin women: Implications for psychotherapy. In C. Vance (Ed.), *Pleasure and danger: Exploring female sexuality* (pp. 149-163). London: Routledge & Kegan Paul.

Espin, O. M. (1987). Issues of identity in the psychology of Latina lesbians. In the Boston Lesbian Psychologies Collective (Eds.), *Lesbian psychologies: Explorations and challenges* (pp. 35-51). Urbana: University of Illinois.

Espin, O. M. (1997). Crossing borders and boundaries: The life narratives of immigrant lesbians. In B. Greene (Ed.), *Ethnic and cultural diversity among lesbians and gay men* (pp. 191-215). Thousand Oaks, CA: Sage.

Esterberg, K. G. (1994). Being a lesbian and being in love: Constructing identity through relationships. *Journal of Gay & Lesbian Social Services, 1,* 57-82.

Esterberg, K. G. (1996). Gay cultures, gay communities: The social organization of lesbians, gay men, and bisexuals. In R. C. Savin-Williams & K. M. Cohen (Eds.), *The lives of lesbian, gay men, and bisexuals: Children to adults* (pp. 377-391). Ft. Worth, TX: Harcourt Brace.

Esterberg, K. G. (1997). *Lesbian and bisexual identities: Constructing communities, constructing selves.* Philadelphia: Temple University Press.

Ettebrick, P. L. (1993). Who is a parent? The need for a lesbian conscious family law. *New York Law School Journal of Human Rights, 10,* 513-553.

Evall, J. (1991). Sexual orientation and adoptive matching. *Family Law Quarterly, 25,* 347-379.

Faderman, L. (1984-1985). The new "gay" lesbians. *Journal of Homosexuality, 10,* 85-95.

Faderman, L. (1991). *Odd girls and twilight lovers: A history of lesbian life in twentieth century America.* New York: Columbia University Press.

Faderman, L. (1992). The return of butch and femme: A phenomenon in lesbian sexuality of the 1980s and 1990s. *Journal of the History of Sexuality, 2,* 578-596.

Fajer, M. A. (1992). Can two real men eat quiche together? Storytelling, gender-role stereotypes, and legal protection for lesbians and gay men. *University of Miami Law Review, 46,* 511-651.

Falbo, T., & Peplau, L. A. (1980). Power strategies in intimate linkups. *Journal of Personality and Social Psychology, 38,* 618-628.

Falco, K. L. (1991). *Psychotherapy with lesbian clients.* New York: Brunner/Mazel.

Falk, P. J. (1989). Lesbian mothers: Psychosocial assumptions in family law. *American Psychologist, 44,* 941-947.

Falk, P. J. (1994). The gap between psychosocial assumptions and empirical research in lesbian-mother child custody cases. In A. E. Gottfried & A. W. Gottfried (Eds.), *Redefining families: Implications for children's development* (pp. 131-156). New York: Plenum.

Faria, G. (1994). Training for family preservation practice with lesbian families. *Families in Society, 75,* 416-422.

Fassinger, R. E. (1991). The hidden minority: Issues and challenges in working with lesbians and gay men. *Counseling Psychologist, 19,* 157-176.

Fassinger, R. E. (1995). From invisibility to integration: Lesbian identity in the workplace. *Career Development Quarterly, 44,* 148-166.

Fassinger, R. E., & Miller, B. A. (1996). Validation of an inclusive model of sexual minority identity formation on a sample of gay men. *Journal of Heterosexuality, 32,* 53-78.

Fay, R. E., Turner, C. E., Klassen, A. D., & Gagnon, J. H. (1989). Prevalence and patterns of same-gender sexual contact among men. *Science, 243,* 338-348.

Federation of Parents and Friends of Lesbians and Gays. (1984). *Read this before coming out to your parents.* Washington, DC: Author.

Feinberg, L. (1993). *Transgender liberation: A movement whose time has come.* New York: World View Forum.

Fertitta, S. (1984). *Never married women in the middle years: A comparison of lesbians and heterosexuals.* Unpublished doctoral dissertation, Wright University, Los Angeles.

Ficarrotto, T. (1990). Racism, sexism, and erotophobia: Attitudes of heterosexuals toward homosexuals. *Journal of Homosexuality, 19,* 111-116.

Firestein, B. A. (1996a). Bisexuality as paradigm shift: Transforming our disciplines. In B. A. Firestein (Ed.), *Bisexuality: The psychology and politics of an invisible minority* (pp. 263-303). Thousand Oaks, CA: Sage.

Firestein, B. A. (Ed.). (1996b). *Bisexuality: The psychology and politics of an invisible minority.* Thousand Oaks, CA: Sage.

Fisher, S. K. (1993). A proposed Adlerian theoretical framework and intervention techniques for gay and lesbian couples. *Individual Psychology, 49,* 438-449.

Fishman, J., & Linde, R. (1983). Informed consent: Making appropriate choices about AIDS from an informed perspective. *Gay Community News, 10,* 8-9.

Flaks, D. K., Ficher, I., Masterpasqua, F., & Joseph, G. (1995). Lesbians choosing motherhood: A comparative study of lesbian and heterosexual parents and their children. *Developmental Psychology, 31,* 105-114.

FM-2030. (1989). *Are you a transhuman?* New York: Warner.

Ford, C. S. (1948). Sexual behavior among primitive peoples. In D. P. Geddes & E. Currie (Eds.), *About the Kinsey report: Observations by 11 experts.* New York: New American Library.

Ford, C. S., & Beach, F. A. (1951). *Patterns of sexual behavior.* New York: Harper & Row.

Forstein, M. (1986). Psychodynamic psychotherapy with gay male couples. In T. S. Stein & C. J. Cohen (Eds.), *Contemporary perspectives on psychotherapy with lesbians and gay men* (pp. 103-137). New York: Plenum.

Fowlkes, M. R. (1994). Single worlds and homosexual lifestyles: Patterns of sexuality and intimacy. In A. S. Rossi (Ed.), *Sexuality across the lifespan* (pp. 151-184). Chicago: University of Chicago.

Fox, R. C. (1995). Bisexual identities. In A. R. D'Augelli & C. J. Patterson (Eds.), *Lesbians, gay, and bisexual identities*

over the lifespan (pp. 48-86). New York: Oxford University Press.

Fox, R. C. (1996). Bisexuality in perspective: A review of theory and research. In B. A. Firestein (Ed.), *Bisexuality: The psychology and politics of an invisible minority* (pp. 3-50). Thousand Oaks, CA: Sage.

Francher, J. S., & Henkin, J. (1973). The menopausal queen: Adjustment to aging and the male homosexual. *American Journal of Orthopsychiatry, 43,* 670-674.

Franzen, T. (1993). Differences and identities: Feminism and the Albuquerque lesbian community. *Signs, 18,* 891-906.

Freedman, M. (1971). *Homosexuality and psychological functioning.* Belmont, CA: Brooks Cole.

Freud, S. (1953). Three essays on a theory of sexuality. In S. Strachey (Ed. and Trans.), *The standard edition of the complete psychological works of Sigmund Freud* (Vol. 7). London: Hogarth. (Original work published 1905)

Freud, S. (1955). Historical notes: A letter from Freud [to an American mother about her homosexual son, written 1935, uncovered by Alfred Kinsey]. *American Journal of Psychiatry, 108,* 787-789.

Freund, K. (1977). Should homosexuality arouse therapeutic concern? *Journal of Homosexuality, 2,* 235-249.

Friend, R. A. (1980). GAYging: Adjustment and older gay males. *Alternative Lifestyles, 3,* 231-248.

Friend, R. A. (1987). The individual and social psychology of aging: Clinical implications for lesbians and gay men. *Journal of Homosexuality, 14,* 307-331.

Friend, R. A. (1990). Older lesbian and gay people: Responding to homophobia. *Marriage and Family Review, 14,* 241-263.

Friend, R. A. (1991). Older lesbian and gay people: A theory of successful aging. In J. A. Lee (Ed.), *Gay midlife and maturity* (pp. 99-118). New York: Haworth.

Frieze, I. H., Hymer, S., & Greenberg, M. S. (1984). Describing the victims of crimes and violence. In A. Kahn (Ed.), *Victims of crime and violence: Final report of the APA Task Force on the Victims of Crime and Violence* (pp. 19-78). Washington, DC: American Psychological Association.

Fygetakis, L. M. (1997). Greek American lesbians: Identity odysseys of honorable good girls. In B. Greene (Ed.), *Ethnic and cultural diversity among lesbians and gay men* (pp. 152-190). Thousand Oaks, CA: Sage.

Gagnon, J. H., & Simon, W. (1967). *Sexual deviance.* New York: Harper & Row.

Gagnon, J. H., & Simon, W. (1973). *Sexual conduct: The social sources of human sexuality.* Chicago: Aldine.

Galassi, F. S. (1991). A life-review workshop for gay and lesbian elders. *Journal of Gerontological Social Work, 16,* 75-68.

Garnets, L., Hancock, K. A., Cochran, S. D., Goodchilds, J., & Peplau, L. A. (1991). Issues in psychotherapy with lesbians and gay men: A survey of psychologists. *American Psychologist, 46,* 964-972.

Garnets, L., Herek, G. M., & Levy, B. (1992). Violence and victimization of lesbians and gay men. In G. M. Herek & K. T. Berrill (Eds.), *Violence against lesbians and gay men* (pp. 207-226). Newbury Park, CA: Sage.

Garnets, L. D., & Kimmel, D. C. (1993a). Introduction. In L. D. Garnets & D. C. Kimmel (Eds.), *Psychological perspectives on lesbian and gay male experiences* (pp. 1-51). New York: Columbia University Press.

Garnets, L. D., & Kimmel, D. C. (1993b). Cultural diversity among lesbians and gay men. In L. D. Garnets & D. C. Kimmel (Eds.), *Psychological perspectives on lesbian and gay male experiences* (pp. 331-337). New York: Columbia University Press.

Garnets, L. D., & Kimmel, D. C. (Eds.). (1993c). *Psychological perspectives on lesbian and gay male experiences.* New York: Columbia University Press.

Gartrell, N. (1981). The lesbian as a "single" woman. *American Journal of Psychotherapy, 34,* 502-510.

Gartrell, N. (1984). *Issues in psychotherapy with lesbian women* (Work in progress series). Wellesley, MA: Wellesley College, Stone Center.

Gebhard, P. H. (1972). Incidence of overt homosexuality in the U.S. and Western Europe. In J. J. Livingood (Ed.), *NIMH task force on homosexuality: Final report and background papers* (pp. 22-29) (DHEW Publication No. [HSM] 72-9116). Rockville, MD: National Institute of Mental Health.

Gebhard, P. H., & Johnson, A. B. (1979). *The Kinsey data: Marginal tabulations of the 1938-1963 interviews conducted at the Institute for Sex Research.* Philadelphia: Saunders.

Germain, C. B. (1991). *Human behavior and the social environment.* New York: Columbia University Press.

Germain, C. B., & Gitterman, A. (1980). *The life model of social work practice* (2nd ed.). New York: Columbia University Press.

Ginsburg, G. (1988). Roles, scripts and prototypes in personal relationships. In S. W. Duck (Ed.), *Handbook of personal relationships* (pp. 23-39). New York: John Wiley.

Gluth, D. R., & Kiselica, M. D. (1994). Coming out quickly: A brief counseling approach to dealing with gay and lesbian adjustment issues. *Journal of Mental Health Counseling, 16,* 163-173.

Gochros, J. S. (1985). Wives' reactions to learning that their husbands are bisexual. *Journal of Homosexuality, 11,* 101-113.

Gochros, J. S. (1989). *When husbands come out of the closet.* New York: Haworth.

Gock, T. (1985, August). *Psychotherapy with Asian/Pacific gay men: Psychological issues, treatment approach and therapeutic guidelines.* Paper presented at the meeting of the Asian-American Psychological Association, Los Angeles, CA.

Gock, T. (1986, August). *Issues in gay affirmative psychotherapy with ethnically/culturally diverse populations.* Paper presented at the meeting of the 94th Annual Convention of the American Psychological Association, Washington, DC.

Goffman, E. (1963). *Stigma: Notes on the management of spoiled identity.* Englewood Cliffs, NJ: Prentice Hall.

Gold, M. A., Perrin, E. C., Futterman, D., & Friedman, S. B. (1994). Children of gay or lesbian parents. *Pediatrics in Review, 15,* 354-358.

Golden, C. (1987). Diversity and variability in women's sexual identities. In the Boston Lesbian Psychologies Collective (Eds.), *Lesbian psychologies* (pp. 19-34). Urbana: University of Illinois.

Golden, C. (1990, August). *Our politics and our choices: The feminist movement and sexual orientation.* Paper presented at the meeting of the American Psychological Association, Boston.

Golden, C. (1994). Our politics, our choices: The feminist movement and sexual orientation. In B. Greene & G. M. Herek (Eds.), *Lesbian and gay psychology: Theory, research, and clinical application.* Thousand Oaks, CA: Sage.

Golden, C. (1996). What's in a name? Sexual self-identification among women. In R. C. Savin-Williams & K. M. Cohen (Eds.), *The lives of lesbians, gays, and bisexuals: Children to adults* (pp. 229-249). Ft. Worth, TX: Harcourt Brace.

Goldman, J. (1992, September). Coming out strong. *California Lawyer, 13,* 30-36, 86-67.

Gomez, J., & Smith, B. (1990, Spring). Taking the home out of homophobia. *Outlook, 8,* 32- 37.

Gonsiorek, J. C. (1981-1982). Introduction: Present and future directions in gay/lesbian mental health. *Journal of Homosexuality, 7,* 5-20.

Gonsiorek, J. C. (1991). The empirical basis for the demise of the illness model of homosexuality. In J. C. Gonsiorek & J. D. Weinrich (Eds.), *Homosexuality: Research implications for public policy* (pp. 115-136). Newbury Park, CA: Sage.

Gonsiorek, J. C. (1993). Threat, stress, and adjustment: Mental health and the workplace for gay and lesbian individuals. In L. Diamant (Ed.), *Homosexual issues in the workplace* (pp. 242-263). Washington, DC: Taylor & Francis.

Gonsiorek, J. C. (1995). Gay male identities: Concepts and issues. In A. R. D'Augelli & C. J. Patterson (Eds.), *Lesbians, gay, and bisexual identities over the lifespan* (pp. 24-47). New York: Oxford University Press.

Gonsiorek, J. C. (1996). Mental health and sexual orientation. In R. C. Savin-Williams & K. M. Cohen (Eds.), *The lives of lesbian, gay men, and bisexuals: Children to adults* (pp. 462-478). Ft. Worth, TX: Harcourt Brace.

Gonsiorek, J. C., Sell, R. L., & Weinrich, J. D. (1995). Definition and measurement of sexual orientation. *Suicide and Life-Threatening Behavior, 25,* 40-51.

Gonsiorek, J., & Weinrich, J. (1991). The definition and scope of sexual orientation. In J. C. Gonsiorek & J. Weinrich (Eds.), *Homosexuality: Research implications for public policy* (pp. 1-12). Newbury, CA: Sage.

González, F. J., & Espin, O. M. (1996). Latino men, latino women, and homosexuality. In R. P. Cabaj & T. S. Stein (Eds.), *Textbook of homosexuality and mental health* (pp. 583-601). Washington, DC: American Psychiatric Press.

Gottman, J. M., & Krokoff, L. J. (1989). Marital interaction and satisfaction: A longitudinal view. *Journal of Consulting and Clinical Psychology, 57,* 47-52.

Gottman, J. S. (1990). Children of gay and lesbian parents. In F. W. Bozett & M. B. Sussman (Eds.), *Homosexuality and family relations* (pp. 177-196). New York: Harrington Park.

Gough, H. G. (1960). *Manual for the CPI: California Psychological Inventory.* Palo Alto, CA: Consulting Psychologists Press.

Graber, E. (1989). A spectacle in color: The lesbian and gay subculture of jazz age Harlem. In M. B. Duberman, M. Vicinus, & G. Chauncey (Eds.), *Hidden from history: Reclaiming the gay and lesbian past* (pp. 318-331). New York: New American Library.

Grace, J. (1992). Affirming gay and lesbian adulthood. In N. J. Woodman (Ed.), *Lesbian and gay lifestyles: A guide for counseling and education* (pp. 33-47). New York: Irvington.

Graham, D., Rawlings, E. I., Halpern, H. S., & Hermes, J. (1984). Therapists' needs for training in counseling lesbians and gay men. *Professional Psychology, 15,* 482-496.

Gramick, J. (1984). Developing a lesbian identity. In T. Darty & S. Potter (Eds.), *Women-identified women* (pp. 31-44). Palo Alto, CA: Mayfield.

Granvold, D. K., & Martin, J. I. (in press). Family therapy with gay and lesbian clients. In C. Franklin & C. Jordan (Eds.), *Family practice: Brief and systemic methods.* Pacific Grove, CA: Brooks/Cole.

Gray, H., & Dressel, P. (1985). Alternative interpretations of aging among gay males. *Gerontologist, 25,* 83-87.

Greeley, G. (1994). Service organizations for gay and lesbian youth. *Journal of Gay and Lesbian Social Services, 1,* 111-130.

Green, D., & Clunis, M. (1989). Married lesbians. In E. Rothblum & E. Coles (Eds.), *Loving boldly: Issues facing lesbians* (pp. 41-49). New York: Harrington Park.

Green, G. D., & Bozett, F. W. (1991). Lesbian mothers and gay fathers. In J. C. Gonsiorek & J. D. Weinrich (Eds.), *Research implications for public policy* (pp. 197-214). Newbury Park, CA: Sage.

Green, R. (1992). *Sexual science and the law.* Cambridge, MA: Harvard University Press.

Green, R., Mandel, J. B., Hotvedt, M. E., Gray, J., & Smith, L. (1986). Lesbian mothers and their children: A comparison with solo parent heterosexual mothers and their children. *Archives of Sexual Behavior, 15,* 167-184.

Green, S. K. (1981). Attitudes and perceptions about the elderly: Current and future perspectives. *Aging and Human Development, 13,* 95-115.

Green, S., Dixon, P., & Gold-Neil, V. (1993). The effects of a gay/lesbian panel discussion on college students' attitudes toward gay men, lesbians, and persons with AIDS. *Journal of Sex Education and Therapy, 19,* 47-63.

Greene, B. (1994a). Lesbian and gay sexual orientations: Implications for clinical training, practice, and research. In B. Greene & G. M. Herek (Eds.), *Lesbian and gay psychology: Theory, research, and clinical applications* (pp. 1-24). Thousand Oaks, CA: Sage.

Greene, B. (1994b). Lesbian women of color: Triple jeopardy. In L. Comas-Diaz & B. Greene (Eds.), *Women of color* (pp. 389-427). New York: Guilford.

Greene, B. (1995). Lesbian couples. In K. Jay (Ed.), *Dyke life: From growing up to growing old—a celebration of the lesbian experience* (pp. 97-106). New York: Basic Books.

Greene, B. (1996). Lesbians and gay men of color: The legacy of ethnosexual mythologies in heterosexism. In E. D. Rothblum & L. A. Bond (Eds.), *Preventing heterosexism and homophobia* (pp. 59-70). Thousand Oaks, CA: Sage.

Greene, B. (Ed.). (1997a). *Ethnic and cultural diversity among lesbians and gay men.* Thousand Oaks, CA: Sage.

Greene, B. (1997b). Ethnic minority lesbians and gay men: Mental health and treatment issues. In B. Greene (Ed.), *Ethnic and cultural diversity among lesbians and gay men* (pp. 216-239). Thousand Oaks, CA: Sage.

Greene, B. (1997c). Preface. In B. Greene (Ed.), *Ethnic and cultural diversity among lesbians and gay men* (pp. xi-xv). Thousand Oaks, CA: Sage.

Greene, B., & Boyd-Franklin, N. (1996). African American lesbians: Issues in couples therapy. In J. Laird & R.-J. Green (Eds.), *Lesbians and gays in couples and families: A handbook for therapists* (pp. 251-271). San Francisco: Jossey-Bass.

Greene, B., & Herek, G. M. (Eds.). (1994). *Lesbian and gay psychology: Theory, research, and clinical applications.* Thousand Oaks, CA: Sage.

Griffin, C., Wirth, M., & Wirth, A. (1986). *Beyond acceptance: Parents of lesbians and gays talk about their experiences.* Englewood Cliffs, NJ: Prentice Hall.

Grimm, D. (1987). Toward a theory of gender: Transsexualism, gender, sexuality, and relationships. *American Behavioral Scientist, 31,* 66-85.

Grossman, A. H. (1997). Growing up with a "spoiled identity": Lesbian, gay, and bisexual youth at risk. *Journal of Gay & Lesbian Social Services, 6,* 43-56.

Groves, P. A., & Ventura, L. A. (1983). The lesbian coming out process: Therapeutic considerations. *Personnel and Guidance Journal, 62,* 146-149.

Grube, J. (1990). Natives and settlers: An ethnographic note on early interaction of older homosexual men with younger gay liberationists. *Journal of Homosexuality, 20,* 119-136.

Gumaer, J. (1987). Understanding and counseling gay men: A developmental perspective. *Journal of Counseling and Development, 66,* 144-146.

Gutiérrez, F., & Dworkin, S. (1992). Gay, lesbian, and Afro-American: Managing the integration of identities. In S. Dworkin & F. Gutiérrez (Eds.), *Counseling gay men and lesbians: Journey to the end of the rainbow* (pp. 141-156). Alexandria: VA: American Association for Counseling & Development.

H., Pamela. (1989). Asian American lesbians: An emerging voice in the Asian American community. In Asian Women United of California (Eds.), *Making waves: An anthology of writings by and about Asian American women* (pp. 282-290). Boston: Beacon.

Haan, N. (1989). Personality at midlife. In S. Hunter & M. Sundel (Eds.), *Midlife myths: Issues, findings, and practice implications* (pp. 145-156). Newbury Park, CA: Sage.

Hadden, S. (1966). Treatment of male homosexuals in groups. *International Journal of Group Psychotherapy, 16,* 13-22.

Haldeman, D. C. (1994). The practice and ethics of sexual orientation conversion therapy. *Journal of Consulting and Clinical Psychology, 62,* 221-227.

Hall, M. (1986). The lesbian corporate experience. *Journal of Homosexuality, 12,* 59-75.

Hall, M. (1989). Private experiences in the public domain: Lesbians in organizations. In J. Hearn, D. L. Sheppard, P. Tancred-Sheriff, & G. Burrell (Eds.), *The sexuality of organization* (pp. 125-138). Newbury Park, CA: Sage.

Hall, M., & Gregory, A. (1991). Subtle balances: Love and work in lesbian relationships. In B. Sang, J. Warshow, & A. Smith (Eds.), *Lesbians at midlife: The creative transition* (pp. 122-133). San Francisco: Spinsters.

Halley, J. E. (1994). Sexual orientation and the politics of biology: A critique of the argument from immutability. *Stanford Law Review, 46,* 503-568.

Halpern, D. (1993). Minorities and mental health. *Social Science and Medicine, 36,* 597-607.

Hammadock, S. (1988). Lesbian sexuality in the framework of psychotherapy: A practical model for the lesbian therapist. In E. Cole & E. D. Rothblum (Eds.), *Women and sex therapy: Closing the circle of sexual knowledge* (pp. 207-219). New York: Harrington Park.

Hammersmith, S. K., & Weinberg, M. S. (1973). Homosexual identity: Commitment, adjustments, and significant others. *Sociometry, 36,* 56-78.

Hammond, N. (1988). Lesbian victims of relationship violence. *Women and Therapy, 8,* 89-105.

Hanley-Hackenbruck,. P. (1989). Psychotherapy and the "coming out" process. *Journal of Gay & Lesbian Psychotherapy, 1,* 21-39.

Hanley-Hackenbruck, P. (1993). Working with lesbians in psychotherapy. *Review of Psychiatry, 12,* 59-83.

Hanscombe, G., & Forster, J. (1982). *Rocking the cradle.* Boston: Alyson.

Hare, J. (1994). Concerns and issues faced by families headed by a lesbian couple. *Families in Society, 75,* 27-35.

Hare, J., & Richards, L. (1993). Children raised by lesbian couples: Does context of birth affect father and partner involvement? *Family Relations, 42,* 249-255.

Harris, M. B., & Turner, P. H. (1985-1986). Gay and lesbian parents. *Journal of Homosexuality, 12,* 101-113.

Harry, J. (1982a). Decision making and age differences among gay couples. *Journal of Homosexuality, 8,* 9-21.

Harry, J. (1982b). *Gay children grown up.* New York: Praeger.

Harry, J. (1983). Gay male and lesbian relationships. In E. Macklin & R. Rubin (Eds.), *Contemporary families and alternative lifestyles: Handbook on research and theory* (pp. 216-234). Beverly Hills, CA: Sage.

Harry, J. (1984). *Gay couples.* New York: Praeger.

Harry, J. (1993). Being out: A general model. *Journal of Homosexuality, 26,* 25-39.

Harry, J., & DeVall, W. B. (1978). *The social organization of gay males.* New York: Praeger.

Harry, J., & Lovely, R. (1979). Gay marriages and communities of sexual orientation. *Alternate Lifestyles, 2,* 177-200.

Hart, J., & Richardson, D. (Eds.). (1981). *The theory and practice of homosexuality.* London: Routledge & Kegan Paul.

Hart, M., Roback, H., Tittler, B., Weitz, L., Walston, B., & McKee, E. (1978). Psychological adjustment of nonpatient homosexuals: Critical review of the research literature. *Journal of Clinical Psychiatry, 39,* 604-608.

Hartman, A. (1993). Out of the closet: Revolution and backlash. *Social Work, 38,* 245-246, 360.

Harvey, S. M., Carr, C., & Bernheine, S. (1989). Lesbian mothers: Health care experiences. *Journal of Nurse-Midwifery, 34,* 115-119.

Hawkeswood, W. G. (1990, November). *I'm a Black man who just happens to be gay: The sexuality of Black gay men.* Paper presented at the American Anthropological Association Annual Meeting, New Orleans.

Hayes, L. (1991). Financial planning for retirement. In B. Sang, J. Warshow, & A. Smith (Eds.), *Lesbians at midlife: The creative transition* (pp. 245-257). San Francisco: Spinsters.

Hays, J. (1991). Cracker Barrel comes under fire for ousting gays. *Nation's Restaurant News, 25,* 1.

Healy, T. (1993). A struggle for language: Patterns of self-disclosure in lesbian couples. *Smith College Studies in Social Work, 63,* 247-263.

Hedgpeth, J. M. (1979-1980). Employment discrimination law and the rights of gay persons. *Journal of Homosexuality, 5,* 66-78.

Hellman, R. E. (1996). Issues in the treatment of lesbian women and gay men with chronic mental illness. *Psychiatric Services, 47,* 1093-1098.

Helfand, K. L. (1993). Therapeutic consideration in structuring a support group for the mentally ill gay/lesbian population. *Journal of Gay and Lesbian Psychotherapy, 2,* 65-76.

Heller, S. (1990, October 24). Gay- and lesbian-studies movement gains acceptance in many areas of scholarship and teaching. *Chronicle of Higher Education,* p. A4.

Hemmings, C. (1996). From lesbian nation to transgender liberation: A bisexual feminist perspective. *Journal of Gay, Lesbian, and Bisexual Identity, 1,* 37-59.

Hencken, J., & O'Dowd, W. (1977). Coming out as an aspect of identity formation. *Gay Academic Union Journal, 1,* 18-26.

Henry, G. (1941). *Sex variants: A study of homosexual patterns.* New York: Harpers.

Hepworth, D. H., & Larsen, J. A. (1993). *Direct social work practice.* Pacific Grove, CA: Brooks/Cole.

Herdt, G. H. (1989). Gay and lesbian youth, emergent identities, and cultural scenes at home and abroad. *Journal of Homosexuality, 17,* 1-42.

Herdt, G. H. (1990). Developmental discontinuities and sexual orientation across cultures. In D. P. McWhirter, S. A. Sanders, & J. M. Reinisch (Eds.), *Homosexuality/ heterosexuality: Concepts of sexual orientation* (pp. 28-38). New York: Oxford University Press.

Herdt, G. H. (1992). "Coming out" as a rite of passage: A Chicago study. In G. H. Herdt & A. Boxer (Eds.), *Gay culture in America: Essays from the field* (pp. 29-65). Boston: Beacon.

Herdt, G. H. (1993). The causes of homosexuality. *Anthropology UCLA, 2,* 1-19.

Herdt, G. H., & Boxer, A. (1992). Introduction: Culture, history, and life course of gay men. In G. Herdt (Ed.), *Gay culture in America: Essays from the field* (pp. 1-28). Boston: Beacon.

Herdt, G. H., & Boxer, A. (1993). *Children of the horizons: How gay and lesbian teens are leading a way out of the closet.* Boston: Beacon.

Herek, G. M. (1988). Heterosexuals' attitudes toward lesbians and gay men: Correlates and gender differences. *Journal of Sex Research, 25,* 451-477.

Herek, G. M. (1989). Sexual orientation. In H. Tierney (Ed.), *Women's studies encyclopedia* (Vol. 1, pp. 344-346). New York: Greenwood.

Herek, G. M. (1990). The context of anti-gay violence: Notes on cultural and psychological heterosexism. *Journal of Interpersonal Violence, 5,* 316-333.

Herek, G. M. (1991). Myths about sexual orientation: A lawyer's guide to social science research. *Law and Sexuality: A Review of Lesbian and Gay Legal Issues, 1,* 133-172.

Herek, G. M. (1992a). Homophobia. In W. R. Dynes (Ed.), *Encyclopedia of homosexuality* (pp. 552-555). New York: Garland.

Herek, G. M. (1992b). Psychological heterosexism and anti-gay violence: The social psychology of bigotry and bashing. In G. M. Herek & T. Berrill (Eds.), *Hate crimes: Confronting violence against lesbians and gay men* (pp. 149-169). Newbury Park, CA: Sage.

Herek, G. M. (1993). Documenting prejudice against lesbians and gay men on campus: The Yale Sexual Orientation Survey. *Journal of Homosexuality, 25,* 15-30.

Herek, G. M. (1995). Psychological heterosexism in the United States. In A. R. D'Augelli & C. J. Patterson (Eds.), *Lesbian, gay, and bisexual identities over the lifespan: Psychological perspectives* (pp. 321-346). New York: Oxford University Press.

Herek, G. M., Gillis, J. R., Cogan, J. C., & Glunt, E. K. (1997). Hate crime victimization among lesbian, gay, and bisexual adults: Prevalence, psychological correlates, and methodological issues. *Journal of Interpersonal Violence, 12,* 195-215.

Herek, G. M., & Glunt, E. (1988). An epidemic of stigma: Public reactions to AIDS. *American Psychologist, 43,* 886-891.

Herek, G. M., & Glunt, E. (1993). Interpersonal contact and heterosexuals' attitudes toward gay men: Results from a national survey. *Journal of Sex Research, 30,* 239-244.

Herek, G. M., Kimmel, D. C., Amaro, H., & Melton, G. B. (1991). Avoiding heterosexist bias in psychological research. *American Psychologist, 46,* 957-963.

Herrell, R. K. (1992). The symbolic strategies of Chicago's gay and lesbian pride parade. In G. Herdt (Ed.), *Gay culture in America: Essays from the field* (pp. 225-252). Boston: Beacon.

Herron, W. G., Kinter, T., Sollinger, I., & Trubowitz, J. (1981-1982). Psychoanalytic psychotherapy for homosexual clients: New concepts. *Journal of Homosexuality, 7,* 177-192.

Hersch, P. (1988, January). Coming of age on city streets. *Psychology Today,* pp. 28-32.

Herzer, M. (1985). Kertbeny and the nameless love. *Journal of Homosexuality, 12,* 1-26.

Hetherington, C., & Orzek, A. (1989). Career and life planning with lesbian women. *Journal of Counseling and Development, 68,* 52-57.

Hetrick, E. S., & Martin, A. D. (1984). Ego-dystonic homosexuality: A developmental view. In E. S. Hetrick & T. S. Stein (Eds.), *Innovations in psychotherapy with homosexuals* (pp. 2-21). Washington, DC: American Psychiatric Press.

Hetrick, E. S., & Martin, A. D. (1987). Developmental issues and their resolution for gay lesbian adolescents. *Journal of Homosexuality, 14,* 25-44.

Hidalgo, H. A. (1984). The Puerto Rican lesbian in the United States. In T. Darty & S. Potter (Eds.), *Women-identified women* (pp. 105-115). Palo Alto, CA: Mayfield.

Hirschfeld, M. (1948). *Sexual anomalies: The origins, nature and treatment of sexual disorders.* New York: Emerson.

Hodges, A., & Hutter, D. (1979). *With downcast gays: Aspects of homosexual liberation* (2nd ed.). Toronto: Pink Triangle.

Hoeffer, B. (1981). Children's acquisition of sex-role behavior in lesbian mothers' families. *American Journal of Orthopsychiatry, 51,* 536-643.

Holden, J. M., & Holden, G. S. (1995). The sexual identity profile: A multidimensional bipolar model. *Individual Psychology, 51,* 102-113.

Hollander, J. (1989). Restructuring lesbian social networks: Evaluation of an intervention. *Journal of Gay and Lesbian Psychotherapy, 1,* 63-72.

Hollander, J., & Haber, L. (1992). Ecological transition: Using Bronfenbrenner's model to study sexual identity change. *Health Care for Women International, 13,* 121-129.

Holtzen, D. W., & Agresti, A. A. (1990). Parental responses to gay and lesbian children: Differences in homophobia, self-esteem, and self-role stereotyping. *Journal of Social and Clinical Psychology, 9,* 390-399.

Holtzen, D. W., Kenny, M. E., & Mahalik, J. R. (1995). Contributions of parental attachment to gay or lesbian disclosure to parents and dysfunctional cognitive processes. *Journal of Counseling Psychology, 42,* 350-355.

Hom, A. Y. (1992). *Family matters: A historical study of the Asian Pacific lesbian network.* Unpublished master's thesis, University of California, Los Angeles.

Hong, S. M. (1984). Australian attitudes towards homosexuality: A comparison with college students. *Journal of Psychology, 117,* 89-95.

Hooker, E. (1957). The adjustment of the male overt homosexual. *Journal of Projective Techniques, 211,* 18-31.

Hooker, E. (1967). The homosexual community. In J. H. Gagnon & W. Simon (Eds.), *Sexual deviance* (pp. 167-184). New York: Harper & Row.

Hooyman, N. R., & Lustbader, W. (1986). *Taking care: Supporting older people and their families.* New York: Free Press.

Hopcke, R. H. (1992). Midlife, gay men, and the AIDS epidemic. *Quadrant, 25,* 101-109.

House, R. M., & Holloway, E. L. (1992). Empowering the counseling professional to work with gay and lesbian issues. In S. H. Dworkin & F. J. Gutiérrez (Eds.), *Counseling gay men and lesbians: Journey to the end of the rainbow* (pp. 307-323). Alexandria, VA: American Association for Counseling and Development.

Howard, J. A., Blumstein, P., & Schwartz, P. (1986). Sex, power, and influence tactics in intimate relationships. *Journal of Personality and Social Psychology, 51,* 102-109.

Hu, S., Pattatucci, A. M. L., Patterson, C., Li, L., Fulker, D. W., Cherny, S. S., Kruglyak, L., & Hamer, D. (1995). Linkage between sexual orientation and chromosome Xq28 in males but not females. *Nature Genetics, 11,* 248-256.

Huggins, S. L. (1989). A comparative study of self-esteem of adolescent children of divorced lesbian mothers and divorced heterosexual mothers. In F. W. Bozett (Ed.), *Homosexuality and the family* (pp. 123-135). New York: Harrington Park.

Humphreys, L. (1973). *Out of the closets: The sociology of homosexual liberation.* Englewood Cliffs, NJ: Prentice Hall.

Hunt, B. (1993). What counselors need to know about counseling gay men and lesbians. *Counseling and Human Development, 26,* 1-12.

Hunter, J. (1990). Violence against lesbian and gay male youth. *Journal of Interpersonal Violence, 5,* 295-300.

Hunter, S. (1994, November). *Crisis versus transition: How to assess which one fits your midlife clients.* Paper presented at the National Association of Social Workers/Texas Annual Conference, Dallas.

Hunter, S., & Sundel, M. (Eds.). (1989). *Midlife myths: Issues, findings, and practice implications.* Newbury Park, CA: Sage.

Hunter, S., & Sundel, M. (1994). Midlife for women: A new perspective. *Affilia: Journal of Women and Social Work, 9,* 113-129.

Huston, M., & Schwartz, P. (1995). The relationships of lesbians and gay men. In J. Wood & S. Duck (Ed.), *Under-studied relationships: Off the beaten track* (pp. 89-121). Thousand Oaks, CA: Sage.

Hutchins, L. (1996). Bisexuality: Politics and community. In B. A. Firestein (Ed.), *Bisexuality: The psychology and politics of an invisible minority* (pp. 240-259). Thousand Oaks, CA: Sage.

Hutchins, L., & Káahumanu, L. (1991). *Bi any other name: Bisexual people speak out.* Boston: Alyson.

Hyde, J. S. (1985). Women and language. In J. S. Hyde (Ed.), *Half the human experience* (pp. 211-230). Lexington, MA: D. C. Heath.

Icard, L. (1985-1986). Black gay men and conflicting social identities: Sexual orientation versus racial identity. *Journal of Social Work and Human Sexuality, 4,* 83-93.

Icard, L. D. (1996). Assessing the psychosocial well-being of African American gays: A multidimensional perspective. *Journal of Gay & Lesbian Social Services, 5,* 25-49.

Icard, L. D., Longres, J. F., & Williams, J. H. (1996). An applied research agenda for homosexually active men of color. *Journal of Gay & Lesbian Social Services, 5,* 139-164.

Irwin, P., & Thompson, N. L. (1977). Acceptance of the rights of homosexuals: A social profile. *Journal of Homosexuality, 3,* 107-121.

Isay, R. A. (1990). Psychoanalytic theory and the therapy of gay men. In D. P. McWhirter, S. A. Sanders, & J. M. Reinisch (Eds.), *Homosexuality/heterosexuality: Concepts of sexual orientation* (pp. 283-303). New York: Oxford University Press.

Island, D., & Letellier, P. (1991). *Men who beat the men who love them.* New York: Haworth.

Jackson, K., & Brown, L. B. (1996). Lesbians of African heritage: Coming out in the straight community. *Journal of Gay & Lesbian Social Services, 5,* 53-67.

Jacobs, H. (1994). A new approach for gay and lesbian domestic partners: Legal acceptance through relational property theory. *Duke Journal of Gender Law & Policy, 1,* 159-172.

Jacobs, M. A., & Brown, L. B. (1997). American Indian lesbians and gays: An exploratory story. *Journal of Gay and Lesbian Social Services, 6,* 29-41.

Janoff-Bulman, R. (1979). Characterological versus behavioral self-blame: Inquiries into depression and rape. *Journal of Personality and Social Psychology, 37,* 1798-1809.

Janus, S. S., & Janus, C. L. (1993). *The Janus report on sexual behavior.* New York: John Wiley.

Jay, K. (1995, Winter). Lesbian New York. *Harvard Gay & Lesbian Review, 2,* 19-22.

Jay, K., & Young, A. (Eds.). (1972). *Out of the closets: Voices of gay liberation.* New York: Jove.

Jeffreys, S. (1994). The queer disappearance of lesbians: Sexuality in the academy. *Women's Studies International Forum, 17,* 459-472.

Jenny, C., Roesler, T. A., & Poyer, K. C. (1994). Are children at risk for sexual abuse by homosexuals? *Pediatrics, 1,* 41-44.

Jensen, L., Gambles, D., & Olsen, J. (1988). Attitudes toward homosexuality: A cross-sectional analysis of predictors. *International Journal of Social Psychiatry, 34,* 47-57.

Johansson, W. (1990a). Discrimination. In W. R. Dynes (Ed.), *Encyclopedia of homosexuality* (pp. 320-323). New York: Garland.

Johansson, W. (1990b). Law, United States. In W. R. Dynes (Ed.), *Encyclopedia of homosexuality* (pp. 692-698). New York: Garland.

Johansson, W. (1990c). Prejudice. In W. R. Dynes (Ed.), *Encyclopedia of homosexuality* (pp. 1031-1033). New York: Garland.

Johansson, W. (1990d). Psychology. In W. R. Dynes (Ed.), *Encyclopedia of homosexuality* (pp. 1078-1080). New York: Garland.

Johnson, B. (1990). Survey reveals male and female differences in sexual behaviors of older adults. *Contemporary Sexuality, 24,* 3.

Johnson, J. (1982). Influence of assimilation on the psychosocial adjustment of Black homosexual men (Doctoral dissertation, California School of Professional Psychology, 1982). *Dissertation Abstracts International, 42,* 4620B.

Johnston, J. (1973). *Lesbian nation: The feminist solution.* New York: Simon & Schuster.

Jones, B. E., & Hill, M. J. (1996). African American lesbians, gay men, and bisexuals. In R. P. Cabaj & T. S. Stein (Eds.), *Textbook of homosexuality and mental health* (pp. 549-561). Washington, DC: American Psychiatric Press.

Jones, D., & Willette, A. (1995, October 19). Critics claim Disney's gay policy is anti-family. *USA TODAY,* p. B1.

Jones, I. E., Farina, A., Hastorf, A. H., Markus, H. J., Miller, D. T., & Scott, R. A. (1984). *Social stigma: The psychology of marked relationships.* New York: Freeman.

Káahumanu, L. (1992). It's official! The 1993 March on Washington for Lesbian, Gay, and (Yes) Bisexual Rights and Liberation. *Anything That Moves: Beyond the Myths of Bisexuality, 4,* 22-24.

Kahn, M. J. (1991). Factors affecting the coming out process for lesbians. *Journal of Homosexuality, 21,* 47-70.

Kanuha, V. (1990). Compounding the triple jeopardy: Battering in lesbian of color relationships. *Women and Therapy, 9,* 169-184.

Karls, J. M., & Wandrei, K. E. (1994a). *PIE manual: Person-in-environment system.* Washington, DC: NASW.

Karls, J. M., & Wandrei, K. E. (1994b). *Person-in-environment system.* Washington, DC: NASW.

Kaufman, P. A., Harrison, E., & Hyde, M. L. (1984). Distancing and intimacy in lesbian relationships. *American Journal of Psychiatry, 141,* 530-533.

Kaupman, G. (1991, February 29). Cracker Barrel waffles on anti-gay policy. *Southern Voice,* p. 1.

Kehoe, M. (1985). *Lesbians in literature and history.* New York: Haworth.

Kehoe, M. (1986). Lesbians over 65: A triple invisible minority. *Journal of Homosexuality, 12,* 139-152.

Kehoe, M. (1989). *Lesbians over 60 speak for themselves.* New York: Harrington Park.

Kelley, H. H. (1983). Love and commitment. In H. H. Kelley, E. Berscheid, A. Christensen, J. H. Harvey, T. L. Huston, G. Levinger, R. McClintock, L. A. Peplau, & D. R. Peterson (Eds.), *Close relationships* (pp. 265-314). New York: Freeman.

Kelley, H. H., Berscheid, E., Christensen, A., Harvey, J. H., Huston, T. L., Levinger, G., McClintock, E., Peplau, L. A., & Peterson, D. R. (1983). *Close relationships.* New York: Freeman.

Kelley, H. H., & Thibaut, J. W. (1978). *Interpersonal relations: A theory of interdependence.* New York: John Wiley.

Kelly, J. (1975). Brothers and brothers: The gay man's adaptation to aging (Doctoral dissertation, Brandeis University, 1974). *Dissertation Abstracts International, 36,* 3130A.

Kelly, J. (1977). The aging male homosexual: Myth and reality. *Gerontologist, 17,* 328-332.

Khayatt, D. (1994). Surviving school as a lesbian student. *Gender and Education, 6,* 47-61.

Kimmel, D. C. (1977). Psychotherapy and the older gay man. *Psychotherapy: Theory, Research and Practice, 14,* 386-393.

Kimmel, D. C. (1978). Adult development and aging: A gay perspective. *Journal of Social Issues, 34,* 113-130.

Kimmel, D. C. (1979-1980). LIfe-history interviews of aging gay men. *International Journal of Aging and Human Development, 10,* 239-248.

Kimmel, D. C., & Sang, B. E. (1995). Lesbians and gay men in midlife. In A. R. D'Augelli & C. J. Patterson (Eds.), *Lesbian, gay, and bisexual identities over the lifespan: Psychological perspectives* (pp. 190-214). New York: Oxford University Press.

Kinsey, A. C., Pomeroy, W. B., & Martin, C. E. (1948). *Sexual behavior in the human male.* Philadelphia: W. B. Saunders.

Kinsey, A. C., Pomeroy, W. B., Martin, C. E., & Gebhard, P. H. (1953). *Sexual behavior in the human female.* Philadelphia: W. B. Saunders.

Kirk, M., & Madsen, H. (1989). *After the ball: How America will conquer its fear and hatred of gays in the 90's.* New York: Doubleday.

Kirkpatrick, M. (1988). Clinical implications of lesbian mother studies. In E. Coleman (Ed.), In *Integrated identity for gay men and lesbians: Psychotherapeutic approaches for emotional well-being* (pp. 201-211). New York: Harrington Park.

Kirkpatrick, M. (1989). Middle age and the lesbian experience. *Women's Studies Quarterly, 1-2,* 87-86.

Kirkpatrick, M. (1990). Homosexuality and parenting. In J. Spurlock & C. B. Robinowitz (Eds.), *Women's progress: Promises and problems* (pp. 205-222). New York: Plenum.

Kirkpatrick, M. (1991). Lesbian couples in therapy. *Psychiatric Annals, 21,* 491-496.

Kirkpatrick, M., Smith, C., & Roy, R. (1981). Lesbian mothers and their children: A comparative survey. *American Journal of Orthopsychiatry, 51,* 545-551.

Kite, M. E. (1984). Sex differences in attitudes towards homosexuals: A meta-analytic review. *Journal of Homosexuality, 10,* 69-89.

Kite, M. E. (1994). When perceptions meet reality: Individual differences in reactions to lesbians and gay men. In B. Greene & M. Herek (Eds.), *Lesbian and gay psychology: Theory, research, and clinical applications* (pp. 25-53). Thousand Oaks, CA: Sage.

Kite, M. E., & Deaux, K. (1986). Attitudes toward homosexuality: Assessment and behavioral consequences. *Basic and Applied Social Psychology, 7,* 137-162.

Kitzinger, C. (1987). *The social construction of lesbianism.* London: Sage.

Kitzinger, C. (1991). Lesbian and gay men in the workplace: Psychosocial issues. In M. J. Davidson & J. Earnshaw (Eds.), *Vulnerable workers: Psychosocial and legal issues* (pp. 223-257). New York: John Wiley.

Kitzinger, C. (1995). Social constructionism: Implications for lesbian and gay psychology. In A. R. D'Augelli & C. J. Patterson (Eds.), *Lesbian, gay, and bisexual identities over the lifespan: Psychological perspectives* (pp. 136-161). New York: Oxford University Press.

Kitzinger, C. (1996). Speaking of oppression: Psychology, politics, and the language of power. In E. D. Rothblum & L. A. Bond (Eds.), *Preventing heterosexism and homophobia* (pp. 3-19). Thousand Oaks, CA: Sage.

Kitzinger, C., & Coyle, A. (1995). Lesbian and gay couples: Speaking of difference. *Psychologist, 8,* 64-69.

Kitzinger, C., & Perkins, R. (1993). *Changing our minds: Lesbian feminism and psychology.* New York: New York University Press.

Kitzinger, C., & Wilkinson, S. (1995). Transitions from heterosexuality to lesbianism: The discursive production of lesbian identities. *Developmental Psychology, 31,* 95-104.

Klein, F. (1990). The need to view sexual orientation as a multivariate dynamic process: A theoretical perspective. In D. P. McWhirter, S. A. Sanders, & J. M. Reinisch (Eds.), *Homosexuality/heterosexuality: Concepts of sexual orientation* (pp. 277-282). New York: Oxford University Press.

Klein, F. (1993). *The bisexual option* (2nd ed.). New York: Harrington Park.

Klein, F., Sepekoff, B., & Wolf, T. J. (1985). Sexual orientation: A multi-variable dynamic process. *Journal of Homosexuality, 11,* 35-49.

Klinger, R. L., & Cabaj, R. P. (1993). Characteristics of gay and lesbian relationships. *Review of Psychiatry, 12,* 101-125.

Klinkenberg, D., & Rose, S. (1994). Dating scripts of gay men and lesbians. *Journal of Homosexuality, 26,* 23-35.

Kochman, A. (Speaker). (1993). *AIDS and the elderly* (Cassette Recording No. ASA3-691). San Francisco: American Society on Aging.

Kochman, A. (1997). Gay and lesbian elderly: Historical overview and implications for social work practice. *Journal of Gay & Lesbian Services, 6,* 1-10.

Kooden, H. (1997). Successful aging in the middle-aged gay man: A contribution to developmental theory. *Journal of Gay & Lesbian Social Services, 6,* 21-43.

Kooperman, L. (1994). A survey of gay and bisexual men age 50 and older: AIDS related knowledge, attitude, belief, and behavior. *AIDS Patient Care, 8,* 114-117.

Krafft-Ebing, R. (1892). *Psychopathia sexualis.* Philadelphia: Davis.

Krajeski, J. P. (1984). Psychotherapy with gay and lesbian patients. In E. S. Hetrick & T. S. Stein (Eds.), *Innovations in psychotherapy with homosexuals* (pp. 76-88). Washington, DC: American Psychiatric Association.

Krestan, J., & Bepko, C. (1980). The problem of fusion in the lesbian relationship. *Family Process, 19,* 277-290.

Kronenberger, G. K. (1991). Out of the closet. *Personnel Journal, 70,* 40-44.

Kurdek, L. A. (1987). Sex role self-schema and psychological adjustment in coupled homosexual and heterosexual men and women. *Sex Roles, 17,* 549-562.

Kurdek, L. A. (1988a). Correlates of negative attitudes toward homosexuals in heterosexual college students. *Sex Roles, 18,* 727-739.

Kurdek, L. A. (1988b). Perceived social support in gays and lesbians in cohabiting relationships. *Journal of Personality and Social Psychology, 54,* 504-509.

Kurdek, L. A. (1988c). Relationship quality of gay and lesbian cohabiting couples. *Journal of Homosexuality, 15,* 93-118.

Kurdek, L. A. (1989). Relationship quality in gay and lesbian cohabiting couples: A 1-year follow-up study. *Journal of Social and Personal Relationships, 6,* 39-59.

Kurdek, L. A. (1991a). Correlates of relationship satisfaction in cohabiting gay and lesbian couples: Integration of contextual, investment, and problem-solving models. *Journal of Personality and Social Psychology, 61,* 910-922.

Kurdek, L. A. (1991b). Sexuality in homosexual and heterosexual couples. In K McKinney & S. Sprecher (Eds.), *Sexuality in close relationships* (pp. 177-191). Hillsdale, NJ: Lawrence Erlbaum.

Kurdek, L. A. (1991c). The dissolution of gay and lesbian couples. *Journal of Social and Personal Relationships, 8,* 265-278.

Kurdek, L. A. (1992). Relationship stability and relationship satisfaction in cohabiting gay and lesbian couples: A prospective longitudinal test of the contextual and interdependence models. *Journal of Social and Personal Relationships, 9,* 125-142.

Kurdek, L. A. (1993). The allocation of household labor in homosexual and heterosexual cohabiting couples. *Journal of Social Issues, 49,* 127-139.

Kurdek, L. A. (1994a). Areas of conflict for gay, lesbian, and heterosexual cohabiting couples: What couples argue about influences relationship satisfaction. *Journal of Marriage and the Family, 56,* 923-934.

Kurdek, L. A. (1994b). The nature and correlates of relationship quality in gay, lesbian, and heterosexual cohabiting couples: A test of the contextual, investment, and discrepancy models. In B. Greene & G. M. Herek (Eds.), *Lesbian and gay psychology: Theory, research, and clinical applications* (pp. 133-135). Thousand Oaks, CA: Sage.

Kurdek, L. A. (1995a). Developing changes in relationship quality in gay and lesbian cohabiting couples. *Developmental Psychology, 31,* 86-94.

Kurdek, L. A. (1995b). Lesbian and gay couples. In A. R. D'Augelli & C. J. Patterson (Eds.), *Lesbian, gay, and bisexual identities over the lifespan: Psychological perspectives* (pp. 243-251). New York: Oxford University Press.

Kurdek, L. A. (1997). Relation between neuroticism and dimensions of relationship commitment: Evidence from gay, lesbian, and heterosexual couples. *Journal of Family Psychology, 11,* 109-124.

Kurdek, L. A., & Blisk, D. (1983). Dimensions and correlates of mothers' divorce experiences. *Journal of Divorce, 6,* 1-24.

Kurdek, L. A., & Schmitt, J. P. (1986a). Early development of relationship quality in heterosexual cohabiting, gay, and lesbian couples. *Developmental Psychology, 22,* 305-309.

Kurdek, L. A., & Schmitt, J. P. (1986b). Interaction of sex role self concept with relationship quality and relationship beliefs in married, heterosexual cohabiting, gay and lesbian relationships. *Journal of Personality and Social Psychology, 51,* 365-370.

Kurdek, L. A., & Schmitt, J. P. (1986c). Relationship quality of gay men in closed or open relationships. *Journal of Homosexuality, 12,* 85-99.

Kurdek, L. A., & Schmitt, J. P. (1986d). Relationship quality of partners in heterosexual married, heterosexual cohabiting, and gay and lesbian relationships. *Journal of Personality and Social Psychology, 51,* 711-720.

Kurdek, L. A., & Schmitt, J. P. (1987). Perceived emotional support from family and friends in members of homosexual, married, and heterosexual cohabitating couples. *Journal of Homosexuality, 14,* 57-68.

Laird, J., & Green, R.-J. (Eds.). (1996). *Lesbians and gays in couples and families: A handbook for therapists.* San Francisco: Jossey-Bass.

Landau, A. D. (1994). Employment discrimination against lesbians and gays: The incomplete legal response of the United States and the European Union. *Duke Journal of Comparative and International Law, 4,* 335-361.

Lander, P. S., & Charbonneau, C. (1990). The new lesbian in midlife: Reconstructing sexual identity. In J. Hurtig et al. (Eds.), *Michigan Discussions in Anthropology, 9,*1-14.

Laner, M. R. (1978). Growing older male: Heterosexual and homosexual. *Gerontologist, 18,* 496-501.

Laner, M. R., & Laner, R. H. (1980). Sexual preference or personal style? Why lesbians are disliked. *Journal of Homosexuality, 5,* 339-356.

Larsen, K. S., Cate, R., & Reed, M. (1983). Anti-Black attitudes, religious orthodoxy, permissiveness, and sexual information: A study of the attitudes of heterosexuals toward homosexuality. *Journal of Sex Research, 19,* 105-118.

Larson, P. C. (1982). Gay male relationships. In W. Paul, J. D. Weinrich, J. C. Gonsiorek, & M. E. Hotvedt (Eds.), *Homosexuality: Social, psychological, and biological issues* (pp. 219-232). Beverly Hills, CA: Sage.

LaTorre, R. A., & Wendenberg, K. (1983). Psychological characteristics of bisexual, heterosexual, and homosexual women. *Journal of Homosexuality, 9,* 87-97.

Laumann, E. D., Gagnon, J. H., Michael, R. T., & Michaels, S. (1994). *The social organization of sexuality: Sexual practices in the United States.* Chicago: University of Chicago.

Lazarus, R. S., & Folkman, S. (1984). *Stress, appraisal, and coping.* New York: Springer-Verlag.

Leavy, R., & Adams, E. (1986). Feminism as a correlate of self-esteem, self-acceptance, and social support among lesbians. *Psychology of Women Quarterly, 10,* 321-326.

Lee, D. B., &Saul, T. T. (1987). Counseling Asian men. In M. Scher, M. Stevens, G. Good, & G. A. Eichenfield (Eds.), *Handbook of counseling and psychotherapy with men* (pp. 180-191). Newbury Park, CA: Sage.

Lee, J. A. (1977). Going public: A study in the sociology of homosexual liberation. *Journal of Homosexuality, 3,* 49-78.

Lee, J. A. (1987). What can homosexual aging studies contribute to theories of aging? *Journal of Homosexuality, 13,* 43-71.

Lee, J. A. (1990). Aging. In W. Dynes (Ed.), *Encyclopedia of homosexuality* (pp. 26-29). New York: Garland.

Lee, J. A. (1991). Can we talk? Can we really talk? Communication as a key factor in the maturing homosexual couple. In J. A. Lee (Ed.), *Gay midlife and maturity* (pp. 143-168). New York: Haworth.

Lee, J. A. (1993). Special problems of older gay employees. In L. Diamant (Ed.), *Homosexual issues in the workplace* (pp. 218-223). Washington, DC: Taylor & Francis.

Lee, J. A., & Brown, R. G. (1993). Hiring, firing, and promoting. In L. Diamant (Ed.), *Homosexual issues in the workplace* (pp. 45-62). Washington, DC: Taylor & Francis.

Lemp, G., Neri, G., & the San Francisco Department of Public Health, AIDS Office. (1991). *The Young Mens's Survey.* Presentation to the San Francisco Health Commission.

Leslie, D., & Mac Neill, L. (1995). Double positive: Lesbians and race. In J. Adelman & G. M. Enguidanos (Eds.), *Racism in the lives of women: Testimony, theory, and guides to antiracist practices* (pp. 161-169). New York: Harrington Park.

LeVay, S. (1991). A difference in hypothalamic structure between heterosexual and homosexual men. *Science, 253,* 1034-1037.

Lever, J., Kanouse, D. E., Rogers, W. H., Carson, S., & Hertz, R. (1992). Behavior patterns and sexual identity of bisexual males. *Journal of Sex Research, 29,* 141-167.

Levine, H., & Evans, N. J. (1991). The development of gay, lesbian, and bisexual identities. In N. J. Evans & V. A. Wall (Eds.), *Beyond tolerance: Gays, lesbians, and bisexuals on campus* (pp. 1-24). Alexandria, VA: American College Personnel Association.

Levine, M. P. (1979). Employment discrimination against gay men. *International Review of Modern Sociology, 9,*151-163.

Levine, M. P. (1992). The life and death of gay clones. In G. Herdt (Ed.), *Gay culture in America: Essays from the field* (pp. 68-86). Boston: Beacon.

Levine, M. P., & Leonard, R. (1984). Discrimination against lesbians in the workforce. *Signs, 9,* 700-710.

Levinger, G. C. (1979). A social psychological perspective on marital dissolution. In G. Levinger & O. C. Moler (Eds.), *Divorce and separation* (pp. 37-63). New York: Basic Books.

Levinson, D., Darrow, C. N., Klein, E. B., Levinson, M. H., & McKee, B. (1978). *The seasons of a man's life.* New York: Knopf.

Levy, E. F. (1992). Strengthening the coping resources of lesbian families. *Families in Society, 73,* 23-31.

Lewis, S. (1979). *Sunday's women: Lesbian life today.* Boston: Beacon.

Lie, G., & Gentlewarrier, S. (1991). Intimate violence in lesbian relationships: Discussion of survey findings and practice implications. *Journal of Social Service Research, 15,* 41-59.

Lie, G., Schilit, R., Bush, J., Montagne, M., & Reyes, L. (1991). Lesbians in currently aggressive relationships? *Violence and Victims, 6,* 121-135.

Likosky, S. (1992). *Coming out: An anthology of international gay and lesbian writings.* New York: Pantheon.

Linde, R. (1994). Impact of AIDS on adult gay male development: Implications for psychotherapy. In S. A. Cadwell, R. A. Burnham, & M. Forstein (Eds.), *Therapists on the front-*

line: Psychotherapy with gay men in the age of AIDS (pp. 25-31). Washington, DC: American Psychiatric Press.

Liu, P., & Chan, C. C. (1996). Lesbian, gay, and bisexual Asian Americans and their families. In J. Laird & R.-J. Green (Eds.), Lesbians and gays in couples and families: A handbook for therapists (pp. 137-152). San Francisco: Jossey-Bass.

Lockhart, L. L., White, B. W., Causby, V., & Isaac, A. (1994). Letting out the secret: Violence in lesbian relationships. Journal of Interpersonal Violence, 9, 469-492.

Logan, C. R. (1996). Homophobia? No, Homoprejudice. Journal of Homosexuality, 31, 31-51.

Loiacano, D. K. (1989). Gay identity issues among Black Americans: Racism, homophobia, and the need for validation. Journal of Counseling and Development, 68, 21-25.

Longino, H. (1988). Science as social knowledge: Values and objectivity in scientific inquiry. Princeton, NJ: Princeton University Press.

Longres, J. F. (1995). Human behavior and the social environment (2nd ed.). Itasca, IL: F. E. Peacock.

Lopez, G., & Chism, N. (1993). Classroom concerns of gay and lesbian students. College Teaching, 41, 97-103.

Lott-Whitehead, L., & Tully, C. T. (1993). The family lives of lesbian mothers. Smith College Studies in Social Work, 63, 266-280.

Loulan, J. (1986). Psychotherapy with lesbian mothers. In T. S. Stein & C. J. Cohen (Eds.), Contemporary perspectives on psychotherapy with lesbians and gay men (pp. 103-137). New York: Plenum.

Lucco, A. J. (1987). Planned retirement housing preferences of older homosexuals. Journal of Homosexuality, 14, 35-56.

Lundy, S. E. (1993). Abuse that dare not speak its name: Assisting victims of lesbian and gay domestic violence in Massachusetts. New England Law Review, 28, 273-311.

Lynch, F. R. (1992). Nonghetto gays: An ethnography of suburban homosexuals. In G. Herdt (Ed.), Gay culture in America: Essays from the field (pp. 165-201). Boston: Beacon.

Lynch, J. M., & Reilly, M. E. (1986). Role relationships: Lesbian perspectives. Journal of Homosexuality, 12, 53-69.

MacIntosh, H. (1994). Attitudes and experiences of psychoanalysis in analyzing homosexual patients. Journal of the American Psychoanalytic Association, 42, 1183-1207.

Mallon, G. P. (1992a). Gay and no place to go: Assessing the needs of gay and lesbian adolescents in out-of-home settings. Child Welfare, 71, 547-556.

Mallon, G. P. (1992b). Serving the needs of gay and lesbian youth in residential treatment centers. Residential Treatment for Children and Youth, 10, 47-61.

Malyon, A. K. (1981-1982). Psychotherapeutic implications of internalized homophobia in gay men. Journal of Homosexuality, 7, 56-59.

Manalansan, M. F., IV. (1996). Double minorities: Latino, Black, and Asian men who have sex with men. In R. C. Savin-Williams & K. M. Cohen (Eds.), The lives of lesbian, gay men, and bisexuals: Children to adults (pp. 393-425). Ft. Worth, TX: Harcourt Brace.

Marcus, E. (1988). The male couple's guide to living together. New York: Harper & Row.

Marecek, J., Finn, S. E., & Cardell, M. (1982-1983). Gender roles in the relationships of lesbians and gay men. Journal of Homosexuality, 8, 45-50.

Marín, G., & Marín, B. V. (1991). Research with Hispanic populations (Applied Social Research Methods Series, Vol. 23). Newbury Park, CA: Sage.

Marks, G., Bundek, N. I., Richardson, J. L., Ruiz, M. S., & Maldonado, N. (1992). Self-disclosure of HIV infection:

Preliminary results from a sample of Hispanic men. Health Psychology, 11, 300-306.

Marmor, J. (1980). Overview: The multiple roots of homosexual behavior. In J. Marmor (Ed.), Homosexual behavior: A modern reappraisal (pp. 3-22). New York: Basic Books.

Marsiglio, W. (1993). Attitudes toward homosexual activity and gays as friends: A national survey of heterosexual 15- to 19-year old males. Journal of Sex Research, 30, 12-17.

Martin, A. D., & Hetrick, E. S. (1988). The stigmatization of the gay and lesbian adolescent. Journal of Homosexuality, 15, 163-183.

Martin, D., & Lyon, P. (1992). The older lesbian. In B. Berzon & R. Leighton (Eds.), Positively gay (pp. 111-120). Berkeley: Celestial Arts.

Martin, D., & Lyon, P. (1995). Lesbian liberation begins. Harvard Lesbian & Gay Review, 2, 15-18.

Martin, H. P. (1991). The coming-out process for homosexuals. Hospital and Community Psychiatry, 42, 150-162.

Martin, J. I. (1995). Gay and lesbian faculty in social work: Roles and responsibilities. Journal of Gay & Lesbian Social Services, 3, 1-12.

Martin, J. I., & Knox, J. (1997). Self-esteem instability and its implications for HIV prevention among gay men. Health and Social Work, 22, 264-273.

Martin, J. L. (1988). Psychological consequences of AIDS-related bereavement among gay men. Journal of Consulting and Clinical Psychology, 56, 856-862.

Mason, H. R. C., Marks, G., Simoni, J. M., Ruiz, M. S., & Richardson, J. L. (1995). Culturally sanctioned secrets? Latino men's nondisclosure of HIV infection to family, friends and lovers. Health Psychology, 14, 6-12.

Matteson, D. R. (1987). The heterosexually married gay and lesbian parent. In F. W. Bozett (Ed.), Gay and lesbian parents (pp. 138-161). New York: Praeger.

Matteson, D. R. (1996). Psychotherapy with bisexual individuals. In R. P. Cabaj & T. S. Stein (Eds.), Textbook of homosexuality and mental health (pp. 433-449). Washington, DC: American Psychiatric Press.

Mattison, A. M., & McWhirter, D. P. (1990). Emotional impact of AIDS: Male couples and their families. In B. Voeller, J. M. Reinisch, & M. Gottlieb (Eds.), AIDS and sex: An integrated biomedical and biobehavioral approach (pp. 401-419). New York: Oxford University Press.

Mattison, A. M., & McWhirter, D. P. (1995). Lesbians, gay men, and their families: Some therapeutic issues. Psychiatric Clinics of North America, 18, 123-137.

Mauro, T. (1996, May 21). Colo. ruling called historic. USA TODAY, p. A1.

Mayerson, P., & Lief, H. (1965). Psychotherapy of homosexuals: A follow-up study of nineteen cases. In J. Marmor (Ed.), Sexual inversion (pp. 302-344). New York: Basic Books.

Mays, V. M. (1985). Black women working together: Diversity in same sex relationships. Women's Studies International Forum, 8, 67-71.

Mays, V. M., & Cochran, S. D. (1986, August). The Black lesbian relationship project: Relationship experiences and the perception of discrimination. Paper presented at the meeting of the 94th Annual Convention of the American Psychological Association, Washington, DC.

Mays, V. M., & Cochran, S. D. (1988). The Black women's relationship project: A national survey of Black lesbians. In M. Shernoff & W. Scott (Eds.), The sourcebook on lesbian/gay health care (2nd. ed., pp. 54-62). Washington, DC: National Lesbian and Gay Health Foundation.

Mays, V., Cochran, S., & Rhue, S. (1993). The impact of perceived discrimination on the intimate relationships of Black lesbians. *Journal of Heterosexuality, 25,* 1-14.

McAllan, L. C., & Ditillo, D. (1994). Addressing the needs of lesbian and gay clients with disabilities. *Journal of Rehabilitation Counseling, 25,* 26-35.

McConaghy, N. (1981). Controlled comparison of aversion therapy and covert sensitization in compulsive homosexuality. *Behavior Research and Therapy, 19,* 425-434.

McDaniel, M. A. (1989). *Preservice adjustment of homosexual and heterosexual military accessions: Implications for security clearance suitability* (Rep. No. PER-TR-89-04, 21). Washington, DC: Department of Defense.

McDonald, G. J. (1982). Individual differences in the coming out process for gay men: Implications for theoretical models. *Journal of Homosexuality, 8,* 47-60.

McDougall, G. J. (1993). Therapeutic issues with gay and lesbian elders. *Clinical Gerontologist, 14,* 45-57.

McGrath, E. (1990, August). *New treatment strategies for women in the middle.* Paper presented at the annual convention of the American Psychological Association, Boston.

McIntosh, M. (1981). The homosexual role. In K. Plummer (Ed.), *The making of the modern homosexual* (pp. 44-49). London: Hutchinson.

McKirnan, D., & Peterson, P. (1986, October 2). Preliminary social issues survey results available. *Windy City Times,* pp. 2, 8.

McKirnan, D. J., & Peterson, P. L. (1989). Alcohol and drug use among homosexual men and women: Epidemiology and population characteristics. *Addictive Behaviors, 14,* 545-553.

McPherson, D. (1993). Gay parenting couples: Parenting arrangements, arrangement satisfaction, and relationship satisfaction (Doctoral dissertation, Pacific Graduate School of Psychology, 1993). *Dissertation Abstracts International, 54,* 3859B.

McWhirter, D. P., & Mattison, A. M. (1988). Psychotherapy for gay male couples. In J. De Cecco (Ed.), *Gay relationships* (pp. 161-168). New York: Harrington Park.

McWhirter, D. P., & Mattison, A. M. (1994). Male couples. In R. P. Cabaj & T. S. Stein (Eds.), *Textbook of homosexuality and mental health* (pp. 319-337). Washington, DC: American Psychiatric Press.

Metz, M. E., Rosser, B. R. S., & Strapko, N. (1994). Differences in conflict-resolution styles among heterosexual, gay, and lesbian couples. *Journal of Sex Research, 31,* 293-308.

Metz, P. (1997). Staff development for working with lesbian and gay elders. *Journal of Gay & Lesbian Services, 6,* 35- 45.

Meyer, C. L. (1992). Legal, psychological, and medical considerations in lesbian parenting. *Law and Sexuality, 2,* 237-264.

Meyer, I. H. (1995). Minority stress and mental health in gay men. *Journal of Health and Social Behavior, 36,* 38-56.

Meyer, J. (1990). Guess who's coming to dinner this time? A study of gay intimate relationships and the support for those relationships. *Marriage & Family Review, 14,* 59-82.

Meyer, P., Tapley, E. K., & Bazargan, M. (1996). Depression in HIV symptomatic gay and bisexual men. *Journal of Gay & Lesbian Social Services, 5,* 69-85.

Michael, R., Gagnon, J. H., Laumann, E. N., & Molata, G. (1994). *Sex in America.* Boston: Little, Brown.

Mickens, E. (1994). *The 100 best companies for gay men and lesbians.* New York: Pocket.

Miller, B. (1978). Adult sexual resocialization: Adjustments towards a stigmatized identity. *Alternative Lifestyles, 1,* 207-234.

Miller, B. (1979a). Gay fathers and their children. *Family Coordinator, 28,* 544-552.

Miller, B. (1979b). Unpromised paternity: Life-styles of gay fathers. In M. P. Levine (Ed.), *Gay men: The sociology of male homosexuality* (pp. 239-252). New York: Harper & Row.

Miller, B. (1986). Identity resocialization in moral careers of gay husbands and fathers. In A. Davis (Ed.), *Papers in honor of Gordon Hirabayashi* (pp. 197-216). Edmonton, Alberta: University of Alberta.

Miller, N. (1989). *In search of gay America.* New York: Atlantic Monthly Press.

Miller, N. (1992). *Out in the world.* New York: Simon & Schuster.

Minnigerode, F. A. (1976). Age-status labeling in homosexual men. *Journal of Homosexuality, 1,* 273-276.

Minnigerode, F., & Adelman, M. (1976, October). *Adaptations of aging homosexual men and women.* Paper presented at the Convention of the Gerontological Society, New York.

Minnigerode, F., & Adelman, M. (1978). Elderly homosexual women and men: Report of a pilot study. *Family Coordinator, 27,* 451-456.

Minnigerode, F. A., Adelman, M. R., & Fox, D. (1980). *Aging and homosexuality: Physical and psychological well-being.* Unpublished manuscript, University of San Francisco.

Minton, H. L., & McDonald, G. J. (1983-1984). Homosexual identity formation as a developmental process. *Journal of Homosexuality, 9,* 91-104.

Mintz, E. (1966). Overt male homosexuals in combined group and individual treatment. *Journal of Counseling Psychology, 20,* 193-198.

Miranda, J., & Storms, M. (1989). Psychological adjustment of lesbians and gay men. *Journal of Counseling and Development, 68,* 41- 45.

Mitchell, V. (1988). Using Kohut's self psychology in work with lesbian couples. *Women & Therapy, 8,* 157-166.

Mitchell, V., & Helson, R. (1990). Women's prime of life: Is it the 50s? *Psychology of Women Quarterly, 14,* 451-470.

A model foster-care policy. (1985, May 28). *Boston Globe,* p. 14.

Money, J. (1988). *Gay, straight, and in-between.* New York: Oxford University Press.

Monteiro, K. P., & Fuqua, V. (1994). African American gay youth: One form of manhood. *High School Journal, 77,* 20-36.

Montgomery, L., & Collins, J. (1989, January 8). Prejudice and presumption: Views of victims' lifestyle blur truth in gay-bashing case. *Dallas Times Herald,* pp. A1, A16, A17.

Moraga, C., & Hollibaugh, A. (1985). What we're rollin around in bed with. In A. Snitow, C. Stansell, & S. Thompson (Eds.), *Powers of desire: The politics of sexuality* (pp. 394-405). New York: Monthly Review Press.

Morales, A. T., & Sheafor, B. W. (1995). *Social work: A profession of many faces.* Boston: Allyn & Bacon.

Morales, E. S. (1990). Ethnic minority families and minority gays and lesbians. *Marriage and Family Review, 14,* 217-239.

Morales, E. S. (1992). Counseling Latino gays and Latina lesbians. In S. Dworkin & F. Gutiérrez (Eds.), *Counseling gay men and lesbians: Journey to the end of the rainbow* (pp. 125-139). Alexandria, VA: American Association for Counseling and Development.

Morales, E. S. (1996). Gender roles among Latino gay and bisexual men: Implications for family and couple therapy. In J. Laird & R.-J. Green (Eds.), *Lesbians and gays in couples and families: A handbook for therapists* (pp. 272-297). San Francisco: Jossey-Bass.

Morin, S. F., & Schultz, S. J. (1978). The gay movement and the rights of children. *Journal of Social Issues, 34,* 137-148.

Morris, R., Baker, C., & Huscroft, S. (1992). Incarcerated youth at risk for HIV infection. In R. J. DiClemente (Ed.), *Adolescents and AIDS: A generation in jeopardy* (pp. 52-70). Newbury Park, CA: Sage.

Morrow, D. F. (1993). Social work with gay and lesbian adolescents. *Social Work, 38,* 655-660.

Morrow, D. F. (1996). Coming-out issues for adult lesbians: A group intervention. *Social Work, 41,* 647-656.

Morrow, S. L., & Hawxhurst, D. M. (1989). Lesbian partner abuse: Implications for therapists. *Journal of Counseling and Development, 68,* 58-62.

Moses, A. E., & Hawkins, R. O., Jr. (1986). *Counseling lesbian women and gay men: A life issues approach.* Columbus, OH: Merrill.

Murphy, B. (1989). Lesbian couples and their parents: The effects of perceived parental attitudes on the couple. *Journal of Counseling and Development, 68,* 46-51.

Murphy, B. C. (1994). Difference and diversity: Gay and lesbian couples. *Social Services for Gay and Lesbian Couples, 1,* 5-31.

Murray, S. O. (1992). Components of gay community in San Francisco. In G. Herdt (Ed.), *Gay culture in America* (pp. 107-146). Boston: Beacon.

Myers, M. F. (1981-1982). Counseling the parents of young homosexual male patients. *Journal of Homosexuality, 7,* 131-143.

Myers, M. F. (1989). *Men and divorce.* New York: Guilford.

Mylott, K. (1994). Twelve irrational ideas that drive gay men and women crazy. *Journal of Rational-Emotive and Cognitive Behavioral Therapy, 12,* 61-70.

Myron, N., & Bunch, C. (Eds.). (1975). *Lesbianism and the women's movement.* Baltimore: Diana.

Nakajima, G. A., Chan, Y. H., & Lee, K. (1996). Mental health issues for gay and lesbian Asian Americans. In R. P. Cabaj & T. S. Stein (Eds.), *Textbook of homosexuality and mental health* (pp. 563-581). Washington, DC: American Psychiatric Press.

Nakayama, T. K., & Corey, F. C. (1993). Homosexuality. In R. Kastenbaum (Ed.), *Encyclopedia of adult development* (pp. 208-115). Phoenix: Oryx.

Nardi, M. P. (1992a). Cultural diversity in men's friendships. In M. P. Nardi (Ed.), *Men's friendships* (pp. 173-185). Newbury Park, CA: Sage.

Nardi, P. M. (1992b). That's what friends are for: Friends as family in the gay and lesbian community. In K. Plummer (Ed.), *Modern homosexualities: Fragments of lesbian and gay experience* (pp. 108-120). London: Routledge.

Nardi, P. M., & Sherrod, D. (1994). Friendship in the lives of gay men and lesbians. *Journal of Social and Personal Relationships, 11,* 185-199.

National Association of Social Workers. (1984). What non-gay therapists need to know to work with gay and lesbian clients. *Practice Digest, 7,* 28-31.

National Association of Social Workers. (1996). *The NASW code of ethics.* Washington, DC: Author.

National Gay and Lesbian Task Force, Policy Institute. (1991). *Count and counter hate crimes: A fact sheet on violence against lesbians and gay men.* Washington, DC: Author.

National Gay and Lesbian Task Force. (1994). *Lesbian, gay and bisexual rights in the U.S.: A chart of states, cities, counties and federal agencies whose civil rights laws, ordinances, and policies bar discrimination based on sexual orientation.* Washington, DC: Author.

National Gay and Lesbian Task Force. (1997, June). *Employment non-discrimination bill introduced.* Press release, on-line.

Neisen, J. H. (1987). Resources for families with a gay/lesbian member. In E. Coleman (Ed.), *Integrated identities for gay men and lesbians: Psychotherapeutic approaches for emotional well-being* (pp. 239-251). New York: Harrington Park.

Neisen, J. H. (1990). Heterosexism: Redefining homophobia for the 1990s. *Journal of Gay & Lesbian Psychotherapy, 1,* 21-35.

Neisen, J. H. (1993). Healing from cultural victimization: Recovery from shame due to heterosexism. *Journal of Gay & Lesbian Psychotherapy, 2,* 49-63.

Nemeyer, L. (1980). Coming out: Identity congruence and the attainment of adult female sexuality (Doctoral dissertation, Boston University, 1980). *Dissertation Abstracts International, 41,* 1924B.

Nestle, J. (1992). *The persistent desire: A femme-butch reader.* Boston: Alyson.

Newman, B. S. (1989). The relative importance of gender role attitudes to male and female attitudes toward lesbians. *Sex Roles, 21,* 451-465.

Nichols, M. (1987). Doing sex therapy with lesbians: Bending a heterosexual paradigm to fit a gay lifestyle. In the Boston Psychologies Collective (Eds.), *Lesbian psychologies* (pp. 242-260). Urbana: University of Illinois.

Nichols, M. (1988a). Bisexuality in women: Myths, realities, and implications for therapy. *Women and Therapy, 7,* 235-252.

Nichols, M. (1988b). Low sexual desire in lesbian couples. In S. Leiblum & R. C. Rosen (Eds.), *Sexual desire disorders* (pp. 387-412). New York: Guilford.

Nichols, M. (1989). Sex therapy with lesbians, gay men, and bisexuals. In S. R. Leiblum & R. C. Rosen (Eds.), *Principles and practice of sex therapy: Update for the 1990s* (2nd ed., pp. 269-297). New York: Guilford.

Nicoloff, L. K., & Stigliz, E. A. (1987). Lesbian alcoholism: Etiology, treatment, and recovery. In the Boston Lesbian Psychologies Collective (Eds.), *Lesbian psychologies: Explorations and challenges* (pp. 283-293). Urbana: University of Illinois.

Norris, W. P. (1992). Liberal attitudes and homophobic acts: The paradoxes of homosexual experience in a liberal institution. In K. Harbeck (Ed.), *Coming out of the classroom closet: Gay and lesbian students, teachers and curriculum* (pp. 81-120). Binghamton, NY: Harrington Park.

Nurius, P. S. (1983). Mental health implications of sexual orientation. *Journal of Sex Research, 19,* 119-136.

Nyberg, E., & Alston, J. (1976). Analysis of public attitudes toward homosexual behavior. *Journal of Homosexuality, 2,* 99-107.

Obear, K. (1991). Homophobia. In N. J. Evans & V. A. Wall (Eds.), *Beyond tolerance: Gays, lesbians, and bisexuals on campus* (pp. 39-78). Alexandria, VA: American College Personnel Association.

Ochs, R. (Ed.). (1995). *The bisexual resource guide.* Cambridge, MA: Bisexual Resource Center.

Ochs, R. (1996). Biphobia: It goes more than two ways. In B. A. Firestein (Ed.), *Bisexuality: The psychology and politics of an invisible minority* (pp. 217-239). Thousand Oaks, CA: Sage.

Olsen, M. R. (1987). A study of gay and lesbian teachers. *Journal of Homosexuality, 13,* 73-81.

Olson, E. D., & King, C. A. (1995). Gay and lesbian self-identification: A response to Rotheram-Borus and Fernandez. *Suicide and Life-Threatening Behavior, 25,* 35-39.

O'Neil, M. (1990). A mirror to our souls: Working with older adults with AIDS and HIV illness. In B. Genevay & R.

Katz (Eds.), *Countertransference and older clients* (pp. 54-68). Newbury Park, CA: Sage.

Orion Center. (1986). *Survey of street youth.* Seattle, WA: Author.

Ostrow, D. G. (1996). Mental health issues across the HIV-1 spectrum for gay and bisexual men. In R. P. Cabaj & T. S. Stein (Eds.), *Textbook of homosexuality and mental health* (pp. 859- 879). Washington, DC: American Psychiatric Press.

Owlfeather, M. (1988). Children of grandmother moon. In W. Roscoe (Ed.), *Living for the spirit: A gay American Indian anthology* (pp. 97-105). New York: St. Martin's.

Padesky, C. A. (1989). Attaining and maintaining positive lesbian self-identity: A cognitive therapy approach. In E. D. Rothblum & E Cole (Eds.), *Lesbianism: Affirming non-traditional roles* (pp. 145-156). New York: Haworth.

Page, S., & Yee, M. (1985). Conception of male and female homosexual stereotypes among university students. *Journal of Homosexuality, 12,* 109-118.

Patterson, C. J. (1992). Children of lesbian and gay men. *Journal of Sex Research, 30,* 62-69.

Patterson, C. J. (1995). Lesbian mothers, gay fathers, and their children. In A. R. D'Augelli & C. J. Patterson (Eds.), *Lesbian, gay, and bisexual identities over the lifespan: Psychological perspectives* (pp. 262-290). Oxford: Oxford University Press.

Patterson, D. G., & Schwartz, P. (1994). The social construction of conflict in intimate same-sex couples. In D. D. Cahn (Ed.), *Conflict in personal relationships* (pp. 3-26). Hillsdale, NJ: Lawrence Erlbaum.

Pattison, E. M., & Pattison, M. L. (1980). "Ex-gays": Religiously mediated change in homosexuals. *American Journal of Psychiatry, 137,* 1553-1562.

Paul, J. P. (1984). The bisexual identity: An idea without social recognition. *Journal of Homosexuality, 9,* 45-65.

Paul, J. P. (1985). Bisexuality: Reassessing our paradigms of sexuality. *Journal of Homosexuality, 9,* 45-63.

Paul, J. P. (1996). Bisexuality: Exploring/exploding the boundaries. In R. C. Savin-Williams & K. M. Cohen (Eds.), *The lives of lesbian, gay men, and bisexuals: Children to adults* (pp. 436-461). Ft. Worth, TX: Harcourt Brace.

Paul, J. P., Hays, R. B., & Coates, T. J. (1995). The impact of the HIV epidemic on U.S. gay male communities. In A. R. D'Augelli & C. J. Patterson (Eds.), *Lesbians, gay, and bisexual identities over the lifespan: Psychological perspectives* (pp. 347-397). New York: Oxford University Press.

Pearlman, S. F. (1987). The saga of continuing clash in lesbian community, or will an army of ex-lovers fail? In the Boston Lesbian Psychologies Collective (Eds.), *Lesbian psychologies: Explorations and challenges* (pp. 313-326). Urbana: University of Illinois.

Pearlman, S. F. (1989). Distancing and connectedness: Impact on couple formation in lesbian relationships. *Women and Therapy, 8,* 77-88.

Pederson, W. B. (1994). HIV risk in gay and lesbian adolescents. *Journal of Gay & Lesbian Social Services, 1,* 131-147.

Peplau, L. A. (1981). What homosexuals want in relationships. *Psychology Today, 15,* 28, 34, 37-38.

Peplau, L. A. (1982-1983). Research on homosexual couples: An overview. *Journal of Homosexuality, 8,* 3-21.

Peplau, L. A. (1983). Roles and gender. In H. H. Kelly, E. Berscheid, A. Christensen, J. H. Harvey, T. L. Huston, G. Levinger, E. McClintock, L. A. Peplau, & D. R. Peterson (Eds.), *Close relationships* (pp. 220-264). San Francisco: Freeman.

Peplau, L. A. (1991). Lesbian and gay relationships. In J. C. Gonsiorek & J. D. Weinrich (Eds.), *Homosexuality: Research findings for public policy* (pp. 177-196). Newbury Park, CA: Sage.

Peplau, L. A. (1993). Lesbian and gay relationships. In L. D. Garnets & D. C. Kimmel (Eds.), *Psychological perspectives on lesbian & gay male experiences* (pp. 395-419). New York: Columbia University Press

Peplau, L. A., & Cochran, S. D. (1981). Value orientations in the intimate relationships of gay men. *Journal of Homosexuality, 6,* 1-19.

Peplau, L. A., & Cochran, S. D. (1990). A relational perspective on homosexuality. In D. P. McWhirter, S. A. Saunders, & J. M. Reinisch (Eds.), *Homosexuality/heterosexuality: Concepts of sexual orientation* (pp. 321-349). New York: Oxford University Press

Peplau, L. A., Cochran, S. D., & Mays, V. M. (1986, August). *Satisfaction in the intimate relationships of Back lesbians.* Paper presented at the 94th Annual Convention of the American Psychological Association, Washington, DC.

Peplau, L. A., Cochran, S. D., & Mays, V. M. (1997). A national survey of the intimate relationships of African American lesbians and gay men: A look at commitment, satisfaction, sexual behavior, and HIV disease. In B. Greene (Ed.), *Ethnic and cultural diversity among lesbians and gay men* (pp. 11-38). Thousand Oaks, CA: Sage.

Peplau, L. A., & Gordon, S. L. (1983). The intimate relationships of lesbians and gay men. In E. R. Allgeier & N. B. McCormick (Eds.), *The changing boundaries: Gender roles and sexual behavior* (pp. 226-244). Palo Alto, CA: Mayfield.

Peplau, L. A., Padesky, C., & Hamilton, M. (1982). Satisfaction in lesbian relationships. In D. Perlman & S. Duck (Eds.), *Intimate relationships: Development, dynamics and deterioration* (pp. 13-42). Beverly Hills, CA: Sage.

Peplau, L. A., Veniegas, R. C., & Campbell, S. M. (1996). Gay and lesbian relationships. In R. C. Savin-Williams & K. M. Cohen (Eds.), *The lives of lesbian, gay men, and bisexuals: Children to adults* (pp. 250-273). Ft. Worth, TX: Harcourt Brace.

Peters, D. K., & Cantrell, P. J. (1993). Gender roles and role conflict in feminist lesbian and heterosexual women. *Sex Roles, 28,* 379-392.

Peterson, J. L. (1992). Black men and their same-sex desires and behaviors. In G. Herdt (Ed.), *Gay culture in America: Essays from the field* (pp. 147-164). Boston: Beacon.

Peterson, J. L. (1995). AIDS-related risks and same-sex behaviors among African American men. In G. M. Herek & B. Greene (Eds.), *AIDS, identity, and community: The HIV epidemic and lesbians and gay men* (pp. 85-104). Thousand Oaks, CA: Sage.

Peterson, P. L., & McKirnan, D. J. (1987, June 25). A profile of older gay males: A perspective from the social issues survey. *Windy City Times,* pp. 2, 8.

Pharr, S. (1988). *Homophobia A weapon of sexism.* Inverness, Scotland: Chardon.

Pierce, D. (1995, March). *Lesbian/gay adoption services in the United States: Policy and practice implications.* Paper presented at the 41st Annual Program Meeting of the Council on Social Work Education, San Diego, CA.

Pies, C. A. (1990). Lesbians and the choice to parent. *Marriage and Family Review, 14,* 137-154.

Pincus, A., & Minahan, A. (1973). *Social work practice: Model and method.* Itasca, IL: Peacock.

Plummer, K. (1975). *Sexual stigma: An interactionist account.* London: Routledge & Kegan Paul.

Pogrebin, L. C. (1983). The secret fear that keeps us from raising free children. *Interracial Books for Children, 14,* 10-12.

Polikoff, N. D. (1991). Educating judges about lesbian and gay parenting: A simulation. *Law and Sexuality, 1,* 173-198.

Ponse, B. (1978). *Identities in the lesbian world: Social construction of the self.* Westport, CT: Greenwood.

Ponse, B. (1980). Lesbians and their worlds. In J. Marmor (Ed.), *Homosexual behavior: A modern reappraisal* (pp. 157-175). New York: Basic Books.

Poor, M. (1982). Older lesbians. In M. Cruikshank (Ed.), *Lesbian studies: Present and future* (pp. 57-69). New York: Feminist Press.

Pope, M. (1995). The "salad bowl" is big enough for us all: An argument for the inclusion of lesbians and gay men in any definition of multiculturalism. *Journal of Counseling & Development, 73,* 301-304.

Pope, M., & Schulz, R. (1990). Sexual attitudes and behavior in midlife and aging homosexual males. *Journal of Homosexuality, 20,* 169-177.

Pope, R. L., & Reynolds, A. L. (1991). Including bisexuality: It's more than just a label. In N. J. Evans & V. A. Walls (Eds.), *Beyond tolerance: Gays, lesbians and bisexuals on campus* (pp. 205-212). Alexandria, VA: American College Personnel Association.

Poussaint, A. (1990, September). An honest look at Black gays and lesbians. *Ebony,* pp. 124, 126, 130-131.

Price, J., & Telljohann, S. (in press). School counselor's perceptions of adolescent homosexuals. *Journal of School Health.*

Proctor, C. D., & Groze, V. K. (1994). Risk factors for suicide among gay, lesbian, and bisexual youths. *Social Work, 39,* 504-513.

Quam, J. K. (1993). Gay and lesbian aging. *SIECUS Report, 21,* 10-12.

Quam, J. K., & Whitford, G. S. (1992). Adaptation and age-related expectations of older gay and lesbian adults. *Gerontologist, 32,* 367-374.

Quinn, F. X. (1997, May). Maine's governor signs bill extending rights to gays. *Dallas Voice,* p. 24.

Ramos, J. (1994). *Companeras: Latina lesbians.* New York: Routledge & Kegan Paul.

Rand, C., Graham, D. L., & Rawlings, E. (1982). Psychological health and factors the court seeks to control in lesbian mother custody trials. *Journal of Homosexuality, 8,* 27-39.

Randall, C. E. (1989). Lesbian phobia among BSN educators: A survey. *Journal of Nursing Education, 28,* 302-306.

Rangaswami, K. (1982). Difficulties in arousing and increasing heterosexual responsiveness in a homosexual: A case report. *Indian Journal of Clinical Psychology, 9,* 147-151.

Raphael, S., & Robinson, M. (1984). The older lesbian: Love relationships and friendship patterns. In J. T. Darty & S. Potter (Eds.), *Women-identified women* (pp. 67-82). Palo Alto, CA: Mayfield.

Raymond, J. G. (1986). *A passion for friends: Toward a philosophy of female affection.* Boston: Beacon.

Reece, R. (1987). Causes and treatments of sexual desire discrepancies in male couples. *Journal of Homosexuality, 14,* 157-172.

Reid, J. D. (1995). Development in late life: Older lesbian and gay lives. In A. R. D'Augelli & C. J. Patterson (Eds.), *Lesbians, gay, and bisexual identities over the lifespan: Psychological perspectives* (pp. 215-240). New York: Oxford University Press.

Reilly, M. E., & Lynch, J. M. (1990). Power-sharing in lesbian relationships. *Journal of Homosexuality, 19,* 1-30.

Reiss, B. F. (1980). Psychological tests in homosexuality. In J. Marmor (Ed.), *Homosexual behavior: A modern reappraisal* (pp. 296-311). New York: Basic Books.

Remafedi, G., Farrow, J. A., & Deisher, R. W. (1993). Risk factors for attempted suicide in gay and bisexual youth. In L. D. Garnets & D. C. Kimmel (Eds.), *Psychological perspective on lesbian and gay male experiences* (pp. 486-499). New York: Hemisphere.

Renzetti, C. (1992). *Violent betrayal: Partner abuse in lesbian relationships.* Newbury Park, CA: Sage.

Results of poll. (1989, June 6). *San Francisco Examiner,* p. A19.

Reynolds, A. J. (1989). Social environmental conceptions of male homosexual behavior: A university climate analysis. *Journal of College Student Development, 30,* 62-69.

Rhoads, R. A. (1994a, February). *College lives and identities: Selves in transition.* Paper presented at the 15th Annual Ethnography in Education Research Forum, University of Pennsylvania, Philadelphia.

Rhoads, R. A. (1994b). *Coming out at college: The struggle for a queer identity.* Westport, CT: Bergin & Garvey.

Rhoads, R. A. (1995). Learning from the coming-out experiences of college males. *Journal of College Student Development, 36,* 67-74.

Rich, A. (1980). Compulsory heterosexuality and lesbian existence. *Signs, 5,* 631-660.

Ricketts, W., & Achtenberg, R. (1990). Adoption and foster parenting for lesbians and gay men: Creating new traditions in families. *Marriage & Family Review, 14,* 83-118.

Risman, B., & Schwartz, P. (1988). Sociological research on male and female homosexuality. *Annual Review of Sociology, 14,* 125-147.

Rivera, R. R. (1991). Sexual orientation and the law. In J. C. Gonsiorek & J. D. Weinrich (Eds.), *Homosexuality: Research implications for public policy* (pp. 81-100). Newbury Park, CA: Sage.

Roberts, B. C. (1997). "The many faces of bisexuality": The 4th International Bisexual Symposium. *Journal of Gay, Lesbian, and Bisexual Identity, 2,* 65-76.

Robinson, B. E., Walters, L. H., & Skeen, P. (1989). Response of parents to learning that their child is homosexual and concern over AIDS: A national study. *Journal of Homosexuality, 18,* 59-80.

Robinson, C. S. (1994). Counselling gay males with AIDS: Psychosocial perspectives. *Journal of Gay & Lesbian Social Services, 1,* 15-32.

Robinson, K. E. (1991). Gay youth support groups: An opportunity for social work intervention. *Social Work, 36,* 458-459.

Rodriguez, F. I. (1996). Understanding Filipino male homosexuality: Implications for social services. *Journal of Gay & Lesbian Social Services, 5,* 93-113.

Rofes, E. E. (1983). *"I thought people like that killed themselves": Lesbians, gay men and suicide.* San Francisco: Grey Fox.

Rofes, E. (1989). Opening up the classroom closet: Responding to the educational needs of gay and lesbian youth. *Harvard Educational Review, 59,* 444-453.

Rogers, S. M., & Turner, C. F. (1991). Male-male sexual contact in the U.S.A.: Findings from five sample surveys, 1970-1990. *Journal of Sex Research, 48,* 491-519.

Rohrbaugh, J. B. (1992). Lesbian families: Clinical issues and theoretical implications. *Professional Psychology: Research and Practice, 23,* 467-473.

Rose, S. (1996). Lesbian and gay love scripts. In E. D. Rothblum & L. A. Bond (Eds.), *Preventing and homophobia* (pp. 151-173). Thousand Oaks, CA: Sage.

Rosenberg, K. P. (1994). Notes and comments: Biology and homosexuality. *Journal of Sex & Marital Therapy, 20,* 147-151.

Rosenfeld, C., & Emerson, S. (1995). *Transgender clients: A basic introduction for counseling professions.* Manuscript submitted for publication.

Ross, M. W. (1983). *The married homosexual man.* Boston: Routledge & Kegan Paul.

Ross, M. W., Paulsen, J. A., & Stalstrom, O. W. (1988). Homosexuality and mental health: A cross-cultural review. In M. W. Ross (Ed.), *The treatment of homosexuals with mental health disorders* (pp. 131-151). New York: Harrington Park.

Roth, S. (1985). Psychotherapy issues with lesbian couples. *Journal of Marital and Family Therapy, 11,* 273-286.

Roth, S. (1989). Psychotherapy with lesbian couples: Individual issues, female socialization and the social context. In M. McGoldrick, C. Anderson, & F. Walsh (Eds.), *Women in families: A framework for family therapy* (pp. 286-307). New York: Norton.

Roth, S., & Murphy, B. C. (1986). Therapeutic work with lesbian clients: A systematic therapy view. In M. Ault-Riche (Ed.), *Women and family therapy* (pp. 78-89). Rockville, MD: Aspen.

Rothblum, E. D. (1990). Depression among lesbians: An invisible and unresearched phenomenon. *Journal of Gay & Lesbian Psychotherapy, 1,* 67-87.

Rothblum, E. D. (1994). "I only read about myself on bathroom walls": The need for research on the mental health issues of lesbians and gay men. *Journal of Consulting and Clinical Psychology, 2,* 213-220.

Rothblum, E. D., & Brehony, K. A. (1993). *Boston marriages: Romantic but asexual relationships among contemporary lesbians.* Amherst: University of Massachusetts Press.

Rotheram-Borus, M. J., Rosario, M., & Koopman, C. (1991). Minority youths at high risk: Gay males and runaways. In M. E. Colton & S. Gore (Eds.), *Adolescent stress* (pp. 181-200). New York: Aldine.

Rotheram-Borus, M. J., Rosario, M., Meyer-Bahlburg, H. F. L., Koopman, C., Dobkins, S. C., & Davies, M. (1992). *Sexual and substance use behaviors among homosexual and bisexual male adolescents in New York City.* Unpublished manuscript, HIV Center for Clinical and Behavioral Studies, New York State Psychiatric Center.

Rotheram-Borus, M. J., Rosario, M., Van Rossem, R., Reid, H., & Gillis, R. (1995). Prevalence, course, and predictors of multiple problem behavior among gay and bisexual male adolescents. *Developmental Psychology, 31,*75-85.

Rothschild, M. (1991). Life as improvisation. In B. Sang, J. Warshow, & A. Smith (Eds.), *Lesbians at midlife: The creative transition* (pp. 91-98). San Francisco: Spinsters.

Rowell, R. (1997). Developing AIDS services for Native Americans: Rural and urban contrasts. *Journal of Gay & Lesbian Social Services, 6,* 85-95.

Rubenfeld, A. R. (1994). Sexual orientation and custody. *Human Rights, 21,* 14-17.

Rubenstein, W. B. (1991). We are family: A reflection on the search for legal recognition of lesbian and gay relationships. *Journal of Law & Policy, 89,* 100-105.

Rubenstein, W. B. (1996). Lesbians, gay men, and the law. In R. C. Savin-Williams & K. M. Cohen (Eds.), *The lives of lesbian, gay men, and bisexuals: Children to adults* (pp. 331-343). Ft. Worth, TX: Harcourt Brace.

Rudolph, J. (1988). Counselor's attitudes toward homosexuality: A selective review of the literature. *Journal of Counseling & Development, 67,* 165-168.

Rupp, L. J. (1992). "Imagine my surprise": Women's relationships in historical perspective. In W. R. Dynes & S. Donaldson (Eds.), *Studies in homosexuality: Lesbianism* (pp. 261-280). New York: Garland.

Rusbult, C. E. (1983). A longitudinal test of the investment model: The development (and deterioration) of satisfaction and commitment in heterosexual involvements. *Journal of Personality and Social Psychology, 45,* 101-117.

Russell, G. M. (1995). *The psychological effects of Amendment 2 on lesbians, gay men, and bisexuals in Colorado.* Unpublished manuscript.

Rust, P. C. (1992). The politics of sexual identity: Sexual attraction and behavior among lesbian and bisexual women. *Social Problems, 39,* 366-387.

Rust, P. C. (1993a). "Coming out" in the age of social constructionism: Sexual identity formation among lesbian and bisexual women. *Gender & Society, 7,* 50-77.

Rust, P. C. (1993b). Neutralizing the political threat of the marginal woman: Lesbians' beliefs about bisexual women. *Journal of Sex Research, 30,* 214-228.

Rust, P. C. (1995). *Bisexuality and the challenge to lesbian politics: Sex, loyalty, & revolution.* New York: New York University Press.

Rust, P. C. (1996a). Finding a sexual identity and community: Therapeutic implications and cultural assumptions in scientific models of coming out. In E. D. Rothblum & L. A. Bond (Eds.), *Preventing and homophobia* (pp. 87-123). Thousand Oaks, CA: Sage.

Rust, P. C. (1996b). Monogamy and polyamory: Relationship issues for bisexuals. In B. A. Firestein (Ed.), *Bisexuality: The psychology and politics of an invisible minority* (pp. 127-148). Thousand Oaks, CA: Sage.

Rust, P. C. (1996c). Sexual identity and bisexual identities: The struggle for self-description in a changing sexual landscape. In B. Beemyn & M. Eliason (Ed.), *Queer studies: A lesbian, gay, bisexual, and transgender anthology* (pp. 64-86). New York: New York University Press.

Saghir, M. T., & Robins, E. (1973). *Male and female homosexuality.* Baltimore: Williams & Williams.

Saghir, M. T., & Robins, E. (1980). Clinical aspects of female homosexuality. In J. Marmor (Ed.), *Homosexual behavior* (pp. 280-295). New York: Basic Books.

Sang, B. (1990). Reflections of midlife lesbians on their adolescence. *Journal of Women and Aging, 2,* 111-117.

Sang, B. (1991). Moving toward balance and integration. In B. Sang, J. Warshow, & A. Smith (Eds.), *Lesbians at midlife: The creative transition* (pp. 206-214). San Francisco: Spinsters.

Sang, B. (1992). Counseling and psychotherapy with midlife and older lesbians. In S. Dworkin & F. Gutiérrez (Eds.), *Counseling gay men and lesbians: Journey to the end of the rainbow* (pp. 35-48). Alexandria, VA: American Association for Counseling and Development.

Sang, B. (1993). Some existential issues of midlife lesbians. In L. D. Garnets & D. C. Kimmel (Eds.), *Psychological perspectives on lesbian and gay male experiences* (pp. 500-516). New York: Columbia University Press.

Sang, B., Warshow, J., & Smith, A. (1991). *Lesbians at midlife: The creative transition.* San Francisco: Spinsters.

Sarbin, T. R., & Karols, K. E. (1988). *Nonconforming sexual orientations and military suitability* (Rep. No. PERS-TR-89-002). Monterey, CA: Defense Personnel Security Research and Education Center.

Sauerman, T. H. (1984). *Coming out to your parents.* Los Angeles, CA: Federation of Parents & Friends of Lesbians and Gays.

Saunders, J. M. (1990). Gay and lesbian widowhood. In R. J. Kuys (Ed.), *Keys to caring: Assisting your gay and lesbian clients* (pp. 224-243). Boston: Alyson.

Savin-Williams, R. C. (1989). Gay and lesbian youths and their parents. *Empathy, 2,* 41-42.

Savin-Williams, R. C. (1990a). Coming out. In W. R. Dynes (Ed.), *Encyclopedia of homosexuality* (pp. 251-254). New York: Garland.

Savin-Williams, R. (1990b). *Gay and lesbian youth: Expressions of identity.* New York: Hemisphere.

Savin-Williams, R. (1994). Verbal and physical abuse as stressors in the lives of lesbian, gay male, and bisexual youths: Associations with school problems, running away, substance abuse, prostitution, and suicide. *Journal of Consulting and Clinical Psychology, 62,* 260-269.

Savin-Williams, R. (1995). An exploratory study of pubertal maturation timing and self-esteem among gay and bisexual male youths. *Developmental Psychology, 31,* 56-64.

Savin-Williams, R. C. (1996). Ethnic- and sexual-minority youth. In R. C. Savin-Williams & K. M. Cohen (Eds.), *The lives of lesbian, gay men, and bisexuals: Children to adults* (pp. 152-165). Ft. Worth, TX: Harcourt Brace.

Savin-Williams, R. C., & Cohen, K. M. (Eds.). (1996). *The lives of lesbians, gays, and bisexuals: Children to adults.* Ft. Worth, TX: Harcourt Brace.

Scallen, R. M. (1981). An investigation of paternal attitudes and behavior in homosexual and heterosexual fathers (Doctoral dissertation, California School of Professional Psychology, Los Angeles, 1981). *Dissertation Abstracts International, 42,* 3809B.

Schaffer, B., & DeBlassie, R. R. (1984). Adolescent prostitution. *Adolescence, 19,* 689-696.

Schaie, K. W., & Willis, S. L. (1991). *Adult development and aging* (3rd ed.). New York: HarperCollins.

Schilit, T., Lie, G., & Montagne, M. (1990). Substance abuse as a correlate of violence in intimate lesbian relationships. *Journal of Homosexuality, 19,* 51-65.

Schmitt, J. P., & Kurdek, L. A. (1987). Personality correlates of positive identity and relationship involvement in gay men. *Journal of Homosexuality, 13,* 101-109.

Schneider, B. (1984). Peril and promise: Lesbian's workplace participation. In J. T. Darty & S. Potter (Eds.), *Women-identified women* (pp. 211-230). Palo Alto, CA: Mayfield.

Schneider, B. (1986). Coming out at work: Bridging the private/public gap. *Work and Occupations, 13,* 463-487.

Schneider, M. (1986). The relationships of cohabiting lesbian and heterosexual couples: A comparison. *Psychology of Women Quarterly, 10,* 234-239.

Schneider, M. (1989). Sappho was a right-on adolescent: Growing up lesbian. *Journal of Homosexuality, 17,* 111-130.

Schneider, S. G., Farberow, N. L., & Kruks, G. N. (1989). Suicidal behavior in adolescent and young adult gay men. *Suicide and Life-Threatening Behavior, 19,* 381-394.

Schoenberg, R. (1989, April). *Unlocking closets in the ivory tower: Lesbian/gay identity formation and management in college.* Paper presented at the meeting of the American College Personnel Association, Washington, DC.

Schoonmaker, C. V. (1993). Aging lesbians: Bearing the burden of triple shame. In N. D. Davis, E. Cole, & E. D. Rothblum (Eds.), *Faces of aging* (pp. 21-31). New York: Harrington Park.

Schreurs, K. M. G., & Buunk, B. P. (1996). Closeness, autonomy, equity, and relationship satisfaction in lesbian couples. *Psychology of Women Quarterly, 20,* 577-592.

Schwanberg, S. L. (1996). Health care professionals' attitudes toward lesbian women and gay men. *Journal of Homosexuality, 31,* 71-83.

Sears, J. T. (1989). The impact of gender and race on growing up lesbian and gay in the South. *National Women's Studies Association Journal, 1,* 422-457.

Sears, J. T. (1994). Challenges for educators: Lesbian, gay, and bisexual families. *High School Journal, 77,* 138-156.

Seil, D. (1996). Transsexuals: The boundaries of sexual identity and gender. In R. P. Cabaj & T. S. Stein (Eds.), *Textbook of homosexuality and mental health* (pp. 743-762). Washington, DC: American Psychiatric Press.

Sell, R. L., Wells, J. A., Valleron, A. J., Will, A., Cohen, M., & Umbel, K. (1990, June). *Homosexual and bisexual behavior in the United States, the United Kingdom and France.* Paper presented at the Sixth International Conference on AIDS, San Francisco.

Sell, R. L., Wells, J. A., & Wypij, D. (1995). The prevalence of homosexuality in the United States, the United Kingdom and France: Results of population-based surveys. *Archives of Sexual Behavior, 24,* 234-248.

Seltzer, R. (1992). The social location of those holding antihomosexual attitudes. *Sex Roles, 26,* 391-398.

Serdahely, W., & Ziemba, G. (1984). Changing homophobic attitudes through college sexuality education. *Journal of Homosexuality, 10,* 109-116.

Serovich, J. M., Skeen, P., Walters, L. H., & Robinson, B. E. (1993). In-law relationships when a child is homosexual. *Journal of Homosexuality, 26,* 57-75.

Shachar, S. A., & Gilbert, L. A. (1983). Working lesbians: Role conflicts and coping strategies. *Psychology of Women Quarterly, 7,* 272-284.

Shallenberger, D. (1994). Professional and openly gay: A narrative study of the experience. *Journal of Management Inquiry, 3,* 119-142.

Sherrill, J. M., & Hardesty, C. A. (1994). *The gay, lesbian, and bisexual students' guide to colleges, universities, and graduate schools.* New York: New York University Press.

Shifrin, F., & Solis, M. (1992). Chemical dependency in gay and lesbian youth. *Journal of Chemical Dependency Treatment, 5,* 67-76.

Shilts, R. (1987). *And the band played on.* New York: St. Martin's.

Shively, M. G., & De Cecco, J. P. (1977). Components of sexual identity. *Journal of Homosexuality, 3,* 41-48.

Shively, M. G., Jones, C., & De Cecco, J. (1983-1984). Research on sexual orientation: Definition and methods. *Journal of Homosexuality, 9,* 127-136.

Shon, S. P., & Ja, D. Y. (1982). Asian families. In M. McGoldrick, J. K. Pearce, & J. Giordano (Eds.), *Ethnicity and family therapy* (pp. 208-229). New York: Guilford.

Siegel, K., & Krauss, B. (1991). Living with HIV infection: Adaptive tasks of seropositive gay men. *Journal of Health and Social Behavior, 32,* 17-32.

Silber, L. (1990). Negotiating sexual identity: Non-lesbians in a lesbian feminist community. *Journal of Sex Research, 27,* 131-139.

Silberman, B., & Walton, R. (1986, March). *Life satisfaction factors and older lesbians.* Paper presented at the National Lesbian/Gay Health Conference, Washington, DC.

Silverstein, C. (1981). *Man to man: Gay couples in America.* New York: William Morrow.

Silverstein, C. (Ed.). (1991a). *Gays, lesbians, and their therapists.* New York: Norton.

Silverstein, C. (1991b). Psychological and medical treatments of homosexuality. In J. C. Gonsiorek & J. D. Weinrich (Eds.), *Homosexuality: Research implications for public policy* (pp. 101-114). Newbury Park, CA: Sage.

Simon, W., & Gagnon, J. H. (1967). Homosexuality: The formation of a sociological perspective. *Journal of Health and Social Behavior, 8,* 177-185.

Simon, W., & Gagnon, J. H. (1986). Sexual scripts: Permanence and change. *Archives of Sexual Behavior, 15,* 97-120.

Simoni, J. M. (1996). Pathways to prejudice: Predicting students' heterosexist attitudes with demographics, self-esteem, and contact with lesbians and gay men. *Journal of College Student Development, 37,* 68-78.

Singerline, H. (1994). OutRight: Reflections on an out-of-school gay youth group. *High School Journal, 77,* 133-137.

Siporin, M. (1979). *Introduction to social work practice.* New York: Macmillan.

Slater, B. R. (1993). Violence against lesbian and gay male college students. *Journal of College Student Psychotherapy, 8,* 177-202.

Slater, S., & Mencher, J. (1991). The lesbian family life cycle: A contextual approach. *American Journal of Orthopsychiatry, 6,* 372-382.

Sleek, S. (1996, June). Ethical dilemmas arise treating AIDS patients. *APA Monitor, 27,* 30.

Slusher, M. P., Mayer, C. J., & Dunkle, R. E. (1996). Gays and Lesbians Older and Wiser (GLOW): A support group for older people. *Gerontologist, 36,* 118-123.

Smalley, S. (1988). Dependency issues in lesbian relationships. In E. Coleman (Ed.), *Psychotherapy with men and women* (pp. 125-135). New York: Haworth.

Smith, A. J. (1990). Working with the lesbian community: The dilemma of overlapping relationships. In H. Lemary & N. Porter (Eds.), *Feminist ethics in psychotherapy* (pp. 92-96). New York: Springer.

Smith, A. (1997). Cultural diversity and the coming-out process: Implications for clinical practice. In B. Greene (Ed.), *Ethnic and cultural diversity among lesbians and gay men* (pp. 279-300). Thousand Oaks, CA: Sage.

Smith, B. (1992). Toward a Black feminist criticism. In G. Hull, P. Scott, & B. Smith (Eds.), *All the women are White, all the Blacks are men, but some of us are brave* (pp. 157-175). Old Westbury, NY: Feminist Press.

Smith, J. (1988). Psychotherapy, homosexuality, and homophobia. *Journal of Homosexuality, 5,* 59-74.

Smith-Rosenberg, C. (1975). The female world of love and ritual: Relations between women in nineteenth century America. *Signs, 1,* 19-27.

Snyder, M. (1981). On the self-perpetuating nature of social stereotypes. In D. Hamilton (Ed.), *Cognitive processes in stereotyping and intergroup behavior* (pp. 183-211). Hillsdale, NJ: Lawrence Erlbaum.

Sohier, R. (1985-1986). Homosexual mutuality: Variation on a theme by E. Erikson. *Journal of Homosexuality, 12,* 25-38.

Sophie, J. (1985-1986). A critical examination of stage theories of lesbian identity development. *Journal of Homosexuality, 12,* 39-51.

Sophie, J. (1987). Internalized homophobia and lesbian identity. *Journal of Homosexuality, 14,* 53-65.

Stark, L. (1991). Traditional gender role beliefs and individual outcomes: An explanatory analysis. *Sex Roles, 9-10,* 639-650.

Starr, B., & Weiner, M. (1981). *The Starr-Weiner report on sex and sexuality in the mature years.* New York: McGraw-Hill.

Stein, E. (1990). Conclusion: The essentials of constructionism and the construction of essentialism. In E. Stein (Ed.), *Forms of desire: Sexual orientation and the social constructionist controversy* (pp. 325-354). New York: Routledge & Kegan Paul.

Stein, M. (1983). *In midlife: A Jungian perspective.* Dallas: Spring.

Stein, T. S. (1993). Overview of new developments in understanding homosexuality. *Review of Psychiatry, 12,* 9-40.

Stein, T. S., & Cohen, C. J. (1984). Psychotherapy with gay men and lesbians: An examination of homophobia, coming-out, and identity. In E. S. Hetrick & T. S. Stein (Eds.), *Innovations in psychotherapy with homosexuals.* Washington, DC: American Psychiatric Association.

Stein, T. S., & Cohen, C. J. (Eds.). (1986). *Psychotherapy with lesbians and gay men.* New York: Plenum.

Stewart, T. A. (1991, December 16). Gay in corporate America. *Fortune,* pp. 43-56.

Stokes, J. P., McKirnan, D. J., Doll, L., & Burzette, R. G. (1996). Female partners of bisexual men: What they don't know might hurt them. *Psychology of Women Quarterly, 20,* 267-284.

Stokes, J. P., Taywaditep, K., Vanable, P., & McKirnan, D. J. (1996). Bisexual men, sexual behavior, and HIV/AIDS. In B. A. Firestein (Ed.), *Bisexuality: The psychology and politics of an invisible minority* (pp. 149-168). Thousand Oaks, CA: Sage.

Storms, M. D. (1980). Theories of sexual orientation. *Journal of Personality and Social Psychology, 38,* 783-792.

Strommen, E. F. (1989). "You're a what?" Family members' reactions to the disclosure of homosexuality. *Journal of Homosexuality, 18,* 37-58.

Strommen, E. F. (1990). Hidden branches and growing pains: Homosexuality and the family tree. *Marriage & Family Review, 14,* 9-34.

Sullivan, T. R. (1994). Obstacles to effective child welfare service with gay and lesbian youth. *Child Welfare, 73,* 291-304.

Sussal, C. M. (1993). Object relations couple therapy with lesbians. *Smith College Studies in Social Work, 63,* 301-317.

Swigonski, M. E. (1995). The social service needs of lesbians of color. *Journal of Gay & Lesbian Social Services, 2,* 67-83.

Talamini, J. T. (1982). *Boys will be girls: The hidden world of the heterosexual male transvestite.* Washington, DC: University Press of America.

Tasker, F., & Golombok, S. (1995). Adults raised as children in lesbian families. *American Journal of Orthopsychiatry, 65,* 203-215.

Teague, J. B. (1992). Issues relating to the treatment of adolescent lesbians and homosexuals. *Journal of Mental Health Counseling, 14,* 422-439.

Telljohann, S. K., & Price, J. H. (1993). A qualitative examination of adolescent homosexuals' life experiences: Ramifications for secondary school personnel. *Journal of Homosexuality, 26,* 41-55.

Thoits, P. (1985). Self-labeling processes in mental illness: The role of emotional deviance. *American Journal of Sociology, 91,* 221-249.

Tierney, W. G. (1992). *Enhancing diversity: Toward a better campus climate* (Report). University Park: Pennsylvania State University, Committee on Lesbian and Gay Concerns.

Toder, N. (1992). Lesbian couples in particular. In B. Berzon & R. Leighton (Eds.), *Positively gay* (pp. 50-63). Berkeley, CA: Celestial Arts.

Tofoya, T. N. (1996). Native two-spirit people. In R. P. Cabaj & T. S. Stein (Eds.), *Textbook of homosexuality and mental health* (pp. 603-617). Washington, DC: American Psychiatric Press.

Tofoya, T. N. (1997). Native gay and lesbian issues: The two-spirited. In B. Greene (Ed.), *Ethnic and cultural diversity among lesbians and gay men* (pp. 1-10). Thousand Oaks, CA: Sage.

Tremble, B., Schneider, M., & Appathurai, C. (1989). Growing up gay or lesbian in a multicultural context. *Journal of Homosexuality, 17,* 253-267.

Triandis, H. C., Kurowski, L. L., & Gelfand, M. J. (1994). Workplace diversity. In H. C. Triandis, M. D. Dunnette, & L. M. Housh (Eds.), *Handbook of industrial and organizational psychology* (Vol. 4, 2nd ed., pp. 769-827). Palo Alto, CA: Consulting Psychologists Press.

Troiden, R. R. (1979). Becoming homosexual: A model of gay identity acquisition. *Psychiatry, 42,* 362-373.

Troiden, R. R. (1989). The formation of homosexual identities. *Journal of Homosexuality, 17,* 43-73.

Troiden, R. R., & Goode, E. (1980). Variables related to the acquisition of a gay identity. *Journal of Homosexuality, 5,* 383-392.

Trosino, J. (1993). American wedding: Same-sex marriage and the miscegenation analogy. *Boston University Law Review, 73,* 93-120.

Trujillo, C. (Ed.). (1991). *Chicana lesbians: The girls our mothers warned us about.* Berkeley, CA: Third Woman.

Tully, C. (1983). *Social support systems of a selected sample of older women.* Unpublished doctoral dissertation, Virginia Commonwealth University, Richmond.

Tully, C. (1988). Caregiving: What do midlife lesbians view as important? *Journal of Gay and Lesbian Psychotherapy, 1,* 87-103.

Tully, C. (1994). To boldly go where no one has gone before: The legalization of lesbian and gay marriages. *Journal of Gay and Lesbian Social Services, 1,* 73-87.

Turner, J. S., & Helms, D. B. (1991). *Lifespan development* (4th ed.). Ft. Worth, TX: Holt, Rinehart & Winston.

Turner, P. H., Scadden, L., & Harris, M. B. (1990). Parenting in gay and lesbian families. *Journal of Gay and Lesbian Psychotherapy, 1,* 55-66.

Udis-Kessler, A. (1996). Identity politics: Historical sources of the bisexual movement. In B. Beemyn & M. Eliason (Ed.), *Queer studies: A lesbian, gay, bisexual, and transgender anthology* (pp. 52-63). New York: New York University Press.

Unger, R., & Crawford, M. (1992). *Women & gender.* New York: McGraw-Hill.

Unterberger, G. L. (1993). Counseling lesbians: A feminist perspective. In R. J. Wicks & R. D. Parsons (Eds.), *Clinical handbook of pastoral counseling* (Vol. 2, pp. 228-265). Mahwah, NJ: Paulist.

Uribe, V. (1994). The silent minority: Rethinking out commitment to gay and lesbian youth. *Theory into Practice, 33,* 168-172.

Uribe, V., & Harbeck, K. M. (1992). Addressing the needs of lesbian, gay, and bisexual youth: The origins of PROJECT 10 and school-based intervention. *Journal of Homosexuality, 22,* 9-28.

U.S. Bureau of the Census. (1990). *Population reports, preliminary figures (1990).* Washington, DC: Government Printing Office.

U.S. Bureau of the Census. (1994). *Census 1990.* Washington, DC: Government Printing Office.

Vaillant, G. (1977). *Adaptation to life.* Boston: Little, Brown.

Vance, C. S. (1988). Social construction theory: Problems in the history of sexuality. In A. van Kooten Niekerk & T. van der Meer (Eds.), *Homosexuality, which homosexuality?* (pp. 13-34). Amsterdam: Jhr. Mr. J. A. Schorerstichting.

Wahler, J., & Gabbay, S. G. (1997). Gay male aging: A review of the literature. *Journal of Gay & Lesbian Social Services, 6,* 1-20.

Walker, L. M. (1993). How to recognize a lesbian: The cultural politics of looking like you are. *Signs, 18,* 866-890.

Wall, V. A., & Evans, N. J. (1991). Using psychosocial developmental theories to understand and work with gay and lesbian persons. In N. J. Evans & V. A. Wall (Ed.), *Beyond tolerance: Gays, lesbians and bisexuals on campus* (pp. 25-38). Alexandria, VA: American College Personnel Association.

Walters, A. S., & Phillips, C. P. (1994). Hurdles: An activity for homosexuality education. *Journal of Sex Education & Therapy, 20,* 198-203.

Walters, K. L. (1997). Urban lesbian and gay American Indian identity: Implications for mental health service delivery. *Journal of Gay & Lesbian Social Services, 6,* 43-65.

Ward, K. (1997, January). Now plans day of action for same-sex marriage. *National Now Times,* pp. 1, 14.

Warren, C. A. B. (1974). *Identity and community in the gay world.* New York: John Wiley.

Warshow, J. (1991). How lesbian identity affects the mother/daughter relationship. In B. Sang, J. Warshow, & A. J. Smith (Eds.), *Lesbians at midlife: The creative transition* (pp. 80-83). San Francisco: Spinsters.

Waterman, C. K., Dawson, L. J., & Bologna, M. J. (1989). Sexual coercion in gay male and lesbian relationships: Predictors and implications for support services. *Journal of Sex Research, 26,* 118-124.

Weeks, J. (1983). The problem of older homosexuals. In J. Hart & D. Richardson (Eds.), *The theory and practice of homosexuality* (pp. 177-185). London: Routledge & Kegan Paul.

Weeks, J. (1991). *Against nature: Essays on history, sexuality, and identity.* London: Rivers Oram.

Weinberg, M. S. (1970). The male homosexual: Age-related variations in social and psychological characteristics. *Social Problems, 17,* 527-537.

Weinberg, M. S., & Williams, C. J. (1974). *Male homosexuals: Their problems and adaptations.* New York: Oxford University Press.

Weinberg, M. S., Williams, C. J., & Pryor, D. W. (1994). *Dual attraction: Understanding bisexuality.* New York: Oxford University Press.

Weinrich, J. D. (1988). The periodic-table model of the gender transpositions: Part II. Limerent and lusty sexual attractions and the nature of bisexuality. *Journal of Sex Research, 24,* 113-129.

Weinstein, D. L. (1992). Application of family therapy concepts in the treatment of lesbians and gay men. In D. L. Weinstein (Ed.), *Lesbian and gay men: Chemical dependency treatment issues* (pp. 141-155). New York: Haworth.

Weitz, R. (1989). Uncertainty and the lives of persons with AIDS. *Journal of Health and Social Behavior, 30,* 270-281.

Wellings, K., Field, J., Johnson, A., & Wadsworth, J. (1994). *Sexual behavior in Britain: The national survey of sexual attitudes and lifestyles.* New York: Penguin.

Wells, J. W., & Kline, W. B. (1987). Self-disclosure of homosexual orientation. *Journal of Social Psychology, 127,* 191-197.

Weston, K. (1991). *Families we choose.* New York: Columbia University Press.

Whisman, V. (1991, August). *Different from whom? Competing definitions of lesbianism.* Paper presented at the annual meetings of the American Sociological Association, Cleveland, OH.

Whitehead, H. (1981). The bow and the burden strap: A new look at institutionalized homosexuality in native North America. In S. B. Ortner & H. Whitehead (Eds.), *Sexual meanings: The cultural construction of gender and sexuality* (pp. 80-115). New York: Cambridge University Press.

Whitford, G. S. (1997). Realities and hopes for older gay males. *Journal of Gay & Lesbian Social Services, 6,* 79-95.

Whitney, C. (1990). *Uncommon lives: Gay men and straight women.* New York: Plume.

Williams, W. L. (1986). *The spirit and the flesh: Sexual diversity in American Indian culture.* Boston: Beacon.

Williams, W. L. (1996). Two-spirit persons: Gender nonconformity among native American and native Hawaiian youths. In R. C. Savin-Williams & K. M. Cohen (Eds.), *The lives of lesbians, gays, and bisexuals: Children to adults* (pp. 416-435). Ft. Worth, TX: Harcourt Brace.

Winkelpleck, J. M., & Westfeld, J. S. (1982). Counseling considerations with gay couples. *Personnel and Guidance Journal, 60,* 294-296.

Winnow, J. (1989, Summer). Lesbians working on AIDS: Assessing the impact on health care for women. *OUT/LOOK, 5,* 10-18.

Wolf, D. (1979). *The lesbian community.* Berkeley: University of California Press.

Wolf, D. G. (1982). *Growing older: Lesbians and gay men.* Berkeley: University of California Press.

Wolf, T. J. (1985). Marriages of bisexual men. *Journal of Homosexuality, 11,* 135-148.

Wolf, T. J., & Klein, F. (1988). Ericksonian hypnosis and strategic interventions for sexual orientation confusion. In E. Coleman (Ed.), *Integrated identity for gay men and lesbians: Psychotherapeutic approaches for emotional well-being* (pp. 67-76). New York: Harrington Park.

Wolfson, E. (1991). Civil rights, human rights, gay rights: Minorities and the humanity of the different. *Harvard Journal of Law & Public Policy, 14,* 21.

Wooden, W. S., Kawasaki, H., & Mayeda, R. (1983). Lifestyles and identity maintenance among gay Japanese-American males. *Alternate Lifestyles, 5,* 236-243.

Wooden, W. S., & Parker, J. (1982). *Men behind bars: Sexual exploitation in prison.* New York: Plenum.

Woodman, N. J. (1987, September). *Lesbian women in their midyears: Issues and implications for practice.* Paper presented at the health/mental health conference of the National Association of Social Workers, New Orleans, LA.

Woodman, N. J. (Ed.). (1992). *Lesbian and gay lifestyles: A guide for counseling and education.* New York: Irvington.

Woodman, N. J., & Lenna, H. R. (1980). *Counseling with gay men and women: A guide for facilitating positive life-styles.* San Francisco: Jossey-Bass.

Woods, J. D., & Lucas, J. (1993). *The corporate closet: The professional lives of gay men in America.* New York: Free Press.

Woolsey, C. (1991, October 7). Digital pioneers program to fight AIDS, ignorance. *Business Insurance,* p. 80.

Wyers, N. L. (1987). Homosexuality in the family: Lesbian and gay spouses. *Social Work, 32,* 143-148.

Zacks, E., Green, R., & Morrow, J. (1988). Comparing lesbian and heterosexual couples on the circumplex model: An initial investigation. *Family Process, 27,* 471-484.

Zastrow, C., & Kirst-Ashman, K. (1990). *Understanding human behavior and the social environment* (2nd ed.). Chicago: Nelson-Hall.

Zavos, M. A. (1995). Sexual orientation law in the 1990s. *Trial, 31,* 27-32.

Zicklin, G. (1995). Deconstructing legal rationality: The case of lesbian and gay family relationships. *Marriage & Family Review, 21,* 55-76.

Zimmerman, B. (1984). The politics of transliteration: Lesbian personal narratives. *Signs, 9,* 663-682.

INDEX

See also Heterosexism
Price, J. H., 134
Pride Day parades, 45, 46
Prime Timers, 167
Proctor, C. D., 129
Project 10, Los Angeles Unified School District, 134, 135-136
Promiscuity, bisexual stereotypes, 27
Prostitution:
    adolescent, 130, 131
    male, 4, 77, 130
Pryor, D. W., 65, 95, 96, 106, 107
Psychological heterosexism, 25-31, 33-34
Psychotherapy. *See* Human services professionals

Quam, J. K., 161, 167
Queer Nation, 42, 52
Queer (term), 9

Racial/ethnic groups. *See* Minorities, racial/ethnic
Racism, 23, 46, 48, 101
Rape, 130, 135
Raphael, S., 163
Reid, H., 129
Relationships. *See* Couples; Linkups; Marriages
Religion:
    "curing" homosexuality through, 173
    See also Catholic Church; Spirituality
Research:
    children of lesbian/gay parents, 122-123
    difficulties, 17-19
    essentialism vs. social constructionism, 5-6
    lacking for bisexuals, 128, 175
    lesbian and gay parents, 118-122
    life course development stages, 127-128
    sexual orientation, 11-17
Residential treatments, 134-135
Retirement communities, 167
Rice queens, 94
Richards, L., 119
Robins, E., 157
Robinson, B. E., 77
Robinson, M., 163
Rofes, E. E., 136
Rosario, M., 129, 131
Rothblum, E. D., 146
Rotheram-Borus, M. J., 129, 131
Rubyfruit Jungle (Brown), 165
Rust, P. C., 50, 51, 96
Ryan, C., 143, 144, 145-146, 147, 149

Saghir, M. T., 157
Sang, B., 142-143, 146, 147-148, 150, 152
Savin-Williams, R., 128

Scallen, R. M., 121
Schneider, M., 128
School systems:
    heterosexism in, 26-30, 118, 132, 133-134, 135-136
    See also Colleges
Schulz, R., 152
Schwartz, P., 98, 105-106, 106
Scripts:
    best friend, 97
    courtship, 94
    gender-blended, 98
    mentor/apprentice, 96
    race-relevant, 97-98
    traditional, 94, 96-97
Self-blame, 32
Self-esteem:
    and friendship, 144, 162
    in children/adolescents, 123, 129, 130, 131, 132
    in midlife, 142, 154
    in older adulthood, 157, 165
    passing and, 85
    physical attractiveness and, 152-153, 154, 156
Self-hatred. *See* Internalized oppression
Self-identity:
    adolescent development, 128-129
    assessment tools, 18
    at midlife, 147-148, 151
    conflict in relationships and, 100, 111
    experimentation prior to, 160
    older adulthood and, 159-160
    sexual orientation and, 15, 16
    See also Coming out; Disclosure; Sexual orientation identity
Senior Action in a Gay Environment (SAGE), 167
Senior Gay and Lesbian Citizens/PROJECT RAINBOW, 167
Sepekoff, B., 12
Serial monogamy, 95
Service organizations:
    for adolescents, 135, 136-137
    for lesbian and gay parents, 121, 123-124
    for older adults, 167
Sexual behavior:
    as individual choice, 6, 29, 64, 66
    causes, 5-6, 177
    compatibility and, 107
    defined, 3
    determining sexual orientation through, 15, 65
    menopause and, 146
    midlife, 146, 148, 152-153
    nonbiased terminology for, 9
    older adulthood and, 163
    sexual desire vs., 15, 51, 66
Sexual desire, sexual behavior vs., 15, 51, 66
Sexual Identity Formation (SIF) model, 58-59, 60-61, 65, 70

ABOUT THE AUTHORS

Ski Hunter is Professor, School of Social Work, University of Texas at Arlington. She teaches human behavior and the social environment, adult development, and personal linkups. Recent areas of her scholarship include lesbians and gay men and midlife. She coedited the book *Midlife Myths* in 1989 and is currently working on a manuscript on midlife women. She has made many presentations on these topics before professional groups during the past several years.

Coleen Shannon is Associate Professor, School of Social Work, University of Texas at Arlington. Her areas of teaching and scholarship include stress management, biofeed-

back, supervision, and clinical practice with lesbians and gay men. In addition, she is an instructor for training programs in biofeedback, engages in direct delivery of biofeedback services, and provides supervision for advanced credentialing. She is a board member of the Biofeedback Certification Institute of America.

Jo Knox is Assistant Professor, School of Social Work, University of Alabama. She teaches research and evaluation and direct practice in social work. Her areas of scholarship include HIV prevention, military and veteran's family mental health issues, and social services for diverse populations.

221

James I. Martin is Associate Professor, School of Social Work, New York University, where he teaches direct practice and research. He previously has maintained a private practice in clinical work, treating mainly gay and lesbian clients. His areas of scholarship include HIV prevention, gay and lesbian issues in social work, and the application of self psychology to social work practice. He is a member of the Council on Social Work Education Commission on Gay Men and Lesbian Women.